Art Education
SOCIAL for JUSTICE

EDITORS: Tom Anderson
David Gussak
Kara Kelley Hallmark
Allison Paul

Contents

K-12 Focus

Higher Education and Teacher Preparation

International Perspectives

Appendix

Preface

Art for Life is a *Way* of Life,
Or,
Personal Revelations: Why I Needed to Work on this Book

Eight months ago I was asked to help Tom and Kara in editing the chapters in this book. Given that I am not an art educator but an art therapist, I thought I could provide an unbiased eye in reviewing these chapters on the authors' abilities to communicate to the general reader a clear and uncomplicated yet academic treatise on the topics. I also felt that because I thought I was intimate with the concept of how art can be used to underscore, heighten, and reflect social interaction that I could provide a practiced and educated eye to how art can be used to elevate and promote awareness of social justice. I have been an art therapist for many years, using art therapy to encourage change and healing with correctional populations. After many years of providing art therapy in a prison, my work shifted to higher education. Over the past 11 years, as an educator in two separate universities, my focus shifted from the practice of providing art therapy in prison to an academic, research-based focus, studying the effectiveness of art therapy in prison. Although I made sure art therapy was still provided to the inmate populations through graduate interns, I essentially moved from the field into a lab. As I edited these chapters, I was once again familiarized with the importance of one-to-one, field-based interactions through art. What also reasserted itself was that the interaction within the art facilitation process is just as valuable to the artist facilitator as it is to those who are the participants.

Although I have been loathe to present personal ruminations for an academic audience, and I have stressed the importance to my students of avoiding first person references in professional studies and publications, I broke this golden rule when writing this preface. A lot has happened over the past 8 months of editing to facilitate these changes, and I felt that this

section provided the perfect venue to explore those changes. Editing this text erased for me many of the boundaries that I thought existed between art education and art therapy. It also personalized research for me and it caused me to reflect on the instrumental connections between art and life. I came into this as an art therapist whose academic training encouraged academic objectivity and a separation between academic disciplines; my recent experiences have allowed me to explore another perspective. My story of this change has three parts—my transition from faculty member to department chair, my work with prisons, and my work on this book.

A number of years ago, I was hired as a faculty member for the Florida State University, Department of Art Education. This department comprises three programs—art education, art administration, and art therapy. I teach for the art therapy program. I had previously taught for a university where the art therapy program was housed in the psychology department. The FSU Department of Art Education was a unique experience for me; I now teach for a department that focuses on art, in an environment where I no longer have to explain the importance of creative expression. However, I [initially] felt like I had to defend the therapeutic value of art, the actual formal application of how art therapy can be healing. Although I worked closely with the other art education faculty—serving on art education and arts administration doctoral committees, chairing my own doctoral students' committees, and eventually teaching doctoral seminars that included students from all three programs—I fundamentally remained an art therapist, with a clear line drawn between my field and the other two. However, several actions virtually coincided that allowed me to realize the convergence of the three programs' foci within my own epistemological

Preface. Art for Life is a *Way* of Life, Or, Personal Revelations: Why I Needed to Work on this Book

v

perspective: my role in developing the newly developed statewide Arts in Corrections program and the Inmate Mural Arts Program, becoming the new Chair for the Florida State University Department of Art Education, and editing these chapters.

Arts in Corrections

Over the past 5 years, I have been working with a team of art therapy graduate students conducting research on the effectiveness of art therapy in prison; recently, this research translated directly to application. In the summer of 2007, the Florida Department of Corrections, as a response to several arts in corrections programs around the state as well as the research conducted by our art therapy program on the effectiveness of art therapy in prisons, formed a workgroup whose task was to explore the possibility of establishing a statewide Arts in Corrections (AiC) program. Because of the research we had been conducting, I was asked to be the chairperson of this newly implemented workgroup composed of members from the Florida Department of Corrections and from various arts communities throughout the state. The AiC would have several components that would focus on the product of creative endeavors, to evoke problem solving, socialization, and control, as well as an art therapy component, to address mental health needs through the art process—skills that would aid the inmates' adjustment to the society to which they may eventually be released; essentially, this program promoted social justice through art.

Shortly after the Secretary of the Department of Corrections signed the Executive Summary and policy, an Advisory Group was formed whose chief goal was to implement this new and innovative program. Leslie Neal, a member of the workforce and president and founder of Art Springs, a dance and arts program that provided services to prison inmates in South Florida, was asked to co-chair the AiC Advisory Group.

Since we received this optimistic nod from the Department of Corrections administration, the AiC program has been faltering due to change in administrative personnel, political foci, and fiscal and budgetary concerns, yet it continues to address the need for the arts in the prison system. One of the projects that we developed was the Inmate Mural Arts Program (IMAP) as a cooperative effort between the Florida State University Department of Art Education/Art Therapy Program and the various correctional institutions with which we would contract. This project was designed to produce large, outdoor murals completed by groups of inmates who had

to work together to create such grand results. Facilitated by art therapy students, this program produced its first successful mural the summer of 2008 on the 22 x 47 ft. external wall of the chapel of a large men's prison in rural Florida. In the fall of 2008, the IMAP team completed a mural for a small South-Georgia community with jail inmates. This 35 x 50 ft. mural was painted on the side of a downtown building, in a community known for its large outdoor murals. This piece became a bridge that connected these jail residents with the small-town community, and turned the inmates from objects to real, creating beings. These acts achieved social justice. The IMAP team has since been asked to develop a similar mural in a women's prison in rural Florida.

Through these endeavors we were able to use the art as an agent of change, of evoking and promoting social justice. We used the art as a bridge between the disenfranchised and the outside world. In order for us to succeed, we relied not only on art therapy, but also on education and administration. To develop the AiC and IMAP we needed to know about policy and develop our own administrative skills. We negotiated at all levels, and in order to succeed, we had to learn about, and work with, the bureaucratic structure. But the success of the implemented programs, and ultimately the development of highly visible products, relied on our *educational skills*; it was no longer about how therapeutic the artmaking process was, but about how aesthetically significant the final art product was. To do this, we had to be able to teach artistic and creative techniques. The success of these programs would ultimately promote awareness of the prison culture, and allow those inside to gain skills that would promote individuality and success. In order to achieve success for social justice through the arts in prison, we had to rely on all three programmatic foci. This [collaborative advantage] soon became even clearer when I became the new chair of the Department of Art Education.

Becoming Chair of Several Symbiotic Programs

In the fall of 2008, I became chair of the department and began to understand the close relationships between our art therapy, arts administration, and art education programs. The previous chair, recognizing the symbiotic nature of the three programs, felt that the department needed a unifying theme. While trying to figure out what we had in common, to make explicit our common goals, as a department we decided that the title of the Anderson and Milbrandt (2005) text, *Art for Life*, was an apt description. With permission from the authors, this became our rallying cry. Shortly after this decision was made, I became department chair.

As I familiarized myself with the nuances of administration and the responsibilities and contributions of all of the programs, I realized that the motto *Art for Life* was a description that bound the programs together. It is a vision that we had already embraced as a department, but just never put into formal words. The motto provides an easy way, a shortcut, to explain to others what our department was about, and each program reflects it clearly.

The art therapy program focuses on how the arts can promote healing in a variety of different settings from preschool to geriatric care, public to special needs schools, medical to psychiatric, correctional settings to hospice. The projects and studies that emerge from this program evaluate the effectiveness of art for these settings, and provide strategies on how the art can help facilitate health and wellness. The art education program educates students to be more than teachers in the public classrooms. They learn the value of providing an appreciation of aesthetics, expressive tools, and strategies for success. The student teachers and developing art educators and professors learn that their place goes beyond the walls of the brick-and-mortar classroom, into the world at large. It is no coincidence that many of the contributors for this text either were former students for this program, or have worked closely with the program's faculty and graduates. The arts administration program provides skills that surpass policy comprehension and development. This program focuses on the development, implementation, and sustainability of arts programming within different communities, settings, and cultures. Understanding the impact of arts programming within a variety of social strata, graduates from this program can provide services for the underserved as well as the elite. As contributors to all communities and environments, those who graduate carry with them the inherent belief that art is for life.

Adopting the *Art for Life* mantra did not change the focus of the department; it just provided an easier way of communicating our focus. Understanding how each program contributes to the fundamental belief that art education, arts administration, and art therapy are all ideally intended to do something valuable in people's lives beyond as well as within schools, eased my transition from faculty member to administrator.

Editing the Chapters

Among all of these professional changes, administrative responsibilities, and dawning realizations, I was asked to help with this book. Although I began this task with one idea on what needed to be done, I ended with an entirely different perspective. However, as I reflect upon the task's completion, the two viewpoints may not be entirely separate.

My initial response to editing these chapters was to appraise them for flow and comprehension. When I began reviewing these chapters, I realized that a shift had to be made, from objective, distance discourse to a narrative presence. This was a difficult transition to make; however, as I reviewed the chapters, I soon realized how appropriate such an approach was, and that it was indeed a valid means of academic presentation. As I accepted these chapters, I came to recognize that such a different and more personally framed paradigm is legitimate; the narratives and first person accounts are indeed worthy of academic attention and hold their own merit.

In addition, through these writings, the notion of art education/ therapy/administration for social justice became even clearer in my mind, coalescing with one purpose. These numerous chapters forced me to reevaluate the relationships between the art educator and the classroom, the artist and the media, the art educator and other art teachers, and the art teacher and culture. It became clear how the artist and art educator can facilitate social justice through various media, promote change and clarity, and generate healing, trust, and bridge building. These chapters ranged from the profoundly personal to the academically oriented and from a focus on the individual to a global perspective: art therapy, arts administration, and art education having the common goal of social justice—an important piece of Art for Life.

It was only through narrative discourse that the simultaneously personal and global import of what was being done could be communicated. While the authors talked of their own experiences, it was not difficult to see how these experiences could be applied to various situations—that the philosophies that guided these actions could be adopted by all of us. Taken individually, some of these chapters make wonderful stories; as a whole, these chapters provide a blueprint for how art can permeate our social fabric.

It is with profound gratitude that I thank Tom and Kara for asking for my help in editing these chapters, and I thank the authors for granting the privilege of taking their thoughts and ideas and manipulating them to make them clearer and more reader-friendly while making sure that I would not change their meanings. Special thanks need to be given to Allison Paul, with whom I worked closely with during the process. Beginning as a graduate student whose role was to organize the drafts and initiate and complete correspondence with the authors, she soon displayed a dedication, clarity, and work ethic that rightly earned her the moniker of co-editor.

Through reading and editing these chapters, I learned a great deal of the important role the art educator and artist facilitator plays in today's society to facilitate justice. I dare anyone to read this book and not walk away with an intense awareness of what Art for Life truly means.

REFERENCES
Anderson, T., & Milbrandt, M.K. (2002). *Art for life: Authentic instruction in art*. New York: McGraw Hill, Publishers.

Introduction and Theoretical
FOUNDATIONS

An Introduction to *Art Education for Social Justice*

Tom Anderson

What is this Book?

It is through our stories that we know ourselves and the world around us. In that context, this is a book mostly of stories by and about educators who have used aesthetic strategies, art education strategies, to achieve or maintain social justice. The settings for the stories are schools and universities, community and service learning contexts, and correctional settings. The stories usually include suggestions for readers who are interested in constructing social justice in their own art educational contexts.

To set the foundation for the stories and curricula that follow, I will first address how we are defining *social justice* for the purposes of this book, and then I will examine some potential roles for aesthetically framed educational activities toward the ends of social justice.

The concept of social justice seems almost always to be tied to some notion of social equity; that is, people's perceptions of whether they have been granted equal access or equal opportunity, been treated fairly, and/or granted the respect they feel they deserve. Inherent in this understanding of social justice is a power relationship. Further, this power inequity is normally related to socially constructed positions of privilege and peripheralization frequently centered on race, ethnicity, gender, sexual orientation, and differing abilities or upon the amount of resources each party in a relationship has. These resources can be physical (land, oil, grain); fiscal (money, stocks, and such); or personal (intellectual, emotional, or physical strength).

Opportunities and lack of opportunities, resources and lack of resources, and the consequent social conditions and institutional structures attending to and fostering those inequities are root causes of misunderstandings, resentments, and conflict between people. When people see each other primarily in terms of stereotypes and symbolic reifications of privilege and marginalization or wealth and poverty rather than—first—as people, it leads to objectification: "That's just a beggar, dike, rich bitch, greedy landlord, sharecropper, tenement dweller, honky," and worse. Such characterizations are stereotypes that encourage distance, misperception, and fear between people who perceive themselves as different from each other in their fundamental humanness, each seeing the other group not as *us*, or even *like us*, but as *other*. This estrangement frequently leads to social strife between individuals and groups, and ultimately to wars. Privilege and peripheralization as a power relationship, while it has racial, ethnic, gender, and other components, almost always manifests itself in the disparity between those who have resources and those who don't, which usually sets the conditions for social justice or social abuse. This being a book of stories, I'll illustrate this point with one of my own.

Understanding Social Justice: A Personal Account

In Bali, Indonesia, as in many places in the world, economic disparity between the indigenous people and the visitors/tourists can be extreme. I visited Bali in 2005. As a tall, white man with a camera, I was immediately recognized as an outsider, and I couldn't walk 100 steps down the street in Ubud or Sanur without being approached by a local person who had a strategy to relieve me of my money. Almost certainly, however, each offered me something in exchange: "Taxi?" they would say, making a driving motion with their arms. "Massage? Manicure? Pedicure? Step into my shop? Good paintings!" These people were not panhandlers, but they obviously wanted just one thing from me: my money. They weren't interested in who I was as a person, but merely saw me as a stereotype tourist, thus as a vehicle of opportunity for their own personal gain. I was not, to them, a real/whole person, but just a symbolic form: a moving money target, an opportunity, to be scanned and maximized for gain before I moved out of range. These folks, many of them desperately poor, recognized full well, just by the fact that I was there from somewhere else, that by their standards I was wealthy beyond belief. And they wanted some of what I had. My humanity was beside the point.

Conversely, it was easy for me to think of the Balinese, who constantly were approaching me, as an annoyance. It would have been easy for me not to see them as people with souls, with families to feed and problems with their kids. It would have been easy to frame them simply as an irritation, like gnats, to be brushed away. I could have slipped into seeing them not really even as people, or at least not as people like me. I could have framed them as vagrants and ne'r-do-wells or even as beggars as did one outraged, burly Australian, who, when he was approached by a local woman with a baby in one arm and her other hand out to him, shouted indignantly at her, "Get a bloody job!!!"

That incident stopped me cold. I wanted to remind that man that he was a visitor in Bali. "Even if you don't understand local mores and values," I wanted to tell him, "at least show the people some human respect." On my high horse, I was thinking, "How could he know what these people are up against?" My immediate second thought was, "How could I?" My wife and I wrestled with how to afford respect and humanity to people who wanted nothing from us but our money. We talked about the dilemma of objectification on both sides of the social equation and decided to deal directly with the problem of what we saw as being pestered. We took to looking directly at the person who was trying to sell us something and simply saying in a straightforward, pleasant way: "No thank you." This humanized the asker in our eyes, and in most cases, it neutralized the asker's insistence that we buy something. In fact, many of the people started saying, "You're welcome," then directing their attention elsewhere. Possibly our act of making contact humanized us their eyes, too. In this way, we both made a small step toward deobjectifying the other, and a very small step, to be sure, but a step toward social justice.

Art's Role in Fostering Social Justice

The arts are forms of communication between human beings about things that count (Anderson & Milbrandt, 2005; Dewey, 1958/1934; Gardner, 1994; Goodman, 1978; Langer, 1980). The important things that define culture and its values have always been presented and represented though rituals supported and framed by the arts, whether that be a Gelede festival in West Africa (R. Anderson, 1990) or contemporary performance art (Garoian, 2001; Gomez-Pena, 2008). R. Anderson (1990), in fact, defined art as "culturally significant meaning encoded in an affecting sensuous medium" (p. 238). In that capacity, for Dissanayake (1988), art serves a basic, biological, survival function in that it facilitates the social cooperation that is a primary means for our survival as a species. It does this by *aesthetically* displaying (thus causing us to pay attention), thus making concrete a group's core values and beliefs through ritual, ceremony, and other public presentations.

Kechuk Dance. A ritual dance performed in Bali, Indonesia, telling traditional stories as paradigms of correct action for optimal living.

So if art is communication from one human being to another about things that count, what better content than social justice? Precious few things count more than how we treat our fellow human beings and the kinds of relationships we have with them. The right of human beings to be treated fairly, equally, and with dignity and respect is a core value defining what it means to be civilized. It's the root of all social good, and potentially the root of all social progress (Dewey, 1963/1938).

The little bit of progress my wife and I made toward human tolerance in Bali was particularly significant for me because I was there for the 10th anniversary of the *Kids' Guernica Peace Mural Project* (T. Anderson, 2000; Kids' *Guernica*: International Children's Peace Mural Project, 2008), a project which I co-founded with colleagues from Japan, based on the principle of developing tolerance and understanding between individuals and between cultures, using art and art education as the means. While it was a start, I realized my simple act of making contact didn't fundamentally change the relationship each party had to basic resources and opportunities, which was problematic to me, and the causes and solutions to social inequity weighed ever more heavily on my shoulders during the time I was there. What more could I do in my professional role as an art educator to promote social justice?

Framing Art Education for Social Justice

Another insight came during a seminar and retreat, hosted by Doug Boughton and Kerry Freedman, in which the participants argued and tested the place of aesthetics in visual culture art education. Kevin Tavin took his nowwell-known position that the centering of aesthetics and aesthetic contemplation is antiquated and defunct in visual culture education. But I came to an almost opposite position, that in its essence, *art education deals in aesthetic capital as the common denominator for all that we do.* Whether we are visual culture advocates, formalists, essentialists, advocates of art for life, art therapists, arts administrators, researchers, or teachers, *our common content is art and visual artifacts, that is, aesthetically framed artifacts and performances.*

A focus that centers the aesthetic as a means of ingress to content that counts, such as social justice, requires that we leave behind Kant's (1964) idea that the aesthetic is a heightened emotional response, a keen, finely honed type of appreciation engaged *for its own sake.* Certainly many contemporary artists have left this behind already. Fred Wilson, for example, in his piece *Mining the Museum*, placed slave shackles alongside fine silver service to point out that not all lives were the same in colonial America. Barbara Kruger, in her piece *I Shop, Therefore I am*, playing on Descartes' famous "I think therefore I am," invited us to think about identity construction in the consumer culture. She is suggesting that power in the consumer culture rests more deeply on the Cartesian cultural identity, which encourages the split between human beings and nature and allows for rampant consumerism and industrialization that follows from it. In her piece *We Have Received Orders Not to Move*, she depicted a bent-over woman with pins in her, as though she's a voodoo doll. Who put in the pins and why? Is it The Man? Certainly, these aesthetically framed examples challenge given relationships of power, building on the aesthetic for the extrinsic purpose of social justice. They are not art for its own sake.

Wheel, Hock E Aye Vi Edgar Heap of Birds.
Inspired by Native American architectural forms and the Big Horn medicine wheel in Wyoming … artist Hock E Aye Vi Edgar Heap of Birds covered the forked red tree forms with text and imagery related to the history of Indian people in the United States and indigenous peoples elsewhere. Each tree addresses a specific theme, from conflict over resources to global cooperation among indigenous peoples. (Denver Art Museum Home Page, 2008)

Following from the example of socially concerned artists, can art education, too, foster an understanding and serve the purposes of social justice? I believe it can, if it embraces both extrinsic (premodern and postmodern) as well as intrinsic (modern) purposes for art and education (Anderson & Milbrandt, 2005; Dissanayake, 1988; Paskow, 2004). In premodern societies, the aesthetic's role was to cause people to pay attention to things that counted. That continues today, not only in Barbara Kruger's or Fred Wilson's work, but also in every day life. Singing, ceremonial clothing, ritual performance, chalices, murals, menorahs, and a myriad of other artifacts and performances bring our focus to the Christmas pageant, the Gelede festival, or Chanukah. Serrano's *Piss Christ*, the seated Buddha at the Todaiji Temple in Nara, or an Iroquois false face mask all reference values and understandings beyond themselves. Even high modernists Gottlieb and Rothko reflected that art has to be about something other than itself (T. Anderson, 1989).

Attaining social justice through art education entails taking an instrumentalist, reconstructionist stance (Anderson & Milbrandt, 2005). Whether intentionally or not, visual artifacts present us with differing worldviews and sets of beliefs that represent human beings' ways of being, believing, and doing. From a social justice perspective, artworks and visual culture can be used as sensitive instruments to guide us to human understandings that engage both the intellect and the emotions, toward the ends of social reconstruction and social justice. That is our focus in this book. *Art education for social justice, as framed here, centers art forms, visual artifacts, performances, and educational activities that encourage social equity and the opportunity for all people to achieve their vocational, professional, personal, social, and economic goals in the world.* This entails using the aesthetic as the central strategy for exposing, deconstructing, disarming, and acting out against those aspects of culture that promote inequity, that are socially and psychologically manipulative, one-sided, dishonest, or repressive, as well as for constructing visions that provide or potentially provide equal opportunities for all. Such aesthetic strategies include but are not limited to critique, visual exploration, artmaking, and various forms of social activism in the school and in the community.

Our Focus on Action

Taking up social justice in art education necessitates a focus on action. The theoretical groundwork of social inequity and social reconstruction is a well-trodden path that I will come back to briefly in the literature review, but here, we see no reason to walk the same philosophical path yet again. So the focus in this book is not on reinventing the theories of social reconstruction through art, nor in reinterpreting or reiterating those theories. Rather, our purpose is to present examples of those who are walking the talk. Primarily, we present accounts of those who have actually engaged in social justice art education in community and K–12 contexts. Also, we present lesson plans that make it possible for the reader to do the same. The value in this approach is that each story may serve as a model and inspiration for others, as a call to action, as a roadmap to further social justice endeavors. Our collaborators in this book tell stories that give meaning and substance to the theory, that provide the data from which theory can be constructed. In that spirit, I will tell the part of my story that led me to this book.

Leading to This Book: My Story

I grew up in the age of late modernism, a time when much of the understanding of the communal sense of art had been lost. In modernism the individual, not the society, was centered, and art and design reflected this social reality (T. Anderson, 1997a). It was the age of artist as hero. Creative individual expression reigned supreme. The traditional artistic qualities of elaboration and crafting skill were demoted to secondary status except as they serviced creativity. Skillfully crafted artifacts of communal belief were devalued to the level of mere craft, and the artist who continued to act as medium for communal belief was reduced to a mere craftsperson, because his/her work lacked the essential modernist artistic quality of individual creativity. Unlike in traditional societies, where the aesthetic response was an attention-getting device—only the first step in serving an extrinsic social purpose—in modernism, the aesthetic response was the highest purpose and end-goal of art (Greenberg, 1961).

For advocates of social justice through the arts, those were hard times. Functionalist meanings in art were largely co-opted by the corporate manipulations of advertising and commercial design on one hand, and denied by modern, universalist, "high" artists and critics on the other. But fortunately, art and design for social justice was bubbling just below the surface, waiting to break though the crust of modernism. Budding postmodernists questioned whether the modernist idea of the "free" individual—rising above and rejecting tradition, escaping from the repression of the traditions of culture—is desirable or even possible (Bowers, 1987). How good is it, they asked, for individuals to deny, devalue, ignore, or obscure their societies' collective values, mores, institutions, and ways of doing things? How much is lost when an individual fails to acknowledge that he or she is the bearer of tradition? Tradition provides patterns that make communication and collective living possible. To a large degree, tradition determines how one thinks, what one thinks about, and in what ways. These postmodernists (Neo-Marxists, bioregionalists, social reconstructionists, and other activists concerned with social justice and environmental balance) began to seek ways to reconnect the arts and society. Their primary means was recentering the artful artifact (a painting, a performance, a building) in the life of the community.

That was where I entered the flow. As a young man growing up in a modernist social climate, attending art school in Montana, I wondered how to connect my love of art with the other things I really cared about, namely social justice and ecological balance. I kept hitting the wall with my teachers and mentors, until I moved to Eugene, Oregon, and found the town full of street murals and a graduate art education program of activist art educators led by June King McFee and Vincent Lanier. Encouraged by socially framed

People's History of Telegraph Park, 1968, Berkeley, CA.

art education and the painted walls of Eugene, I became a street muralist.

In the late 1960s many social activist artists discovered the walls of their towns and cities as canvases for their expression. First in New York, Chicago, and Los Angeles, and social activist centers like Berkeley, Madison, and Eugene, then spreading everywhere, even to little towns in rural Minnesota, community murals took hold (T. Anderson, 1984). These community murals were instrumentalist in intent with a purpose beyond being pretty or decorative. Usually, the purpose was socially reconstructionist, focused on content such as the civil rights struggle; gender, class, and economic equality; the war in Vietnam; ecological balance and bioregionalism; the right to health care and a good education; and other social justice issues. Rather than being universalist, these murals were locally specific in form and content, rising from the aesthetic of the local community and addressing the local community's issues, values, mores, and aesthetic sensibilities. This was an intrinsically social art, relying on local support for ideas, financing, and even execution.

Immersed in the liberal social culture of Eugene, Oregon, I began to coordinate street mural projects, and later as a high school teacher in western and southern Oregon, I worked with my students to paint social justice murals in the schools. In my doctoral program, at the University of Georgia, I wrote my dissertation on contemporary American street murals using the Feldman (1970) method of critical analysis as my research strategy. I found the Feldman strategy to be excellent in some respects, but too modernist to effectively address extrinsic social purposes of art. Thus, I spent several years thinking how to modify Feldman's model. I ended up with an alternate structure that more intrinsically incorporates crucial socially contextual information, and situates the work in its authentic context, asking of the work not only what it *is*, but also what it is *for* (T. Anderson, 1995), resulting in a critical structure *focused not only on the work but also on its context.*

Shortly after I was hired by Florida State, a Japanese art educator, Abe Toshifumi, was touring the influential art education programs in the United States. He turned up at Florida State University, and I offered him lodging at my home for a few nights. His English was not good, and my Japanese was non-existent. During that first day he'd frequently stop in the middle of a sentence, say "Just a moment," then flip through the Japanese-English dictionary, find his word, and continue on. Communication was a slow business. On the way to my house, we stopped in at a grocery store, where Toshifumi bought a bottle of sake. Then we went home where we watched the Paul Simon Africa concerts on a VHS tape checked out from the library. After plenty of Paul Simon, Ladysmith Black Mambaso, and warm sake, either I became fluent in Japanese or Toshifumi became fluent in English or it didn't matter. We swapped stories about our kids, wives, salaries, and colleagues with ease and comfort. We drew pictures and didn't seem to need the dictionary.

Among my first journal articles, rising from my dissertation, were some about the contemporary American street mural movement, so when Toshifumi left, I gave him some photocopies of journal articles, including one titled "Contemporary American Street Murals: Their Defining Qualities and Significance for Art Education" (T. Anderson, 1984). After that, for about 10 years, Toshifumi and I corresponded regularly and even saw each other a couple times in Japan. Then one day, early in summer 1995, I got a call. "Hi Tom, this is Abe." "Abe San, how are you?" I responded. "Fine," he said. Then cutting to the chase, as he does, he said, "I read about your work with murals carefully and I have an idea. The 50th anniversary of the bombing of Hiroshima is in August. Do you think we could do children's murals from America and Japan as a bridge of peace?" "Oh my god! That's only 2 months from now," I thought. But out loud, I said, "This is a terrific idea. We'll do it!" That was the beginning of the *Kids' Guernica Peace Mural Project*, and I never made a better professional snap decision in my life.

The initial concept was for the mural exchange to be between the US and Japan. Children in the US executed the first mural. I took that mural to

The first Kids' *Guernica* Peace Mural, executed in Tallahassee, FL, Summer 1995.

Japan where Japanese children studied it and executed a mural in response. Then the murals were displayed together in Donari-cho on August 6, 1995, the 50th anniversary of the atom bomb being dropped on Hiroshima. As the project evolved, however, it became apparent to all of us that peace in the world is not simply a Sino-American issue. Consequently, Professor Abe

and Arts Japan brought France, Korea, Papua New Guinea, India, and Nepal into the project, and I recruited teams in Kuwait, Canada, Australia, and other parts of the US to participate. As the project has evolved (sometimes with and sometimes without me), teams have executed a peace mural made jointly by Palestinian and Israeli kids, a mural developed in Afghanistan during the conflict, and one made in the US only weeks after 9/11. As of this writing, nearly 15 years after we started, we continue to recruit peace mural sites. The project now has grown to include more than 200 murals from more than 60 countries.

The project statement says we believe that in spite of the fact that the children and sponsors of this project are of different cultural backgrounds, certain human drives and concerns are universal. One such desire is to live safely in peace, free from war or the threat of war. We also believe that since art is at root an instrument of culture, children of different countries participating in this study will express these universal concerns differently, each according to their own locally specific needs and criteria. Finally, we believe that the power and potential of the project lies in this idea of unity of purpose and diversity of approach. By examining the multiple paths we all take to reach common goals it is our hope that understanding, tolerance, and respect for one another will grow. As expressed in the project statement, we hope this may be a path to world peace.

We determined that cooperative community mural making was a natural vehicle for this peace project since community murals are instrumentalist in nature, focusing on social or community related issues to be addressed and/or acted upon through aesthetic means. Of particular significance for this project is the fact that community murals emphasize group identity and cooperative problem solving. For more information on this project the reader can read the chapter by Fischer and Kaneda later in this volume or go to www.kidsguernica.org. We welcome your participation.

Art and Social Reconstruction

Concurrently with the peace mural project, I was working on a book with Melody Milbrandt, 8 years in the making, called *Art for Life*. In *Art for Life*, Melody and I took a social reconstructionist stance and addressed social justice both in the content we chose and in our suggested teaching and learning processes. Almost all the artists and movements we feature in the book focus on social justice, from Buddhist monks making peace mandalas, to artists from within the art establishment such as social activist artist Bill Viola, whom we feature in our chapter on technology, and Barbara Kruger who deals with issues such as authorship/authority, truth, and power.

We also have a chapter—a sample curriculum unit—devoted to Krzysztof Wodiczko, a Polish-born designer and artist who uses his art to engender debate about social problems, hoping to make people think about solutions. We focus in particular on his invention of a homeless vehicle, of which he made a prototype for the Whitney Biennial in 2000. Another featured artist is Fred Wilson, an artist I mentioned earlier, who reconstructs our collective historical narrative focused on social justice for African Americans.

There are many other artists who work for social justice and who have inspired me: for example, Carrie Mae Weems, who explores gender roles and racism (Lowe, 2007), and Hank Willis Thomas, whose work explores "the relationship between advertising and the black male body. In the 19th century, slaves were prized for their robustness and strength. Commercial uses of black men's bodies place similar values on them, and in so doing, have the huge potential of devaluing their very humanity" (The Story, n.d., para 1). The Guerrilla Girls (2003, 2008) also take on sexism and racism through their art. Guillermo Gomez-Pena (n.d.) takes on cultural stereotyping and Mexican American border crossing in his art performances. Judith Baca (The Social and Public Art Resource Center, 2008) is best known for her large-scale public murals involving extensive community organizing and participation, addressing multi-cultural audiences, for example the Great Wall of Los Angeles, which brought attention to the contributions of California's cultural minorities. These and other artists who have stood up for social justice in their work have been an inspiration to me.

The Point: Art, Education, and Relationship

It is through these experiences and influences that I've come to believe that the core of art is fundamentally about the state of being human, and what that means, as communicated from one human being to another. In essence, art is symbolic communication about human relationships. In that context, and to bring my story to a point, I think art education can serve an important role in helping all of us—teachers and students alike—develop relationships through which we come to understand ourselves and others. These are relationships that constitute community, not only locally, not only with those who share our immediate interests, but community in the larger sense of understanding our place in the web of all peoples, everywhere. In spite of the fact that we are all tribal by nature (having loyalty most naturally to our own group), we also need to understand that across tribes, across economic boundaries, across ethnicities, we are all essentially human; we all have the same biocultural impulses, the same drive to seek love and meaningful work and pleasure; and we all have the same fears that we'll be abused or misunderstood or left alone.

Certainly, our traditional ancestors understood the most important values, traditions, and beliefs were to be carried on the elegant wings of aesthetic form. But the problem, from a social perspective, is that people express these important things differently, in different cultures. In short, art is not a universal language. The impulse for aesthetically framed communication is universal, but art forms themselves are locally and culturally specific: different in different cultures. This fact potentially contributes to the condition of seeing others' artifacts as foreign and exotic, and by extension, the people who made them as not like us—as *Other*. So the task across cultures, both in making and receiving, is to engage sincerely the universally expressive impulse of humankind through its myriad culturally specific art forms toward the end of mutual understanding as a way to humanize and de-objectify each other—to see each other not as stereotypes (rich bitch or beggar), but simply as people, much like ourselves in our shared basic humanity. Unwrapping and interpreting aesthetic forms for meaning with the goals of social justice in place can help us to understand ourselves and others better, setting the foundations for cross cultural and interclass relationships, giving us an avenue to pursue more intelligent, meaningful, and humane action in the arena of life.

Maybe it is too dramatic to claim that social justice can be achieved through the arts, thus that the world can be saved through art. Maybe I should make the more modest claim that the arts can provide windows and mirrors on the world helping us to understand what needs fixing, if we are so inclined. However, I could also reverse the argument and ask, if the world is not to be saved by art, then by what? Artists and art educators have the skills to create aesthetically framed objects and performances that can move people to action. This instrumentalism has been proven through time by the Catholic Church and Hitler among others, and has been one of the most important goals of art and design through all of human history. So I'm going to go out on an idealistic limb, here; *I suggest, as something of a manifesto, that we use the proven power of art (education) for good: to achieve relationships that foster tolerance and respect between individuals, between groups of people, and between nations. I propose we use art (education) as a principled instrument of social justice, where possible, and use the power of art education to communicate relationships that reflect social justice that follows from a faith in art's power to change the world.* This volume was conceived with these ends in mind, and my fellow editors and the authors of following chapters share the one overarching purpose of achieving social justice through art and education.

Literature on Social Justice: A Personal View

Broadly speaking, there are many inspirational writers who engage the cause of social justice. Stalwarts, for me, have been Richard Anderson (1990), James Banks (2001), Chet Bowers (1974, 1987, 2001), Paulo Friere (1970, 1973), Henry Giroux, (Arnowitz & Giroux, 1991; Giroux & Simon, 1989), Tich Nhat Hanh (2008), bell hooks (1994), Ivan Illich (1970), Lucy Lippard (1984, 1990), Neil Postman (1992), and of course John Dewey (1958/1934, 1963/1938). There also are a lot of good, contemporary, practical sources advocating social justice on the Web, such as the *Architecture for Humanity Project* (2008), which addresses homelessness as a result of natural destruction, including tsunami reconstruction, Katrina reconstruction efforts, and other projects such as a rural center of excellence in socially isolated and economically depressed Tanzania, and the Kids with Cameras project for the disenfranchised children of the Calcutta brothels. Another excellent site is *Teaching Tolerance* (2008), sponsored by The Southern Poverty Law Center to oppose hate, bigotry, and bias in all their forms. In addition to the website, this group puts out an excellent free hard copy journal for K–12 education. At another website a number of socially concerned artists and projects are represented (Free Dimension, n.d.). Finally, I want to mention the Adbusters (n.d.) website, which does a terrific job of turning manipulative advertising techniques against the advertisers themselves to promote economic justice through truthful representation.

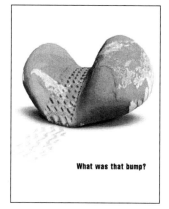

What was that bump?

Adbusters spoof ad, accessed at www. adbusters.org/gallery/spoofads, August 4, 2008.

Social Justice and Art Education

Personally, in art education I first found my social justice inspiration studying with June King McFee (McFee, 1961; McFee & Degge, 1977), under whose tutelage other socially concerned art educators developed, including Blandy and Congdon (1991) and Chalmers (1996). Laura Chapman (1986, 1978) was another art educator who embedded social justice concepts in her work and was huge influence on me. Another strongly influential figure in my development of a social justice sensibility was Edmund Burke Feldman (1970) with his anthropological approach to the field.

Recently, much good work has been done in art education focused on social justice. It is beyond the scope of this essay to address all that literature, but describing some of it will give a sense of the parameters and direction of theory and practice in this arena. Foundationally, art education for social justice takes a contextualist, instrumentalist position that art must be about and for something other than just being decorative for its own sake. Many theorists and practitioners now favor dismantling composition (elements of design) and technique as the central conceptual structure for instruction in art education, and are constructing in their place theme-based, content-oriented instruction in which techniques follow from the need to express something meaningful outside the classroom, something about life.

Many theme-based advocates are social reconstructionists, who center social justice as a primary concern in the content they advocate and teach (Anderson & Milbrandt, 2005). In this context, Powell and Speiser (2005) have edited a fine, mostly practical book on international efforts to address social change through the arts. Desai and Chalmers (2007), more theoretically, engaged in a dialogue about the relationship between art education in schools and society toward a pedagogy of social justice, providing a rationale as well as resources for the task, and examples of social justice art education in action. Like Desai and Chalmers, Pistolesi (2007) argued against formalized school art focused only on compositional and technical skills development in favor of teaching to culturally engaged issues based curricula in art, in this case, peace and war. Gude (2007), too, took formalized school art to task in advocating the forming of the self through investigating community themes encountering difference, attentive living, and empowered experiencing and making. Keifer-Boyd, Amburgy, and Knight (2007) took on unexamined privilege and power in their examination of visual culture education and how it shapes the ways we know ourselves and the world. Desai (2000) discussed the imaging of difference and the politics of representation in multicultural art education. Arnold (2005) described strategies, guiding questions, and lesson ideas for confronting violence through the arts. Colman (2006) reported on her experience as an artist/educator-in-residence at three peace and human rights summer camps for Israeli and Palestinian teenagers. In a similar vein, Cohen-Evron (2005) wrote about five art teachers in Israel and their approaches to dealing with violent conflict between Israelis and Palestinians. Belliveau (2005) addressed bullying in school through an anti-bullying drama project.

Probably the source most consistently focused on the issues of social justice in art education is *The Journal of Social Theory in Art Education*. Every issue of this yearly journal, from its start in the 1990s, has been focused on various aspects of art education for social justice. Picking just one issue, for example, we find an article on teaching for peace and justice (Congdon, 1993), the politics and power relations of choosing and buying a T-shirt in a postmodern world (jagodzinski, 1993), montage as a democratizing strategy for personal expression (Garoian, 1993) and feminism and censorship in art education (Lang, Helgadottir, Blaikie, & Tarlow-Calder, 1993). In another issue I had an article called "Art, Education, and the Bomb: Reflections on an International Children's Peace Mural Project" (T. Anderson, 1997b). In the same issue Ballengee-Morris (1997) reported on the development of Appalachian mountain students' development of a cultural sense of self through locally specific curricula. Examples of articles from another issue include Schellin's (1990) "Art Education in the Time of AIDS," and Snider's (1990) "Feminism as Metaphor," as well as 10 other theme-based articles. Other issues are similarly packed with equally relevant social justice literature. Just this past year, Keifer-Boyd, Emme, & jagodzinski (2008) edited a terrific book reprinting classic articles from the *Journal* through the first 25 years.

The Journal of Cultural Research in Art Education, while not specifically dedicated to it, frequently has had content focused on social justice in art education. I edited an issue focused on constructing peace following the events of September 11, 2001 (T. Anderson, 2002). Some of the contributors included Sandell (2002) who wrote "Same Time Next Year? Reflections on Post-Cataclysmic Art Education," Lankford (2002) who wrote about nurturing humaneness through art education, and Gussak (2002) who wrote about art therapy's potential role in building a bridge of peace. In other issues of *JCRAE*, Bastos and Hutzel (2004) and Bastos (2007) have

reported on their attempt to address racial issues through community art in the Art-in-the-Market program. Whitehead (2005) described the implementation of democratic practices in a large, culturally diverse university classroom, Hutzel and Cerulean (2003) discussed the building of community and environmental responsibility through the development of a "Procession of the Species," and Carpenter (2003) described Pat's Barbershop as a safe, aesthetically constructed, educational place where African Americans can talk straight. Also, Hanes and Nintze (2008) examined how art education might be used to cultivate peace in times of war.

Service-learning is an important focus of art education for social justice. Russell and Hutzel (2007) wrote about promoting students' social and emotional learning through service-learning projects that serve the larger community. Hutzel (2007a) also used the teaching of a computer graphics class as a service learning activity, as a democratic activity, used for the purpose of constructing community, in the Dewian sense, by reaching out to an at-risk student population in an inner city neighborhood. Buffington (2007b) advocated addressing big ideas such as power, community, diversity, and the environment through service learning (university to middle school outreach) in art education. Jeffers (2005) offered an extended look into challenges and reciprocal benefits of service learning to both the community and learners extending the service.

Closely related to service learning, community-based art education (Congdon, Blandy, & Bolin, 2001) also frequently focuses on social justice. For example, Garoian (2001) examined social empowerment through performance art. Irwin and Kindler (1999) provided a forum for examining art education partnerships for community construction beyond the boundaries of the school. Hutzel (2007b) described a participant action study in the West End neighborhood in Cincinnati that sought to change local youths' perceptions through an asset-based art curriculum. Maxine Greene (1995) richly illustrated how art education may serve to engender the power of agency to participants in the construction of a just community. Drawing inspiration from June King McFee, Darts (2006) described the development of a curriculum based on the idea that the arts can facilitate an ethic of care that can transform individuals and communities, and Venable (2005) described the role art therapy and art education can play with incarcerated youth.

Visual culture art education, in its focus on the meaning of art rather than aesthetic appreciation, frequently enters into concerns related to social justice. For example, Freedman (2000) focused on social perspectives on art education in the US toward the end of teaching visual culture in a democracy, while Tavin (2002) explored the meaning and impact of advertising on children and adolescents. Duncum (2006) explored the effects of violent media on young people.

Another common focus of social justice art education is cross-culturalism, multiculturalism, and cultural border-crossing issues. Multicultural art education may or may not deal directly in social justice issues but frequently provides a conceptual foundation for social justice through art. For example, Gall (2008) addressed a strategy to overcome teachers' fear to address cultural diversity. Garber (1995) wrote a classic border-crossing article in which she set the teaching of art in particular cultural contexts. Fattal (2006) suggested a strategy of de-objectifying those of other cultures through an aesthetic focus on food in its personal, community, and larger cultural contexts. Stokrocki (2001) explored a similar strategy, focusing on family and family values. And Stuhr (1994) examined multiple paradigms of multiculturalism in relation to art education and social reconstruction.

Gay and lesbian concerns and gender bias are other foci of social justice in art education. For example Lampela (2005) addressed the writing of effective lesson plans focused on the works and issues of lesbian and gay artists, and Sanders (2007) focused on contemporary and near contemporary broadcast and film productions autoethnographically in relation to queer identity construction. The *International Journal of Art & Design* (Stanley, 2007) devoted an entire issue to lesbian and gay issues in art, design, and mass media. Closely related, gender issues are important in the literature on social justice. For example, Garber (2003) described a course focused on Myra Sadker Day and a feminist perspective on gender bias.

Focused on action, practical curricula have been developed addressing social justice through art education, such as Silverman's (2007) focus on postcards (from both an aesthetic/receptive perspective and creative/production perspective as a source of visual dialogue for cultural tolerance. Buffington (2007a) developed an instructional unit on the Heidelberg Project, an inner-city aesthetic/housing project in Detroit that gives African Americans there a sense of ownership and community. Increasingly, practical curricula can also be found online, for example a site (Art and Social Justice Curriculum Project, 2007) that describes a yearlong project in two Oakland, California, public schools to address social justice through learning in the arts, or the site developed at the University of Iowa that addresses identity and social justice and activism for 9th through 12th grades (Williams, 2008).

Our Contribution to the Literature

It is the editors' sincere hope that this volume meaningfully enhances and expands the literature in art education for social justice, in theory, and, since we are calling for action and providing models of action, especially in practice. Particularly apparent to me in editing the chapters in this book, is the focus of almost all of the authors on collaborative activity: on establishing and maintaining relationships through the messy business of art for life. Art education for social justice is action-oriented, taking place in the social arena toward the social ends of tolerance, equity, fairness, and decency, which make for respect and justice between one human being and another. We deeply appreciate the valuable efforts of the authors who have contributed here and hope their work will inspire you to continue the conversation, and to work for social justice through art education.

REFERENCES

Adbusters. (n.d.). Retrieved December 1, 2008, at http://www.adbusters.org/

Anderson, R. (1990). *Calliope's sisters: A comparative study of philosophies of art.* Englewood Cliffs, NJ: Prentice Hall.

Anderson, T. (1984). Contemporary American street murals: Their defining qualities and significance for art education. *Journal of Multicultural and Cross-cultural Research in Art Education, 2,* 14–22.

Anderson, T. (1989). Interpreting works of art as social metaphors. *Visual Arts Research, 15*(2), 42–51.

Anderson, T. (1995). Toward a cross-cultural approach to art criticism. *Studies in Art Education, 36*(4), 198–204.

Anderson, T. (1997a). Toward a postmodern approach to art education, in J. Hutchens & M. Suggs (Eds.), *Art education: Content and practice in a postmodern era.* Reston, VA: National Art Education Association.

Anderson, T. (1997b). Art, education, and the bomb: Reflections on an International Children's Peace Mural Project. *Journal of Social Theory in Art Education, 17,* 71–97.

Anderson, T. (2000). The Guernica children's peace mural project. *The International Journal of Art and Design Education, 19*(2), 141–152.

Anderson, T. (Ed.). (2002). *Journal of Cultural Research in Art Education,* 19–20.

Anderson, T. & Milbrandt, M. (2005). *Art for life: Authentic instruction in art.* New York: McGraw-Hill.

Architecture for Humanity Project (2008). Updated May, 2008, retrieved May 27, 2008, http://architectureforhumanity. org/projects.htm

Arnold, A. (2005). Confronting violence through the arts: A thematic approach. *Art Education, 58*(4), 13–19, 33.

Arnowitz, S., & Giroux, H. (1991). *Postmodern education: politics, culture, and social criticism.* Minneapolis: University of Minnesota.

Art and Social Justice Curriculum Project. (2007) Constructed April 11, 2007, retrieved May 27, 2008, http://center. cca.edu/about/news/46

Ballengee-Morris, C. (1997). A mountain cultural curriculum: Telling our story. *Journal of Cultural Research in Art Education, 17,* 98–116.

Banks, J., & McGee-Banks, C. (Eds.). (2001). *Multicultural education: Issues and perspectives.* Boston: Allyn & Bacon.

Bastos, F. (2007). Art in the market program: Ten years of community-based art education. *Journal of Cultural Research in Art Education, 25,* 51–63.

Bastos, F., & Hutzel, K. (2004). The Art in the Market project: Addressing racial issues through community art. *Journal of Cultural Research in Art education, 22,* 86–98.

Belliveau, G. (2005). An arts-based approach to teach social justice: Drama as a way to address bullying in schools. *The International Journal of Arts Education, 1*(2), 136–189.

Blandy, D., & Congdon, K. (1991). *Pluralistic approaches to art criticism.* Bowling Green, Ohio: Bowling Green State University Popular Press.

Bowers, C. (2000). *Let them eat data: How computers affect education, cultural diversity* and the prospects of ecological sustainability. Athens, GA. University of Georgia Press.

Bowers, C. (1987). Elements of a post-liberal theory of education. New York: Teachers College Press.

Bowers, C. (1974). *Cultural literacy for freedom.* Eugene, OR: Elan.

Buffington, M. (2007b). Art to bring about change: The work of Tyree Guyton. *Art Education, 60*(4), 33–38.

Buffington, M. (2007b). The big idea: Service learning and art education. *Art Education, 60*(6), 40–45.

Carpenter II, S. (2003). Never a dull moment: Pat's Barbershop as educational environment, hypertext, and place. *Journal of Cultural Research in Art Education, 21,* 5–18.

Chalmers, G. (1996). *Celebrating pluralism: Art, education, and cultural diversity.* Los Angeles: The Getty Education Institute for the Arts.

Chapman, L. (1986). *Instant art, instant culture: The unspoken policy for American schools.* New York: Teachers College Press.

Chapman, L. (1978). *Approaches to art in education.* New York: Harcourt Brace Jovanovich.

Cohen-Evron, N. (2005). Students living within violent conflict: Should art educators play it safe or face difficult knowledge? *Studies in Art education, 46*(4), 309–322.

Colman, A. (2006). Integrating human rights and the visual arts: A peace education project for Israeli and Palestinian teenagers. *International Journal of Education through Art, 2*(1), 43–59.

Congdon, K. (1993). Art teaching for peace and justice. *Journal of Social Theory and Art Education, 13,* 13–36.

Congdon, K., Blandy, D., & Bolin, P. (Eds.) (2001). *Histories of community-based art education.* Reston, VA: National Art Education Association.

Darts, D. (2006). Art education for a change: Contemporary issues and the visual arts. *Art Education, 59*(5), 6–12.

Desai, D. (2000). Imaging difference: The politics of representation in multicultural art education. *Studies in Art Education, 41*(2), 114–129.

Desai, D., & Chalmers, G. (2007). Notes for a dialogue on art education in critical times. *Art Education, 60*(5), 6–12.

Denver Art Museum Home Page. (2008). http://www.denverartmuseum.org/ explore_art/collections/objectDetails/ objectId--107955

Dewey, J. (1963/1938). *Experience and education.* New York: Collier.

Dewey, J. (1958/1934). *Art as experience.* Bantam: New York.

Dissanayake, E. (1988). *What is art for?* Seattle, WA: University of Washington Press.

Duncum, P. (2006). Attractions to violence and the limits of education. *The Journal of Aesthetic Education, 40*(4), 21–38.

Fattal, L. (2006). Sabor Latino: Bodegas of aesthetic ideas. *Art Education, 59*(1), 38–45.

Feldman, E. (1970). *Becoming human through art.* Englewood Cliffs, NJ: Prentice Hall.

Free Dimension, (n.d.). Website for social justice activism through art. Retrieved June 12, 2008.

Freedman, K. (2000). Social perspectives on art education in the U.S.: Teaching visual culture in a democracy. *Studies in Art Education, 41*(4), 314–329.

Freire, P. (1973). *Education for critical consciousness.* New York: Seabury.

Freire, P. (1970). *Pedagogy of the oppressed.* New York: Herder and Herder.

Gall, D. (2008). Navigating a way through plurality and social responsibility. *International Journal of Art & Design Education, 27*(1), 19–26.

Garber, E. (1995). Teaching art in the context of culture: A study in the borderlands. *Studies in Art Education, 36*(4), 218–232.

Garber, E. (2003). Teaching about gender issues in the art education classroom: Myra Sadker Day. *Studies in Art Education, 45*(1), 56–72.

Gardner, H. (1994). *The arts and human development.* New York: Basic Books.

Garoian, C. (1993). Linear perspective and montage: Two dominating paradigms in art education. *Journal of Social Theory and Art Education, 13*, 57–86.

Garoian, C. (2001). Remote control: Performing memory and cultural history, in K. Congdon, D. Blandy, & P. Bolin (Eds.), *Histories of community-based art education*. Reston, VA: National Art Education Association.

Giroux, H., & Simon, R. (1989). *Popular culture, schooling, and everyday life*. Westport, CN: Bergin & Garvey.

Gomez Pena, G. (2008) Gomez-Pena's lapocha nostra. Retrieved 5/27/08, from http://www.pochanostra.com/home/

Goodman, N. (1978). *Ways of worldmaking*. Indianapolis, IN: Hackett.

Greenberg, C. (1961). *Art and culture: Critical essays*. Boston: Beacon.

Greene, M. (1995). *Releasing the imagination: Essays on education, the arts, and social change*. San Francisco: Jossey-Bass.

Gude, O. (2007). Principles and possibility: Considerations for 21st-century art and culture curriculum. *Art Education, 60*(1), 6–17.

Guerrilla Girls. (2003). *Bitches, bimbos, and ballbusters: The Guerrilla Girls' illustrated guide to female stereotypes*. New York: Penguin.

Guerrilla Girls. (2008). Guerrilla Girls: Reinventing the "f" word: feminism, 2008. http://www.guerrillagirls.com/

Gussak, D. (2002). Art therapists as bridge builders of peace. *Journal of Cultural Research in Art Education, 19–20*, 94–102.

Hanes, J. & Nintze, J. (2008). Cultivating peace in times of war. *Journal of Cultural Research in Art Education, 26*, 51–64.

Hanh, T. N. (2008). *The world we have*. Berkeley, CA: Parallax.

hooks, b. (1994). *Teaching to transgress: Education as the practice of freedom*. London: Routledge.

Hutzel, K., & Cerulean, S. (2003). Taking art education to the streets: The "Procession of the Species" as Community Arts. *Journal of cultural Research in Art Education, 21*, 36–43.

Hutzel, K. (2007a). A service-learning approach to teaching computer graphics. *Art Education, 60*(1), 33–38.

Hutzel, K. (2007b). Reconstructing a community, reclaiming a playground: A participatory action research study. *Studies in Art Education, 48*(3), 299–315.

Illich, I. (1970). *Deschooling society*. New York: Harper & Row.

Irwin, R., & Kindler, A. (Eds.) (1999). *Beyond the school: Community and institutional partnerships in art education*. Reston, VA: National Art Education Association.

jagodzinski, j. (1993). The war of labels: An art educator in search of a sign. *Journal of Social Theory and Art Education, 13*, 87–112.

Jeffers, C. (2005). *Spheres of possibility: Linking service learning and the visual arts*. Reston, VA: National Art Education Association.

Kant, I. (1964). *Critique of judgment*. Oxford: Claredon.

Keifer-Boyd, K., Emme, M., & jagodzinski, j. (2008). *InCite, inSight, inSite: Journal of Social Theory in Art Education: The first 25 years*. Reston VA: National Art Education Association.

Keifer-Boyd, K., Amburgy, P., & Knight, W. (2007). Unpacking privilege: Memory, culture, gender, race, and power in visual culture. *Art Education, 60*(3), 19–24.

Kids' Guernica: International Children's Peace Mural Project. (2008). Updated 5/14/2008, retrieved 5/27/08, from http://www.kids-guernica.org/index.html

Lampela, L. (2005). Writing effective lesson plans while utilizing the work of lesbian and gay artists. *Art Education, 58*(2), 33–39.

Lang, H., Helgadottir, G., Blaikie, F., & Tarlow-Calder, P. (1993). Feminism and censorship. *Journal of Social research and Art Education, 13*, 113–156.

Langer, S. (1980). *Philosophy in a new key*. Cambridge, MA. Harvard University Press.

Lankford, L. (2002). Nurturing humaneness. *Journal of Cultural research in Art Education, 19-20*, 47–52.

Lippard, L. (1990). *Mixed blessings: New art in a multicultural America*. New York: Pantheon.

Lippard, L. (1984). *Get the message? A decade of art for social change*. New York: E. P. Dutton.

Lowe, L. (2007). Visual arts: Carrie Mae Weems' cryptic works beg for interpretation. Posted 2/18/07, retrieved 5/27/08, from http://www.rochester.edu/College/humanities/news/index.php?article=548

McFee, J. (1961). *Preparation for art*. San Francisco: Wadsworth.

McFee, J., & Degge, R. (1977). *Art, culture, and environment*. San Francisco: Wadsworth.

Paskow, A. (2004). *The paradoxes of art: A phenomenological investigation*. Cambridge, UK: Cambridge University Press.

Pistolesi, E. (2007). Art education in the age of Guantanamo. *Art Education, 60*(5), 20–24.

Powell, C., & Speiser V. (Eds.). (2005). *The arts, education and social change*. New York: Peter Lang.

Postman, N. (1992). *Technopoly: The surrender of culture to technology*. New York: Knopf.

Russell, R., & Hutzel K. (2007). Promoting social and emotional learning through service learning art projects. *Art Education, 60*(3), 6–11.

Sandell, R. (2002). Same time next year? Reflections on post-cataclysmic art education. *Journal of Cultural Research in Art Education, 19–20*, 13–19.

Sanders III, J. (2007). Queer visual culture texts. *Visual Arts Research, 33*(1), 44–55.

Schellin, P. (1990). Art education in the time of AIDS. *Journal of Cultural Research in Art Education, 10*, 83–93.

Silverman, J. (2007). Postcards from another's home: Visual dialogues for cultural tolerance. *Art Education, 60*(6), 17–24.

Snider, A. (1990). Feminism as metaphor. *Journal of Social Research in Art Education, 10*, 125–127.

Stanley, N. (Ed.) (2007), *The International Journal of Art & Design Education, 26*(1).

Stokrocki, M. (2001). Guerrero family art traditions, in K. Congdon, D. Blandy, & P. Bolin, (Eds.) *Histories of community-based art education*. Reston, VA: National Art Education Association.

The Social and Public Art Resource Center. (2008). The Great Wall resource portal. Updated and retrieved 5/27/08, from http://sparcmurals.org:16080/sparcone/index.php?option=com_content&task=view&id=20&Itemid=52

The Story. (n.d.). Hank Willis Thomas. Retrieved 5/27/08, from *http://thestory.org/photo-galleries/hank-willis-thomas*

Stuhr, P. (1994). Multicultural art education and social reconstruction. *Studies in Art Education, 35*(3), 171–178.

Tavin, K. (2002). Engaging advertisements: Looking for meaning in and through art education. *Visual Arts Research, 28*(2), 38–47.

Teaching Tolerance. (2008). Updated May, 2008, retrieved May 27, 2008, from *http://www.tolerance.org/index.jsp*

Venable, B. (2005). At-risk and in-need: Reaching juvenile offenders through art. *Art Education, 58*(4), 48–53.

Williams, R. (2008). Art, identity, social justice, and human rights (an art education curriculum), constructed 2008, retrieved May 27, 2008, from http://www.uiowa.edu/~artlearn/ASJHR/ArtSocialJustice.htm.

Whitehead, J. (2005). Democratic community and cultural diversity. *Journal of Cultural Research in Art Education, 23*, 118–126.

Social Justice through a Curriculum Narrative: Investigating Issues of Diversity

Christine Ballengee-Morris, Vesta A. H. Daniel, and Patricia L. Stuhr

Multiculturalism in the United States of America

Part of the discussion of diversity issues must be grounded in the concept of multiculturalism. Since the turn of the 19th century, people have been interpreting multiculturalism through various lenses (e.g. sociocultural, political, academic, and pedagogical), all of which are biased. The evolution of terms, specifically the word *multicultural*, is being questioned as reality continually shifts. History provides our foundation and defines our vocabulary for considering the term *multicultural*. It also provides a focused vision, and through critical reflection and analysis, reveals the nature of conflicts surrounding the term multicultural. Through this type of analysis, the evolving term *multicultural* now includes intercultural, intracultural, and crosscultural, and their intersections and complexities. The breadth of these conceptual changes surrounding the term *multicultural* is profoundly affected by and, in turn [these changes] affect visual culture and education as represented through the arts, contemporary media and artifacts, and associated narratives.

Although multiculturalism is presented primarily in terms of educational reform, the broader concept of multiculturalism is not new. Multiculturalism is a reality because of our ancestors' nomadic lifestyles. *National Geographic*'s 1999 article on "Global Culture" (Swerdlow, 1999) visualized and described the nomadic nature of our predecessors. Nomadic life demanded that humans develop adaptations to the new environments they encountered. These diverse environmental adaptations helped groups of humans create varied cultural systems. While traveling, groups of humans encountered others and their different lifestyles. Their reactions to these encounters were many and complex: among them, curiosity, avoidance, fear, violence, joy, trading, sharing, feasting, uniting, negotiation, creation of community, assimilation, and enculturation.

Today humans are still mobile (nomadic) beings; however, much of the traveling is via virtual networks: television, radio, films, and computer technology. For these reasons, the dimensions of the challenge of multiculturalism are larger for people, especially educators who use these virtual depictions and narratives to teach the issues and implications of this topic to students.

Multiculturalism and School Reform

The complex issues of cultural diversity are often studied as a part of the school reform movement known as Multicultural Education. *Multicultural Education* is a concept, philosophy, and a process that originated in the 1960s as part of the Civil Rights Movement to combat racism (Sleeter & Grant, 1987). It was then, and still is, an educational process dedicated to providing more equitable opportunities in social, political, and especially educational arenas for disenfranchised individuals and groups to gain. This is an ideal, like the ideal of democracy, which may never be completely met; however, it is still seen by many as a worthy and necessary educational goal for a more just and equitable society (Sleeter & Grant, 1987). All forms of education act as social intervention and the implementation of these forms reconstructs society in various ways. Notably the practice

KEY CONCEPTS

- Social Reconstructionism
- Visual Culture
- Community
- Narratives
- Terrorist

of multicultural art education has been characterized by a broad-brush approach to limitations such as generalizations and stereotypes. However, through narratives individual, local, national, and global differences and similarities are emphasized and generalized categories are harder to preserve. The narrative enables us to pay attention to particular points through attention to particular details.

Concepts of multiculturalism in art education are continually in process in order to encourage social justice and thriving, constructive communities. Process rather than product should be the consequence of curriculum guided by democratic social goals and values. These goals and values are meant to confront the "racial class, gender, and homophobic biases woven into the fabric of society" (Bigelow, Harvey, Karp, & Miller, 2001, p. 1). This process helps explain and confront colonialist practices that stem from one group of people having power over another group's "... education, language(s), culture(s), lands and economy" (Ballengee-Morris, 2000, p. 102). Moreover, these goals and values provide for classroom practices that are built on empathy, democracy, and social justice. Strategies for reaching these goals can be found in the processes of constructing positive and supportive communities. Through our deliberations on the development of multicultural curriculum, we advocate that it is guided by democratic social goals and values. These goals and values should: (1) be grounded in the lives of students; (2) provide a critical lens to view all social and cultural systems; (3) establish a safe environment in which to do critical inquiry; (4) incite an investigation of bias; (5) present justice for all as a goal; (6) provide for participatory and experiential involvement; and (7) be hopeful, joyful, kind, visionary, affirming, activist, academically rigorous, integrated, culturally sensitive, and utilize community resources (Daniel & Collins, 2002; Ballengee-Morris & Stuhr, 2001; Bigelow, Harvey, Karp, & Miller, 2001).

Good curricula and teaching, particularly in the area of multiculturalism, should connect with the students' narratives, needs, experiences, and communities. Students need to understand that their identities are constructed by the stories that they tell about themselves and the stories that are told about them (Cohen-Evron, 2005). It is important for students to investigate how their lives connect to and are limited by the broader society. Students need critical skills to address social issues and to think through how some groups may benefit or suffer from the colonial practices and decisions of other people. When it is possible to do so, students should move,

conceptually and physically, outside of the classroom to link with real-world communities, issues, and problems in order to practice these critical skills. This type of critical investigation is not without threat or danger; thus, teachers must be empathetic, practical, and cautious in creating mentally and physically safe environments in which learning can occur. It is necessary to examine biases that lead to prejudice, discrimination, and colonialism through the exploration of history, current social issues, and visual culture. Students need to recognize their own biases and those of others in order to see the connections between power and wealth and injustice. The concept of justice and equitable opportunities for all are important goals. To help students in understanding these goals, it is necessary to create opportunities in which they can actively participate in and experience these concepts firsthand. Examining and producing visual culture imagery and objects that lead to and end in an understanding of justice and the complexities of social, political, and economic relations are valuable goals for education.

Toward reaching these goals, the classroom should serve as a microcosm for a democratic society, in which students are cared for and enabled to care for each other. Caring about students and enabling them to care about others helps them to create an environment in which they may feel safe and secure and allows them to be hopeful, joyful, kind, visionary, and affirming. These are qualities that we would like to see employed in the larger democratic society. Our goal is for students to envision themselves as capable of valuing their lives, embracing integrity, and being advocates and activists for justice. This is possible only through an integrated curriculum that is academically demanding and conceptually connected to students' lives. Visual culture provides a stimulating component to integrated curriculum by posing images and objects that characterize complexity, ambiguity, contradiction, paradox, and multiple perspectives. In this way, students learn that real life is messy and issues are not solved by having one right answer. Solutions involve discussion, compromise, negotiation, arbitration, mediation, cultural sensitivity, and openness to community resources, multiple representations, and re-representations (Bigelow, Harvey, Karp, & Miller, 2001; Daniel, 2001).

Curriculum needs to go beyond the prepackaged curricula formulas and narrow agendas often imposed by state and national guidelines. It should be built on empathy, democracy, and critical practice. The goals and values we proffer provide for a curriculum that is credible, authentic, and practical. It engages students and teachers with a sense of educational purpose and connects students with the visual culture and narratives of the communities that surround them (Bigelow, Harvey, Karp, & Miller, 2001).

We are not of the mind that multicultural school reform and its goals and values represent an answer or a model that can be learned finally and put in place in a prescribed manner within a static curriculum. Rather, teachers and students should learn to look at their own as well as the cultural construction of others through and in visual culture. Using a critical perspective, the community of learners may come to understand that what has been socially learned can also be unlearned or changed by individuals within the group or community, if it is deemed necessary to do so.

Change in the community can be energized or deterred by its cultural identity and connections. Cultures are not discrete entities but are connected to peoples' lives and driven by their choices. People within groups, who are part of a state or nation and who are influenced by global events and media, carry the responsibility of their rights and can be blamed for inaction. We live in a global world and our daily lives are impacted by that reality. It is also important to understand that our lives are connected to and influence the lives of others. How we make meaning of the narratives that are constructed locally, nationally, and globally through visual culture needs to be a part of the art education curricula. Desai (2005) has suggested the importance of "charting the global networks that connect economic, social, political process to aesthetic production, thereby opening spaces for students to examine the relationship between local and global" (p. 305). Getting people to think critically about their own and their group's narratives and actions and whom they are empowering or disenfranchising through their personal narratives, life, actions, and work (which includes making and interpreting the meaning of visual culture), is important (Ballengee-Morris & Stuhr, 2001). The action or inaction of each person ultimately affects all persons.

History, Heritage, and Tradition

The dynamic and interactive concepts of history, heritage, tradition, and culture need to be defined from a social anthropological perspective to facilitate the understanding of multicultural art and visual culture education. *History* can be understood as an oral or written story of a particular people's past. It is the past collective experiences and personal and dialogic narratives of sociocultural groups as they were recorded by, often privileged, representatives of that group. *Heritage* can be explained as what we have inherited from a specific sociocultural group's history and utilize in our

lives. *Traditions* are the practices based in heritage that tie the culture of lived experiences of a person within a group to certain narratives (real or fictional), such as songs, art and visual culture, food, and clothing. History, heritage, and traditions do not exist only in the past. These concepts are continually being constructed and reconstructed in the present to make them meaningful and relevant for people's lives. Individuals' varied experiences within the history, heritage, tradition, and culture of the groups to which they belong is what produces diversity (Ballengee-Morris & Stuhr, 2001; Chanda & Daniel, 2000).

Culture

Perhaps the most misunderstood concept is culture. It is often thought to be a static, esoteric entity that is outside of an individual's lived experience. According to Daniel (2001), culture is made up of what we do and what we value. David Morris said that "[C]ulture is the heritage of the future" (Morris, in personal communication, 2000). Culture provides a dynamic blueprint for how we live our lives and confines our possibilities for understanding and action. This is one reason that it is so important to learn about the culture and values of others. Multicultural education helps us see broader possibilities for ways of thinking about life and death and the available choices for action. We all have cultural connections because we all live and exist within social groups. How we live our lives is influenced by aspects of our personal sociocultural identity as lived within a particular nation or nations by global issues. The conditions possible for individuals' social and cultural change are in part determined by the governing system of the nation or nations in which one lives or of which one is a citizen. This larger political system often is referred to as the national culture or macroculture. Nations' governmental systems are continually subject to change, depending upon the current political, social, and economic conditions. We are all influenced by global issues and the economic and political state of the world, represented through visual culture, most often at a virtual level (Ballengee-Morris & Stuhr, 2001).

Personal Cultural Identity

The aspects of one's personal cultural identity include: age; gender and sexuality; social and economic class (education, job, family position); exceptionality (giftedness, differently abled, health); geographic location (rural, suburban, urban, as well as north, south, east, west, or central); religion; political status; language; ethnicity (the aspect most people concentrate on when they think about culture); and racial designation (Ballengee-Morris & Striedieck, 1997; Banks & Banks, 1993; Gollnick & Chinn, 1998; Sleeter & Grant, 1987; Stuhr, 1995). These aspects of our personal cultural identity are shared, often through stories with different social groups and are often greatly influenced by the national culture(s) in which the group exists. A person's existence and participation within these groups are often the bases for positions of power and acts of discrimination. The various aspects of a person's cultural identity are in transition and dynamic. Recognizing our own sociocultural identity and our biases makes it easier to understand the multifaceted cultural identities of others, including how it might help clarify why and how they might respond as they do (Ballengee-Morris & Stuhr, 2000). Ultimately, all we can ever understand is a part of a cultural group based on a member's temporal experience as they report or express it (Scott, Stuhr, & Krug, 1995). Because partial, temporal understandings of a group are all that exist, it is not possible to come to a complete understanding of a homogeneous culture. For example, there is no such thing as "an" African American culture or "a" Native American culture or "a" Jewish culture. All of these groups can be viewed ethnically, culturally, or spiritually and within the groupings there are vast differences. The label Native American includes over 500 tribes; traditionalists, Christians, and combinations; urban, rural, and reservation settings. There is no single cultural group that could be understood through memorizing its characteristics. The more that is learned about the narratives of various members of a particular group's history, heritage, traditions, and cultural interactions, the more complexly and richly one can understand the social and cultural groups to which they belong (Stuhr, 1999).

National and Global Culture

National cultural identity often is fragmented into region, state, province, county, and local community levels where institutions, laws, and policies exist and change. National culture is primarily political and is the site where cultural beliefs and values are formed, sanctioned, and/or penalized. "[T]his process occurs within a hegemonic power structure to create order and conformity that mediates the uncertainty and conflict of everyday life and social and environmental changes" (Ballengee-Morris & Stuhr, 2000, p. 3). National culture identities have history, heritage, and traditions associated with them. These identities are continually being constructed and reconstructed in accordance with the current political

opinions. It is also important to note that individuals often, voluntarily or involuntarily, attend to images and artifacts of visual culture. An example of this would be the collective image presented by three major figures in U.S. national government: Condoleezza Rice, Colin Powell, and Brigadier General Vincent Brooks (see Figure 1).

Figure 1. Photographs by Associated Press: Condoleezza Rice, Colin Powell, and Brigadier General Vincent Brooks.

All of these individuals are African American and have portrayed in the past or do currently portray the war in Iraq as a fact, to be consumed in a way that makes us feel the US is in control and we are all safe. These spokespersons have presence, power, and authority. This collective image is very complex. What questions about this collective visual culture image does this raise? They are all great role models; however, in the United States imagery that represents race is still a formidable component. Given this, the following questions may be important in exploring the nature and impact of visual culture. What is the national agenda behind the placement and visibility of these individuals? If these individuals are viewed as icons connected with the war, do they serve as an effective military recruiting tool for other African Americans and people of color and should they be used in this way?[1] Another example involving visual culture that exposed issues of race and social class in the US was presented during media representations of hurricane Katrina in August 2005. As government officials and news media personnel discussed issues raised by the ineffective process of evacuating and sheltering the poor, they often presented the plight of these survivors from a racist lens. In one report, white people *found* food and black people *looted*. Issues were raised concerning the major television networks' collusion in representing race and poverty from a racist point of view.[2]

The media representation of race is meant to recruit and show equality. The two photographs, in this situation, affirm the stereotypes that white is good and black is bad. The representations and the dialogic narratives within the local, national, and global communities not only affect students today, but also influence how they make meaning concerning people and events during their lives.

Investigating and critiquing our understanding(s) of our national culture(s) is an ongoing process that may help us and/or students to identify and to recognize our ethnocentric perspectives at the national, regional, state, and local levels. Individuals also may travel to other countries to visit and to live, either willingly or unwillingly; perceptual aspects of their previous national culture(s) journey with them. These nomadic notions color and affect their understandings of the new national culture(s) that may be encountered. This inquiry process is important because it creates the potential for critique of national culture at all levels and opens up possibilities of becoming familiar with the national cultures of others, especially when the nomadic understandings and experiences of others are allowed to be expressed. The process is also significant because it facilitates the understanding of the foundations of democracy, its potential, and its risks in achieving our goals of educating responsible, accountable, active members of society through the arts and visual culture education.

Global culture is largely fueled by economics and affects all national cultures. It functions through mass media (television, radio, newspapers, telephones, faxes, etc.) and computer technology (e-mail, World Wide Web, etc.) to produce hegemonically constructed, shared, and virtual cultural experiences. Global culture directly or indirectly affects most individuals on the planet, especially the youth. It involves the commodification and control of personal and national culture at an international level. One of the mainstays of this cultural level is visual culture, along with the history, heritage, and traditions that are created by capitalist manufacturers' desires for global sales. The merchandise of global culture could be products, ideology or politics, war, religion, and spirituality. Mass media merchandising can be a positive and useful tool when co-opted for educational purposes such as *Sesame Street*, saving endangered species (Ballengee-Morris & Stuhr, 2001).

The personal, national, and global aspects of culture make up a fluid and dynamic mesh of an individual's cultural identity. They are wholly integrated into one's personality and experience. In our discussion of the personal, national, and global aspects of cultural life, these aspects have been separated and discussed individually. Personal, national, and global cultures are integrated and continually affect each other's everyday life. We believe the purpose of multicultural school reform is to help students identify and deal with cultural complexity and issues of power as associated with social affiliations and narratives about personal, national, and global cultural identity(ies).

Curricular Considerations

When a particular concept is addressed in the classroom, it is more meaningful if it is posed as an issue or question for students to investigate. It then becomes the driving force of the curriculum. A concept that is relevant to students' lives, organizations. and agencies that help children and that is worthy of study in art education is terrorism (Cohen-Evron, 2005). There are many organizations and agencies with assistive information about helping children and families cope with the stress of war, terrorism, and other crises such as the American Psychological Association (www.apa.org), National Association of School Psychologists (www.nasponline.org), and National Center for Post Traumatic Stress Disorder (www.ncptsd.org/facts/specific/fs_children.html). These websites can also provide teachers with a rationale for teaching about complex concepts inherent in the current social condition of the world. Terrorist threats and attacks on the US and the realities of war as seen in the media each day are frightening experiences for all Americans, especially children. They may be especially fearful because children worry that threatened or actual military actions in the Middle East will result in more 9/11 situations here in the US. Terrorism affects students and teachers at personal, communal, national, and global cultural levels. These narratives might have intense psychological and physical affects on our students. Investigating the concept of terrorism can also inform students of the causes and deterrents associated with it and help to alleviate their misconceptions, fears, and, even possibly, physical distress. Teachers and other adults need to help students feel safe at a time when the world is perceived and viewed through selective media stories as a dangerous place. It is important to help students understand current events factually and realistically. By exploring a concept such as terrorism through visual culture teachers can help students to investigate how events do or do not impact their lives, and to deal responsibly with the emotions they engender. Not all students will be affected by the study of the concept of terrorism in the same way. Emotions evoked through visual culture imagery may be intense: fear, loss of control, anger, isolation, loss of stability, and confusion. Students who have suffered personal loss, or have been exposed to terrorist acts or military actions, are more likely to feel intensified emotions and be more vulnerable. Students whose parents or acquaintances are in the military or are first responders may also be more strongly affected. Consideration of community, postcolonialism, and social justice provide us with lenses to address the issues/questions concerning terrorism within a nation that espouses democracy as the backbone of our national beliefs. All children, however, are likely to be affected in some way by war or terrorism involving our country. On the National Association School Psychologists' (NASP) website, there is a section called *Children and Fear of War and Terrorism*, which states that students:

> … may have trouble understanding the difference between violence as entertainment and the real events taking place on the news. Today's children live in the world of *Armageddon, Independence Day, Air Force One*, and cartoon Super Heroes. Some of the modern media violence is unnervingly real. Youngsters may have difficulty separating reality from fantasy, cartoon heroes and villains from the government soldiers and real terrorists. Separating the realities of war from media fantasy may require adult help. (www.nasponline.org, #10)

Figure 3. Does the fear of terrorism justify discriminatory behaviors? (www.crf.usa.org/terror/terrorism_links.htm)

Figure 4. Who is a terrorist? (crf-usa.org/terror/terrorism_links.htm)

Figure 2. Who gets to identify who a terrorist is? (Photographs by Associated Press)

For example, issues/questions dealing with the concept of terrorism might be: Who gets to identify who a terrorist is (Figure 2)? Does the fear of terrorism justify discriminatory behaviors (Figure 3)? Who is a terrorist (Figure 4)? How is terrorism related to colonialism (Figure 5)? These types

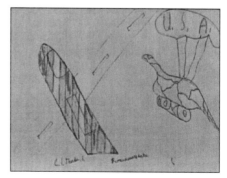

Figure 5. *Bronuasuartake*, Drawing by Jeremy Meisel, age 8, influenced by Desert Storm.

of questions require that both students and teachers consider their own beliefs, values, knowledge, and life experiences. Such questions also provide an opportunity to look at the influences of visual culture on each of these variables. Even small children can investigate such issues or questions, if they are made relevant to the children's life experiences. The complex concept of terrorism is one that could be explained and explored through a related notion of conflict. For instance, it might be more engaging and sensible for children to address the concept of terrorism or conflict by exploring visual imagery found in familiar items such as toys, cartoons, television programs, video and computer games, nightly news, and mall arcades. Students may also have overheard adult conversations that focused on social concerns such as terrorism. Teachers can be assisted in the process of developing curricula by turning to websites and videos by organizations such as Teaching Tolerance, TIME for Kids, and Media Awareness, among other resources.[3]

It is important for teachers and other adults to acknowledge that they do not like terrorists or war. The importance of keeping and bringing peace to situations and areas disturbed by terrorists and war activity is also important to acknowledge. Letting students know that we are all frightened and dislike the unsettling and disturbing images we see in the media and news is important to acknowledge. However, it is equally important to help students imagine, envision, and represent the possibility for a more peaceful, kind, and socially responsible world. Both students and teachers need to feel socially connected, and should be encouraged to help each other through this difficult period of our history to brighter, peaceful world. Although our government and media may not clearly define through the images, they show the difference between terrorism and war; it is important that, as educators and those informed about visual representation, these distinctions are made clear. It is important that teachers stop students from stereotyping people from other cultures or countries. It is also important to help students understand that bullying and harassment are not acceptable behaviors and that these forms of action do not improve safety for any group of people or society, but rather contribute to an environment that condones terrorist activity. Teachers and students need to jointly plan, imagine, and represent creative solutions for a terror-free world.

Children may play "war," pretend to blow things up, or include images of violence in artwork and writing. This may be upsetting to adults under current circumstances, but it is a normal way for children to express their awareness of events around them. Gently redirect children away from violent play or efforts to "replay" the terrorist attacks, but don't be overly disapproving unless the play is genuinely aggressive. Talk with children about their art or written images and how they feel. Share your reactions. Help them to consider the consequences of war or terrorist acts—what happens if a building blows up or a bomb explodes? For children who seek pretend play as an outlet, encourage role-playing of the doctors, firemen, policemen, etc. who have helped to save lives. If a child seems obsessed with violent thoughts or images for more than a few days, talk to a mental health professional. (www.nasponline. org, # 5)[4]

Educators should investigate the facts about developments in the war and protections against terrorism. It is important that students' questions be answered with information and not speculation. Teachers should be prepared to communicate with community members by providing a rationale for addressing the concept of terrorism and letting parents know if their child is exhibiting undue stress over the topic. This will help parents understand what their children are learning about their world and concepts such as terrorism, which can foster thoughtful discussion at home and create a sense of safety and security.

The process of constructing curriculum narrative with social justice as a goal can help students to view images in a thoughtful manner so that they will develop democratic ways of thinking and become informed consumers. By learning about the ways in which the visual arts can influence people, children can be prepared to decide how they will allow themselves to be influenced. They can learn early how civic leaders use stories and imagery to represent themselves and influence people's voting choices. To promote social justice, children should begin to learn about the ways in which groups of people are represented in their stories and imagery. Through art education, children can come to understand the damaging effects of misrepresentation and visual stereotypes (Freedman & Stuhr, 2005).

REFERENCES

Ballengee-Morris, C., & Streidieck, I. M. (1997). A postmodern feminist perspective on visual arts in elementary teacher education. In D.R. Walling (Ed.), *The role of the arts and humanities in postmodern schooling*. Bloomington, IN: Phi Delta Kappa.

Ballengee-Morris, C. (2000). A sense of place: Allegheny Echoes. In K. Congdon, D. Blandy, & P. Bolin (Eds.), *Making invisible histories of art education visible*. Reston, VA: National Art Education Association.

Ballengee-Morris, C., & Stuhr, P. L. (2000). Heritage, traditions, and culture in a changing world. *Art Education, 54*(4), 6–13.

Ballengee-Morris, C., & Stuhr, P. L. (2001). Multicultural art and visual culture education in a changing world. *Art Education, 54*(4), 6–13.

Banks, A. J., & Bank, C. A. (1993). *Multicultural education: Issues and perspectives* (2nd ed.). Needham Heights, MA: Allyn & Bacon.

Bigelow, B., Harvey, B., Karp, S., & Miller, L. (2001). *Rethinking our classrooms, volume two: Teaching for equity and justice*. Milwaukee, WI: Rethinking Schools Limited.

Boughton, D., Freedman, K., Hausman, J., Hicks, L., Madeja, S., Metcalf, S., Rayala, M., Smith-Shank, D., Stankiewicz, M., Stuhr, P., Tavin, K., & Vallence, E. (2002). Art education and visual culture. *NAEA Advisory*. Reston, VA: National Art Education Association.

Chanda, J., & Daniel, V. (2000). ReCognizing works of art: The essences of contextual understanding. *Art Education, 53*(2), 6–11.

Cohen-Evron, N. (2005) Students living within a violent conflict: Should art educators "play it safe" or face "difficult knowledge"? *Studies in Art Education, 46*(4), 309–322.

Daniel, V. (2001). Art education as a community act: Teaching and learning through the community. *Conference Proceedings for the New prospects of Art Education in Theory and Practice Symposium*, National Taiwan Normal University, Taipei.

Daniel, V., & Collins, C. (2002). Community visions. In C. Basualdo (Ed.), *Face Your World* (pp.81–94). Columbus, OH: Wexner Center for the Arts/The Ohio State University.

Desai, D. (2005). Places to go: Challenges to multicultural art education in a global economy. *Studies in Art Education, 45*(4), 293–308.

Freedman, K., & Stuhr, P. L. (2005). Curriculum and visual culture. In M. Day & E. Eisner (Eds.), *Handbook of Art Education Research*. Reston, VA: National Art Education Association.

Gollnick, D.M., & Chinn, P.C. (1998). *Multicultural education in a pluralistic society* (5th ed.). Columbus, OH: Charles E. Merrill Publishing Company.

Sleeter, C., & Grant, C. (1987). An analysis of multicultural research in the United States. *Harvard Educational Review, 57*(4), 421–445.

Stuhr, P. L. (2007). Miracle's gate: Altar for a white buffalo. *Journal of Cultural Research in Art Education, 24*(1), 29–39.

Scott, A. P., Krug, D., & Stuhr, P. (1995). A conversation about translating the indigenous story. *Journal of Multicultural and Cross-Cultural Research in Art Education, 13*(1), 29–45.

Stuhr, P. (1995). A social reconstructionist multicultural art curriculum design: Using the powwow as an example. In R. W. Neperud (Ed.), *Context Content and Community in Art Education: Beyond Postmodernism*. New York: Teachers College Press. (pp. 193–221).

Stuhr, P. L. (1999). Multiculturalism Art Education: Context and Pedagogy. *FATE, Journal of the College Art Association, 22*(1), 5–12.

Swerdlow, J. L. (1999). Global culture. *National Geographic, 196*(2), 2–5.

ENDNOTES

[1] African Americans make up 12% of the general population of the US. 21% serve in the U.S. military. 30% are Army enlisted. www.commondreams.org

[2] For visuals and further commentaries see www.salon.com/news

[3] www.Mediaawareness.ca/eng/ www.nctvv.org/National Coalition on TVViolence www.timefor kids.comTIME for Kids

[4] Adapted from *Children and War—Responding to Operation Desert Storm* by Debby Waddell and Alex Thomas (Helping Children Grow Up in the 90s, National Association of School Psychologists, 1992) and modified from material posted on the NASP website following the September 2001 terrorist attacks.

Aligning Our National Visual Arts Standards with the Social Justice Aims of Art Education

Elizabeth M. Delacruz

This chapter considers ideas about the social justice oriented aims of art education in the 21st century, with attention to conceptualizations both offered by and missing from our *National Visual Arts Standards*. The *National Visual Arts Standards* attempt to describe and guide preparation, staff development, curriculum design, instruction, student learning, scheduling, and assessment in arts education. They also function to publicly define the nature, purpose, and value of arts education in the United States. Published by the National Art Education Association in 1994, the *Visual Arts Standards* are a component of the *National Standards for Arts Education* (1994), which also include dance, music, and theater standards. My insights and suggestions are based on contemporary and longstanding scholarly writings about and practices in art and art education; my past 28 years of teaching art in K–12, higher education, and other settings (early childhood settings, community sites, museums, etc.); and my reflections about the practices of the teachers and arts advocates with whom I have worked all these years.

All of the art teachers I have ever known believe that they are making a difference in the world. Like me, my art teacher friends believe that works of art embody the values and achievements of diverse peoples and civilizations, and that the creation and study of those works provides a means through which young people come to a deeper understanding of what it means to be human. For cultural anthropologist Ellen Dissanayake (2003), the creation and cultural utilization of art not only involve processes of *making special*; they also give biological, cultural, and evolutionary advantage to

KEY CONCEPTS
- National Visual Arts Standards
- 21st Century
- Social Justice
- Technology
- Community Arts Partnerships

human societies. Philosophers, historians, and art education theorists have similarly observed that artworks embody something quite significant, and that systematic study of the contents and contexts of art from diverse societies provides both a justification and a guide for those involved in art education.

Such is also the view articulated throughout the *National Visual Arts Standards* (1994), which attempt to describe the core values of the visual arts education community:

All peoples, everywhere, have an abiding need for meaning—to connect time and space, experience and event, body and spirit, intellect and emotion. [The arts] connect each new generation to those who have gone before, equipping the newcomers in their own pursuit of the abiding questions: Who am I? What must I do? Where am I going? (p. 1)

These somewhat romantic and idealized views seem distant from more recent politically charged discourse in visual arts education, that is, those social-theory oriented formulations about the *critical* functions of art education in contemporary life, the challenge to art teachers to tackle difficult social issues in the classroom, and the assertion that art education should be a catalyst for change toward more equitable societal institutions and practices.

I have been a contributor to this kind of academic discourse about the moral underpinnings of art education. I am both compelled by and wary of such directives, noting that a great bulk of it emanates from individuals employed in university settings. I have spent too much time working in and with public school K–12 art programs and teachers to believe that art teachers are well positioned or secure enough in their schools and communities to carry out such politically charged mandates without considerable efforts, sacrifices, risks, and assistance from their counterparts in university settings (Delacruz, 1990, 2000).

At the same time I am an idealist. I believe that art teachers can and do make a difference, that they are agents of social change, and that they are greatly needed and highly relevant, now more than ever. With some degree of optimism, I consider here how our national visual arts standards *might* support a 21st-century framework for art education—one that regards art as both an embodiment of human values *and* as a means for social reconstruction. I connect the aims of art education as expressed in our national standards to notions of art education that align with the ideas of social justice, citizenship, and global civil society,[1] now more possible due to the proliferation and ubiquity of creative *networked* digital media. My thesis is that art education in the 21st century needs to foster local and global citizenship.

Why Art? Why Citizenship? Why Now?

In answer to the question "What benefits does an art education provide?" the *National Visual Arts Standards* acknowledge the influence of the arts "in their power to create and reflect cultures, in the impact of design on virtually all we use in daily life, and in the interdependence of work in the arts with the broader worlds of ideas and action (1994, p. 3). As this important policy document asserts, "If our civilization is to continue to be both dynamic and nurturing, its success will ultimately depend on how well we develop the capacities of our children, not only to earn a living in a vastly complex world, but to live a life rich in meaning" (pp. 1–2). From the point of view of a multicultural educator like me, a life rich in meaning is one that is deepened and broadened by a sense of connection to others and enriched by an impetus to civic action, or public engagement (Delacruz, 2005). The creation of art and the study of works of art of culturally diverse people facilitate such a connection, fostering the development of communal identity, intercultural understanding, empathy, and compassion (Delacruz, 1995, 2003; Lankford, 2002; Zimmerman, 2002). This view, also reflected in our national standards, relies on the belief that "an education in the arts benefits *society* because students of the arts gain powerful tools for understanding human experiences, both past and present. They learn to respect the (often very different) ways others have of thinking, working, and expressing themselves" (1994, p. 35). These diverse ways of thinking, embodied in arts as a form of personal and cultural storytelling (Blandy & Kellman, 2004), may be explored and examined in the art room, and it is through the sharing of these diverse stories (life narratives and experiences) that individuals bond with one another within and across communities and cultural divisions. In this view, art educators provide both a special *place* within their schools and the *means through which* the development of student humaneness is nurtured (Lankford, 2002). Coupled with cultivation of a sense of social justice, political savvy, and a disposition toward civic engagement, visual arts education becomes a tool for social change.

In the aftermath of September 11, 2001, rising ethnic and religious conflicts worldwide, and mounting concerns about threats to democracies and the growing global ecological crisis, recent writings in art education have focused on the aims of art education in an increasingly complex, volatile, fragile, and interconnected world. Students are keenly aware of and concerned with local, regional, national, and world conditions. In a survey not too long ago of her local high school art students, my former doctoral dissertation advisee at the University of Illinois and now visiting Assistant Professor at a peer university, Rebecca Plummer Rohloff found that her students cared deeply about issues of war, violence, poverty, divorce, racism, sexism, body image, homophobia, consumerism, the environment, and just about everything else adults also care about (personal communication). An art education responsive to student concerns, needs, and aspirations must engage these kinds of contemporary social issues and conditions. Anderson (1985) has long advocated the position that art education needs to be socially relevant. Blandy and Kellman (2004) argued that art education programs should address economic, social, psychological, technological, and public health problems associated with globalization. Similarly, in Zimmerman's (2002) view, art education programs should establish links between local communities, national concerns, and international issues. Numerous writings about the social and moral aims of art education posit that art education should foster cross-cultural understandings, social responsibility, critical inquiry, and democratic polity (Blandy, 2004; Stuhr, 1994)—ideas that have been decades in the making within the discipline of art education (Blandy & Congdon, 1987; Chapman, 1978; Hamblen, 1990; McFee &

Degge, 1977; Lanier, 1969). Underlying these notions is a belief in the capacity of art to transform people and the social institutions they build.

Our *National Visual Arts Standards* also argue for this instrumental view—that the arts are fundamental, and that they are transformative. These standards clearly articulate a multicultural orientation that "The cultural diversity of America is a vast resource for arts education, and should be used to help students understand themselves and others. The visual, traditional, and performing arts provide a variety of lenses for examining the cultures and artistic contributions of our nation and others around the world" (1994, p. 9). Our standards explicitly ask teachers to "attend to issues of ethnicity, national custom, tradition, religion, and gender" in their curricular constructions (p. 9). Valued outcomes of an arts-standards driven program of study embrace intercultural and interdisciplinary connections. For example, suggestions offered in the national standards mention possibilities for the study of shifts in the American social consciousness in the 20th century, African Americans' contributions to the civil rights movement, and the politics of ancient Japanese society. These national standards also connect art education to notions of citizenship: "We recognize an obligation to provide our children with the knowledge and skills that will equip them to enter society, work productively, and make their contributions as citizens" (p. 7).[2]

Schools have tremendous potential to serve as incubators for civil society. Schools once were widely shared public places in their communities and neighborhoods. Community members gathered in local schools for evening classes, cooperative extension programs, club meetings, public debates, elections, immigrant resources and services, performances from local and touring groups, athletic events, picnics, potluck dinners, and all sorts of civic activities (Boyte, 2002). Although still used for some public functions, schools are considerably less accessible today, locked down in response to threats of random violence, staffed with law enforcement officials in search of weapons and drugs, and encumbered with user fees and regulations limiting who can and cannot use school facilities for political, religious, or other specific non-school purposes. Moreover, schools are not viewed as particularly accessible places serving the needs of disenfranchised groups within communities.

Scholars note the decline of available public spaces for the development of civic friendships, especially as local schools moved away from being social centers for their communities (Boyte, 2002). Similarly, social critics have observed a general erosion of civil society in the US, brought about also by increased mobility and migration patterns (Fraser, 2005), social fragmentation (Boyte, 2002), expansion of governmental and corporate control of private life (Rieff, 1999), narrowing of the voluntary sector to service and advocacy (Sirianni & Friedland, n. d.), decrease in charitable giving and membership in voluntary social and civic-minded associations (Putnam, 2000), and an ascendance of single issue politics (Miller, 1999). Schools have a unique opportunity to reverse this trend by providing a place to bring people together and serve as a catalyst for social change, civic friendship, and public engagement of lasting significance. Art education, as much as any subject area in the standardized school curriculum, has the capacity to facilitate such a mission and do it well.

A careful reading of the *National Visual Arts Standards* (1994) reveals the underlying belief that art education has the capacity to foster social change: "The arts are often an impetus for change, challenging old perspectives from fresh angles of vision, or offering original interpretations of familiar ideas" (p. 1). As noted in these standards, the power of art to transform and enrich personal lives is also the power of art to transform societies: "Our way of life in the modern world and the success of our children in it depend on creating a society that is both literate and imaginative, competent and creative" (p. 12).

High-Tech/Low-Tech Strategies

If the role of schools is to foster an imaginative citizenry dedicated to the kind of civic life envisioned in an open, just, democratic society, and if art education has both the potential and a moral obligation to provide educational experiences that lead students to become creative and savvy contributors to these aims, then art educators must promote active student engagement with individuals and communities beyond their immediate circle of friends and families. Two strategies for fostering civic connections in art education include utilizing new technologies in the art classroom[3] for the formation of student collective public opinion and possible social action, and creating local school-community art partnerships aimed at enriching and improving community life for individuals beyond the classroom. Both strategies—one high-tech, the other low-tech—are predicated on the notion of creating a *culture of caring*.

Technology

New technologies provide a powerful and potentially different form of education than traditional methods of teaching. Our *National Standards for Arts Education* recognize that, "existing and emerging technologies will always be a part of how changes in the arts disciplines are created, viewed, and taught" (1994, p. 10). These standards are clear not only in their understanding of the power of new technologies, but also in their insistence that art education benefits from technological advancements: "The transforming power of technology is a force not only in the economy but in the arts as well" (p. 6). Our national standards also recognize the complexity of technology in our contemporary age of global media: "In a world exploding with information and experience, in which media saturate our culture with powerful images and messages at every turn, it is critical that young people be provided with tools not only for understanding that world, but also for contributing to it and making their own way" (p. 12).

Encompassing all curricular areas, but within the arts and humanities in particular, new technologies provide a means of facilitating personal creativity, inquiry, reflection, and commentary (both creative and critical) about things that matter to people worldwide. This includes both the production of varied forms of creative expression about the stuff of life, and the study of diverse creative cultural practices worldwide: "The arts help all students to develop multiple capabilities for understanding and deciphering an image- and symbol-laden world" (*National Visual Arts Standards*, 1994, p. 3). New technologies provide students with unprecedented access to artworks, images, visual experiences, and symbol systems from around the world. Unfortunately, our national standards for arts education fail to recognize the power of technology to transform individuals and society in the same ways that art is thought to transform society. A few observations offered in this section speak about the potential of technology to foster social justice.

Contributing productively to society means not only creating or studying cultural productions, but also engaging the difficult processes of critically analyzing new global digital media (Delacruz, in press), and working to challenge and dismantle institutions and practices that perpetuate social inequities, injustice, and cultural violence. Beyond production and consumption of artistic expressions, now available within a globalized network of technologies, communications, and *virtual* experiences, technology pedagogy in the visual arts classroom has the potential to engage students in social issues and practices that facilitate cross-cultural exchange and collective social action, through (using Web 2.0 terminology) online peer-to-peer (P2P) social networking and cultural production. Media guru Howard Rheingold (2000, 2007) wrote extensively about the impact of electronic social networking on the development of online creative, civic-minded social networks (*virtual communities* in his vernacular), made possible by advancements in computer technologies. He noted that the eager adoption of Web publishing, digital video production and distribution, social networking, multiplayer role-playing games, and creative utilization of other Internet-based media by millions of young people around the world demonstrates the strength of their desire, unprompted by adults, to learn and adapt digital media to their own purposes and pleasures.

Many students already know more about technology than most of their teachers. The implications of this are clear to Rheingold: "The tools for cultural production and distribution are in the pockets of 14 year olds. This does not guarantee that they will do the hard work of democratic self-governance: the tools that enable the free circulation of information and communication of opinion are necessary but not sufficient for the formation of public opinion" (2007, ¶2). Creative digital media and electronic communication networks enable but do not guarantee civic engagement aimed at social justice, or what I call cultural citizenship. Although highly capable, youth may not be self-inclined to participate in work for the common good, without specific guidance from teachers.

Cultural citizenship relies on development of two moral capacities—the capacity to pursue rationally a conception of the good and the capacity for an effective sense of justice (Bridges, 2002). Technology, by virtue of its anywhere, anytime state of existence richly supports a globalized sphere of citizen inquiry, the formation of collective public opinion, and civic action toward the public good (Kellner, n. d.). Public opinion affects the behaviors of public institutions (governmental agencies), of privatized commerce industries (Habermas, 1974), and of single individuals, including students, in local settings. Procedures for developing public opinion in the classroom are well known in education. These procedures call for a process of inquiry that adheres to principles of rational debate and consensus building (Oliver, 1980), processes I find highly relevant to networked electronic communication systems. Development of the kind of public opinion in the classroom or in online discourse that leads to social justice oriented public engagement requires more than rationalization and debate; it requires a classroom context that facilitates what educational scholar Nel Noddings calls a culture of caring (2005). Classroom conversations and online expressions must focus on things that matter to students and other people, things that are deeply *felt*. Moreover, they must be followed by collective plans of action that involve others, informed by the processes of rational deliberation, consensus building, empathy, and compassion. Creating warm and caring classroom conditions facilitates an impetus to form alliances across divisions of race, gender, class, ethnicity (a goal explicitly mentioned in the *National Visual Arts Standards*), and a host of other differences that divide students from one another, and instills a desire to take collective action on behalf others.

Community-Arts Based Partnerships and Initiatives

As seductive and exciting as new technologies are, I also favor low-tech local approaches to the creation of caring communities. Community-arts based partnerships involve an alliance of local organizations, cultural creatives, and civic minded individuals; require the cultivation of cross cultural friendships; and extend the reach of art teachers further into their local communities. They also require political knowledge of local conditions and structures, and time, a most valuable commodity for a K–12 art teacher. This section concludes with a couple examples from my own recent community-arts based public work that exemplifies how a civic partnership approach reflects our *National Visual Arts Standards*, contributes to social justice, promotes civil society, and brings prominence to the role of the visual arts in community life.

In my hometown, an economically stressed community of about 12,000 residents in east central Illinois, about 15 miles from the university where I teach, 67% of children in the public schools meet the requirements for free and reduced lunch, the community experiences a 30% mobility rate each year, and the Rantoul City Schools have failed to meet NCLB national testing standards. Such statistics mean that these children are poor, their lives lack stability, and the local schools struggle to meet the needs of its students. Working with Anne Sautman, Director of Education at the Krannert Art Museum, and with a Rantoul High School art teacher, Laura Billimack, we launched a High School internship program called *ARTspeak* 3 years ago. Jointly funded by Rantoul Township High School (RTHS) and the Krannert Art Museum, *ARTspeak* enrolls 12 culturally diverse students each year in a 16-week paid internship in which they come to the Krannert,

study its multicultural holdings, make art that expresses their own cultural identities, and lead art activities with youth in the community. Recently a technology component was added in which the High School art interns will also work with the English teacher, a technology specialist in the school, to produce an art/literary magazine and a website about Rantoul's growing multicultural population. Through publicity and presentations, this program communicates to the wider community about the combined power of art-plus-youth to do things of value to others. This educational experience feeds back into Laura's classroom conversations, student personal creative work, examinations of multicultural art, and increased interest in art in the local community. The growing popularity of the program is such that high school students from outside the art curriculum are now contacting Billimack, expressing interest in the program.

Building on these successes and relationships, a local artist/community arts educator (Lindsey Scott) and I sought and were awarded $10,000 National Endowment for the Arts Challenge America Fast Track Grant to oversee the painting of a community mural at a Rantoul Latino outreach center called Cultivadores.[4] David Requa, a former music teacher and current superintendent of RTHS, was on the Mural Advisory Team. The grant involved minority youth working with a local muralist, Glen Davies, in the painting of the community mural, which celebrates Rantoul's changing cultural makeup. This mural project was accompanied by a $25,000 companion grant written for Cultivadores after several brainstorming sessions with local artists, educators, youth, and community people, and awarded by the Lowe's Charitable and Educational Foundation to install a community garden adjacent to the Rantoul Community Mural. We broke ground for the Rantoul Community Garden and Mural Project in April 2008. The first mural was completed that summer, additional murals have been added, and the garden project is ongoing at the writing of this chapter.

Through the efforts of several individuals over a yearlong planning process, Cultivadores, a not-for-profit youth empowerment and social advocacy agency, is now in the business of art education, in partnership with local artists, art educators, community members, the NEA, and a major corporation. The fusion of energy and vision from these diverse individuals creates its own momentum, publicity, and good will in this community. The garden is being promoted as a "gift from the Latino community" to the greater Rantoul community, and in March 2008 Cultivadores received a

4-year commitment from the Village Board of Rantoul for $21,000 per year to use for operating expenses. Cultivadores plans to fill its building exterior and interior with murals, all painted by Rantoul youth working with area artists. Other murals are now appearing in sites in Rantoul. A website for Cultivadores is also in planning stages, along with a sharing of the ongoing work in a traveling photo-documentary exhibition.

Conclusions and Caveats

Creating conditions that foster a culture of caring is a daunting task for teachers, given the current bureaucratic, accountability-driven orientations of schools. Talking, listening, creative self-expression, critical inquiry, and community building are time consuming, unpredictable, and difficult to assess by any of the current standardized measurements favored in schools today. Social reconstruction is similarly a formidable goal for art education. Political action aimed toward social justice and social change is messy and difficult work. Art teachers should not be doing this work alone and university art educators are in a unique position to provide direct and sustained leadership, write grants, and help design, promote, and facilitate the kind of art education advocated here—side-by-side with the K–12 art teacher.[5]

I have established in this chapter some ways that the *National Visual Arts Standards* could support a social reconstructionist vision of art education. Although somewhat outdated and limited in many ways, and too generalized and expansive in other ways, our national standards provide a political document that art teachers may use to explain the nature and value of their work to those in need of such explanation. In the current standardized, test-driven, post-No Child Left Behind educational environment, it makes sense to talk about standards and performance indicators in these ways insofar as these standards articulate a set of authoritative statements about our goals, along with strategies for determining how well we are meeting those goals. On the other hand, our national arts standards fail to adequately engage our moral obligation to engage the social, economic, and cultural injustices, issues, and conditions that underlie the incredibly complicated problems that exist throughout the world today. In this regard, our national standards are also out of touch with a considerable body of art that is produced today by culturally diverse civic-minded activist artists in the US and throughout the world.

Not every art teacher will find the problems-based social reconstructionist-oriented interpretation of our national standards, as argued in this chapter, appealing. Nor do all teachers necessarily have the kind of access to new technologies needed to launch into the kinds of initiatives suggested earlier in this chapter. Moreover, few will have guaranteed access to interested university personnel and inter-institutional partnerships discussed in the examples given in this chapter. I always found teaching art during my K–12 years rather lonely and isolating, and I made sure that I located art teaching positions near major universities so that I could have access to university resources, people, and opportunities for professional development and renewal. Not every art teacher has that kind of mobility. At the same time, every art teacher does have close allies close by, including other teachers in their school and other people in their communities that believe like they do that creativity, culture, community, and children are important. Every art teacher has an opportunity to connect with their state and national professional art and educational organizations for professional renewal (Delacruz, 2000). And every art teacher has the time in their curriculum to engage students in conversations and activities that embrace aspects of our social lives that really matter to young people, their families, and communities, with or without these national standards.

Anderson, T. (1985). Toward a socially defined studio curriculum. *Art Education, 38*(5), 16–18

Blandy, D. (2004). Commentary: Folklife, material culture, education, and civil society. *Visual Arts Research*, (58), 3–8.

Blandy, D., & Congdon, K. G. (1987). *Art in a democracy.* New York: Teachers College Press.

Blandy, D., & Kellman, J. (2004). Editorial: A special issue on diverse populations. *Visual Arts Research*, (58), 1–2.

Boyte, H. C. (2002). *A different kind of politics: John Dewey and the meaning of citizenship in the 21st century.* Retrieved August 15, 2005, from http://www.cpn.org/crm/contemporary/different.html

Bridges, T. (2002). *Civic friendship, communitarian solidarity, and the story of liberty.* Retrieved August 15, 2005, from http://www.civsoc.com/nature/nature10.html

Chapman, L. H. (1978). *Approaches to art in education.* San Diego: Harcourt.

Delacruz, E. M. (1990). Revisiting curriculum conceptions: A thematic perspective. *Visual Arts Research, 16*(2), 10–25.

Delacruz, E, M. (1995). Multiculturalism and the tender years: Big and little questions. In C. M. Thompson (Ed.), *The visual arts and early childhood learning* (pp. 101–106). Reston VA: National Art Education Association.

Delacruz, E. M. (2000). Making a difference. In K. Keifer-Boyd, K. Fehr, & D. Fehr (Eds.), *Realworld readings: Things your professor never told you about art education* (pp. 11–20). New York: Falmer Press.

Delacruz, E. M. (2003). Racism American style and resistance to change: Art education's role in the Indian mascot issue. *Art Education, 56*(3),13–20.

Delacruz, E. M. (2004). Teachers' technology working conditions and the unmet promise of technology. *Studies in Art Education, 46*(1), 6–19.

Delacruz, E. M. (2005). Commentary: Art education in civil society. *Visual Arts Research, 31*(2), 3–9.

Dissanayake, E. (2003). *The core of art: Making special. Journal of the Canadian Association for Curriculum Studies, 1*(2), 3–9.

Fraser, N. (2005). *Transnationalizing the Public Sphere.* Retrieved February 10, 2007, from http://www.republicart.net/disc/publicum/fraser01_en.htm

Gross, E. F. (2004). Adolescent Internet use: What we expect, what teens report. *Journal of Applied Developmental Psychology, 25*(6), 633–649.

Habermas, J. (1974, Autumn). The public sphere: An encyclopedia article. (S. Lenox & F. Lenox, Trans.). *New German Critique*, 3, pp. 49–55.

Hamblen, K. A. (1990). Beyond the aesthetic of cash-culture literacy. *Studies in Art Education, 31*(4), 216–225.

Horrigan, J., & Rainie, L. (2006). *The Internet's growing role in life's major moments.* Retrieved February 10, 2007, from http://www.pewinternet.org/

Kellner, D. (n. d.). *Habermas, the public sphere, and democracy: A critical intervention.* Retrieved August 15, 2005, from http://www.gseis.ucla.edu/faculty/kellner/kellner.html

Korten, D. C. (2000). *The civil society: An unfolding cultural struggle.* Keynote address presented to the Fourth International Conference of the International Society for Third-Sector Research in Dublin, Ireland. July 5, 2000. Retrieved August 15, 2005, from http://www.cyberjournal.org/cj/authors/korten/CivilizingSociety.shtml

Lanier, V. (1969). The teaching of art as social revolution. *Phi Delta Kappan, 1*(6), 314–319.

Lankford, E. L. (2002). Nurturing humaneness. *Journal of Cultural Research in Art Education* (19/20), 47–52.

McFee, J. K., & Degge, R. (1977). *Art, culture, and environment.* Belmont, CA: Wadsworth.

Miller, D. W. (1999). Perhaps we bowl alone, but does it really matter? *The Chronicle of Higher Education*, July 16, 1999.

National standards for arts education: What every young American should know and be able to do. (1994). Reston, VA: Music Educators National Conference.

National visual arts standards. (1994). Reston, VA: National Art Education Association.

Noddings, N. (2005) *'Caring in education', the encyclopedia of informal education.* Retrieved December 1, 2007, from www.infed.org/biblio/noddings_caring_in_education.htm

Oliver, D. (1980). Jurisprudential inquiry: Clarifying public issues. In B. Joyce & M. Weil (Eds.), *Models of teaching, 2nd edition* (pp. 260–276). Englewood Cliffs, NJ: Prentice-Hall.

Putnam, R. (2000), *Bowling alone: The collapse and revival of American community.* New York: Simon and Schuster.

Rheingold, H. (2007). *The tools of cultural production are in the hands of teens.* Blog dated January 1, 2007. Retrieved February 10, 2007, from http://www.smartmobs.com/archive/2007/01/01/the_tools_of_cu....html

Rheingold, H. (2000). *The virtual community: Homesteading frontier.* (Revised edition). Cambridge, MA: MIT Press.

Rieff, D. (1999). The false dawn of civil society. *The Nation* (February 22, 1999). Retrieved August 15, 2005, from http://www.thenation.com/doc/19990222/Riefff/

Sirianni, C., & Friedland, L. (n. d.). Civil Society. In *Civic Dictionary.* Retrieved August 15, 2005, from http://www.cpn.org/tools/dictionary/civilsociety.html

Stuhr, P. (1994). Multicultural art education and social reconstruction. *Studies in Art Education, 35*(3), 171–178.

Zimmerman, E. (2002). Intercultural education offers a means to promote tolerance and understanding. *Journal of Cultural Research in Art Education* (19/20), 68–80.

[1] An inclusive definition of civil society is offered here as *that realm of private voluntary associations and public agencies or institutions working toward the public good.* This definition includes schools (Delacruz, 2005).

[2] Implicit in the assertion that all children become productive citizens is the requirement that all children have equitable access to educational resources and outcomes. Children, families, neighborhoods, and communities across the country suffer from abominable social inequities, and this condition is without moral justification in the richest, most powerful nation on earth.

[3] Until K–12 schools and teachers are adequately supported in their efforts to integrate emerging electronic technologies into their instructional practices, the "promise of technology" is both unrealizable and frustrating (Delacruz, 2004).

[4] The Rantoul community mural and community garden were developed in collaboration with Rantoul-born artist and community art educator/activist now living in East St. Louis, Lindsey Scott.

[5] Gaps between higher education and K–12 divisions of the profession are beyond the scope of this chapter, other than to share the following. My art teacher friends sometimes comment to me that university art educators are largely "missing in action" and involved in esoteric concerns of little relevance to K–12 art teachers' real world needs and issues. That K–12 art teachers make such an observation was also shared at a March 2008 Higher Education Division business meeting at the Annual Convention of the National Art Education Association by our current NAEA President, Barry Shauck. The 2008 Higher Education Division Director Melody Milbrandt set up through the Regional Directors a series of cross disciplinary Issues Forums for the 2009 NAEA Convention held in Minneapolis. These issues forums were an attempt to initiate conversations and bridge gaps between Higher Education and other NAEA Divisions, including but not limited to Elementary and Secondary Divisions.

Community
EDUCATION

The Women's Studio Workshop: A Room of Her Own

Kara Kelley Hallmark

When given the opportunity to investigate art and social justice, I knew that I had to talk about the Women's Studio Workshop. The workshop is a place where art and social justice are intertwined so intimately that often the actions are understated, less obvious than those of other outspoken conscious-raising groups or the picketing efforts of driven activists. However, there are many aspects of the daily goings-on at the workshop that could easily qualify as efforts toward leveling the playing field for all. Perhaps most significantly is the core mission of the workshop to create opportunities for women artists to work and learn. There is much literature on the merits of this topic and debate about whether an all-woman space is necessary or if it is even a good thing for women. This essay is not designed to cover that material. Rather, this is a series of partial conversations and observations that led to my overall perception of the workshop as a positive experience for women artists.

In an effort to combine my academic background in art education and women's studies, I went in search of an all-woman arts organization to investigate for my doctoral research. I discovered a residential art space called the Women's Studio Workshop in Rosendale, New York, and learned that not only was this workshop run by and for women, but this was a place that survived the political backlash that the women's movement underwent in the 1980s (Evans, 2003; Rosen, 2000). Eureka! Without hesitation, I picked up the phone and called the main number. This was the occasion that I first met Ann Kalmbach, the Executive Director. When I told her about my research, she replied, "Great you found us! When can you come

KEY CONCEPTS
- Community Art
- Women's Studies
- Residential Art Community
- All-woman Art Space
- Feminism

up?" I felt her openness and warmth instantly. I soon learned that it was Ann who was the captain of this ship. Throughout my research, her dedication to the workshop was boundless and her presence a constant.

Straight away I made flight reservations into Stewart Airport, just a few miles from Rosendale. During my first visit, I was a wide-eyed novice-researcher soaking up everything around me like a sponge, photographing with my digital camera and my mind and documenting initial perceptions in the form of abbreviated sentences, scribbles, crudely drawn charts, and tape-recorded interviews. Subsequent trips were conducted in a more orderly fashion with a specific agenda in mind, meanwhile attempting to maintain an organic nature to my visit, allowing for schedule changes, and the unexpected conversation, impromptu meal, cup of tea, or walk in the woods (Dewey, 1934). I completely immersed myself into the community of the workshop by staying on-site, sharing communal household responsibilities, and volunteering in the office and studios, returning to the workshop for a total of three visits (Anderson, 2000; Creswell, 1998; Eisner, 1997; Naples, 2003).

A Kernel of an Idea

The history of the workshop is firmly rooted in the history of women artists and women in society over the past 30 years. Although the workshop was established in the early 1970s during the height of the Women's Liberation Movement, interestingly all four of the founding artists said that they were not active participants in the larger women's movement. However, they all experienced challenges as women art students and then as women artists and educators. Co-founders Anita and Babs expressed anger and even deep disappointment in the lack of opportunities that they faced as young women artists. Anita reached a level of frustration that nearly caused her to leave art school, and Babs was told that she would lose her faculty position when a man of equal qualifications came along. They decided to take action. Four women artists—Ann, Tana, Anita, and Babs—co-founded the Women's Studio Workshop. These four women came together out of friendship and their common experiences as women and as artists.

They all gave me their own version of how the workshop was initiated and how Anita procured the funding. By the time I sat down to talk with Anita about that first grant, I had already talked to the others and even several of the staff members. When talking with Babs, she asked me, "Has Anita told you that this was her idea?" I shook my head and she continued, "No, I didn't think so. If Anita does something great, she won't be the one to tell you. So, I'll tell you." I told Anita that Babs said this and she blushed and chuckled as she started to tell me about that first grant.

I was working in the library, which was actually pretty wonderful … but I started to think wow, here you are and you aren't making art. So, I somehow learned that you could write a grant … I started to think about what we could do. I wanted to do something for Barbara, my mentor, and for Ann my dear buddy … we had been drawing and making art together and going to arts activities together, so there was that kernel of a thought. I wrote the grant as if we were going to create a communal living situation. Um, I wish that I could think of a model to tell you but I didn't have a model myself. I was thinking about these communities that were self-contained where stuff was made by hand with a craft quality and an aesthetic quality. This was in England and other communities sprang up around it. I wasn't thinking about craft since we were focused on fine art, but I was thinking about a living community where we could do artistic work and discuss it and discuss ideas … I remember being extremely shocked that I got a phone call at the library where I was working and they said that they wanted to come up and see us. So they came up to meet us. It would never happen that way today, because we hadn't actually done anything. Then we had the meeting and they told us that we had to come up with something that was more concrete.

So after the men left, we got together and talked about what we were going to do. Fortunately, Ann and Tana were getting concrete learning in printmaking and we made a statement about how it's difficult for women artists to find space and money to make art and they gave us the money. (Hallmark, 2007, pp. 84–85)

With that first grant, they rented a house in town and began offering art classes to the local community, meanwhile making art in every spare moment. Over the years, the workshop evolved into a residential artist community and the facilities expanded when they bought a few houses across town. They broadened the scope of the organization to include a rigorous artist intern program for recent women BFA graduates, provide grants for established women artists, collaborate with local schools in the art-in-education program for both girls and boys, and offer international art experiences. However, what initially motivated the creation of the workshop—the need for women to have space to create—remains today the center of what the workshop is all about.

A Room of Her Own

Both the artists-in-residence and the interns talked about how the workshop gave them access to materials, space, and opportunities to learn what they may not have elsewhere. More importantly, they talked about how the artist-in-residence program gave them the opportunity to have a room of their own, even if just for a while. During my first visit, my focus was centered on how an all-woman artist space might be different, maybe even better, than a co-ed one. I discovered that the workshop is pro-woman, not anti-man. Although male artists have participated in the past, Ann said that this was problematic, especially concerning the living quarters for the interns and artists. She stressed how important it was for the women to feel comfortable. After a short pause Ann said, "After all the male artists have plenty of places to work." I continued to ask her about what makes an all-woman space different.

KARA: Is there something unique about the energy that it's all women?

ANN: I don't know.

KARA: Is that because it's all you know?

ANN: Yeah. Sometimes I go out in the world and it's like only the men talk and they aren't saying an interesting thing.

KARA: I do find it interesting to be in a woman centered space and like we were talking about last night, to be in a nurturing space. Although I know you said that you stay away from that characterization.

ANN: It's a hard one … It isn't valued. (Hallmark, p. 93)

During another trip to the workshop, I revisited the issue with Ann. I was interested to learn that she had considered the topic over the past several months since our last conversation.

KARA: Last time I was here you and I talked a lot about the workshop being a separatist community and whether or not that is good.

ANN: I think about this a lot now.

KARA: Do you?

ANN: Yes, because I think, well first of all, I just went through this long process with the Board about our mission that says "all people" and how do you say that when the title is the Women's Studio Workshop? And, now I'm like, it's pretty old fashioned and what does it mean in contemporary terms? (Hallmark, p. 94)

When I asked Babs about male artists in the space, she declared, "Well mostly I think that they make the women feel uncomfortable. After all we can empty our own trash" (Hallmark, p. 95). Anita told me a story about a confrontation she had with a male artist who was offended that the residency did not accept male applications. She recalled being deeply disturbed by his comments and felt that she had to defend the workshop. Tana told me stories about when they tried to open the doors to male artists and how the dynamics in classes and the studio shifted dramatically, alienating the women artists somewhat. Here again, without having an overt feminist agenda, the workshop proved itself to be a woman-centered space.

The Artists-in-Residence

The artists-in-residence all expressed sentiments about their comfort level with the studio spaces. Staying at the workshop allowed the artists to work all hours of the night without the safety concerns of traveling to and from another location. This was something that artist-in-residence Karmen and I talked about as she led me through the silkscreen studio to the third-floor artist apartment. The apartment felt like a secret getaway with a cozy couch and a small kitchen naturally lit by skylights with a deck off of the back. I met with Karmen, a photographer who was at the workshop for a 6-week residency after she had already been at the workshop for several weeks.

Born in Greece, Karmen was the product of a restrictive education that placed her into an academic track to study law. After immigrating to the United States with her husband she felt the freedom to pursue an education in the arts. Although her teachers were male, she felt that they were supportive and introduced women artists in the curriculum. At the workshop she was away from her life as teacher and wife and Karmen had the time and space to create a large body of work that kept her in the

Karmen, Third-Floor Artist Apartment in Main House.

Jessica, Printmaking Studio.

of work while I'm here which is great. It's great being around all these women and hearing their stories and Tana is in her own little world and to hear Anita talk about grant writing and to make connections with the interns and stuff. When you are an artist you own your own business you are an entrepreneur ... I would like to be a professional artist ... but I'm interested in arts administration and the organization itself.

KARA: So, when you say you want to be a professional artist, do you mean you want to be able to support yourself with your artwork?

JESSICA: Yeah. It would be really nice to get that financial reward for my work.

KARA: In order to validate your work?

JESSICA: Yeah.

KARA: Do you self identify as a feminist?

JESSICA: See, I think that it's different for my generation. I don't think that it's an issue anymore. I don't want to make it an issue. That's intense to call yourself a feminist, especially with the history and with what that word means to a lot of people who think that it's negative. I don't think that it is but there are a lot of people out there that say it is ... but, yes and no I guess.

KARA: Do you notice anything different about working in an all-woman space?

JESSICA: Yes, I like it. There is definitely a different energy working in a space with all women then if you are in there with five other guys.

KARA: How does that affect how you work or how you are feeling?

darkroom for the majority of the time. She expressed feelings of isolation about this but said that the daily potluck lunch and eating dinner with the other artists helped her through this and provided the ability for her to focus on her work when she was alone in the studio. Karmen, a self-identified feminist, talked about her experience at the workshop in relationship to being part of a group, "Being in a community with artists makes me feel great about being an artist. Being around all women made it very intimate" (Hallmark, p. 99).

Jessica was Karmen's roommate during that residence, during which the two met for the first time. However, I observed that they interacted like old buddies and seemed comfortable moving through the artist apartment that they shared. I found myself talking with Jessica off and on throughout this trip. She was always smiling and eager to talk about almost anything.

KARA: When you leave the workshop what do you want to take away from this experience and where do you go from here?

JESSICA: Well, I want to produce an amazing body of work. I'll be here for 5 weeks. I'm producing at least three bodies

JESSICA: Well, I guess it depends on the personalities too. But, if there are guys in the room then the women act differently and it's nice not having them and having to bring that to the table … Well, I was always close with my mom so I wasn't that worried about it being strange … when I first looked at the workshop online I thought—oooh how lucky and I was excited that there was something just for us [women]. My guy friends were like, what we can't come? Oh, we want to come! I feel very lucky that this is an opportunity … to have the time to work without having to wait tables or some other kind of part time job is really great. (Hallmark, pp. 99–102)

A Quiet Feminism

The feminist label was difficult for some of the women to embrace at the workshop. A few of the artists expressed that the term was too divisive and implied a feeling of anti-man. However, everyone I talked to, even those adverse to the term strongly agreed that they endorse feminist ideals, defined as supporting women's equality in economic, political, and in every other way that men experience society. Although the women were not overtly proclaiming a feminist agenda or participating in public political activity, the workshop was founded on giving opportunities to women, which permeates everything that they do.

Ann said that she couldn't help but take the role of social worker and recognized that people probably perceive her to be a feminist, although she does not call herself that. Tana and Anita both felt that the term suggests an association with the political consciousness-raising groups of the 1970s, which they did not participate in. However, they all agreed that indeed the workshop is an agent for social change and that in contemporary terms they are feminists. Of the four founders, Babs was the only one who boldly proclaimed to be a feminist. She maintained strong feelings about the role of the workshop in the lives of women artists:

When we started we had problems with the name, lots of people said, "Don't you know that calling yourself the women's studio workshop is making it more divisive?" I would just say, "Back off … we are just trying to even the score." I mean people would come up to us and say things. It was just awful. I think that if

nothing else—well once in awhile we have troubles. People would say that women don't need to be a separate group. But we do need it. I can see how things are better and different than they used to be but it's not all better. It isn't. (Hallmark, pp.106–107)

Ellen is a past intern who never really left the workshop. After her 6-month internship, she continued working until returning to graduate school. Today, Ellen is married and has recently completed her MFA and she regularly volunteers at workshop events. Late one afternoon, Ann told me about Ellen and that she was on her way over to meet with me for an impromptu interview. I waited for her in the main office while the office staff finished up the day's work. When Ellen walked through the side office door, everyone was thrilled to see her and jumped up to greet her with hugs.

She confidently introduced herself and we walked back into the silk-screen studio to talk. She told me right away that she loves the workshop and when she heard about my project that she just had to drive over and talk to me. Ellen was born in 1975 in Iowa and grew up in a home environment that taught her to voice her opinions and that promoted the idea that women should have equal opportunities in life and society.

Ellen, Silk Screen Studio.

KARA: You talked about expressing ideas of being a woman in your artwork as a younger student, do you still do that?

ELLEN: I came here about 6 months after graduating [and] my work really changed. And, I had to think about how I was in an all female environment and then I realized that it wasn't an issue for me anymore.... It was a level of comfort ... I could just focus on what I wanted and it started to become and still is very much so to this day about the environment and natural surroundings. And you can also understand why that started happening while I was at the workshop. My praise for the workshop is that it is feminism at its best. It's not hitting you over the head with it, we're not running around with picket signs and t-shirts or anything like that. It's just an organization full of women doing something. Doing what they want to be doing and doing it quietly, well I don't know if that's the word but doing it without shouting, I am woman. (Hallmark, pp. 108–109)

What Does It All Mean?

Many of the artists said that having the time and space to create a large body of work was the best thing about the workshop. Jessica said that she was relieved when she got the grant to come to the workshop, rather than waiting tables. Several of the intern artists casually mentioned that they too wondered about what odd jobs they might have to do if they were not on staff at the workshop. In *A Room of One's Own*, Woolf (1929) referred to a place where women have the freedom and space to work, with the financial resources for the time to work creatively, fully developing their own geniuses. She recognized the importance of wealth and the lack thereof among women and their potential creativity, questioning the role of foremothers and how they may have contributed to the perpetuation of female poverty.

Karmen was happy to take a break from the chores of her daily life as a teacher and wife. She cautioned me against misinterpreting that she was unhappy with her life, but said that she found it difficult to complete a large body of work at one time with the demands of daily life. De Beauvoir (1952) wrote about the life and activities of women, mired with the daily chores of life, confined by their daily duties as prescribed by society, religion, and their roles as daughters, wives, and mothers. This daily life kept them too busy for things such as intellect, dreams, and philosophy.

Although Ellen was raised in a feminist-centered household, she was still deeply affected by her experience at the workshop. Being in an all-woman space allowed her to explore woman-focused themes in her artwork, where previously she felt unable to do so. Frueh and Raven (1991) endorsed a woman's artist community and wondered about a woman's ability to function within the mainstream art world, asking "does entering the mainstream, still white, male, and Eurocentric, lead to a cultural democracy or to the disappearance of dynamic, valuable differences?" (p. 8). Frueh and Raven claimed that a separatist environment is the only way to completely be free from patriarchal structures.

hooks (1995) called for a resurgence of feminist action by way of consciousness-raising groups, gatherings, and public meetings in feminist practice. She explained that in order for women to create, whether visual or literary art, time is needed for reverie and contemplation. Although the woman artist is more accepted than she was several decades ago, hooks said that society still does not accept the time and space she needs to develop creatively. She pointed out that the Women's Liberation Movement expanded opportunities for women artists, but remained limited to Caucasian women with economic means. hooks concluded that women need environments where they can work, create, and closely explore experiences and relationship to artistic production.

Although they do not proclaim a feminist agenda, the Workshop is woman centered, which in and of itself is a political maneuver. As such, the Workshop exudes a quiet feminism that empowers women and creates space for their needs and desires. The workshop is actively working to help bring equality to women artists, which is an act of social justice. A radical feminist agenda claims that the organization of women based on their sex *is* political because the very act of discerning gender for reasons of organization is personal (Dauphinais, Barkan, & Cohn, 1992; Gordon, 1978; Liss, Crawford, & Popp, 2004), meaning, all issues related to the consciousness of recognizing biological difference are personal and political (Humm, 1990).

The Women's Studio Workshop (Main House) (2006).

All of the co-founders and the permanent staff at the Workshop talked about the conflict with the name, Women's Studio Workshop, and limiting the space to women only. Many of them faced direct scrutiny and criticism from the local and art world community. Yet, they all go back to the fact that women still need space to create. All of the artists reportedly felt more comfortable and safe in a woman-centered environment. Some of the women artists felt that it fostered the development of intimate talk and building close friendships. Even those women who did not feel that sex discrimination was something that they had even encountered or had to be concerned with, felt that being in an all-woman art space was special. Overall, the women artists felt that this woman-only art space was a good thing (Hallmark, 2007). Whether working in an all-woman environment is better or worse for women, the workshop certainly is creating space that gives women another opportunity to learn, collaborate, and make art.

REFERENCES

Anderson, T. (2000). Using art criticism strategies in ethnographic research. *Visual Arts Research*, 80–87.

Creswell, J. (1998). *Qualitative inquiry and research design: Choosing among five traditions.* Thousand Oaks, CA: Sage Publications.

Dauphinais, P. D., Barkan, S. E., & Cohn, S. F. (1992). Predictors of rank-and-file feminist activism. *Social Problems, 39*(4), 332–344.

de Beauvoir, S.(1952). *The second sex.* New York: Alfred A. Knopf.

Dewey, J. (1934). *Art as experience.* New York: Putnam.

Eisner, E. (1997). *The enlightened eye: Qualitative inquiry and the enhancement of educational practice.* New York: Macmillan.

Evans, S.M. (2003). *Tidal wave: How women changed America at century's end.* New York: The Free Press.

Frueh, J. & Raven, A. (1991). Feminist art criticism: Its demise and resurrection. *Art Journal, 50*(2), 6–10.

Gordon, J. (1978). Early American women artists and the social context in which they worked. *American Quarterly, 30*(1), 54–69.

Graham, J. (1980). American women artists' groups: 1867–1930. *Woman's Art Journal, 1*(1), 7–12.

Hallmark, K. (2007). *The women's studio workshop: Inside an all-woman art space.* UMI Dissertation Services (UMI Number 3301552).

Harris, A. S. (1973). Women in college art departments and museums. *Art Journal, 32*(4), 417–419.

hooks, b. (1995). *Art on my mind: Visual politics.* New York: The New Press.

Humm, M. (1990). *The dictionary of feminist theory.* Columbus: The Ohio State University.

Liss, M., Crawford, M., & Popp, D. (2004). Predictors and correlates of collective action. *Sex Roles, 50*(11–12), 771–779.

Naples, N. (2003). *Feminism and method: Ethnography, discourse analysis, and activist research.* New York: Routledge.

Rosen, R. (2000). *The world split open: How the modern women's movement changed America.* New York: Penguin.

Schapiro, M. (1972). The education of women as artists: Project *Womanhouse. Art Journal, 31*(3), 268–270.

Sturken, M. (1978). Women artist's group fights discrimination. *Afterimage 5*(9), Retrieved January 18, 2005, from http://www2.rpa.net/~vsw/afterimage/sturken.htm

Tedlock, B. (2000). Ethnography and ethnographic representation. In N. K. Denzin & Y. S. Lincoln (Eds.), *Handbook of qualitative research* (2nd ed.). (pp. 455–487). Thousand Oaks, CA: Sage Publications.

Woolf, V. (1929). *A room of one's own.* New York: Harcourt Brace Jovanovich.

Taft Richardson and the Resurrection of Bones, Children, and a Community

Kristin G. Congdon

Introduction

Taft Richardson was raised and lived much of his life in an African American neighborhood in Tampa, Florida. He was recently forced to leave the house where he created bone sculptures and taught children art. His health is failing, and his mission seems incomplete to him. But I know better. Taft Richardson has given immeasurable gifts to the people who live in his neighborhood; the lessons he offers to the field of art education are as profound and important as any ideas I have experienced in my decades of work in the field. While the best way to understand his teachings is to meet him, I hope to do some justice to his work in this chapter. To do so, I focus on four areas of knowledge: lessons about art, teaching, place (his garden), and community. These topics are all linked. They are also the four reoccurring areas of interest that drive his life.

Lessons about Art

Richardson's artwork (in the object-oriented sense of the word) is primarily sculpture made from bones. He explained that this form of creating emerged after he was eating beef one day and looked down at his plate and saw a giraffe. He understood this to be an answer to his spiritual needs; this was that day that he "found himself." Shortly thereafter, he began to create sculptures using bones from dead animals, particularly road kill. Before this event took place, Richardson felt as if his life hadn't had purpose. He believed that God would help him finding a meaningful path for him to take.

KEY CONCEPTS
- Community Building
- African American Culture
- Folk Art
- Recycling
- Teaching About Art

Richardson understood that this answer to his spiritual needs was found through a common experience. Where one usually throws out the bones left over from a meal, Richardson used them. The act of recycling is common to many artists, especially "folk artists," a term often attributed to Richardson. The act of using something that has been tossed away or disregarded can be a deeply felt act of creativity. For Richardson, his art is a blessing from God that reflects resurrection and rebirth. He considers this understanding his awakening. Suzanne Seriff (1996), one of the curators for the well-regarded exhibition at the International Folk Art Museum in

Taft Richardson with Bone Sculptures. Photo by Bud Lee.

Bone Sculpture by Taft Richardson. Photo by Bud Lee.

Santa Fe titled, *Recycled Reseen: Folk Art from the Global Scrap Heap*, claimed that this idea of turning "trash into treasure" is often spoken about, but rarely examined. Such a process can be a "transformative process" (p. 14). In Richardson's case, he related the recycling of bones not only to the resurrection of Christ but also the forgiveness of sins. The act of making the art can be considered a ritual that cleans and purifies.

He places the bones he picks up in the sun to bleach them clean. He then cares for them, often placing them in his pockets where he can easily experience them as turns them around and around in his fingers. When he is ready to make a sculpture, he knows exactly where each bone will come from and what they will become in their new context. Even the glue that he uses to connect the bones together is made from bones that he crushes and mixes with an adhesive. In this process, a spiritual transformation has taken place.

A similar kind of process takes place when famed folk artist, Thornton Dial, creates as the act of salvaging is profoundly rooted in African American culture and is symbolic of his people. For example, he uses old carpet in his work to make the image of the tiger, which is a metaphor for the African American man. The tiger is king of the jungle, but in this context it was created out of carpet, symbolizing the idea that the proud African American man has been stepped on. The various natural materials he uses such as roots and leaves are mixed in his work with industrial products such as iron and wire to represent a unified wholeness of his experience in the world (Borum, 1993, p. 38). Also symbolically, Charlie Lucas claimed that making art from junk is the "stuff of rebirth" (Gundaker, 1996, p. 81). The act of making something beautiful from that which has been discarded *is* the art in the artwork. The object may be beautiful, but the idea is what is most important. Richardson claimed that he picks bones as his media because it stands for the very basic structure of what it means to live. He thinks about recreating life, much as he understands his Christian God has done. However, he also recognizes that the power to transform is not his; he continually claims that his power and creativity comes from God. "All my creativity," he explained, "comes from the highest Source." Thus, in the act of creating, he finds himself aligned with the spiritual world.

Many other African American artists also work with recycled objects. For example, Martha Jackson-Jarvis is aware of the power of cemetery decorating. Objects related to the deceased are often placed on a grave in order to communicate with the dead and the world beyond. She also

Art Education for Social Justice

acknowledged the "phenomenon of yard dressing, … [where] the objects are sanctified by the labor of those who made them" (Beardsley, 1998, pp. 94-95). According to Robert Farris Thompson, those in the Kongo believe that broken vessels placed on gravesites become whole again in the afterworld (Gundaker, 1996, p. 80). For both Jackson-Jarvis and Richardson, life histories reside in the recycled objects and they are brought to life—in another context—through recycling. This process of renewal is imperative, not only to Richardson's artwork, but also to his teaching.

Lessons about Teaching

The resurrection of the bones, explained Richardson, is about the resurrection of Christ, but it is also akin to the resurrection of the children in his neighborhood. If he (with God working through him) has the power to re-create the bones of dead animals into beautiful transcendent artworks, he recognizes that he (with God's energy) also has the power to re-cast local children into healthy, contributing individuals (Congdon, 2006). He remembered the neighborhood of his youth, where residents lived peacefully with one another and where being poor did not mean being impoverished. When a freeway through Tampa was built so close to his home, it changed the community, as is common in so many neighborhoods across the United States (Congdon, 2004). Greatly disturbed by the youths' involvement with drugs and crime, he wanted to interest the children in a "better path" (Congdon & Bucuvalas, 2006, p. 193). Although he has nine children of his own, his paternal feelings extend to children all over his neighborhood. He often weaves small pieces of their hair into his long white beard to symbolically represent his connection with the children who look to him for guidance. He teaches these neighborhood children to draw, paint, and make masks; he uses his bone sculptures for inspiration.

Many things can be learned about good art educational practices from Taft Richardson. Richardson links his artwork to his educational work. Both are about lifting something (bones and children) up from a devalued position. People ignore the decaying bones of animals, and they ignore the wellbeing of children in poor neighborhoods. He grounds his ideas about art in religion, which he finds most meaningful. He indicated that he learned about art in church; it comes from an understanding of "Our Father who *art* in Heaven." By seeing art as something connected to God, Richardson places the act of creating (and re-creating) in a place and space that has the most potential power. He effectively uses this creative power that comes

from God to capture the attention and respect of his students. They listen and they learn because Richardson's words and activities come from a place that promises to transform their lives, their neighborhood, and their place in the world.

In Richardson's mind, there is no greater group of people than teachers. In the summer of 2006, I was teaching a 1-week Florida Humanities seminar for Florida teachers. I invited Richardson the artist/educator to talk to my group. He was greatly moved by the fact that teachers might be interested in his work. He insisted that the class come to his home instead of him going to the seminar room in St. Petersburg. A group of children played the drums when the bus pulled up to his modest but amazing home. An exhibition of neighborhood artwork lined the fence in his garden. Chairs were set up in his garden for the group to sit and drinks were placed in a cooler. In his home, teachers found a guest book and an exhibition of his work. He repeatedly told the members of the seminar group how honored he was to have them visit. The teachers were greatly affected by the reception and felt that they had never been so honored. Others commented that at first they did not want to go because they felt the neighborhood was dangerous and had planned to stay on the bus. However, when they got to Richardson's yard they were so overwhelmed by the children playing the drums and the artist/teacher's welcome, that they changed their minds. Several of the teachers said that he had reminded them of why they wanted to be teachers in the first place and that the visit transformed them. Many of the teachers wrote about the power of his garden in their final evaluations.

Lessons about Gardens

According to Taft Richardson, gardens can educate. Orr (2006) noted that most people fail to notice that the built environment can be "a powerful and pervasive kind of instruction" (p. B7) and recognized that they "heal faster in the presence of natural beauty" as they have "an inborn sense of harmony that is part of our evolutionary equipment" (p. B8). Richardson reflected this perspective. On a small section of the road where Richardson rented his small house, he grew a lush garden that, for him, represented the Garden of Eden. Gardens and yards created by people of African American heritage can serve a number of activities, many of which honor ancestors (Gundaker 1998). Gardens "…engendered by urban decay have proved effective social organization tools and sites of resistance" (Lippard, 1997, p. 245). For example, after the Los Angeles riots in the 1960s and 1990s, students in the "hood" produced food and *Saber es Poder* (To Know is to Enable) used landscape design to speak in code to people within the public streetscape (Lippard, 1997).

Although Richardson did not technically own the land where he gardened and taught in Tampa, he believed he owned it in ancestral terms because it was his parents' neighborhood and his energy was infused with it. His garden literally covered his yard and the lush greenness was striking amongst the gray industrial buildings surrounding him. His "ownership" of the space was an act of resistance to the city's lack of sensitivity to a space and place where African Americans had previously established homes and a neighborhood of healthy living. Whitt and Slack (1994) suggested that to claim land "is to literally steal community" (pp. 19-20). While Richardson would never use the word "steal" in this context, as he believed his neighborhood already belonged to *him* and not industry, he did recognize the profound nature of being rooted to an ancestral space. He believed that his gardening practices in this space were a way to resist social injustice.

"Materially, humans are skilled makers of a place for themselves in the world" (Sennett, 2008, p. 13). Richardson's place was in his garden, in his Tampa hometown neighborhood, resurrecting bones into sculpture, and teaching children, through art, that the imagination can make anything possible.

Lessons about Community

Reverend Benjamin Chavis coined the term "environmental racism" in 1987. The phrase refers to racial discrimination in environmental policy making—officially making decisions that are disproportionate in the ways in which they negatively affect people of color, include placing toxic waste facilities in minority community, building loud freeways that dissect traditional neighborhoods, and zoning industrial sites in residential spaces primarily occupied by people of color (Di Chiro, 1996). "Numerous studies have demonstrated that it is primarily low-income communities of color that are often targeted for industrial and toxic waste disposal sites" (p. 302). Such was the case with Richardson's neighborhood.

We cannot fully comprehend Richardson's art without understanding the changes he has witnessed in his community. He is not the only artist who has felt the need to work in the neighborhood in which he grew up, one that has become crime ridden and neglected due, in large part, to environmental racism. Purvis Young, from the African American section of Miami

called Overtown, makes art from old boards found on the streets. His work depicts his African American neighbors rising up in defiance. Angels in the sky look out after them. In spite of his economic success, Young could not imagine living anywhere else than his home community (Congdon & Bucuvalas, 2006). Neither can Taft Richardson.

The aesthetic power in what both Young and Richardson create resides in the collaboration process they have with various elements of their communities. This kind of "engagement is about empowerment" (Dunn & Leeson, 1997). In that sense, the artistic act "is a political statement as much as an artistic one" (p. 27). Although Richardson does not overtly focus on the political nature of what he does when he makes art and teaches, he is aware that his neighborhood, his garden, his art, and his teaching are all intertwined and that together they function in a system that is politically grounded. People of color are often disregarded and devalued in political decision-making; his actions work to counteract the negative results of this racism. He knows that beauty can emerge despite despair, neglect, and injustice. He sees it in the bones he rescues, the garden he grows in the midst of urban decay, and the neighborhood children he teaches to move beyond the destructive influences that surround them.

Concluding Thoughts

Taft Richardson's art, teaching, garden, and community building are all part of his life work. One thing easily fused into another. The place where he worked was central to his work. Without it, he claimed, he couldn't effectively teach or make art. Unfortunately, in 2007, he was forced to leave his home just after his wife passed away. In failing health himself, he had gone to live with relatives.

Place is a "central organizing unit to our economy and society" (Florida, 2002, p. 224). Richardson did not require or ask for funds to teach, nor has he aggressively pursued selling his artwork as he sees that his many sculptures belong together as a unit and should contextually be integrated into his garden and home. It is all to be understood together and not in isolation. However, the economy of Richardson's life—that which makes him rich—was doing the work he was led to do through God's guidance. Although the city of Tampa offered him a new space to work with children, as they had long acknowledged the power of his art, he declined. He claimed that it was not the right space and he could not work without his garden.

When he was in his garden-space, there was a brick factory across the street from his rented home. The noises generated from the factory seemed unbearably loud. It was hard to hold a conversation with Richardson through all the noise. He said that at first it sounded like a machine gun was continuously going off, but then it eventually became music. Richardson's way of reframing both sounds and objects, remaking them into something beautiful is his legacy. It is the model of his work that continues strong in the hearts and minds of so many children and adults who watched him peacefully live and work in his neighborhood space. He made beautiful artwork; he taught numerous neighborhood children to paint, draw, and make masks. He taught them to care about themselves and others, to create gardens, and to fight for their communities by living productive and peaceful lives. He taught about the power to transform objects, people, the landscape, and neighborhoods. And Taft Richardson modeled a way for us to see and understand the world, one that he restructured with wisdom and grace.

AFTERWORD

On Sunday, November 30, 2008, Taft Richardson passed away at the age of 65. He will be missed.

REFERENCES

Beardsley, J. (1998). *Art and landscape in Charleston and the Low Country: A project of Spoleto Festival USA*. Washington, DC: Spacemaker Press.

Borum, J. P. (1993). Strategy of the tiger: The world of Thornton Dial. *Folk Art, 18*(4), 34–40.

Congdon, K. G. (2004). *Community art in action*. Worcester, MA: Davis.

Congdon, K. G. (2006). Folkvine.org: Arts-based research on the Web. *Studies in Art Education, 48*(1), 36–51.

Congdon, K. G., & Bucuvalas, T. (2006). *Just above the water: Florida folk art*. Jackson: University Press of Mississippi.

Di Chiro, G. (1996). Nature as community: The convergence of environment and social justice. In W. Cronin (Ed.), *Uncommon ground: Rethinking the human place in nature* (pp. 298–320). New York: W. W. Norton.

Dunn, P., & Leeson, L. (1997). The aesthetics of collaboration. *Art Journal, 56*(1), 26–37.

Florida, R. (2002). *The rise of the creative class and how it's transforming work, leisure, community, and everyday life*. New York: Basic Books.

Gundaker, G. (1998). Introduction: Home ground. In G. Gundaker (Ed.), *Keep your head to the sky: Interpreting African American ground* (pp. 3–23). Charlottesville: University Press of Virginia.

Gundaker, G. (1996). What goes around comes around: Temporal cycles and recycling in African-American yard work. In C. Cerny & S. Seriff (Eds.), *Recycled reseen: Folk art from the global scrap heap* (pp. 72–81). New York: Harry Abrams.

Lippard, L. R. (1997). *The lure of the local: Sense of place in a multicentered society*. New York: The New Press.

Orr, D. W. (2006, October 20). A meditation on building. *The Chronicle of Higher Education*, pp. B6–B8.

Seriff, S. (1996). Folk art from the global scrap heap: The place of Irony in the politics of poverty. In C. Cerny & S. Seriff (Eds.), *Recycled reseen: Folk art from the global scrap heap* (pp. 8–29). New York: Harry Abrams.

Sennett, R. (2008). *The craftsman*. New Haven, CT: Yale University Press.

Unmonumental: The object in the 21st century. (2007). New York: Phaidon Press. In association with the New Museum of Contemporary Art.

Whitt, L. A., & Slack, J. D. (1994). Communities, environments and cultural studies. *Cultural Studies 8*(1), 5–31.

Sidewalk Encounters: Re-envisioning "Problem" Neighborhoods

6

Karen Hutzel and Loring Resler

Children in Weinland Park wave when you drive by. They ask your name. They want to be ballerinas and teachers and basketball players. They are creative and funny and rascally. (Phillips, Columbus Dispatch, July 12, 2007)

Informal sidewalk encounters heightened our awareness of community through a service-learning project in the Weinland Park neighborhood of Columbus, Ohio. Five Ohio State University graduate students in Art Education, one professor, a community partner, and many kids spent a week exploring the assets of this community to inspire the creation of a community art piece. The graduate students, all art teachers from places as far as Alaska and as near as Columbus, had little knowledge of the neighborhood. Their initial encounters were of a strong sense of community in an apartment complex that housed single mothers. The graduate students commented on the village feeling present in this housing complex; older kids looked out for younger ones and referred to each other as brothers and sisters, while the mothers were caring and supervisory of all the children.

We were the outsiders. The children, experts on their community, were our guides. The result was a painted community art piece of multiple canvases, representing community through an environmental encounter at a neighborhood community center, tied together and hung by a wood curtain rod. The art piece reflected many assets in the community, including the natural, human, and social assets discovered during a mapping of the neighborhood. The art piece currently hangs at the neighborhood library

KEY CONCEPTS

- Communicative Action through Pragmatism
- Community-Based Action Research
- Collaborative Artmaking
- Border Crossing
- Service-Learning

and will travel around the community to eventually find its home in the new neighborhood policing center. Several of the graduate students/art educators left with a renewed sense of community and desire to utilize service-learning in their own schools.

Hutzel's First Encounter

As I walked down the sidewalk, a police car passed slowly, stopped, and backed up next to me. The passenger side window was down. The police officer in the driver's seat leaned toward me and asked, "Are you going far down this street?" I hesitated, confused if I was doing something wrong. "No, not far," I said as I considered the short distance I was walking from my car parked on the street to the apartment complex where I was meeting my community partner. "Are you okay?" he asked me. I told him I was, still confused. "Are you sure?" he asked me. "Yes, I'm fine," I said quickly. "Well, be careful." He said it slowly, like a warning of danger.

As I continued to walk and he pulled away, I realized the "problem" he observed. I was a white woman walking by myself in a predominately black neighborhood. My safety was of concern to this white police officer, evidenced through this seemingly caring act, although filled with issues of superiority, racism, and disconnect. He was not walking the sidewalks of this neighborhood. The police car acted as his barrier—a barrier that prevented him from knowing the neighborhood, the people, and their values. My purpose, however, as a professor attempting to connect my students with this neighborhood, was to break through unnecessary yet prevalent borders and barriers, to map the assets of the community in order to inspire the creation of a collaborative art piece. It was an ironic beginning to this journey, an encounter that framed my understanding of the perceptions of this particular neighborhood.

Considering Weinland Park

Weinland Park is one of seven University Area district neighborhoods, a community located just east of The Ohio State University campus. The University Area itself is where many students live, although few call Weinland Park home. The University Area was once home to the majority of Ohio State students, but as of 2003, over half of the students had retreated to the suburbs, the result of two decades of neglect by merchants, property owners, and the university (Pristin, 2003).

Similar to other university communities, this particular part of the University Area is a mixed race, lower-income area that carries with it negative perceptions typical of communities with similar urban locations and economic demographics.

According to U.S. Census Data of 2000, Weinland Park is home to 4,810 people, a 29% drop from 1970's population of 6,746 (Weinland Park Neighborhood Plan, 2006). The neighborhood's youth, ages 19 or younger, represent 36% of the population, an indication of the high percentage of children living in the community. At the same time, 33% of the population is 20 to 29 years old. Therefore, 69% of the population of Weinland Park is under 30 years old. The population's racial demographic is diverse, as 41% of the population is white, while 51% is African American. The median household income of Weinland Park families in 1999 was $15,381, compared to $37,897 for the entire Columbus community. In Weinland Park, 50% of the population is below the poverty level, and the unemployment rate is over 15%. Thirty-eight percent (38%) of the population does not have a high school diploma, while 31% has a high school diploma but no college. Only 9% of the population resides in owner-occupied housing which, when combined with over 600 Section 8 housing units, results in this neighborhood being a rental-oriented, densely-populated community, occupying a mere one-third of a square mile. These statistics are typical of lower-income communities that are situated near college campuses, as they tend to be home to a mix of few college students and many folks with little formal education and lower incomes.

Although the Weinland Park neighborhood is located just a few blocks from the university campus, it feels many miles away. A recent development project opened with the intent of attracting so-called high-caliber students and faculty back to the area. Described as a gateway, it actually created a physical barrier between the university and this neighborhood and gave the obvious impression of a gate. The neighborhood is described as a place to avoid, as one graduate student found when searching the Internet for information about Weinland Park. On the website, City-Data.com, this student located two queries and responses about suggestions for moving near campus. In both cases, the response was to avoid the Weinland Park area. One of the responses indicated that "[t]he only section that is truly bad and should be avoided, near High St. close to OSU … This area is small and called Weinland Park. This is the only neighborhood that is next to, directly north, or south of the University to avoid" (City-data.com, 2007). The implications for such negative perceptions point toward obvious issues of inequality based on race and class, polarizing people into small and avoided areas. Children are not excluded from this polarization, and ultimately begin to recognize their "turf" in such a way as to maintain safety by protecting it and remaining within its boundaries.

We experienced Weinland Park through a service-learning course that focused on an asset-based approach to community development underscored by action research methodologies. This chapter will present results of our collaboration and the random sidewalk encounters we experienced, beginning with a discussion of the theoretical underpinnings of the project, as well as articulating action research and service-learning methodologies.

Theorizing Communicative Action through Pragmatism

Prior to postmodern thinking, Jurgen Habermas (1984) described social life as embedded in the search for meaning through reflection and communication. He proposed an organic approach to developing social and human understanding that accounts for the intersubjectivity of human relations in search of freedom, liberation, and human emancipation. What Habermas (1984) described as "communicative action" has the goal of an "intersubjective mutuality of reciprocal understanding, shared knowledge, mutual trust and accord with one another" (p. 3). The goal for communicative action and liberation is rooted in pragmatism, an empirical methodology of inquiry and action attributed to philosopher Charles Peirce (James, 1907) who recognized the necessity of a reciprocal relationship between thought and behavior. Peirce believed that it is only through action that thought gains depth, clarity, and significance. Thus, theory and practice are bound, mutually informing one another: to theorize without putting that into action is disconnected abstraction; to act without theory is uninformed action (James, 1907). Cornel West (1989) advocated a politically responsive pragmatism that had direct relevance to individual and community transformation through knowledge and action. West challenged theorists to consider the possibilities inherent in learning from oppressed people and suggested a process of reconstructing misperceptions and practices found in traditional systems. Derrida (1976) similarly suggested theoretical processes that seek not to impose perceptions and interpretations of those holding power, but rather participatory and democratic approaches to discovering multiple perspectives in order to develop responsive activities through such cultural learning activities.

Art's role in fostering an understanding of human intersubjectivity and bringing awareness to and capacity for social change is well documented. At the most fundamental level, art serves as a vehicle for articulating group meaning, whether done on an individual or collective scale (Dissanayake, 1992). Community cultural development through the arts acts as a counterbalance to society's current economic climate of exclusion by offering dialogic, embodied images counter to those of commercial culture (Adams & Goldbard, 2001). Direct experience with art closes gaps between communities (Putnam & Feldstein, 2003) through collaboration and multi-level dialogue, effecting social change. Art is a means by which communities can honor culture while working around a social issue toward social transformation, the process leading to emancipation (Adams & Goldbard, 2001; Hutzel, 2007). These theoretical and artistic foundations are embedded in action research and service-learning, which provide methodologies for enacting the goals of transformation and social change through education and research.

Capturing the Action Research Methodology

Action research is not just a tool for solving problems, but is a valuable resource for building a sense of community. (Stringer, 2007, p. 122)

This experience was shaped by an action research methodology that served to establish a sense of community within the group (Stringer, 2007) and explored the potential for collaborative art to create change in the community (Hutzel, 2007). Action research is defined by the collaborative process of examining a shared concern (Kemmis & McTaggart, 1988) with the goal of transformation (Brydon-Miller, 2001) and change through

consensus building (Stringer, 2007). Stringer (2004) identified nine components of action research, including change, reflection, participation, inclusion, sharing, understanding, repetition, practice, and community. We were critical of the degree to which we achieved these nine components in our work, as our physical involvement in the community was limited to one week, diminishing the possibility of reaching success with several of these goals. However, at a basic level the action research approach supported our service-learning agenda as we worked collaboratively, examined authority and power, and recognized multiple voices to include in a collaborative art piece toward the goals of change and understanding. The authors' ongoing involvement in the community may have better attended to the entirety of these goals through additional service-learning courses; Hutzel developed and piloted a computer art service-learning course for neighborhood girls to be taught annually and Resler is collaborating with a neighborhood young adult on a community mural. In both cases, we found ourselves working with many of the same children, and were hopeful this continued involvement would have a greater impact on those particular children as well as on the neighborhood as a whole. In this way, action research continued organically, often without an official beginning or ending (Stringer, 2007).

In our work, we utilized a community-based action research methodology, which "provides a model for enacting local, action-oriented approaches to inquiry, applying small-scale theorizing to specific problems in specific situations" (Stringer, 2007, p. 10). In this model, the researcher acts as a facilitator of a process by which participants engaged in a collective investigation toward the goals of creating understanding and formulating change. Our approach toward this process was to begin with an asset-based mapping activity with children who lived in the neighborhood (Kretzmann & McKnight, 1993; Hutzel, 2007).

Asset-based mapping serves to highlight the existing positive qualities of a community, which can include environmental, human, social, and physical assets (Green & Haines, 2002). This process involved the graduate students, professor, community partner, and kids in the neighborhood walking around the community with cameras. The camera became a significant part of the data collection as it highlighted the visions of the kids, who chose the community assets they wished to photograph. Most significant was the kids' emphasis on photographing people—human assets—of the community and particularly those who participated in this project. With the cameras and final collaborative art piece, we creatively and visually communicated our research results to the community and university in a way that addressed the needs and interests of each (see Stringer, 2007). The asset-based approach to this service-learning project and action research methods challenges traditional learning and research approaches that focus on problems and needs, further confronting the power and authority traditionally held by university representatives working with marginalized communities. In this way, the action research methodology was further enhanced by the course's service-learning foundation.

Framing Our Educational Experience

Our experience in Weinland Park was part of a service-learning course; one of the authors was the professor of this course, and the other was a doctoral student who participated. Resler was an art teacher in south Atlanta before beginning her doctoral work at Ohio State. Hutzel, the professor of the course, taught in urban neighborhoods in Cincinnati, Ohio, before her affiliation with Ohio State. Each of us have taught in urban settings, and felt prepared to encounter the racial dynamics the experience was expected to educe. The course was constructed to utilize service-learning to expose art teachers to this cross-racial and cross-cultural experience and teaching strategy through practical application, theoretical and pragmatic readings, ongoing verbal and online reflection, and a final reflective paper. Service-learning has the potential to promote social justice through practical experiences with multicultural education. It involves a "commitment to appreciating the assets and serving the needs of a community partner, while enhancing student learning and academic rigor through the practice of intentional reflective thinking and responsible civic action" (Duncan & Kopperud, 2008, p. 4). Although many definitions of service-learning focus on "needs" and "problems," this definition allowed room for an asset-based approach to create reciprocity and of "doing with" as opposed to "doing for" (Friere, 1970).

Aside from Resler, the students in the course were part of a mostly online master's degree program in the Art Education Department at Ohio State. The course was designed with an online and onsite component, in which the students began online conversations with neighborhood children in June and were onsite for one week in July to create the art piece. The students were art teachers from Alaska, Chicago, and Knoxville. The online students also brought an understanding of service-learning to the course because they had participated in an online multicultural course with Hutzel in which their course project was to implement a small service-learning activity in their own schools. The pragmatic experience during our week in the community, however, seemed to be necessary to further their understanding of the possibility for service-learning to be a reciprocal exchange and to give up the power and control they are accustomed to having in their school situations. As one of the students wrote after the experience, "Using the asset-based approach, this project belonged to the community (not us). We were merely facilitators who encouraged and guided the learning experience. In the process, the youth became our teachers by sharing their community with us." The process of collaboration required us all to recognize the assets we brought to the experience; the graduate students brought their years of teaching experience and leadership abilities, the youth brought the years of living in the community and youthful ideas, and the professor and community partner brought their understanding of the collaborative process.

The collaborative artmaking strategy (Cooper & Sjostrom, 2006) and asset-based mapping approach helped us all to re-envision this particular neighborhood through the creation of a community within our working group. The collaborative artmaking was central to the community's creation. "Almost everyone understands that a democracy functions best when its citizens are educated and involved. But not everyone understands that art activities can help promote this goal … people often neglect to think about how art has the power to connect us and help us think through community-based issues" (Congdon, 2004, p. 42). Making the art piece was not meant to be the focus of the project; however, completing the art piece itself provided a goal and an outcome to work together.

The approach to collaboratively making art was framed on the same theoretical foundations as the action research and service-learning methodologies. Individual ideas were joined together into one both physically—through the joining of individual art pieces into one finished art piece—and conceptually—as our notions of this particular community coalesced into a positive outlook on the neighborhood. Our sidewalk encounters through the asset-based mapping approach led to developing the collaborative art piece that portrayed the human and environmental assets encountered in the community. A large textured tree, representing the community garden, served as the centerpiece of the collaborative painting. Statements of recognized assets acted as tree branches: "The community garden is beautiful;" "There's a lot of love in this neighborhood;" and "I'm going to that new school in the fall." Around the tree, as if they were falling leaves, were photographs of the participants and neighborhood as witnessed throughout the week and captured by the youth participants. This central tree image was framed by individually-painted flowers bound together in a quilt-like fashion.

Crossing Borders

The sidewalk became an important part of our mapping, serving as a metaphor for the borders and boundaries by which we constructed and defined our sense of place. But just as importantly, the sidewalk offered the means by which to circumvent those perceived borders by providing a pathway for a fluidity of movement and information between neighbors (Johnson, 2001). Sidewalks provided us with a variety of interactions, many of them random: we passed various people, stores, and landscapes, learning to recognize patterns while allowing improvisation. This offered us a path for engagement and perpetual feedback in a constantly changing environment and ultimately provided a broader base from which to make intelligent decisions (Johnson, 2001). This type of engagement was in contrast to the detached exposure offered by our encapsulation in a car. The significance of sidewalks is in their ability to define a grassroots system grounded in local interactions; random engagement creates a type of systemic organism beyond the individual, an intelligence born of responsiveness, of situation, rather than of generalization. This resulted in an emergent intelligence and social transformation (Johnson, 2001). We define sidewalk encounters as those informal exchanges had with others when walking through a neighborhood with an openness to the assets and surroundings in the community.

Our learning involved multiple sidewalk encounters. The professor's sidewalk encounter with the concerned police officer highlighted many misperceptions facing the community. The majority of the graduate students entered into this experience with few, if any, preconceived notions of the environment or population with which they would be working. Through their own sidewalk encounters, they quickly recognized the role of place in informing one's perception and identity. One graduate student was grateful for having no prior knowledge through the media of the neighborhood; another reflected in appreciation of a community member giving her insight into and relieving her apprehension of the neighborhood and its people. Our community partner, Catherine, sensitive to the significance

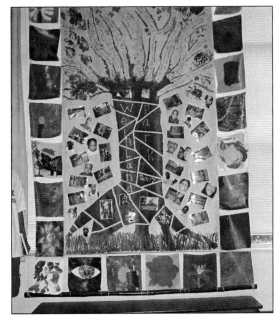

Figure 1. The finished collaborative art piece.

of sidewalk encounters, marched right up to a police officer stationed in front of a new early childhood development center, intent on introducing the community youths and police officer to one another. As a quiet teenage boy and the police officer shook hands, the importance of these informal exchanges became evident.

Catherine arranged for us to meet in a housing complex that housed single mothers and their children in order to engage children that were often underserved in the neighborhood. The heat of the room seemed unbearable the first day, but Catherine's insistence on this location proved to be most important to our engagement in the community. Some of our greatest lessons came from witnessing the warmth and welcoming nature of the residents and their willingness to embrace this project, which overrode any possible concerns regarding safety and inclusion held by graduate students. The dominant community asset recognized by graduate students was that of a community bound by love, trust and support: children look out for one another; mothers share parenting responsibilities and support one another;

Figure 2. The housing complex in Weinland Park.

Figure 3. A budding artist shows off his athletic skills.

and children seek opportunities for growth in community, as evidenced by their creation of their garden and their participation in this community art project. These mothers and children put faces on the theoretical notion of social capital (Putnam, 2000) and underscored theories of collective identity (Apple, 1995) and sense of community (Davidson & Cotter, 1986; Chavis & Wandersman, 1990). Our middle-class values were challenged by a place—this housing complex—that at first seemed lifeless and stale (see Figure 2), but came alive through the social interactions that ran each day.

Sidewalk encounters also invited a wide range of possible interactions and engagements. A young budding artist and potential art educator gained recognition through his athletic ability to walk down the sidewalk on his hands (see Figure 3). In examining their photographs, children commented on the corner market, seen in the background of one picture: "Oh, there's Sam's!" "Yeah, that's where my daddy goes." In another example, a young girl couldn't wait to cross the street to take close-up pictures of the Day Lilies in a neighbor's previously unnoticed garden.

Notions of power and control were immediately dismantled the first day together when Catherine told the children to pick their own college partner. The college students, with somewhat frightened looks, sat quietly as each child pointed to the adult with whom they wanted to spend the day. The youngest in the room quickly took hold of his leadership position when

Figure 4. Walking the sidewalks of Weinland Park.

he stepped up first to point to the shortest and youngest-looking student and said, "I want the little one." The last picked student later commented on feelings of inferiority and a reminder of being picked last for sporting teams in school. With this dismantling of power, we were on our way throughout the neighborhood, following along the sidewalks and dirt paths on a hot and sunny day.

We quickly found that the children of Weinland Park were acutely aware of the boundaries and borders created by the sidewalks defining and articulating their neighborhood, as well as the means by which they could navigate them to create new possibilities for themselves. A tiny, savvy 4-year old, who had grabbed our attention right away, stated his understanding that he could go anywhere he wanted, anytime, as long as he did not go into any alleys. Another young man crossed the sidewalk and a busy street several times each day, between investigating our project, shooting basket-ball alone in the adjacent park, and talking with gang members across the street, uncertain of where he wanted to make his place in the community. During an afternoon of painting later in the week, two young men joined the activity but chose to paint the boundaries defining their gang turf and the associated tags, rather than paint the flowers the other children were painting. In detailing their turf, they politely articulated the boundaries we university-associated people may have unconsciously crossed in coming there; they also identified the boundaries by which they negotiated their existence and safety through a map of their gang turf in their gang colors of blue and black. Their identification and territory was reinforced for us the following morning when we arrived to the site to discover gang initials carved into the gravel for us to recognize. These visual messages reinforced the borders that we had crossed and reconfirmed the boundaries by which the young gang members lived.

Border crossing, although currently discussed in our society as the physical crossing of national borders, is considered in education as cultural and represents varied applications, including the crossing of interdisciplinary and intellectual borders (Metz, 2001). Cultural border crossing has been discussed in education specifically as (1) a means by which to circumvent the unavailability of senior science courses in rural schools (Nielsen & Nashon, 2007); (2) a process by which students can address issues of race, class, and sex to reach higher levels of achievement (Alston, 2004); and (3) a means to explore literacy as a complex and multilayered phenomenon (Thames & York, 2003). Cultural border crossing is also promoted as a process to increase cultural awareness and sensitivity through educational activities that cause students to enter into an exchange with multiple cultures, including their own (Bastos, 2006; Jupp, 2001).

We had all crossed some borders in coming together for this experience. The borders were physical, emotional, intellectual, and personal, creating a slight discomfort in the beginning that eventually dissipated with our focused and collaborative work toward completing our art piece. The borders seemed to become less prevalent as the week progressed, despite the young gang members' reminder of their physical territory. With ongoing involvement, we can only imagine these multiple borders and boundaries we encountered in Weinland Park could eventually dissipate.

Following Up

Although we each had returned to the housing complex a few times after the summer project, during a visit 10 months later, on a warm April afternoon, the children came to our side immediately. Some remembered us well, asking if we would be doing another art piece soon. Others, who were less involved, had to be reminded of who we were. The younger boy who had asserted his leadership early on in our project, did so again, inviting us up to the second floor meeting space in the community room. This (now) kindergartner asked us what we wanted to talk about, and then proceeded to remind us of the details of the art piece, drawing a picture of what it looked like. Two sisters who had participated with Hutzel for 2 days in her computer art course, came up to hug her, and then reminded her of the dogs they had seen in photographs. After further description of the dogs being dressed in "funny clothes," Hutzel finally recalled that these two girls had joined her class for a visit to the William Wegman exhibit at the Wexner Center on campus.

We then visited a family across the alley, three of whose four children had participated in the activity. Their younger daughter was in a photograph in a *Dispatch* article about our work while their son was quoted in the article as wanting to become an art teacher some day. They immediately invited us into their home where they were preparing for a special night for their oldest daughter, who was performing in a play downtown. The father informed us his son was continuing to paint, despite his efforts to get him to use a pencil first. We encouraged him to allow the painting, and asked the boy if he still wanted to go to college to become an artist. While he was shaking his head yes, his younger sister told us from across the room, "We're already artists." We thanked her for the clarification.

REFERENCES

Adams, D., & Goldbard, A. (2001). *Creative culture: The art of cultural development.* New York: The Rockefeller Foundation.

Alston, J. A. (2004). Informed commentary: The many faces of American schooling: Effective schools research and border-crossing in the 21st Century. *American Secondary Education, 32*(2), 79–93.

Apple, M.W. (1995). Is social transformation always progressive? Rightist reconstructions of schooling today. In M. James (Ed.), *Social reconstruction through education: The philosophy, history, and curricula of a radical ideal.* Norwood, NJ: Ablex Publishing Corp.

Bastos, F. M. C. (2006). Border-crossing dialogues: Engaging art education students in cultural research. *Art Education, 59*(4), 20–24.

Brydon-Miller, M. (2001). Research and action: Theory and methods of participatory action research. In D. L. Tolman & M. Brydon-Miller (Eds.), *From subjects to subjectivities: a handbook of interpretive and participatory methods* (pp. 76–79). New York: New York University Press.

Chavis, D. M., & Wandersman, A. (1990). Sense of community in the urban environment: A catalyst for participation and community development. *American Journal of Community Psychology, 18*(1), 55–81.

City-data.com. (2007). Areas to avoid/look for near OSU campus Blog. Retrieved April 22, 2008, from http://www.city-data.com/forum/columbus/117047-areas-avoid-look-near-osu-campus.html

Congdon, K. (2004). *Community art in action.* Worcester, MA: Davis Publications, Inc.

Cooper, M., & Sjostrom, L. (2006). *Making art together: How collaborative artmaking can transform kids, classrooms, and communities.* Boston: Beacon Press.

Davidson, W.B., & Cotter, P.R. (1986). Measurement of sense of community within the sphere of city. *Journal of Applied Social Psychology, 16*(7), 608–619.

Derrida, J. (1976). *Of grammatology.* Baltimore: Johns Hopkins University Press.

Dissanayake, E. (1992). *Homo Aestheticus.* Seattle: The Free Press.

Duncan, D., & Kopperud, J. (2008). *The service-learning companion.* Boston: Houghton Mifflin.

Freire, P. (1970). *Pedagogy of the oppressed.* New York: Continuum.

Green, G.P., & Haines, A. (2002). *Asset building and community development.* Thousand Oaks, CA: Sage Publications.

Habermas, J. (1984). *The theory of communicative action: Reason and the rationality of society.* Boston: Beacon Press.

Hutzel, K. (2007). Reconstructing a community, reclaiming a playground: A participatory action research study. *Studies in Art Education, 48*(3), 299–315.

Johnson, S. (2001). *Emergence: The connected lives of ants, brains, cities, and software.* New York: Scribner.

James, W. (1907). *Pragmatism: A new name for some old ways of thinking.* New York: Longmens, Green and Co.

Jupp, J. C. (2001). The Rio Grande Valley: Border crossing, diversity within diversity, and rethinking categorical language. *Multi-Cultural Review, 10*(2), 34–41.

Kemmis, S., & McTaggart, R. (1988). *The action research planner.* Victoria: Deakin University.

Kretzmann, J. P. & McKnight, J. L. (1993). *Building communities from the inside out: A path toward finding and mobilizing a community's assets.* Chicago: ACTA Publications.

Metz, M. H. (2001). Intellectual border crossing in graduate education: A report from the field. *Educational Researcher, 30*(5), 12–18.

Nielsen, W. S., & Nashon, S. M. (2007). Accessing science courses in rural BC: A cultural border-crossing. *Alberta Journal of Educational Research, 53*(2), 174–188.

Phillips, J. (2007). Budding spirit: Neighborhood's young artists impart their sense of community. *The Columbus Dispatch.* July 12, 2007.

Pristin, T. (2003). Improving the neighborhood at Ohio State. *The New York Times.* April 30, 2003.

Putnam, R. (2000). *Bowling alone.* New York: Touchstone.

Putnam, R., & Feldstein, L. M. (2003). *Better together: Restoring the American community.* New York: Simon & Schuster.

Stringer, E. T. (2004). *Action research in education.* Columbus, OH: Pearson.

Stringer, E. T. (2007). *Action research: Third edition.* Los Angeles: Sage Publications.

Thames, D. G., & York, K. C. (2003). Disciplinary border crossing: Adopting a broader, richer view of literacy. *Reading Teacher, 56*(7), 602–610.

Weinland Park Neighborhood Plan. (2006). City of Columbus, Department of Development, Planning Division.

West, C. (1989). *The American evasion of philosophy.* Madison: University of Wisconsin Press.

Lines of Flight: The Nomadic Teachers of the Beehive Collective's Polinizaciones Project in Colombia and Venezuela

Carolyn Erler

Cross-pollination is the transfer of pollen among different plants or varieties of the same species. (Delaplane & Mayer, 2000, p. 18)

Members of the Beehive Collective are often asked if they raise bees. The answer is no, not exactly. Their focus is cross-pollination. The Beehive Collective is a group of nomadic political artists and teachers who use their own artwork to "cross-pollinate the grassroots" (Beehive Collective, 2004) with radically critical and hopeful ideas. They travel with their artwork folded in their backpacks, which allows them to move freely from site to site in search of new students. Their artworks on fabric banners, or *mantas* as they are known throughout Latin America, are masterful labors of love, densely packed with stories, iconographic images, and visionary messages capable of spanning linguistic and cultural bounds. One of the collective's most-traveled artworks, *Plan Colombia,* has been on the move since 2004. A non-copyrighted image, it has circulated through hands and communities well beyond the purview of the Beehive Collective, which has collectively entrusted it to the organic and holistic winds of cross-pollination. This chapter will trace the line of flight of *Plan Colombia,* and the work of one of its most dedicated teachers, who travels through Colombia and Venezuela under the name of *lunes.*

lunes

Compared to honey bees, some wild bees pollinate certain crops more efficiently because of unique and desirable behaviors. (University of Georgia Honey Bee Program, 2008, p. 1)

KEY CONCEPTS

- The Beehive Collective
- Political Graphics
- Latin America
- Nomadic Art Teaching
- Youth Activism

I met *lunes* in 2004 when we were both students at Florida State University. I was writing about the street theater and agitprop art of the Coalition of Immokalee Workers, a group of Florida-based migrant workers whose successful boycott of Yum! Brands, the multinational fast-food conglomerate, made labor history. A professor urged me to seek out *lunes,* then a graduate student in anthropology and charismatic leader of the FSU chapter of Students for Peace and Social Justice. She gave me his phone number and I dialed.

lunes was in Colombia collecting native plants and herbs for his thesis on Andean ethno-botany. Despite his remote location, like Subcommandante Marcos, he somehow managed to have cell phone reception and wireless Internet. After his return to the United States, we crossed paths at an off-campus warehouse that served as bike shop, art gallery, anarchist library, and unheated living quarters for a handful of politically radical students. At the time, I did not realize he was a local celebrity for the anarchist set, complete with his own Sunday night radio show and entourage at the FSU student station. He was a soft-spoken, articulate, intelligent young man, uncommonly respectful of an "older" woman such as me. It was at this meeting that I learned that he was a member of the legendary political graphic arts group, the Beehive Collective. This meeting with *lunes* made it possible for me to join the collective as a researcher and popular educator in early 2004.

The Beehive Collective

The honey bee hive is known as a super organism. The reason for this classification is that the hive as a whole acts as a single organism, like a dog or a bear. (Royal Gold Farms, 2008)

When I first became a member of the collective, very little had been written in the field of art education about vernacular visual youth culture. Darts (2004, 2008) was one of the first to critically explore the phenomenon of culture jamming, a resistance movement against monoculture and consumerism by means of guerrilla art forms such as graffiti, stenciling, adbusting, hacktivism, postering, and billboard modification (Gelwicks, 2004; Lasn, 1999, 2000). The Beehive Collective is part of this youth culture, but at a much deeper level; it draws strength from the tradition of Latin American political graphics collectives such as the Mexican Taller de Graphica Popular (TGP, Popular Graphic Arts Workshop), founded in 1937. The TGP, which was dedicated to serving the progressive movements of Mexico, was itself rooted in the work of the master printmaker and social critic Jose Guadalupe Posada, who worked during the 1910 Mexican Revolution (Caplow, 2007). When considering the Beehive Collective, it is helpful to understand this duel strain of influence on the group's artwork and far-flung pedagogical mission.

The Beehive Collective is a loosely organized international network of cultural workers and image-based educators whose graphic campaigns are known throughout South America, Central America, and parts of the global North (Hoffman, 2003). Since its founding in 1999 by a small group of anti-globalization activists, the collective has created a trilogy of large-scale graphics—*Free Trade Area of the Americas, Plan Colombia, and Mesoamerica Resiste!*—that chronicle the major economic-political shifts of our time from the standpoint of those whose voices have been silenced by the corporate media (Beehive Design Collective, 2004). The hand-drawn graphics are illustrated narratives based on conversations between Beehive artists and indigenous and peasant farmers, activists, and researchers in Colombia, Mexico, Ecuador, and the United Sates (Hoffman, 2003). The collective's *Plan Colombia* is the product of a grassroots story-gathering project in Colombia initiated by *lunes,* who is Colombian American, in conjunction with North American members of the Beehive Collective (Erler, 2006).

Political Context of "Plan Colombia"

Most bee kills occur when pesticides drift or move from the target area into the apiary or onto crops attractive to the bees. The outcome of drift can be catastrophic. (UGHBP, 2008, p.1)

It is helpful to know the recent history of US-Colombia relations in order to understand the graphic. Since 1999, the US has given some $4.5 billion to a program to fight drug trafficking and leftist guerrillas in Colombia (Center for International Policy [CIP], 2006). Under President G.W. Bush, about half of the program's budget, $306 million (Cooper, 2001; CIP, 2001), went to private defense contractors such as Military Professional Resources Inc. (CIP, 2007; U.S. Department of State, 2001, 2007; Harrop, 2007). Working with the Colombian military, these private armies or so called Enhanced International Peacekeeping Forces (CIP, 2006) undertook large-scale fumigation operations of coca plants using the powerful herbicide, glyphosate. Scientists and indigenous leaders repeatedly warned that the spraying of chemical herbicides to destroy coca fields seriously threaten the rainforests and wildlife of the Amazon and the health of indigenous and small farming communities. The large quantities of glyphosate dropped from the sky killed food crops and caused a series of health problems and water contamination (Knight, 2000), resulting in the biggest humanitarian disaster in the Western Hemisphere, according to the United Nations News Center (2004). Colombian nationals have tried to tell the story of the program's devastating impact on peasant farmers and indigenous peoples (Hart, 2000; Leech, 2007; Refugees International, 2004;

Figure 1. A picture-lecture event.

Amnesty International, 2004). It is this story that the Beehive Collective tells in its monumental banner, *Plan Colombia.*

Picture-Lectures

A Pollinator is an agent that moves pollen, whether it be wind, bees, bats, moths, or birds. (UGHBP, 2008, p. 1)

The Beehive Collective presents *Plan Colombia* graphic in the context of educational events it calls picture-lectures. These are 1–2 hour action-learning sessions in which two or more members of the Collective co-present the graphic as a detailed narrative (Figure 1). A picture-lecture can happen almost anywhere, such as a street, a classroom, a hallway, church basement, or community centers. Members of the collective consciously set out to use the graphic as an educational tool to fill in the gaps of the dominant narrative and expose its inaccuracies (Beehive Collective, 2004).

The presenter, or picture-lecturer, is central to the Beehive event. This person unpacks the meaning of the detailed graphic and relates it to the audience. The picture-lecturer relates to not only the beliefs and attitudes of its audience, but also knows the visual imagery that is meaningful to it. Perhaps because Beehive graphics are stylistically similar to comic books and graphic novels, North American enthusiasts of Beehive graphics tend to be youthful. So too are the picture-lecturers. Blair (2004), a scholar of visual rhetoric, indicated that visual arguments rely on the rhetorical astuteness of the arguer for their success. The persuasive power of *Plan Colombia* lies in the youth and vitality of its Beehive presenters.

Visual Narrative

Honeybees collect nectar and store it as honey in their hives. Nectar and honey provide the energy for the bee's flight muscles and for heating the hive during winter. (National Honey Board, 2008, p. 1)

The *Plan Colombia* banner reads vertically, like a scroll (Figure 1). A work of overwhelming size and power, the banner poses a counter-narrative to the official U.S. position on Colombia. While the U.S. State Department frames the Colombian conflict as one between narco-terrorism and the civilizing forces of democracy, the Beehive Collective holds a mirror up to the US, reflecting the mighty capitalist nation as a wasp or W.A.S.P. nest. Starting at the top of the banner, the narrative (which is also printed in a pamphlet that can be referred to while viewing the banner) begins:

"The long history of colonialism in the Americas, currently manifested in the Andean region as *Plan Colombia,* is a metaphor for the multi-faceted destructive influences of U.S. foreign policy and corporate monoculture on a global scale" (Beehive Collective, 2004, p.2).

Moving downward, Black Hawk helicopters, surveillance satellites, and spy planes crowding the air space over Colombia are illustrated. Most North Americans would recognize these images, since the US is a major military power and these images often fill our TV and movie screens. Through this image, the Beehive Collective (2004) underscores what they see as the problem: "The Multi-layered Multi-Billion Dollar Military Operation: The drug war is a smokescreen for multinational corporations' interests in extraction of the rich biodiversity and natural resources of the Amazon and her peoples" (p. 4).

In the post-9/11 media, crop-dusters became an ominous symbol of potential terrorist attack on the U.S. food supply. The Beehive Collective used this image to illustrate another point of view. The *Plan Colombia* narrative stressed: "Round-up Ultra, a broad-spectrum herbicide manufactured by the U.S. chemical corporation Monsanto, is being sprayed to justify the war on drugs to the American people, but has had devastating effects on both subsistence crops and rainforest habitat" (p. 3).

The fourth scene, "A Swarm of Mosquitoes has landed to Extract the Resources of the Area," focuses on the Cano Limon-Covenas oil pipeline, which spans 500 miles through the rainforest region of Ecuador and Colombia. This is where the most intensive fumigations are taking place. As a result, millions of Colombians are displaced from their homelands as their crops of maize and squash fail. Caught between corporate militias, US-financed counterinsurgency squads, left-wing guerrillas, and defoliating fumigations, the peasant farmers and indigenous people of the land experience "the invasion of colonialism in every aspect of daily life" (Beehive Collective, 2004, p. 3).

The solution to the nightmare depicted in the *Colombia* graphic lies in the work of the ants. In the final scene, titled "The Nightmare Brought to Justice," Leafcutter ants dismantle the twisted pipeline that spells out the European-given name, Colombia. Ants of resistance are busy breaking up the nightmare scenes and taking them back, piece by piece, to the earth. "Composting the nightmare, processing it through the filter of the earth, will assure that what grows back will not be just as destructive" (Beehive Collective, 2004, p. 4). Herein lies the Collective's harsh judgment of historic colonialism and activist solution to present day occurrences of neo-colonialism in the form of market globalization.

Polinizaciones

I contacted *lunes,* hoping to get an update on his work with the graphic, while preparing to write this chapter. We had been out of touch for about 2 years. I e-mailed him this greeting:

"What have you been up to these days? Any involvement with the bees?"

A few hours later, he replied: "I've been living in Colombia for a little over a year. Between us, and the rest of the hive, I am the main person doing everything for the (*Plan Colombia*) project. There are other newer bees from down here doing their own stuff, but I have not been able to get them to document it on the site very much…" (*lunes,* personal communication, May 5, 2008).

I responded: "I'm so happy to hear you're in Colombia. Whereabouts? … You said you are the main person doing the project, plus there are new bees working on it. What were your plans, bee-wise, when you left the US?

Later the same day, he wrote: "Mostly doing beehive and popular education stuff. Right now I am in Bogotá but not in the same place for much time. 2 weeks ago I was in La Guajira and in a week and a half I am on my way to Venezuela for a month or so. All for beehive stuff."

Sensitive to the fact that the Beehive Collective has little respect for academia, I very carefully asked if we could have a fuller dialogue about his teaching in Colombia. I explained that the results could appear in a book about art education and social justice.

He responded: "Sounds hella interesting the only thing is my Internet contact is only so often and in a week I start traveling again (and then) I will have barely any at all. Though if I can help in any other way I am all game." (*lunes,* personal communication, May 6, 2008)

Our correspondence dropped off in the days before he left for Venezuela. I turned my attention to the Beehive Collective website and its *Polinizaciones* blog, "Reportbacks from Colombia." The stated purpose of the blog site is "to share and spread the word of the launching of Polinizaciones." An introduction, probably written by *lunes* (2008), explains:

Polinizaciones is a collaboration between the Beehive and various communities, groups and people in Colombia, Venezuela, Ecuador, & Panama to distribute the hive's graphic trilogy regarding globalization in America, specifically the FTAA, Plan Colombia & Plan Puebla Panama. This past year of 2007 was spent meeting and sharing with just some of the organisms affected in the region by these policies and responding with resistance. In 2008 local ants and bees will swarm the regions interested sharing stories, experiences, the graphics and skills sharing with the creation of new pedagogy tools and cultural resistance.

Yet an integral part of the Beehive's popular education mission is to ensure that the results of their collaborative research process—the finished illustrations—are returned to the communities that are most affected by the realities depicted in the graphics. While people living the daily reality of U.S. intervention in Colombia and the mega-projects of the PPP know quite well what they are experiencing, the graphics serve as a tool to facilitate communication about communities' struggles as well as for fostering dialogue about the realities in different places. In our work with the communities in Colombia and Panamá we will specifically, but not exclusively, use image-based communication tools (Figure 2). The project team will facilitate this graphic-based learning, encouraging the sharing experiences through methods of popular education (Beehive Collective, 2008).

lunes did not agree to a formal dialogue about his teaching, but before leaving for Venezuela, he wrote about his experiences in Colombia on the Polinizaciones blog. I received this, of course, as a gift. However, there was a reason he had chosen to write about his thoughts with the bloggers and not directly with me. His blog essay revealed an otherworldly consciousness that the quick e-mail exchange had not captured. For one thing, he had not mentioned that he was visiting a *resguardo*—an indigenous reserve—with members of the Muisca Federation near Bogotá (Figure 3).

To provide a context for *lunes'* blog essay, the history of the Muisca needs recounting. Archeological evidence dates the Muisca culture to 2500 B.C. A large agrarian society based in the eastern highland savannah of present-day Colombia, the civilization peaked between 1000 and 1550 C.E. After the Spanish conquest, Muisca survivors were forced to live in indigenous shelters (*resguardos*) and work the land for Spanish colonists. In 1810, the newly independent state of Colombia dissolved the shelters, with the exception of the Reservation of Cota, which was purchased by the Muisca community and re-established as a reserve in 1916. Since then, there

Figure 2. Photo of a picture-lecture on the Polinizaciones blog site.

Figure 3. Lunes teaching in Colombia.

has been a process of reconstruction of the indigenous councils. In 2002, the five working councils of Cota, Suba, Bosa, Chia, and Sesquile held the First General Congress of the Muisca People, in which they founded the Great Council of the Muisca People and joined the National Indigenous Organization of Colombia (Nativewiki, 2008; Colombia Support Network, 2007; ONIC, 2008). It was from inside this life-world that *lunes* had replied to my e-mail messages.

Provided is an excerpt from *lunes'* essay, including English translations in parentheses where needed. The full contents of the entry can be read at http://polinizaciones.blogspot.com/

Bajo la sombra del Majuy - Beneath the shade of the Majuy.

May 13, 2008

Lunes

Preparing for another long trip, we have returned from all corners of Colombia to regroup in the savanna of Bacatá (Bogotá). While one would think that we would take this time to rest, that is not the case…. In these weeks we have escaped often from the concrete jungle to be able to get to know, learn, teach and share with our Muisca brothers and sisters in Cota. Even though we have been in Bacatá and the rest of the Savanna on many occasions, this is the first opportunity we have had to meet and visit the hummingbird (a god who takes the form of a hummingbird in Mesoamerican mythology) compañera (girls) of the Muisca nation.

On these visits to the community we did a couple of story tellings (picture-lectures) for different groups on the *resguardo* (reserve), we

participated in *mingas* (community work) planting corn and quinua, we received medicine and council from the elders, and we were able to purge our lil bellies after so much travel. One of the more special experiences was being able to share with the youth of the community who have a musical group. These lil hummingbirds flew up and down and all around with their *sikus, kenas,* guitars, *bombos* and the *charrango* playing music from Bolivia, Peru and from their own culture. The only thing that shined more than the feathers on the hummingbird youth was their consciousness, humility and love for their territory and community. We also helped them care for the sheep and reminded them that the efforts they are making to maintain their customs, traditions and culture is of great importance for their community, the continent and the world.

Even though it has been wonderful meeting the hummingbirds and sharing in the Savanna with its indigenous inhabitants, the problems we have seen affecting communities in other regions were also present here. While the hummingbird youth shine and their elders share with them, many of the hummingbirds in the community have lost their interest in maintaining their customs. This is because of many reasons but the first being the invasion of the Spanish in the Savanna from early on, though more recently there is also the nearby Bogotá and the influence of its materialistic and consumer culture … Another problem is th(at) wealthy folks from Bogotá are taking over agricultural lands (and turning) them into housing subdivisions … This has been a shock for rural folks … While there are many examples of those who maintain the practices of weaving, pottery, music and traditional agriculture, there is a lack of support for the hummingbirds that are active in the struggle of maintaining these practices.

…most inhabitants of Bogotá … believe that the wetlands must be drained, the forests cut down, and the fertile earth paved over. In the midst of this … urbanization … it appears that the largest Muisca and pre-Muisca cemetery has been found. It … could have up to 1,500 tombs, the oldest ones being over 2,000 years old. For the inhabitants of Usme (another Spanish settlement of Muisca origin), about to be consumed by the expansion of Bogotá, this has been great news since they were not in favor of the housing development that was going to be built in the area and until now there seemed no possible way of halting the construction. Now they with other inhabitants of the Savanna are pressuring that the necropolis be recognized as Arqueological Patrimony of the city and the country and that the ancestors of the inhabitants of the Altiplano Cundiboyacense (highlands along the eastern corridor of the Colombian Andes, the ancient territory of the Muisca) are there and need to continue resting as they have done for the last 2,000 years. While it is important to protect, recognize, and value the past, we are not in agreement with the local widespread belief that Muisca culture is a dead culture. Marginalized by invasive actors on the Savanna such as the State and private companies, the Muisca are still present, resisting and surviving in their ancestral territory. While rapidly changing, it is still theirs.

Once we finished this flight, of which many more to come, an elder wrote this about our visit…

We give thanks to life, mother nature and our mother earth (*hicha quaia*) for permitting us to find in our path brothers from another hive that have helped us remember with their experience, nobility and great preoccupation regarding the direction in which we are headed. Poisoning and contaminating all the forms of life in the planet, the cosmos and in the universe.

They have made us remember the word of our elders and have made us realize the importance of our memory and cultural traditions, our mother earth (*hicha quaia*) the valuable traditional medicine, seeds and arts, the labor of the *minga*, of Love of Life. Within our territory and within the great Hive. Learn more of Western Thought to support and strengthen our traditional wisdom as the principal tool to rebuild the path constructed by our elders – a path that will once again take us to our own origin. It will take us to find the truth in our hearts, warmed by the sacred spirit (*hicha quaia*)

ANAXIE <- ITZE QUENE (so it is) (*lunes*, 2008, May 13).

Lines of Flight

Honeybee swarms are one of the most beautiful and interesting phenomena in nature. A swarm starting to issue is a thrilling sight. (Ellis, 2008)

lunes wrote about storytelling, planting crops, and receiving medicine and council from the elders all in the same sentence. This may have been because he perceives these things to be of equal value. However, there is almost no mention of teaching in *lunes'* essay. This suggests a departure from the modern western European concept of teaching.

The essay suggests that teaching and learning can occur naturally when people work together, listen to each other, and regard each other with respect. A deeper theme is the need to leave home—metaphorically and/or physically—to become the *other* of settled, accepted society. As a traveling outsider, a person learns by becoming a guest in the other's house. If, as a guest, you put yourself to good use, then perhaps you can stay. As *lunes'* story shows, pedagogical acts such as story telling occur within a broad network of acts that give meaning and depth to the human encounter. *lunes* seemed to spend much of his time with the Muisca learning about the pressures they face as traditional people surrounded by suburban sprawl, industrial pollution, and the attractions of modern life for the young. The formal teaching moment sprang from this well-prepared ground, for Beehive Collective banners seem to arouse curiosity and merit interest wherever they go (Figures 4 and 5).

Figure 4: "Plan Colombia" detail, "the story of the story." 2003.

Figure 5. Child's drawing inspired by "the story of the story." 2008.

The polinizaciones will continue to spread as *lunes* travels and teaches, offering the tools of the Beehive Collective to people dreaming of flight. As the polinizaciones blog shows, this is already happening. Although *lunes* wrote to me in an e-mail, "There are newer bees from down here doing their own stuff, but I have not been able to get them to document it on the site very much" (personal communication, May 5, 2008), it was evident that the blog grew increasingly popular. After *lunes'* May 13 essay, a bee by the name of Miércoles added two entries, "Tres Alumno de Univalle Libres!!," a rallying cry for the release of three students from prison, on May 14, and "La Privatizacion del Agua," a lengthy essay about the monopolization of fresh drinking water by Coca-Cola and other large corporations, on May 21. Another blogger named Domingo posted an entry on May 4 titled "Sixth Encuentro Tawaintisuyu Abya Yala Pacha Mapu Woumain – Venezuela," which, translated into English, reveals the vision and drive of the indigenous youth movement in Latin America (Figure 6):

> This Sixth Continental Encuentro of Youth Original to Tawaintisuyu, which allows us to give continuity to the project of unification of criteria and strategies of resistance to power, constructing a Good Living, advancing towards the Dignified Living and concreting the dream of the memory of our ancestors of Living Fully, between the original peoples of Abya Yala Pacha Mapu (Mother Earth Tierra y Nature), coexisting dignified and wisely in the millenarian diversity, weaving networks of networks, singing the song of voices, walking over bridges of rainbows, recuperating from the tentacles of the neoliberal global system, that only wants political and economic hegemonies to continue its invasions, genocides, submissions and aculturalization. This space will enable the conditions for exchange and construction of our integration, that comes from our ancestors that have inhabited Abya Yala for thousands of years and today with the collaborating activities, the organizations of indigenous youth that interact in this territory look to strengthen the bond that the borders have deteriorated over time.

The indigenous youth form the four infinite sides of the sun, population of approximately 36 million inhabitants, we call to find each other and be able to articulate our proposals, establish common currents of action and from our own reality support in the general consolidation of the

Figure 7. Picture-lecture in the streets of Bogotá.

Figure 6. An ant waves the flag of solidarity in Domingo's May 4th posting.

Generational movement of Tawaintisuyu Abya Yala Pacha Mapu Woumain in all the continents and the Mother Earth, announcing that:

> "We arose from the immense vastness that founded this opportunity,
> To be still is to be tomorrow,
> Having the ability to move without eluding anything,
> Like the Quetzalcoalt"
> AMARU KNKY
> WE RETURNED AND WE ARE MILLIONS
> THE QUAKE COMES FROM INSIDE, FOR THIS OUR 'N'
> IS THE 'S'
> Welcome! (Domingo, 2008)

The art and teaching of the Beehive Collective finds a home in social climates like this, where young people are politically mobilized and the power of mass action is well understood. Popular education, a concept presented in the US by Paulo Freire but never widely embraced, is the kind of informal, nomadic art teaching that *lunes*, Domingo, Miércoles, and a swarm of other bees practice in the process of cross-pollinating the grassroots (Figure 7). There is a spirit to their teaching that many school-bound educators may look upon as romantic (which may seem as such from a U.S. perspective). However, the world is both more enchanting and brutal than many middle-class people in the US suspect. To quote a pamphlet distributed at a protest by German beekeepers, who attributed these words to Albert Einstein: "If the bee disappeared off the surface of the globe then man would only have four years of life left. No more bees, no more pollination, no more plants, no more animals, no more man" (McLaughlin, 1994, p.1). From this perspective, the bees' flights of radical hope and criticism appear part of a larger adaptive move toward a more sustainable and just world system.

REFERENCES

Amnesty International. (2004, April 23). Colombia: A laboratory of war: Repression and violence in Arauca. *Amnesty International Online Documentation Archive.* Retrieved October 24, 2007, from http://web.amnesty.org/library/index/engamr230042004

Beehive Design Collective. (2008). Reportbacks from Colombia – Polinizaciones blog active! Retrieved May 19, 2008, from http://www.beehivecollective.org/english/polinizaciones.htm

Beehive Design Collective. (2004). *The Beehive Collective's Plan Colombia narrative.* Retrieved November 10, 2005, from www.beehivecollective.org

Blair, A.J. (2004). The rhetoric of visual arguments. In C. Hill & M. Helmers (Eds.), *Defining visual rhetorics* (pp.41–62). Mahwah, NJ: Erlbaum.

Caplow, D. (2007). *Leopoldo Mendez: Revolutionary art and the Mexican print.* Austin: University of Texas Press.

Center for International Policy (2001). Colombia (2001 narrative). Retrieved October 28, 2007, from http://www.ciponline.org/facts/co01.htm

Center for International Policy. (2006). Just the facts: A civilian's guide to U.S. defense and security assistance to Latin America and the Caribbean. Retrieved October 28, 2007, from http://www.ciponline.org/facts/co.htm#military

Center for International Policy. (2007, November). U.S. contractors in Colombia. Retrieved October 28, 2007, from http://www.ciponline.org/colombia/contractors.htm

Colombia Support Network. (2007, May 31). National Indigenous Organization of Colombia (ONIC) on land rights. Retrieved May 18, 2008, from http://colombiasupport.net/news/2007/05/national-indigenous-organization-of.html

Colombia has the biggest humanitarian crisis in the Western Hemisphere, UN says. (2004, May 10). *UN News Centre.* Retrieved October 27, 1007, from http://www.un.org/apps/news/story.asp?NewsID=10691&Cr=colombia&Cr1#

Cooper, M. (2001, March 19). Plan Colombia. *The Nation, 272*(11), 11–18.

Darts, D. (2008). The art of culture war: (Un)popular culture, freedom of expression, and art education. *Studies in Art Education, 49*(2), 103–121.

Darts, D. (2004). Visual culture jam: Art, pedagogy, and creative resistance. *Studies in Art Education, 45*(4), 313–327.

Delaplane, K. S., & Mayer, D. F. (2000). *Cross pollination by bees.* Oxon, U.K.: CAB International.

Domingo. (May 4, 2008). Sixth Encuentro Tawaintisuyu Abya Yala Panch Mapu Woumain—Venezuela. Message posted to http://polinizaciones.blogspot.com/

Ellis, M. (2008). Honey bee swarms. Retrieved May 21, 2008 from University of Nebraska-Lincoln Department of Entomology website: http://entomology.unl.edu/beekpg/beeswarm.shtml

Erler, C.R. (2006). *Learning from the Beehive Collective: A participatory action research study of image-based education in an experimental community.* Unpublished doctoral dissertation, Florida State University, Tallahassee.

Gelwicks, J. (2004). CultureJam: Hijacking commercial culture. *American Studies International, 42*(1), 135–6.

Harrop, F. (2007, June 26). The madness of Plan Colombia. *Real Clear Politics.* Retrieved October 24, 2007, from http://www.realclearpolitics.com/articles/2007/06/the_madness_of_plan_colombia.html

Hart, P. (2000, May/June). Colombia's cocaine shell game: Media are leading the U.S. into a civil war in the name of the "war on drugs." *Fairness & Accuracy in Reporting (FAIR).* Retrieved February 25, 2006 from http//www.fair.org

Hoffman, H. (2003, November 19). The Beehive Collective. *In These Times.* Retrieved November 18, 2007, from http://www.inthesetimes.com/article/113/the_beehive_collective/

Knight, D. (2000, November 21). Plan Colombia: Fumigation threatens Amazon, warn indigenous leaders, scientists. *Inter Press Service News Agency.* Retrieved October 27, 2007, from http://www.commondreams.org/headlines/112100-01.htm

Lasn, K. (1999). *Culure jam: The uncooling of America.* New York: Eagle Brook/William Morrow and Co.

Lasn, K. (2000). The meme machine. *The Ecologist, 30*(2), 44–5.

Leech, G. (2007). *Crude interventions: The United States, Oil, and the New World (Dis)Order.* London, UK: Zed Books.

Lunes. (2008, May 13). Bajo la sombra del Majuy—Beneath the shade of the Majuy. Message posted to http://polinizaciones.com/

Lunes. (2008). Reportbacks from Colombia. *Polinizaciones* [blog]. Retrieved May 10, 2009, from The Beehive Collective website: http://polinizaciones.com/

McLaughlin, C. (1994, January 29). Fearful beekeepers plead for curbs on honey imports. *The Scotsman,* p. 13A.

Nativewiki. (2008). History of the Muisca people. Retrieved May 19, 2008, from http://www.nativewiki.org/Muisca

National Honey Board. (2008). Honey and honey bees: The incredible story. Retrieved May 15, 2009, from http://www.honey.com/consumers/kids/beefacts.asp

National Indigenous Organization of Colombia (ONIC). (2008). Historia social y politica del Movimiento Indigena de Colombia. Retrieved May 19, 2008, from http://www.onic.org.co/historia.shtml

Refugees International (2004, July 30). Forgotten people: Displaced indigenous people of Colombia. Retrieved March 15, 2006, from http://www.refugeesinternational.org/content/article/detail/3093/

Royal Gold Farms. (2008). Honey bee hive structure. Retrieved May 16, 2008, from http://www.royalgoldfarms.com/Web%20Pages/Hive%20Structure.htm

University of Georgia Honey Bee Program. (2008). Protecting pollinators from pesticides. Retrieved May 16, 2008, from University of Georgia, Honey Bee Program website: http://ourworld.compuscrvc.com/homepages/Beekeeping/

U.S. Department of State. (2007). Report to Congress on certain counternarcotics activities in Colombia. Retrieved October 28, 2007, from http://www.ciponline.org/colombia/contractors.htm

U.S. Department of State. (2001, March 14). Plan Colombia. Retrieved October 24, 2007, from http://www.state.gov/p/wha/rls/fs/2001/1042.htm

Making a (Visual/Visible) Difference Because People Matter: Responsible Artists and Artistic Responses to Community

B. Stephen Carpenter II, Pamela G. Taylor, and Min Cho

Public pedagogy requires re-conceptualizing teaching, learning, and curriculum (Ibanez-Carrasco and Meiners, 2004; Slattery, 2006). We believe that such public pedagogy makes a difference in the lives of students and the future of communities. In the context of a postmodern approach to art education that includes visual culture, media studies, and design education, public art pedagogy demands a social justice agenda to ground its theory and practice. Within the service-learning realm, this social justice approach aids students, educators, and community members in developing a sense of personal agency and social responsibility (Boyle-Baise & Langford, 2004) through active participation in thoughtfully organized service experiences (ASLER, 1993).

McFee and Degge (1977) outlined early concepts of community-based art education. Although difficult to define in terms of issues and needs, community-based pedagogy, community-based learning, and/or community-based education link instructional goals, strategies, and activities beyond traditional institutional boundaries (London, 1994; Stephens, 2006; Ulbricht, 2005). In this chapter we point to public pedagogy (Brady, 2006; Ibanez-Carrasco & Meiners, 2004; Slattery, 2006), new genre art education (Green, 1999), service-learning (Taylor, 2002a, 2002b, 2004, 2005; Taylor & Ballengee-Morris, 2004) and community-based art education (London, 1994; McFee & Degge, 1977; Neperud & Krug, 1989; Stephens, 2006; Ulbricht, 2005) to establish a foundation for our concept of art education that "makes a difference."

KEY CONCEPTS
- Community-Based Art Education
- Public Art Pedagogy
- Hunger
- Safe Drinking Water
- Service-Learning

In this chapter, we describe examples of service-learning and community-based art education projects that we have directly or indirectly helped to design, implement, evaluate, and sustain. These examples are based on a social justice agenda and fit the concept of meaningful public art pedagogy. Specifically, the projects offered as examples address public health and education needs such as hunger (Taylor, 2002a) through the Empty Bowls project, and safe drinking water inspired by Potters for Peace. Such sustained projects exemplify the types of artistic responses to community needs that are necessary to advance social justice and a democratic society. Finally, we offer a set of principles taken from personal experiences with, and observations of, these projects along with our research on similar projects to help other artists and educators move forward with meaningful public art pedagogy in their own communities.

Clay, Pottery, and Bowls

Regardless of culture or the times, potters typically work together in communal or studio environments. One reason for this seemingly global aspect of the production of pottery stems from the labor-intensive nature of producing works in clay. Potters must acquire clay, prepare it for use, hand build or wheel throw pots, fire greenware in a kiln, glaze the work, and then fire it a second time. This complex equation does not take into account collecting traditional fuel sources such as wood or peat.

Because the potters' primary responsibility has been to create vessels to hold water or store grains and other foods, potters have traditionally played a central role in their community. Furthermore, they have also been responsible for creating other aspects of domestic living such as roof and floor tiles, dinnerware, and washbasins. These handmade items embody the sense of community from which they were produced and the historical and traditional sense of community that has endured in the artists' clay studios. The notion of the ceramics studio as a communal site has been adopted as part of the operational curricula in undergraduate and graduate clay studios, community art centers, and secondary school art departments (Carpenter, Bey, & Smith, 2007). Indeed, potters and ceramic artists are well situated to engage in responsible community-based educational and social justice practices. Based on this assumption, we offer two examples of artists engaged in responsible community-based work to promote social justice.

Facing Hunger: Empty Bowls

Begun in 1990 in a Michigan high school art class, Empty Bowls is a unique and nationally recognized fundraising project that helps to alleviate hunger (Imagine/RENDER, 2006). It involves artists and communities in creating handmade ceramic bowls used for a simple meal of soup served at a fundraiser for local food banks and similar agencies. Along with the meal, guests witness educational performances and exhibitions. At the end of the event, guests keep their bowls to remind them of the empty bowls of hungry people (Imagine/RENDER, 2006).

Many hands and shared ownership make Empty Bowls events successful.

Empty Bowls events may take many forms such as this "Empty Bowls Full Hearts" Valentine project.

Over the years, numerous and diverse people have engaged in equally valuable and diverse alternatives to the Empty Bowls project. From traditional meals to other fundraising events (i.e. auctions, bridal showers, and holiday packages) and from the concept of bowl as vessel, such as purses and boxes, to metaphoric and non-utilitarian bowls made of woven paper or other porous media, the national Empty Bowls database and a simple Internet search yield numerous awareness and fund raising opportunities.

Our own Empty Bowls experiences included several traditional and nontraditional approaches. For example, while at Radford University, author Taylor (2002a) worked with local potters, university art and art education students, and local children in an after school program to create bowls used for a soup dinner that featured exhibitions, speakers, and a performance by singer songwriter Quinn Loggins. Loggins wrote and performed his Empty Bowls song at the event as well as a subsequent fundraiser in a local music club. At the University of Georgia, Taylor continued her work with Empty Bowls where her art education students created bowls for an established annual event at a local church. Her students also instituted a yearly Valentine's Day event entitled "Empty Bowls Full Hearts" in which they filled their handmade ceramics bowls with candy and sold them at a table in the arts building. Sweethearts of all ages clamored to give "a truer expression of love: the gift of caring for others" (personal communication, February 14, 2004). Author Taylor credits her sister, Pat Taylor Bullard for this idea. Bullard remains involved with hunger fund and awareness raising projects in Tennessee specifically through Lifeworks Foundation.

Author Cho facilitated an on-site Empty Bowls project at a National Service-Learning conference with several Virginia Commonwealth University graduate students where conference participants designed and glazed pre-fired ceramic cereal bowls. Students of many ages learned about the concept of Empty Bowls through various print materials and then created bowl designs with underglazes and underglaze pencils. They dipped their bowls in a clear glaze to make them food safe, fired them at a local ceramics warehouse, and brought them back to the conference for display and purchase. Approximately 90% of the participants who designed their bowls purchased their own creations as a reminder of their experience and to contribute to help alleviate hunger. As a result of this overwhelming response, $1000 was donated to a local hunger organization and homeless shelter.

Research was conducted by Taylor in 2002 that surveyed Empty Bowls facilitators across the country. The survey was intended to gather information about who participated in the events, how the beneficiaries of the event were chosen, and how the motives and benefits of the projects included the ideas of civic and social responsibility. This study focused on the 65% of the Empty Bowls facilitators who responded to the survey and rated the idea of building a stronger sense of community and raising awareness for civic responsibility as their highest motivation for attempting the project. Inspiring a long-term commitment to service is an integral part of social justice education. We believe that Empty Bowls projects affect and transform viewers, patrons, artists, and participants of Empty Bowls projects.

Facing Thirst: Potters for Peace and Other Artists

Worldwide, every 15 seconds, a child dies from a water-related disease and for children under the age of five, these diseases are the leading cause of death (Water Partners International, 2008). According to Canadian news and communications company CTV (2006):

> The world's wealthiest nations must step up and do something about a global water crisis that is crippling economies and spreading disease among millions, according to a new report from the UN…. The report sets out concrete steps to solve what it describes as a 'silent crisis,' because people aren't comfortable talking about water and sanitation issues, and it often garners little media attention…There are nearly 5,000 children that die every day for lack of clean drinking water and a decent toilet. (Retrieved online, March 2, 2007, http://www.ctv.ca/servlet/ArticleNews/story/CTVNews/20061109/water_crisis_061109/20061109?hub=World)

For concerned global citizens, these realities are unacceptable.

Potters for Peace (PfP) is a non-profit organization in which potters make low-cost, point-of-use ceramic water filters, mainly from local materials. The filters, treated with colloidal silver, remove diseases from unsafe, non-potable water. Members of PfP respond to requests around the world from people who do not have clean drinking water, help them establish water filter production facilities, and promote the use of the ceramic water filters in coordination with non-governmental organizations (NGOs) and health organizations. Sadly, on September 3, 2008, Ron Rivera, coordinator of the Potters for Peace ceramic water program, died from a heart attack

as a result of contracting malaria while helping people in Nigeria. Along with numerous other affordable and ecologically responsible projects that have been used successfully around the world, the PfP ceramic water filter is featured in *Design Like You Give a Damn* (Architecture for Humanity, 2006). The filter is "…a low-tech, low-cost, colloidal silver-enhanced ceramic water filter…. Field experience and clinical test results have shown this filter to effectively eliminate approximately 99.88% of most water-born disease agents" (Potters for Peace, 2008).

Further, the PfP ceramic water filter "has been cited by the United Nations' Appropriate Technology Handbook, and tens of thousands of filters have been distributed worldwide by organizations such as International Federation of the Red Cross and Red Crescent, Doctors Without Borders, UNICEF, Plan International, Project Concern International, Oxfam and USAID" (Potters for Peace, 2008). Originally, the filter was designed for general use in developing countries "to be fabricated at the community level and provide potable water to the poorest of the poor" (Potters for Peace, 2008). PfP does not "own any filter facilities, does not sell filters nor does it have the funds to create new facilities. We act as a clearing house of information gathered by staff, researchers, and worldwide contacts" (Potters for Peace, 2006). The efforts of PfP are concentrated on assisting people around the world; however, similar living conditions, needs, and issues exist within the United States.

Poverty and injustice are impediments to positive community development, educational opportunities, and the general health and welfare of residents in the Colonias of Texas. According to Oscar J. Muñoz, Deputy Director of the Center for Housing and Urban Development at Texas A&M University, Colonias residents vary in their exact description depending on the agency providing services to them, but they are largely defined as occupants of unincorporated areas lacking one or more basic services, such as water, wastewater, or paved roads (personal communication, January 11, 2006.) Traditionally, these communities are populated by Hispanic Americans, lie within counties adjacent to the Texas-Mexico border, and are among the poorest neighborhoods in Texas. On average, Colonias residents are estimated to have annual incomes of $10,000 to $14,000 (Burke, Black, & Ellis, 2005). For more information on the Colonias in Texas, visit http://www.pbs.org/klru/forgottenamericans/, a site inspired by the documentary film, *The Forgotten Americans* by Hector Galán. The film originally aired on PBS in 2000.

Most of the nearly 500,000 residents in the Colonias of Texas live with serious health problems caused by a lack of potable water. The majority of Colonias residents only have access to water they can purchase in large quantities and which, without further treatment, is only suitable for flushing toilets. Residents have limited access to water treated through reverse osmosis. As a result of the poor water quality, some children in the Colonias suffer from frequent cases of diarrhea, which negatively affect their success in school. The need for all Colonias residents to have access to potable water presents other problems, as installing water lines from water pumping stations into neighborhoods costs millions of dollars that local jurisdictions either cannot afford or will not install. While a very small number of Texas Colonias received water lines in the past few years, experts agree that most may never have access to safe drinking water.

Author Carpenter was inspired by Potters for Peace and his communications with artists and humanitarians Manny Hernandez and Richard Wukich. He decided to engage in a creative response to the needs of Colonias residents—his fellow citizens in Texas. Carpenter and colleague Oscar J. Muñoz, Deputy Director of the Colonias Program at Texas A&M University (TAMU), established a water filter production project in response to the unsafe water situation in the Colonias of Texas. Their collaboration resulted in a joint educational, research, and social action project called the TAMU Water Project. The project also maintains a blog that provides related information and activities (http://tamuwaterproject.wordpress.com). Now, with the addition of Bryan Boulanger, assistant professor of environmental engineering at Texas A&M University, the TAMU Water Project is a multifaceted initiative focused on the production of ceramic water filters based on the PfP design, and includes related social, community, and educational initiatives. Artists Hernandez and Wukich serve as creative and technical advisors. The TAMU Water Project is a collaborative creative partnership among colleagues and students to promote social justice and improved educational and economic opportunities. A central goal of the TAMU Water Project is to work with Colonias residents to establish self-sustaining facilities that will produce point-of-use ceramic water filters as low-cost, environmentally safe, and effective sources of potable water. To date, the TAMU Water Project has hosted water filter demonstration workshops for K–12 and university students, educators, artists, and Colonias community members, worked with Colonias residents, leaders, and local social services agencies, built two water filter presses, begun production of

Richard Wukich and Manny Hernandez discuss ceramic water filters at a workshop in Bryan, TX.

Oscar Muñoz, Juan Galvan, and Manny Hernandez make a water filter during a public pedagogy demonstration.

filters, and finalized plans to build facilities near community centers within Colonias in Webb County just outside of Laredo, Texas.

In short, the TAMU Water Project is working to directly alleviate poor health related to unsafe drinking water locally, promote education, and encourage economic and community rejuvenation within the Texas Colonias. Carpenter, Muñoz, and Boulanger believe—as do the residents of the Colonias with whom they are working on the project—that improved health, education, and economic benefits will inspire other responses from the community and embody social justice outcomes made possible by this community-based form of art education.

Service-Learning as a Social Justice Agenda

We recognize the work of Becker (1997), Irwin and Kindler (1999), and others who have encouraged art educators to promote and embody social justice within their interpretations of art education. Dean (1999) called on art educators to challenge the limits of their own pedagogy by identifying central questions such as, "…what is the importance of creativity without the confines of the art world and what is the function and value of art and its wider application in society?" (p. 55). Similarly, we are particularly interested in the intrinsic value of art—and artistic skills, knowledge, and ways of knowing—and its wider application to society and communities. This question is central to our interest in the roles and relationships between artists, education, and social justice.

Service-learning is an emerging educational innovation that integrates community service into the academic curriculum. Over the past two decades, many educators embraced this pedagogy for its positive academic, behavioral, and affective outcomes (Follman, 1998; Weiler, LaGoy, Crane, & Rovner, 1998). With increased federal and state support to implement service-learning, more schools include it as part of their curricula (National Center for Education Statistics, 1999).

Primary theoretical underpinnings of service-learning trace back to pragmatist Dewey and his philosophy of experience (Giles & Eyler, 1994). Dewey's thoughts on the interaction of knowledge and skills, with experience serving as the key to learning, are now basic tenets of service-learning (Ehrlich, 1996). Theoretically related is experiential education, which actively engages learners in direct experience and focuses reflection in order to increase knowledge, develop skills, and clarify values (Association for Experiential Education, 2008). In a comparison study on the benefits of service with undergraduate students, researchers found that "student participants [in service-learning] were much more likely than non-participants to strengthen their commitment to the following life goals: promoting racial understanding, participating in community action programs, and influencing social values" (Sax & Astin, 1997, p. 28). Furthermore, a conceptual framework entitled *The Collaborative Service-Learning Model* (Joyce & Weil with Calhoun, 2000) embodied factors of social process learning, such as cooperative learning and learning communities. In this model, students work individually and collaboratively to identify, pledge, and develop solutions for real and academically based problems that address cognitive and social dimensions (Pritchard, 2004).

It is within this dimension that service-learning may best impact issues of social justice. Education through social justice provokes critical thoughts, challenges conventional ideas of equality and economic justice, and ultimately charges students to take on the roles of change agents (Bell, 1997). Like Dean (1999), we strive to extend notions of pedagogy, art, artmaking, art appreciation, creativity, and expression through social justice and service-learning. We want to "extend the purposes of art education to include the power of the arts to educate and to provide the service opportunities that transform and give us meaning in our lives" (Taylor, 2004, p. 124).

Thoughts for Moving Forward

In this final section a set of principles is offered for engaging in community-based forms of pedagogy and cultural work informed by and dedicated to social justice. Based on our personal experiences with the projects described above in combination with our own research, we believe

these principles may help other artists and educators move forward with meaningful public art pedagogy in their own communities. The principles we offer are:

Question what we teach and how it relates to where we are. Art educators Blandy and Hoffman (1993) promoted place-based education grounded in the principles of eco-theory and environmental concerns. More recently, Grunewald (2003) offered a critical place-based pedagogy that:

> ...seeks the twin objectives of decolonization and 'reinhabitation' through synthesizing critical and place-based approaches. A critical pedagogy of place challenges all educators to reflect on the relationship between the kind of education they pursue and the kind of places we inhabit and leave behind for future generations. (p. 3)

For art education, a critical pedagogy of place "might also disconnect from traditional dominant art making and studio practices and establish itself as a site of lived engagement and social action through expanded possibilities for considerations of visual interpretation, performance, and events" (Carpenter and Tavin, forthcoming). That is, the making of art objects and images might become less of a focus than the engagement of arts understandings and practices for responsible community-based and place-based ends. As art educators make important decisions about what is most important for their students to learn, know, understand, and do, we believe that they should also make more explicit connections to lived experiences, places, and communities.

Consider the community as a curriculum with reciprocal learning. Like Owens and Wang (1996), we believe that the community can serve as a curriculum that encourages learners and educators to consider all segments of a community as viable sources for learning. As such, any community can be conceived of as a curriculum to be learned, studied, revisited, and in a constant state of renegotiation. Inherent in service-learning practice is the idea of reciprocity (Roy & Cho, 2006) where learners and the community receive mutual benefits in a reciprocal relationship. As educators and students look toward their communities for learning experiences, they may receive professional, expert, financial, and volunteer support. In the process, they open channels of communication that could foster dialogue and relationships attuned to social justice.

Look inward, outward, backward and forward by continual, critical reflection. Reflection is the keystone of service-learning. Reflection is an internalization of thoughts and actions brought forth through writing, discussions, and artistic practices. Without intended cognitive deliberation on the purposes of the service, it merely mimics an action performed for the benefit of the community. Therefore, any attempt to establish a foundation for an art education that "makes a difference" would require and provoke forms of critical reflection that, like critical pedagogy, would call into question the impact associated with, derived from, and provoked by needs for service and community practices.

Finally, the two examples used in this chapter—Empty Bowls and Potters for Peace/TAMU Water Project—epitomize artistic forms useful in community-based art education for social justice. Clay and ceramics represent an age-old and respected craft with profound and meaningful histories. While function and utility have always been key components of clay and ceramics, personal meanings associated with clay objects are also important. And yet practices similar to Empty Bowls and Potters for Peace challenge and transform idiosyncratic ideas associated with clay objects in order to make a difference on a much broader scale. We believe that such ideas represent only a small portion of the kinds of differences that art and art education associated with social justice and service-learning can make to our human lives.

Alliance for Service-Learning in Education Reform (ASLER). (1993). *Standards of quality for school-based and community-based learning*. Washington, DC: The Alliance for Service-Learning in Education Reform.

Architecture for Humanity (2006). *Design like you give a damn: Architectural responses to humanitarian crises*. K. Stohr & C. Sinclair (Eds.). Metropolis Books.

Association for Experiential Education. (2008). *What is experiential education?* Retrieved April 1, 2008, from http://aee.org/

Becker, C. (1997, March). Training citizen artists. Art and education conference report, *Artweek*, 13–14.

Bell, L. A., (1997). Theoretical foundations for social justice education. In M. Adams, L. A. Bell & P. Griffin (Eds.), *Teaching for diversity and social justice: A sourcebook* (pp. 44–58). New York: Routledge.

Blandy, D., & Hoffman, E. (1993). Toward an art education of place. *Studies in Art Education, 35*(1), 22–33.

Boyle-Baise, M., & Langford, J. (2004). There are children here: Service-learning for social justice. *Equity & Excellence in Education, 37*(1), 55–66.

Brady, J. F. (2006). Public pedagogy and educational leadership: Politically engaged scholarly communities and possibilities for critical engagement. *Journal of Curriculum and Pedagogy, 3*(1), 57–60.

Burke, D., Black, K., & Ellis, P. B. (2005). Texas colonias van project: An aspect of transportation in underserved communities. Retrieved February 2006, from http://swutc.tamu.edu/publications.htm

Carpenter, B. S., Bey, S., & Smith, M. M. (2007). Inspirational clay studio practices and visiting artists: Products and altar installations. *The Journal of Cultural Research in Art Education, 25*, 25–37.

Carpenter, B. S., & Tavin, K. (forthcoming). Art education beyond reconceptualization: Enacting curriculum through/with/by/for/of/in/beyond visual culture, community and public pedagogy. In Erik Malewski (Ed.), *Curriculum studies—the next moment: Exploring post-reconceptualization*. New York: Routledge.

CTV (2006). Richest nations must tackle water crisis: UN. Retrieved March 2, 2007, from http://www.ctv.ca/servlet/ArticleNews/story/CTVNews/20061109/water_crisis_061109/20061109?hub=World

Dean, F. (1999). Moving the mountain: Linking higher art education and communities. In R. Irwin & A. Kindler (Eds.), *Beyond the school: Community and institutional partnerships in art education*, 47–56. Reston, VA: National Art Education Association.

Ehrlich, T. (1996). Foreword in B. Jacob & Associates (Eds.), *Service-learning in higher education: Concepts and practices*. San Francisco: Jossey-Bass.

Follman, J. (1998). *Florida learn and serve: 1996–97 outcomes and correlations with 1994–95 and 1995–96*. Tallahassee, FL: Florida State University, Center for Civic Education and Service.

Giles, D. E., & Eyler J. (1994). The theoretical roots of service-learning. *Michigan Journal of Community Service-learning, 1*(1), 77–85.

Green, G. (1999). New genre public education. *Art Journal*, Spring.

Grunewald, D. A. (2003). The best of both worlds: A critical pedagogy of place. *Educational researcher, 32*(4), 3–12.

Joyce, N., & Weil, M., with Calhoun, C. (2000). *Models of teaching* (6th ed.) Boston: Allyn and Bacon.

Ibanez-Carrasco, F., & Meiners, E. R. (2004). *Public acts: Disruptive readings on making curriculum public*. New York: RoutledgeFalmer.

Imagine/RENDER (2006). Empty bowls. Retrieved September 6, 2008, from http://www.emptybowls.net

Irwin, R., & Kindler, A. (Eds.) (1999). *Beyond the school: Community and institutional partnerships in art education*. Reston, VA: National Art Education Association.

London, P. (1994). *Step outside: Community-based art education*. Portsmouth, NH: Heinemann.

McFee, J. K., & Degge, R. M. (1977). *Art, culture, and environment: A catalyst for teaching*. Belmont, CA: Wadsworth.

National Center for Education Statistics. (1999, September). *Service-learning and community service in K–12 public schools (NCES 1999-043)*. Washington, DC: U.S. Department of Education, Office of Educational Research and Improvement.

Neperud, R., & Krug, D. (1989). People who make things: From the ground up, in *Context, content, and community in art education*. New York: Teachers College Press.

Owens, T., & Wang, C. (1996). Community-based learning: A foundation for meaningful educational reform. Retrieved February 3, 2008, from http://nwrel.org/scpd/sirs/10/t008.html

Potters for Peace (2006). Potters for peace clay water filter assistance guidelines. Retrieved September 6, 2008, from http://s189535770.onlinehome.us/pottersforpeace/?page_id=223

Potters for Peace (2008). Filters. Retrieved September 6, 2008, from http://s189535770.onlinehome.us/pottersforpeace/?page_id=9

Pritchard, F. (2004). *Serve and learn: Implementing and evaluating service-learning in middle and high schools*. Mahwah, NJ: Lawrence Erlbaum Associates.

Roy, R., & Cho, M. (2006). *My world... my art: A handbook on integrating service learning into the art classroom*. Tallahassee, FL: Florida Learn & Serve.

Slattery, P. (2006). *Curriculum development in the postmodern era* (2nd edition). New York: Routledge.

Sax, L. J., & Astin, A. W. (1997). The benefits of service: Evidence from undergraduates. *Educational Record, 78*(3&4), 25–32.

Stephens, P. G. (2006). A real community bridge: Informing community-based learning through a model of participatory public art. *Art Education, 59*(2), 40–46.

Taylor, P. G. (2002a). Singing for someone else's supper: Service-learning and empty bowls. *Art Education, 55*(4) 6–12.

Taylor, P. G. (2002b). Service-learning as postmodern art and pedagogy. *Studies in Art Education, 43*(2), 124–140.

Taylor, P. G. (2004). Service-learning and a sense of place. *The Journal of Cultural Research in Art Education*.

Taylor, P. G. (2005). The children's peace project: Service-learning and art education. *International Education Journal* online (5), 581–586. http://iej.cjb.net

Taylor, P. G., & Ballengee-Morris, C. (2004). Service-learning; A language of "we." *Art Education, 57*(5), 6–12.

Ulbricht, J. (2005). What is community-based art education? *Art Education, 58*(2), 6–12.

Water Partners International (2008). Water facts: Facts about water, drinking water, and water related disease. Retrieved September 6, 2008, from http://www.water.org/waterpartners.aspx?pgID=916

Weiler, D., LaGoy, A., Crane, E., & Rovner, A. (1998). *An evaluation of K–12 service-learning in California: Phase II final report*. Emeryville, CA: RPP International with the Search Institute.

Mosaic-Raising as a Means to Enact Socially Responsive Pedagogy

Lynn Sanders-Bustle

Liberation is a praxis: the action & reflection of men & women upon their world in order to transform it. (Freire, 1970, p. 60)

Freire (1970) understood the importance of action and reflection as catalysts for transformation in not only individuals but also society. I suggest that socially responsive pedagogical practices should not only engage students in theoretical classroom explorations of social issues but that

KEY CONCEPTS
- Community-Based Art Education
- Public Art Pedagogy
- Hunger
- Safe Drinking Water
- Service-Learning

they must also actively involve students in real life engagements in community settings. Real world engagements coupled with creative and critical inquiry processes can begin to challenge and disturb long-held worldviews and inspire reflection and just action.

In this chapter I will reveal challenges, complexities, and possibilities inherent in socially responsive practice as my university art education students and I worked alongside clients at a local outreach center to create a 14 by 75 ft. mirror and tile mosaic on the side of a day shelter. This chapter will provide context for the mosaic project and represent nuances of the project through an evocative retelling, using the voices of participants.

Beginnings: The Mosaic Project Evolves

The mosaic project was a semester-long endeavor to create a tile and mirror mosaic on the side of an outreach center shelter. Nonetheless, nothing about this endeavor was simple; in its complexity it thrives as an effort to create. Some hoped to create possibility, some hoped to create a learning experience, some hoped to beautify a blighted space, some hoped to create a public relations opportunity, and some hoped to create a good grade.

The mosaic project was a joint effort between 11 intermediate art education undergraduates, clients, and staff at a local center and me, the university art educator. "Clients" is the term used by the center to designate those who receive services. The Center is a local organization, which provides poor and homeless citizens with critical services such as food, shelter, job training, and rehabilitation.

The Finished Mosaic.

The center campus is three blocks from a vibrant section of town just off the beaten path. This is the real public space:

> where the experience of which we should be speaking, where voices that we should be listening to … in all of those places where we are even afraid to go, and all of those places that we get to when we make a mistake, take a wrong bus, a wrong subway line. (Wodiczko, n.d., p.11)

The center campus became our second classroom.

The prospect of the project began when the director of the center approached me in the summer of 2005 about the possibility of working with my students to "beautify" the outside wall of a day shelter. In 2001, I had worked with a Philadelphia mosaic artist named Isaiah Zagar whom I credit with teaching me his method. His mosaics captured my attention while attending a conference during that same year. In awe of their magical quality I went on to take his workshop and learn the process later to work with others to create mosaics with groups across two states. Given this experience, it made sense to create one on the shelter wall.

Working with communities to create such works, I came to recognize the power of participatory public art as not only as an accessible opportunity for community members to view art on the streets but as a chance to "invite artists and communities to work together as a cooperative team" (Geiger, 2006, p. 45). In particular, the interactive quality of the mosaic making process allows passersby to involve themselves in a variety of ways— carrying bags of sand, mixing grout, gluing tiles, telling stories, or offering suggestions or commentary—to contribute to raising the mosaic. The term "raising" is a reminder of a time when communities worked together to raise structures, and captures the physical nature of the work of mosaic-making which is highly dependant on manual labor and is often impacted by the forces of nature. It also suggests an uplifting message of possibility, hope, and transformation.

Linking Classroom and Community

The mosaic project became central to my fall 2005 intermediate art education course. In the past the students were required to explore a contemporary issue of their choice such as "culture, race, gender, class, ethnicity, ability, religion, sexual orientation, age, and community" (Gaudelius & Speirs, 2003, p. 2). This semester they were to focus on homelessness and poverty to parallel the real world experiences at the center. Educators understand the value of providing real world experiences for students, recognizing that

> understanding education in contexts broader than schooling has important implications for art education and calls for an examination of alternative venues, initiatives and strategies that facilitate artistic development, encourage aesthetic growth, and promote reflection about the role and value of art in a society. (Irwin & Kindler, 1999, p.1)

This kind of art education has been referred to as community-based (Ulbricht, 2005) or service-learning (Taylor, 2002; Taylor, & Ballengee-Morris, 2004; Buffington, 2007). Like Taylor and Ballengee (2004), I propose that service-learning be a reciprocal endeavor where learning takes place across all participants where "teacher and student or service-learner and community agent are co-learners or co-workers" (Taylor, 2002, p.128).

Additionally, experiences at the center paralleled a series of course activities designed to help students creatively and critically explore, reflect upon, and synthesize new learning. These activities included creating altered/artist books (Drucker, 2004; Sanders-Bustle, 2007) and designing teaching of art criticism lessons for high school art students. Like many who value inquiry-based explorations (Anderson & Milbrandt, 2005; Sullivan, 2005; Sanders-Bustle 2003; Diamond & Mullen, 1999), I saw altered/artists books as important spaces for students to make personal connections, reflect, and express new found learning textually and visually. Inquiry processes are particularly useful when students are dealing with seemingly controversial issues, which make forming and representing personal ideas particularly challenging yet profoundly significant.

Over the semester, class meetings alternated between the center and the university campus. Meetings at the center campus involved students, clients, and occasionally center staff members in design, planning, and studio workshop sessions. The first meeting introduced the project and engaged clients and students in a brainstorming session using magazine images as a way of thinking about the design. During September and October, students taught three workshops in which clients learned how to bash tile, cut mirror, and mold textured clay medallions and grouted globs. The actual raising of the mosaic began in November and was completed by December.

Crafting an Evocative Retelling

In thinking about how to represent the mosaic project, I knew that a traditional research text would not fully capture the richness of participants' voices or the subtle nuances of daily engagements that represent challenges and possibilities inherent in this kind of work. Rather than trying to objectify or tidy up the experience, I wanted readers/viewers to understand how unforeseen events wove in and out of lives of participants, inviting varying interpretations about the process and the significance of the work while providing greater understanding of the project as a whole.

Consequently, as a work intended to inspire socially just efforts, this project will be represented through evocative text. Evocative texts are those that seek to "re-create lived experience and evoke emotional response" (Richardson, 1994, p. 31), to incite empathy or inspire responsive action. The evocation offered in the next section is not meant to be poetic, but rather to offer a chronological retelling as revealed through participants' voices. This will allow space for the reader/viewer to make interpretations while encouraging emotive sensibilities to rise and fall authentically. Voices include the students, clients, center staff members, and me. Participants' voices are represented by quotes transcribed from interviews, my diary, and course documents such as the altered books, written reflections, and e-mails. Finally, five photographs provide additional context and allow the reader/viewer to experience the aesthetic as well as temporal qualities of the project, the space, and the participants' engagements.

An Evocative Retelling:
Raising the Wall/Raising Awareness/Raising Questions

August 23, 2005: First Day of Class
TEACHER EDUCATOR

Aren't we in the job of teacher preparation?

I introduced our semester long inquiry topic: Homelessness and Poverty.

STUDENT   The course was all designed about a social issue and instead of giving us a choice, Dr. Lynn chose to dictate that it was, (I don't mean dictate in a bad way) but to let us know that it was going to be homelessness and that

we could choose our direction that we wanted to go with that particular topic … that social issue.

STUDENTS   Why are we doing this?

Will the homeless shelter count as observation hours?

How do the meetings with community officials at the shelter relate to the mosaic?

We entered our inquiry into homelessness and poverty with different concerns. I wanted, passionately, to provide my students with a real life experience that would inform our social conscience. However, comments pulled from exit slips provided a glimpse into students' initial impressions of what I had proposed. Students were concerned with the practicalities of academia and the relevance of the inquiry. I wondered what kind of bridge they would need to construct to understand the relevance and more importantly the value of our experience at the center.

August 29, 2005: Hurricane Katrina Slams the State
TEACHER EDUCATOR

Normalcy did not return as news revealed the horrors of flooding and the desperate situation that played out in the city of New Orleans and smaller parishes in the region. A cloud of worry hovered over our days, coloring our moods. Our inquiry took on new relevancy. Hundreds of thousands of people became homeless. Over 7,000 filled our local civic center. I posed this question to my students via e-mail: How is the homelessness caused by Hurricane Katrina the same or different from the homelessness that occurs in our town/nation/world on a daily basis?

STUDENTS   I don't think they are very different at all. The homeless in our culture come from all races and backgrounds just like those made homeless by hurricane Katrina. All of them need help to get back on their feet. All of them at some point had a home—or most—and are now homeless.

….how many people live in NY and pass by the homeless as if they do not exist. They don't even see them anymore and when they open their eyes to the human suffering, they become disgusted instead of feeling compassion. Perhaps we will all look back on the hurricane that hit New Orleans and think about the human suffering in a whole new light…. Yet, still I have a hard time finding my way over to the civic center to help. I am afraid because of all the things I hear about the kinds of people delivered here.

Circumstances such as homelessness and poverty are very real for many but can often seem to be about "others." Katrina brought these issues literally closer to our community demanding reaction from us. I continued to engage students in reflective writing activities to help them to think about the many causes of homelessness. I wanted students to recognize the injustice of the flooding that largely targeted an impoverished population and to even accept a certain level of social responsibility. While their reflections acknowledged the horror of the event they did not recognize the larger sociopolitical issues at play in the tragedy. Yet, they expressed empathy and honesty in their reflections as they worked hard to understand. I wanted to build off of their expressions of care and concern to communicate the harder, painful realities of the roots of oppression.

August 30, 2005: Urban Legends Revealed
TEACHER EDUCATOR

Rumors had already started to fly about the people who had come into the city from the superdome. According to the fearful, the local grocery store had been robbed. Over nine cars had been carjacked. This was not the first time I heard this on this day. I would hear it again later in class. Months later a local independent newspaper made public the absurdity of such claims, referring to the tales as urban legends.

I was disturbed by the stories that were being told in the community and repeated in my classroom. These tales were the result of fear and ignorance precipitated by the sudden influx of divergent socio-economic communities. It is the same fear and ignorance which feed stereotypes about the impoverished and the homeless. I so wanted my students to see the connection. I worked carefully to encourage students to consider the source of the tales,

allowing time in class for students to express the fear that played out in the crafting of such tales. I found myself once again carefully navigating between trying to allow my students to work through their ideas while at the same time trying to dispel stereotypical views of the homeless. I felt myself always asking, how much of my opinion should I reveal?

September 6 and 7, 2005: Unexpected Factors
TEACHER EDUCATOR

Thousands were displaced by the storm, with many of them temporarily relocating to higher parishes. Among them was a young man who arrived in my office. He informed me that he was going to use this time to become certified and therefore he wanted to know if he could join my intermediate course. I welcomed him and began describing the mosaic project. Hesitantly and almost in with a sense of guilt, I revealed that homelessness and poverty were our topics for the semester. Given his current state of homelessness, I immediately offered alternative topics for him to explore. Smiling he assured me, "No, I will be fine."

CLIENT/STUDENT

I have been in recovery for a long time, and I am a client and I am one of the longest ladies living here at the center. I am also a student, in art education…I went to Dr. Lynn, and I let her know that I was a client here [at the Center]. And when I saw her response to it, I was okay. My biggest fear was being portrayed as a homeless client and in recovery because my career goals are to be a teacher.

I have learned that unexpected factors that find their way into real life experiences often have the greatest impact. Both of the students represented in the above quotes inspired a sense of urgency and relevance to my work. Each taught me so much about the unique particularities of being without a home and the desperation that accompanies such an existence. The immediacy of their presence heightened my sense of responsibility and informed my actions in profound ways. While theory (critical) had guided the ideology from which I worked, I knew that my practice or acts as a teacher would have a far greater impact. I worked with this in mind often reflecting deeply and sometimes questioning my ability to engage in something so serious.

September 13, 2005: First Design Meeting with Clients at the Center

STUDENT   How about we get a bunch of paper or a few drawing pads and give them out to the clients and ask them to design what they would like to see put onto the mosaic wall. We can take those ideas and make a blended "community" work of art.

STUDENT/CLIENT

On visual brainstorming for the design: First of all, we had to agree on the overall concept. You had college students, and then you had a group of folks in recovery treatment, and most of them with no high school education, trying to talk about their philosophy on life.

STUDENT   It was hard because I had never been put in that situation where I was around, (I don't want to say that type of people), but I didn't feel quite prepared at first. Nothing happened to make me not feel safe, it was just my own personal prejudices.

CLIENT/STUDENT

We didn't want the mosaic to look like happy, happy, and hunky-dory because that was like a slap in the face to the people who spend their nights sleeping on the deck out here, walking the streets all day and all night, maybe not eating for 2 or 3 days. So we had to really look at that hard and say, "Yeah, we want dignity, hope, and inspiration."

It was very important to us that the design evolve from the efforts of all involved.

The group recognized that the finished mosaic would need to reflect a hopeful vision. This was not an easy task. Not only did we have to consider the aesthetic qualities of the design and practical demands related to the mosaic but we had to consider ways to include as many of the participants' thoughts and ideas in its design and creation. This process allowed us to practice our ability to work together for the sake of a larger community. As a class, we had to let go of personal desires—aesthetic and otherwise—to arrive at a solution.

September 15, 2005: The Uncomfortable Nature of Inquiry
TEACHER EDUCATOR

One day back at the university, two students became particularly agitated while expressing opposite views about homelessness and its causes. The discussion got so heated one student stood up out of her chair raising her voice. The other student turned away and threatened to walk out. Experiencing this level of tension for the first time, I diffused the conversation by trying to bring the conversation back to our discussion of our reading from a chapter in *Art for Life* (Anderson & Milbrandt, 2005).

STUDENT REFLECTIONS ON DISCUSSIONS

Sometimes uncomfortable, but we realize the world is not comfortable and as the teacher one must become comfortable with the uncomfortable. I enjoy getting ideas from other people but there were some discussions that I thought were too heated…. I wish the arguments would have been controlled because this class was very emotionally stressful.

I didn't enjoy the biased opinions, and not many open minds for a group of artists.

I didn't particularly enjoy exposing my students to "the uncomfortable." I was often drawn into heated discussions functioning largely as a mediator convincing myself that there was value in that which is uncomfortable. I am reminded of Dewey's (1934) premise that it is only in a state of disequilibrium that we grow. I often questioned my ability to mediate 'heated' discussions. Yet, I asked myself, "Where else will students have the opportunity to reflect upon such difficult issues? Aren't these the same

Making Clay Medallions.

critical issues that will play out in their classrooms as teachers?"

September 22, 2005: First Workshop: Breaking Tiles and Cutting Mirror

CLIENT First, we broke the tiles and stuff. We learned how to cut glass and mirrors. We learned the procedure of it with the hammer: how to shape it and break it down.

STUDENT These went wonderfully! They were fun to lead and the clients really responded to us.

September 23, 2005
TEACHER EDUCATOR

I am in the process of trying to reach the center to see if we need to postpone the second workshop scheduled for this afternoon. As most of you know by now the university will close at 12:30 today on account of the storm.

September 24, 2005: Hurricane Rita Hits

STUDENT Just seeing the devastation around the areas and seeing the communities completely wiped out. And having to do school work and dealing with these issues in classes… you had these emotional sharing of stories and you know you couldn't focus on anything else because of what happened and what you were dealing with on a daily basis because of it. You know no trees went down in my yard and I still had a house but I almost felt guilty about it. So it is emotional, it's very emotional to see a whole city get destroyed because of natural occurrence.

October 6 and October 20, 2005: More Workshops

STUDENT When I did teach them, it amazed me that some of them took it a step further and would be looking around on the ground using even jewelry they had on and just making like elaborate patterns that I would probably never even thought of.

CLIENT If they would not have said that it was mandatory, I might have never showed up. "I ain't did it before, and I ain't going to do it now," but it worked out for the better…. That's one thing I learned: just try something different. I mean, it can't kill you.

STUDENT These people would be so happy that we were there, and we were doing something with them, and you can just tell it just lifted their spirits. And they got to joke around with us, and they got to work on the art and see it develop.

The workshops served as a valuable space to bring diverse individuals together for a common purpose. Opportunities for learning were just as diverse. Art materials and processes served as ambassadors for conversation revealing intersections between experiences as both students and clients agonized over making a clean cut on the mirror or selecting a suitable texture to imprint on clay. Over time, shared life experiences filtered into conversations related to food or music linking lives and surprising some. I could not help but think about the mandatory nature of the workshops for both the clients and the students. In essence, I had forced my students to attend and the clients were also forced to attend. But, on the other hand, where else would these communities ever come together, if not for this experience?

November 6, 2005: Beginning to Raise the Mosaic

TEACHER EDUCATOR

One day, we went out there to start working on the wall, and three students had put a white face on the woman. Well, we really felt strongly that it needed to be a dark face. So we proceeded to re-grout it. That made some students mad, not because we put a black face, but because we changed their work. So it was this issue of community again. This is not your wall. This is the wall for the community.

STUDENT

Throughout the whole mosaic process, it was hard to get along with everybody because they had ideas and you had ideas. Some people felt like they had to take over the whole project, and you just sort of got shoved aside.

CENTER STAFF

I just liked the atmosphere that these people carried. And these youngsters were fired up to really do what was needed. Like when somebody is truly spiritual, you get these vibes; they can lift you.

STUDENT

Some of the students would show up at the end of the day for about a half an hour because they wanted to get their grade [up]. I would go there on all my days off and spend hours and hours. [I felt] disappointments in myself, too. I did it to the point of distraction of my other assignments.

STUDENT

I took for granted that a lot of people were showing up to help after a whole day's work. Just because they are homeless does not mean they are not hard working.

Overwhelmed and still reeling from the stress of two hurricanes some students began to fight with one another about their roles, contributions to the project, and time spent at the site. Ironically at the same time clients, onlookers, and administrative staff sang the praises of the students. I was glad that center clients did not notice the infighting. While I felt good about the response of the center community I was deeply concerned about

Working on the Mosaic.

my students' responses. Our ability to function as a classroom community was faltering. At this point I realized that I had both the well being of the clients and the students to consider. The teaching and learning circle had widened.

November 11, 2005: Veterans Day

STUDENT

I had two men sitting next to each other. One was a WWII vet and one was a Vietnam vet, and they were putting tile up on this wall and talking about their experiences of the war. There are so many stories.

TEACHER EDUCATOR

Working on that wall and sitting there talking to people that walked up…you know, because a lot of them were just telling stories. His mother died in childbirth having him. Told me a story about a healer who healed a woman's feet. About how a snake got into his bed—he believes his mother came from heaven and tied the snake together to save him. Also, when he was 12, he met Charles Manson on a field trip to the penitentiary.

TEACHER EDUCATOR

> Just sitting there…you would have the opportunity to just talk to people, like for hours. Sometimes they would just talk. Some really didn't want to do it [mosaic], but they just wanted to talk. Some worked and talked. For example, I worked beside Louise:
> Very dark hair, pale skin.
> Glittering blue eye shadow. Early twenties, maybe?
> Her father was a Narc agent "Ironic, huh?" she laughed.
> She was a cheerleader, all A's.
> Mom was strict; Dad was strict.
> "I was rebellious?" she guessed.
> Dad started drinking, ran around on his wife—divorced.
> Lost his job.
> Don't know where he is, somewhere. "In Iraq?" she guessed.
> Is a waitress…
> Lonely.
> "I have no children. Surprised?" She added.

The raising of the mosaic provided us with extended periods of time to spend with clients and other passersby who came to participate or just talk. Conversations were especially fascinating and authentic, often taking the form of storytelling and more importantly revealing our commonalities. Students who spent time were lucky enough to experience this. It was proof that communal artmaking is more than the construction of artwork for beautification. Public art experiences can make art accessible to many and can provide a communal space conducive to ever so subtle attempts at social reconstruction! Where were my students? I needed them to spend more time at the wall! They were missing it!

November 17, 2005

TEACHER EDUCATOR

> At a point, I was very angry. I thought we, as a class, had made a commitment. And they were pretty committed early on. We had excellent class discussions. They helped with the design; they led the workshops; they had been highly involved. All of a sudden it's time to get this thing done; it's time to push, and they were nowhere to be found. So I sent them a pretty strong e-mail, saying we had a commitment.

STUDENT/CLIENT

> We had like one guy come into the program, and he was so mad. He was just having all these compulsions to go out and use drugs. And so he starts to work on the wall, just to get his mind off of it. The next thing you knew, he was just captured with the wall, and he started writing poetry. From that point on, everyday, he would come and work on the wall.

TEACHER EDUCATOR

> It felt so much like I was pushing the wall…seeing my students' frustration with this project, and seeing them struggle through it….

CLIENT/STUDENT

> You rarely had any clients just sitting on the sides. They were all doing something. A lot of them were construction workers … Just the students could have never gotten this done without their cooperation and help. It made the clients feel good because they had skills; they were teaching students. "This is how we grout; this is how we mix cement!"

CENTER MANAGER

> When the wall came, it kind of united a group of people who always come together, but it's always been violent. There was no violence this time around. I saw guys that came out there and helped Dr. L that would never do that anywhere else … because they had a feeling that, "This is for me; this is being done for me! Why can't I go out there and share a little work with them?"

I was perplexed that my students were struggling to be a part of the project, while the clients had embraced it. This was an interesting tension for me to consider. I was very happy that the center was finding great value in the work, yet I was frustrated with student participation. Certainly the fact that the mosaic was being raised off the university campus made it less accessible to the students. Yet at the same time it was not far from our campus. At times, I felt as though the project was taking a back seat to other more conventional or measurable assignments such as tests or reports. The assignment was an atypical player in the game of school. In hindsight, I realized I should have put measures in place to perhaps require participation.

November 22, 2005

STUDENT   When we started this project, we thought it was about us in the class. But Dr. L did sit down and talk to us. "We are working with them and it's for both of us."

CLIENT   Are you Christian? What do you believe is happening? Do you think we are nearing the end of the world?

STUDENT   I was working next to one fellow. He was standing with me, putting tile on the wall, and taking pride in it, and smiling, and engaging in conversation. And one of his buddies stopped by, and he says, "Man, Roadster, I ain't seen you smile like this in, God, 10 years." And Roadster said, "I haven't been this happy in 10 years!"

CLIENT   When you are poor you steal, when you are rich you forget where you came from. I've worked hard…I've even picked cotton.

CENTER MANAGER
          The hardest thing was keeping somebody from taking the products. Keep 'em from stealing. Theft is a serious thing in this business.

STUDENT/CLIENT
          And I think that anybody who passed at the time it was going up and saw the people who looked [like]…your picture of a homeless person…out there putting things up and having such a good time, working with people, and being people. They were surprised!

CLIENT   I am embarrassed. I slept behind the Salvation Army last night.

"Yes, it's YOU. YOU'RE here. YOUR dreams matter, too." Isaiah Zagar (Augustine, 1999, 22)

TEACHER EDUCATOR
          I could not turn my brain off. I couldn't sleep. One question that is always in the front of my mind is whether I am pushing my beliefs on students. I try not to say too much to them.

CLIENT   How old are you?

Working on the mosaic in a public space on a daily basis served as a collective experience upon which the diverse motivations and intentions of many were captured as distinct marks. It was as if the diverse and communal concerns of humanity flowed through the space in a temporal yet random and un-choreographed fashion informing our lives in compelling ways demanding reflections, questions, and reaffirming the greater goal of constructing a better world.

"The mirror is endless energy, reflecting everything." Isaiah Zagar (Augustine, 1999, 14)

December, 2005: Mosaic is Complete!

CLIENT/STUDENT
It's a building block, it's an inspiration. It encourages me on bad days at school. It encourages me when I'm tired and [when] I want to give it up. When I go, "I don't know if I can do this," it says, "Yes, you can!"

STUDENT
At times I didn't know who I was working for. The clients? Myself? My class? To tell you the truth, I am still not sure. But, I have realized it is about everyone.

CENTER MANAGER
A lot of the business [people] downtown, they came by because they heard about the mosaic, and they come here to see it. And I would have never had that opportunity to talk to them. The only times that I have had that opportunity [was] to talk to them on the phone when they tell me they got this homeless guy sleeping at the door step. "Can you come over here and do something about this?" But now, I got a chance to see them up close and personal.

STUDENT
I definitely learned tolerance and how to deal with different personalities. It helped me to better process the whole situation and be able to break down those stereotypes and to talk to the clients and understand what was going on.

CLIENT
I think clients enjoyed it. You know a lot of people did because when they were like one man, "Look at this, remember this and that!" And even, like me, some of them didn't take to it at first, but I saw a lot of people that it brought a lot of joy too.

TEACHER EDUCATOR
It's here for you to look at. And I'm glad you enjoy looking at it. If you take great joy in looking at it, then that's it.

STUDENT
And then toward the end, we actually sat down and were able to communicate; we came together. And [we] were able to finish very strong.

The value of the mosaic project is best revealed in the words of those who experienced it some way or another. As a process it served as a way to bring divergent participants together to share stories, to confront differences and to celebrate commonalities. As a public work of art it offered hope, pride, joy, and a sense of the possible. Mirrored and fragmented, yet held together by a common purpose, the mosaic serves as a representation of what's possible in the larger mosaic of human experience.

Final Reflections

Woywood (2004) wrote of the importance of becoming "comfortable (gutsy) enough to take risks" as art educators while posing the question, "Why is this so hard?" (p. 7). The mosaic project was imperfect, risky, and difficult at times, yet powerful in so many ways. It is my hope that this article has provided a rich depiction of the project while revealing the importance of risky endeavors that make them ripe with opportunities for reflection, connection, and transformation.

It was not the goal of this work to valorize the project or provide a model for how to conduct socially responsive pedagogy. Rather, I hope that this work inspires new questions and suggests possibilities for socially responsive pedagogy. Finally, like many (Darts, 2006; Banks 2006), I strongly suggest that the development of a critical conscience should take on greater value as a necessary component of teacher preparation, prompting us to make certain that coursework not only includes a discussion of techniques and skills related to our disciplines but also encourages critical discussions and actions that may often teeter on the margins of "accepted" ways of being in the world. Consequently, our goal as teacher educators becomes one of providing experiences for our students that not only disseminate privileged morsels of wisdom but challenge and ignite their minds with what Giroux (2004) refers to as the "language of possibility" (p. 211).

ACKNOWLEDGMENTS

In community-based art projects there are many contributors. First and foremost, I would like to thank my students, clients, and staff at the center, as well as other community volunteers who helped make the mosaic possible. Furthermore, I would like to especially acknowledge those participants who freely gave of their time to talk with me about their experiences. Additionally, I thank the outreach center administration that invited us to create the mosaic and who provided funding through a local arts grant and Sheena Buruzs and Melanie Rick who selflessly allowed us to use their photographs in the manuscript. I would like gratefully to acknowledge Rosary Lalik who assisted with research and more importantly became a sounding board for my experiences throughout the mosaic project. Her wisdom and guidance served as a steadying force and inspiration for continued reflection. Finally, I would like to thank Isaiah Zagar for selflessly sharing his art and creative process. His spirit and wisdom have inspired and informed the creation of many mosaics.

REFERENCES

Anderson, T., & Milbrandt, M. (2005). *Art for Life: Authentic instruction in art.* New York: McGraw Hill.

Buffington, M. L. (2007). The big idea: Service-learning and art education. *Art Education, 60*(6), 40–45.

Darts, D. (2006). Art education for a change: Contemporary issues and the visual arts. *Art Education, 59*(5), 6–12.

Dewey, J. (1934). *Art as experience.* New York: Perigee.

Diamond, C. T., & Mullen, C. A. (Eds.). (1999). *The postmodern educator: Arts-based inquiries and teacher development.* New York: Peter Lang.

Drucker, J. (2004). *The century of artist's books.* New York: Granary Books.

Freire, P. (1970). *Pedagogy of the oppressed.* New York: Continuum.

Gaudelius, Y., & Speirs, P. (Eds). (2002). *Contemporary issues in art education.* Upper Saddle River, New Jersey: Prentice-Hall.

Giroux, H. (2004). Teachers as transformative intellectuals. In A. Canestrari & B. Marlow (Eds.), *Educational Foundations: An Anthology of Critical Readings* (pp. 205–212). Thousand Oaks, California: Sage Publications.

Geiger P. S. (2006). A real community bridge: Informing community-based learning through a model of participatory art. *Art Education, 59*(2), 40–46.

Irwin, R. L., & Kindler, A. M. (Eds.). (1999). *Beyond the School: Community and institutional partnerships in art education.* Reston, VA: National Art Education Association.

Richardson, L. (1994). Writing: A method of inquiry. In N. Denzin, & Y. Lincoln (Eds.), *Handbook of qualitative research,* pp. 516–529. Thousand Oaks: Sage.

Sanders-Bustle, L. (Ed.). (2003). *Image, inquiry and transformative practice: Engaging learners in creative and critical inquiry through visual representation.* New York: Peter Lang.

Sanders-Bustle, L. (March 2007). *Altered books as spaces for critical and creative inquiry.* Presented at the annual convention of the National Art Education Association, New York.

Taylor, P. H. (2002). Service-learning as postmodern art and pedagogy. *Studies in Art Education, 42*(2), 124–140.

Taylor, P. G., & Ballengee-Morris, C. (2004). Service-learning: A language of we. *Art Education, 57*(5), 13–18.

Sullivan, G. (2005). *Art practice as research: Inquiry in the visual arts.* London: Sage Publications.

Ulbricht, J. (2005). What is community-based art education? *Art Education, 58*(2), 6–12.

Wodiczko, K. (n.d.) Architecture and therapy. Public Broadcasting System: Art in the Twenty First Century. Retrieved September 2005, from http://www.pbs.org/art21/artists/wodiczko/clip2.html

Woywod, C. (2004). A postmodern visual culture art teacher: Finding peace in my opposing roles. In D. Smith-Shank (Ed.), *Semiotics and visual culture: Sights, signs, and significance* (pp. 5–10). Reston, VA: National Art Education Association.

Art Therapy and Social Justice in Post-Katrina Mississippi

Marcia L. Rosal

If we don't stand up for children, then we don't stand for much.—Marian Wright Edelman

Art therapy is a human service profession. Most often art therapy is practiced with the underserved: the impoverished, the child no one else wants to deal with, mothers suffering from the effects of violence, patients with chronic mental illness, the homeless, the imprisoned, and the traumatized. When working with these populations, art therapists find themselves advocating for their clients, fighting alongside them for services, jobs, and social welfare. With so many art therapists practicing with underserved populations does this mean that art therapy is also a social justice profession? If social justice is defined as concern for the poorest members of our society or *concern for people with the least resources to impact improvement in their lives* (see Counselors for Social Justice at http://couselorsforsocialjustice.com) then perhaps it is true that art therapy has inherent qualities that allow the proclamation that art therapy is a social justice profession. Hocoy (2007) stated that "… what makes the art therapist also a social activist is an awareness of the interconnectivity between individual and collective, between a person's suffering and social imbalance…" (p. 31).

Certainly not all art therapists work within the philosophical or political realm espoused herein and graduate art therapy programs do not always advocate the perspective that the profession has a social justice component.

KEY CONCEPTS

- Art Therapy as a Social Justice Profession
- The Use of Art Therapy to Serve Communities After a Disaster
- Development of a Social Justice Art Therapy Program
- Mentoring Graduate Students for Social Justice Interventions
- The Use of Art Therapy with Children After Hurricane Katrina

Advocating this point of view to all who enter the profession is not necessary or even desirable. However, there are times and events that cry out for art therapists to act in a socially responsible manner.

One prominent illustration of this was the aftermath of September 11, 2001. Art therapists across New York, New Jersey, and the Washington DC area volunteered their services to those whose loved ones died in the attacks and to those who witnessed these atrocities (Anderson, 2001). To help people express the unspeakable through images, shapes, and colors had a healing effect for not only the individual, but for his or her community as well.

Gussak (2001–2002) cited numerous other examples of art therapists who exercised socially responsible art therapy:

1. Roje (1995) wrote about art therapy work after the 1994 earthquake in Los Angeles;
2. Byers (1996, 1998) offered art therapy services in the Middle East, particularly the West Bank and Gaza;
3. Jones (1997) used art therapy with survivors and victims of the Oklahoma City bombings; and
4. Stone (1998) used art therapy with South American women victims of torture.

In summary, Gussak found that art therapists work in a socially just manner with individuals under duress due to natural or human-caused tragedies. He also theorized that through art therapy people are encouraged to form supportive communities following a disaster.

Hurricane Katrina and Coastal Mississippi

In 2005, another horrific event took place: Hurricane Katrina. Many Americans watched television coverage of the destruction and neglect of the aftermath of the storm. Nowhere was this coverage more ubiquitous than in New Orleans, Louisiana. Because of the horror in that city, other communities, possibly even more devastated by Katrina, were little-mentioned or not mentioned at all. Areas of New Orleans are poor and predominately African American, but there are other reasons, too, why it received the majority of media attention. New Orleans is a tourist city and many Americans as well as international visitors flock there every year for Mardi Gras, for the Annual Jazz Festival, or for the French Quarter and its many delights such as the local cuisine and Euro-style culture. With so many tourist dollars at stake, it is no wonder that New Orleans commanded the media's attention.

But what happened to coastal Mississippi, which was ground zero during Hurricane Katrina? Not totally ignored by the media and the public, nonetheless many would be hard pressed to know that more than 3 years later, children and teens still live and go to school in trailers. Nearly 15 months post-Katrina, the *New York Times* (Dreifus, 2006) reported that the children in coastal Mississippi were not eating enough; had asthma, allergies, and other respiratory illnesses due to living in Federal Emergency Management Agency (FEMA) trailers; had other somatic complaints such as headaches and stomach aches; and experienced sleeping problems. The article recounted that the stress of the storm set off a myriad of continuous disasters for children and families such as loss of jobs, homes, deaths and even murders of relatives, and parents leaving town to take jobs elsewhere in order for the family to survive. Eighteen months after the storm, the *New York Times* (Dewan, 2007) reported that more than one-third of the children were absent from school 10 more days in one month and that few mental health services were available.

In that context, in this chapter an example of practicing socially responsible art therapy is explored. An art therapy program for the Pass Christian Boys and Girls Club was created post-Hurricane Katrina when mental health services for this devastated community were almost non-existent. Developed and implemented by the Florida State University (FSU) Art Therapy Program, the purpose of the project was two-fold: (1) to serve a population in need and (2) to introduce graduate level art therapy students to responding to a crisis in a socially responsible manner.

Art Therapy Action

In the coastal city of Pass Christian, Mississippi, just about all was lost. All government buildings were destroyed. Leo Chipper McDermott, Mayor of Pass Christian, labeled the devastation "almost annihilation" (personal communication, July 6, 2007). He reported 65% of homes were lost, as well as 100% of businesses, churches, and schools. The only public building that was still useable was the library. If citizens did not flee prior to the storm, they did afterwards. The town was left with no services, no infrastructure, no food, no potable water, and little hope. Mr. McDermott stated that the first year was "just survival." After an assessment of the damage, the mayor determined that it would be 5–7 years before the community of Pass Christian would be rebuilt.

The building that housed the Boys and Girls Club (B&GC) of Pass Christian was also destroyed. About five miles north of Pass Christian in the small community of Delisle, one school was still standing, the Delisle Elementary School. By adding numerous trailers, the school was operational a few months post-Katrina. The children of Pass Christian returned to school in this building. Through the generosity of the principal, the B&GC was permitted access to the school's facilities for its after-school and summer programs. Although this solution was not ideal for the program or the children, the school provided much needed after school care for the families whose parents needed to work and trying to rebuild their lives. Operating in a public school structure was not ideal yet the administrators and teachers of the B&GC prevailed.

One thing that was not yet available and is still only available in a limited capacity is therapy services for the children. One year post-Katrina, there were only two therapists in town, yet the need for therapy services was immense. One of the therapists, a practicing social worker, offered some volunteer hours to the Delisle school, but found the need overwhelming. In speaking with the director of the B&GC, the social worker realized that the call for therapy services was urgent.

Directly after Katrina hit the Gulf Coast, the Red Cross appointed the state of Florida as front-line responders to devastated Mississippi. Emergency personnel from Florida were immediately posted in various communities along the Gulf Coast of Mississippi. As the only art therapy program in the state of Florida, it was clear that part of our mission was to assist the child victims and survivors of the hurricane's destruction in coastal Mississippi. As art therapists, we would create a therapeutic environment that would allow the children to non-verbally express their experiences of the storm and its aftermath and provide avenues of healing through the creative process. By developing the opportunity for graduate art therapy students to volunteer in a Mississippi project, the program would be demonstrating sound social justice principles. It was through the B&GC that this mission was defined.

With a small grant from Communities Healing through the Arts (CHART) and support from the Florida State University (FSU) Department of Art Education, the art therapy program received permission from the Pass Christian B&GC to provide art therapy services to the children. Although the mental health needs were tremendous, the program personnel were able to travel to Pass Christian only twice a semester due to the high cost of travel and the limited availability of grant monies. Since January 2007, graduate art therapy student volunteers accompanied an art therapy faculty member, and traveled to Pass Christian to spend the day working with children. The B&GC requested that we offer services to the youngest children (K–1st grade), grade 3–4 children, and the older children (grades 5–6). For each trip to Pass Christian, an art therapy intervention was developed for the young children and another for those in the upper grade levels. We arrived early on Friday afternoons and worked with the children as a component of the B&GC after-school program. We also hosted an Open Art Therapy Studio for the parents and children of the B&GC on Saturday mornings. The Open Studio allowed parents and children to create art together and provided a safe place for families to commune.

Art Therapy Interventions

Stage One. The purpose of the first stage of the program was to assess the levels of anxiety experienced by the children and to help them regain a sense of safety and control. During the first visit in early 2007, six graduate students each led three small groups of 3 to 5 children (for a total of 37 children; see Figure 1). The student art therapists first had the children decorate a name plate. Next, the children were asked to discuss changes in housing since the hurricane, asked if they had a safe place before the hurricane, and if they have a place where they feel safe now. The older children were asked to draw a safe place. During the discussion, each child spoke about their art piece, were asked where they lived before and where they lived now, and how they created a new place for them to feel safe. The

Figure 1. Pui Wan, a graduate art therapy student, working with a small group at the Boys and Girls Club in Pass Christian, Mississippi.

younger children were asked to draw their dream house: what they would wish for in a home.

Working with the children in the small group format successfully led to the feeling of safety. The majority of children spoke openly about Hurricane Katrina and without provocation from the student art therapists. In her therapy notes, one art therapy student wrote,

They [the children] all brought up the hurricane on their own. S. drew a dog on her name tag and brought up the issue of pets being left behind in the storm. S. said she lived in a FEMA trailer…and said her safe place was her family.

A therapy note from another student therapist revealed that one of the fourth-grade children reported conflicting housing circumstances:

T. stated she lived with grandparents before, during and after hurricane. Mother is in FEMA trailer next door to grandparents while their house is being rebuilt. Stated that she got sick from FEMA trailer and explained that it was some sort of bacteria or something and so she had to move in with grandparents…lived in Texas and Alabama since Katina. The child expressed concern that mother might get sick. Stated water was all the way to third story but wasn't afraid because, 'I'm not scared of snakes.'

The conflicting statements made by the children were indicative of the multiple moves experienced of many families post-Katrina. Such moves and upheaval is difficult for children. Turmoil over place and the tales of multiple losses were common amongst the children of Pass Christian. Therefore, we implemented art interventions to help the children restructure what happened to them post-hurricane and to assist them with regaining a timeline of their experiences.

When we returned for the fourth visit in July 2007, it was hurricane season and the children exhibited anxiety about storms. The focus continued to be on helping the children gain a sense of control. The children were able to select a lidded box to decorate in any way they wished; the box could be used to hold their personal treasures. Immediately they expressed delight to have a box for their personal items and several children mentioned that a box was good to have just in case they had to re-evacuate. Exploring multiple losses was still a theme for many of the children. One art therapy student wrote:

Common themes in the artwork included loss of pets and family. L. got upset at the end of the session because his uncle had died, but he was able to regain comfort and smiled when reflecting on good memories he had with the uncle.

A child penned, "Keep out, Private" on her box and stated that since the hurricane she lived in a crowded space and wanted the box to be just for her. A student art therapist wrote, *"For the older children, privacy and personal space was of a high priority."* A fifth-grade girl stated, "… *it is good to have something to put my stuff inside before a hurricane."* Another student's therapy note read:

All the group members contributed in expressing their feelings about Hurricane Katrina and the impact it has had on them and their

community. They felt unsafe in their neighborhoods as violence has risen and they are scared of family members dying when they go on trips away from home.

Almost 2 years post-Katrina, children still harbored significant fears. Also evident were the lack of community infrastructure and the lack of safety in neighborhoods.

Stage Two. At the beginning of the new academic year, the project moved into the second stage. For the four visits during fall 2007 and spring 2008 semesters, we wanted to focus on helping the children reframe their hurricane experiences and to move forward. The younger children addressed feelings (mad, sad, glad, and scared) to enable them to speak about the past and present experiences in a meaningful way and to identify how past and present events affected them. Developing a focus on the future and formulating personal goals were the older children's objectives. Their theme was "reframing."

The four feeling states were easy for the children to identify and each was able to identify a time when they experienced these feelings (see Figure 2). One of the boys stated that he was sad about the loss of his

Figure 2. An example of the 4 feeling state project. Shown here are drawings of feeling sad and feeling scared.

dogs. The student therapist wrote, *"One [of the dogs] was on the roof because of the water. He said it made him sad and now they were invisible."* For the "sad" picture, another boy drew his house. Then he drew a cross through the house and wrote, "it got hurt" on the picture.

During the November trip, children were given cut out human figures. The students discussed the physical components of feelings and assisted the children in thinking where emotions were experienced in their bodies. One art therapy student wrote:

J. was able to identify some changes in his body with the happy feeling. His first figure represented the happy feeling. His second was to be sad but he avoided picking out a sad color. His second figure did not depict any feeling.

There were other children who chose not to represent sad or scary feelings. However, another child *identified scared in the throat and happy with a heart in the chest* (see Figure 3). When asked what they would do if they were scared, several children understood that when they were scared they could tell teachers, moms, or even call 911. Other children had trouble speaking about happy feelings or times.

The focus on emotions was useful for the children. We continued to develop interventions that helped the children identify, manage, and cope with difficult feelings throughout the spring semester.

Stage Three. Planning for the summer 2008 program is underway. The focus for the summer will be on recreation and helping the children find healthy ways to enjoy leisure time. Construction is underway for the new Pass Christian B&GC building and it will be completed in December 2008 due to a generous donation made by the U.S. Ambassador from Qatar (Jackie, McGee, Director of the Pass Christian B&GC, personal communication, May 4, 2007). Therefore, the third phase of the project will be to create a mural on one wall of the building dedicated to the rebuilding of the club and the lives of the children in Pass Christian. The children will be involved in all aspects of the project. We will begin this process during the fall semester visit and complete the project in summer 2009.

Analysis. The Mississippi project is still in progress. However some preliminary outcomes have been identified. Jackie McGee observed children's behavior problems decreased after participating in art therapy and she reported that both children and parents expressed that the art therapy was

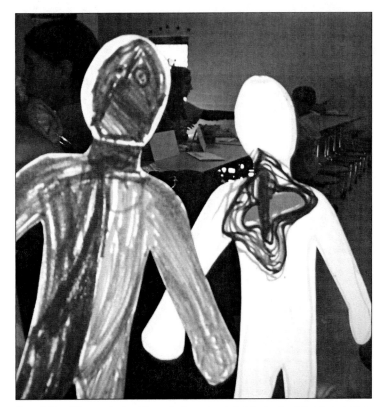

Figure 3. The children used cut-out figures to show where in their bodies they felt various emotions to further understanding of feeling states. Here is an example of one girl's sad/scared and happy figures.

helpful (personal communication, July 6, 2007). The children commented that art therapy was useful in helping them understand their circumstances and feelings.

The art therapy students confirmed that the program was rewarding for them. One student said that she was passionate about giving directly to the children and community of Pass Christian. Another student agreed that she went to help, but she also learned to treasure every moment of her life as well.

Conclusion

The Mississippi project developed by the FSU art therapy program is illustrative of sound social justice art therapy practice. The project was developed in response to a human need caused by a natural disaster. The overwhelmed community of Pass Christian could not offer services to help their children cope with the aftermath of the disaster. Art therapy provided a safe forum for the children to explore what happened to them post-Katrina and to involve them in finding creative solutions to their problems. Finally, the graduate art therapy students experienced firsthand how they could reach out in a socially responsible manner to a devastated community.

REFERENCES

Anderson, F. E. (Ed.) (2001). Art therapists in their own words [Special Section]. *Art Therapy: Journal of the American Art Therapy Association, 18*(4).

Counselors for social justice. http://counselorsforsocialjustice.com

Dewan, S. (2007, February 2). Little progress seen for poorest after hurricane. *New York Times.* Retrieved March 2, 2007, from http://www.nytimes.com

Dreifus, C. (2006, November 21). Attending to sick children along a Gulf Coast still in tatters. New York Times. Retrieved March 2, 2007, from http://www.nytimes.com

Gussak, D. (2001–2002). Art therapists as bridge builders for peace. *Journal of Cultural Research in Art Education, 19 & 20*, 94–101.

Hocoy, D. (2007). Art therapy as a tool for social change. In F. F. Kaplan (Ed.), *Art therapy and social change* (pp. 21–39). Philadelphia, PA: Jessica Kingsley.

Unsung Heroes: Making a Positive Difference through Intergenerational Learning

Debrah Sickler-Voigt

Oftentimes schools do not reflect the individuals who make up our communities. Children are divided by grade level, proportionally fewer males work as teachers than females, and youth seldom interact with individuals (other than their teachers) who come from other generations. To bring an authentic sense of community into our schools, it is necessary for educators to provide youth with a plethora of learning opportunities with individuals who reflect our greater society. During a project called *Discover Middle Tennessee's Wetlands through Art and Exploration*, intergenerational participants worked together to teach children about the community's wetlands. The project provided preservice art educators, who participated in a 3-week community art class, experience in developing theme-based community art projects that involved intergenerational participants. To help us with aspects of the project we were not well-acquainted with, we called upon the expertise of everyday community members, our unsung heroes, who brought their skills and knowledge to our wetlands project.

Review of Literature

Art belongs to everyone, regardless of age (Greenberg, 2004). Intergenerational artmaking in a community brings individuals from different age groups together to make visual statements. Through community art, participants who work together develop shared experiences (Congdon, 2004; Sickler-Voigt, 2006). Members of such a community are

KEY CONCEPTS

- Mentors Play a Significant Role in Educating our Children
- Intergenerational Role Models Can Help Students Achieve More
- Outreach to Adults Living with Hardships and/or Disabilities to Educate our Youth
- Community Learning
- Using Community Art to Discover People's Hidden Talents and Capabilities

interested in fellow participants and take their needs seriously (Hughey, Speer, & Peterson, 1999), and depend on one another to ensure the community's well being. Such a community can best meet the needs of its youth by taking advantage of existing partnerships and creating new ones to empower its residents.

Individual perceptions vary according to the community a person inhabits (Hicks, 1994). Williams and Nussbaum (2001) articulated how it is human nature for an individual to favor one's own group. While American culture celebrates diversity, individuals continue to categorize other people and apply stereotypes. Consequently, some participants who first engage in intergenerational partnerships may feel apprehensive about working with people from different backgrounds. Fortunately, as many of these fears dissolve participants can develop bonds and greater understanding of one another (Mbugua, Wadas, Casey & Finnerty, 2004; Wakefield & Ericson, 2003). In effective partnerships, group members' various communities begin to overlap (The New London Group, 1996), enabling members to bring knowledge from one community into another, and make new meaning.

Mentors within a community inhabit diverse sub-communities formed according to such characteristics as faith, geographical zones, race, work, and special interests. Their diversified life experiences play a significant role in educating children and providing them with quality experiences (Garbarino, 1995; Sickler-Voigt, 2003; Tucker, 1999). Mentors are trustworthy individuals who guide students through various learning processes (Reese, 2006). Working together with mentors correlates with Vygotsky's (1962) theory of Zones of Proximal Development in which an inexperienced partner learns how to achieve a new task and/or overcome a problem by working with an experienced partner.

Methodology

This case study (Stake, 1995) is grounded in Greenwood & Levin's (2000) paradigm of action research. In this case, we were focused on members of a university institution who collaborated to solve problems with typically underserved populations. My role was to teach preservice teachers how to utilize community experts from these underserved populations to learn the skills they need to create community art and provide children with a more balanced representation of society than they normally have at school. The research question that guides this study was: What did the creation of an intergenerational wetland project teach preservice art educators about partnerships, mentoring, and community art?

This study utilized Richardson's (2000) theory of crystallization, which argues that interpreting research data is similar to a crystal because the perspective changes according to the way it is viewed. The story that I tell is my own; however, it has been shaped by my interaction with the participants and review of literature (Fine, Weiss, Weseen & Wong, 2000). I acquired data from a variety of sources including historical documents, photographs, personal observations, student journals (scrapbooks), and qualitative interviews of the participants on audiocassette. I applied Stake's (1995) method for coding interviews to demonstrate how different viewpoints fused together to tell a story and make sense of the experience. To ensure that I accurately portrayed the participants' perspectives I provided participants with a member check. All names of elementary student participants have been concealed to ensure privacy.

Throughout the project, I limited the amount of distance between the researcher and the participants. The participants within this study include volunteers from a local senior center and the Veterans Affairs Tennessee Valley Healthcare System, preservice art education majors, elementary students, and university faculty. Adult participants assured a more realistic sampling of the community than is found in schools. Participants ranged in age from 8 to 86 years old. The eight veteran volunteers were all males. All three senior citizen participants had backgrounds in teaching either

K–12 or college. Research shows that the volunteers chosen for this project belong to groups of people who are sometimes overlooked for their potential contributions to society (Williams & Nussbaum, 2000). Typically, our society views senior citizens and people with hardships and/or disabilities as people who need to be served rather than valuing the services these community members can provide to society (Sommerfield, 1995).

Move Away from your Desk, Explore, and Create!

This project was implemented to provide children with meaningful learning opportunities through art and exploration that would take them away from their desks and out into the community. The plan became a reality through the support of community partners. During the first week of the project, all participants learned about the wetlands at the *Discovery Center at Murfree Spring*. After a quick introduction to the museum, students were led outside by the museum's educator, Gretchen Campbell, to the patio, which was filled with rubber boots for the students to change into. With their boots and gear in place, the students stomped through Murfree Spring and collected environmental samples, made measurements of the water, picked up trash, and discovered animals including tadpoles, crawdads, and turtles. Carrying a variety of samples in their hands, the students entered the museum's science lab. Students took turns conducting experiments, looking through microscopes, and interacting with wetland animals. Upon completion, Mrs. Campbell, who had explained the importance of protecting the animals in the wetlands, instructed the children to return them to the spring. To conclude the tour, Mrs. Campbell led the students out to the boardwalk overlooking acres of wetland habitat. On their walk, students observed a muskrat, birds, a beaver's dam, and more. They also participated in a sound map activity, in which the students listened to the sounds in the wetlands and drew what they heard in their sketchbooks.

The fieldtrip to the Discovery Center left a lasting impression on the elementary students. Jennifer, a sixth-grade student, was aware of the problems associated with polluting the environment and expressed how happy she was to see wildlife in a natural area: "It's just fun to go and it's not disturbed. It's even cooler that the animals aren't scared or anything. They just stay there." Other students were excited by the muskrat they saw. Sean, a fifth grader, stated: "I never heard of a muskrat before and I never did know they exist and I like seeing them swim underwater." Richard, also in

Figure 1. Beaver

Figure 2. Green Frog

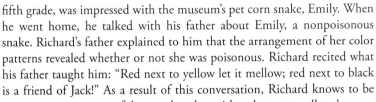

Figure 3. Mallard Ducks

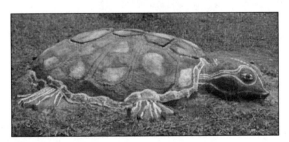

Figure 4. Canadian Goose

Figure 6. Emily the Corn Snake

Figure 5. Red Eared Slider Turtle

fifth grade, was impressed with the museum's pet corn snake, Emily. When he went home, he talked with his father about Emily, a nonpoisonous snake. Richard's father explained to him that the arrangement of her color patterns revealed whether or not she was poisonous. Richard recited what his father taught him: "Red next to yellow let it mellow; red next to black is a friend of Jack!" As a result of this conversation, Richard knows to be careful around snakes with red next to yellow because they are poisonous.

Like the children, the college students benefited from learning about the wetlands from community experts. In addition to visiting the wetlands at Murfree Spring, they met Mrs. Bertha Chrietzburg, an 86-year-old wetland expert and advocate, at the local senior center. Kent, a college student, wrote about his first encounter with Mrs. Chrietzburg in his journal:

> The lady we met with was one of the most caring, concerned environmentalists I have ever met … talk about involved! The lady actually goes out to worksites to make sure they're doing what they're supposed to along the lines of respecting environmental restrictions and code. She has prevented many natural habitats from being destroyed. She still gets out and hikes and is an expert on Tennessee flowers. This was one of the most interesting talks I've ever heard.

Tish, another student, explained: "What I once considered an ugly swamp I can now appreciate its existence." All of the college students were impressed with Mrs. Chrietzburg's knowledge and felt more comfortable teaching about the wetlands after meeting with her. Based on their new knowledge, they developed art lesson plans to teach the children that focused on the theme of the wetlands. We collected the children's designs of geese, ducks, a beaver, a corn snake, a frog, and a turtle made from these art lessons to use as examples for the wetland garden sculptures (See Figures 1–6).

Located adjacent to the student bus pickup and drop off, the garden site was an uninviting drainage ditch surrounded by brick walls. The principal, Mr. Lyles, wanted us to transform it into a beautiful space. On the first day working in the garden, children shoveled red clay and smashed cinder blocks with sledge hammers that would be used to fill the holes and form the concrete wetland animals. The next day the concrete mixer arrived. I had my hesitations because I have never operated a concrete mixer; however, I assumed I could figure it out since I had asked various people for instructions before starting. I made a mess! I dumped way too much concrete into the mixer. As I added water, the mixture gushed out of the machine. A half an hour later, Bill, one of the veteran volunteers, arrived to save the day. He salvaged my mixture and we were able to form the sculptures. Bill had the patience to teach the college students, children, and me about how much concrete to shovel in the mixer and how much water to add. It took 2 weeks to form and paint the large concrete animals.

Toward the end of our project, Dr. Tony Halterlein, a landscaping professor and senior citizen, oversaw the planting of the landscape he designed for our wetland garden. Because we were planting in a drainage ditch, he selected trees and scrubs that could live submerged in water or in a drier environment. The children, college students, veterans, and Dr. Halterlein all bonded together to complete the landscaping in a few hours time.

Using construction and landscaping tools with the mentors appeared to be one of the most rewarding aspects of the project for the children. Joe, a fifth-grade student, explained: "It was really neat because I've never been around veterans. One guy taught me some stuff about planting and another guy taught me about wheelbarrows and concrete." A sixth-grade student, Victoria, enjoyed her experience with the veterans because they would joke with her while working. Billy Bob, another fifth grader, was most proud of learning how to do something new. "I accomplished it. At first, I didn't know how to do it. Then, I knew how to do it and did good on it."

Children were not the only ones who benefited from our group collaboration. Both veteran volunteers and college students commented on their personal gains. John, one of the veterans, stated: "It was something different and I loved every minute of it." He described how he enjoyed working with students and watching others create. Before this experience, John had never created art. He worked diligently on the beaver sculpture. When reflecting on his experience he declared: "We learn from them (the children) and they learn from us... Words do not explain this. Like I said, it's a new beginning

for me. It opened my eyes to new bigger and better things in life, things I didn't know about. Anything is possible." Bill believed if it were not for the children's involvement it would have felt more like work to him. He was impressed with how well they responded to his directions without challenge or conflict. He added: "They're not only impressionable but they want to know more." To summarize his experience, he stated: "I haven't had this much fun in a long time."

This wetland project provided preservice art education majors with experience in implementing a community art project, working with mentors, and teaching. Brooklyn, who worked as a project assistant, acknowledged:

I did not expect for it to be as challenging as it was at times. Beginning this project seemed a little hectic to me because of its massive scale and the number of participants involved. As the plans began to form, my mind's eye could picture the finished product. I began to get excited. I quickly learned that patience is a virtue and you must have lots of it when working with various organizations and people.

Like Brooklyn, the other college students recognized the valuable role that the community members played in making the project successful. Lorielle articulated what she learned about working with mentors: "The advantages are endless because the children learn from them and admire them. It gives the mentors a sense of ability and happiness to help in a way they may have felt incapable before." Another student, Shari, stated: "It makes me very hopeful that people can work together as a group coming from all different backgrounds."

The college students also gained experience using qualitative teaching methods. Some realized how much energy children have and how that energy needs to be constructively channeled to keep students engaged in an activity. Others commented how they were glad no one got hurt and how they learned about the importance of teaching safety procedures. Many felt the most important thing they learned was how to teach children to believe in their own capabilities. Several elementary students admitted how they could not believe that they were able to transform an area in their school into something "magnificent." Josh, a college student, added: "Don't let them (the students) fool you into working for them. Make them do the work. They don't learn anything if you do all the work."

Discussion

The intergenerational component of this project played a significant role in extending learning beyond the wetlands and demonstrating the importance of community mentors. Similar to Prince's (2004) research in which mentors helped reveal students' hidden talents, the elementary and college students discovered new abilities including sensitivity to the environment, teamwork, landscaping, operating construction equipment, painting, and applying mosaics. This project confirmed that regardless of age or status, individuals within a community can make a difference by working together.

While research in the field of education regularly addresses the concerns of youth living with physical and/or mental disabilities (Wachowiak & Clements, 2006), I argue that educators seldom reach out to adults living with hardships and/or disabilities to educate our youth. Like the supervising nurse at the Veterans Affairs hospital, who oversaw our crew of veteran volunteers, stated, it is important to focus on an individual's strengths and capabilities rather than hardships and/or disabilities. Therefore, we chose not to assign labels to their hardships and/or disabilities. The veterans were there to assist us in achieving our goals, which without their wisdom, would not have been possible. In fact, they demonstrated how beneficial people living with hardships and/or disabilities can be in educating our youth.

On the last day of class, I asked the elementary and college students to reflect upon their involvement with the veterans. Billy Bob proudly acknowledged how the veterans used their free time to work with them. Tish stated: "I felt that they appreciated being asked to help. They seemed gracious and happy to be needed. They may have seemed a little timid at first, but their energy and sensitivity to the project was amazing." Becky, another college student, observed:

> They worked long hard days and taught us about more than concrete; they taught us the importance of community involvement. They brought skill and knowledge and incredible work ethic to us. In return, we offered them a sense of belonging. It is in my hope that they realize how important they were to our project and to our community.

Many research studies continue to show the benefits of using senior citizens as community experts (see Barret, 2004; Gildin & Perlstein, 2004). The older adults in this study were vital to educating the college students about the wetlands and landscaping so they could teach this information to the elementary student population. While some senior citizens do receive services from younger generations, our project demonstrated how they are also providers of knowledge. They both inspired and educated the college students. Tish confessed:

> I felt that the wetlands expert, Bertha, played the greatest role to me. Her enthusiasm, dedication, and overall determination to save the wetlands were contagious. She makes you want to stand up and take action for what you believe in.

All participants valued the services our mentors provided, but I was curious to learn if any of them saw possible drawbacks to working with senior citizens or populations experiencing hardships and/or disabilities. Some worried that it might be challenging to work with mentors who do not have experience teaching children. Others were concerned about possible use of foul language. While we only had positive interactions with our volunteers, it is important to remember that it is the teacher's responsibility to keep a watchful eye and guide mentors as needed. This is also beneficial when mentors feel somewhat apprehensive in the beginning of a project due to being in a new environment and/or playing a new role.

Next, I looked for signs of preconceived stereotypes. I did not observe any against the veteran population; however, many college students expressed amazement with Mrs. Chrietzburg's activism for her age. One stated: "It was very inspiring to me to see how passionate she still was at 86 years old." Mrs. Chrietzburg's altruism is impressive; it shows that seniors are fully capable of leading active and inspiring lifestyles. I argue that continued exposure to intergenerational relationships in preservice education will provide students with a more realistic view of senior citizens and persons living with hardships and/or disabilities.

The children's interviews also provided me with insight into their perceptions on the role they played in preparing the preservice art educators for teaching. They felt that gave them a better understanding of what children are like. Jennifer, a sixth-grade student, stated: "Sometimes I hear a lot of adults say young kids are lazy they just sit around and watch TV all day." She believed their work ethic proved their capabilities. They children were actively engaged in learning throughout this project. Jennifer also observed how a student in her class appeared more attentive working outside because it kept his attention. Similarly, Billy Bob stated: "It felt great. I would rather be out here than in the class doing work." This is an important lesson for educators. Children want to learn. Effective learning does not only take place at a desk. Our community project enabled children to learn about the wetlands and transfer their factual knowledge to create a wetland garden using their hands, creativity, and imaginations.

Conclusion

In summary, in this study I found that by recruiting intergenerational community volunteers from places in society one might otherwise not look, we learned new facts and techniques, developed meaningful relationships, and accomplished our goals. Within 3 weeks, the community volunteers became our heroes. Ultimately, this project demonstrated that community mentors, our unsung heroes, can be found in everyday places such as a senior center or hospital facility. Unsung heroes are precious community resources who have the desire and skills to assist teachers in achieving greater educational endeavors for their students. Their services can truly benefit educators who may sometimes feel overwhelmed by large class sizes and/ or lack of experience in a particular subject area. Calling upon their knowledge serves as a basis for developing a healthy sense of community. Future studies, enhanced with extended time allocations and financial support, will be beneficial in further investigating the advantages of intergenerational learning through community art opportunities.

In preservice education, working with intergenerational mentors provides students with a base knowledge of how to secure community support for theme-based instruction and better prepares them for teaching. Becky explained: "Although it was hard work, I feel it best represents how our life will be out in the teaching field. I learned that I can accomplish great tasks with the support of fellow staff, students, and community members." In fact, the class agreed that they plan to implement community art projects when they become certified art educators. Shari's journal, which contained a photograph and written reflection about the rubber boots the students used at the *Discovery Center*, serves as an analogy to summarize our project:

> The boots are symbolic of the wetlands as well as the many people that contributed to our project. They are many colors, many sizes, and yet all so unique. They are ready to serve us and work for us. That is what I experienced from the community, the students, the veterans, the St. Claire senior center, the media, the people that donated supplies and my professor for bringing this all together. The project was meaningful on so many levels and I have learned so much.

Barret, D. B. (2004). Generations together. In A. M. La Porte (Ed.), *Community connections: Intergenerational links in art education* (pp. 129–140). Reston, VA: National Art Education Association.

Congdon, K. G. (2004). *Community art in action*. Worcester, MA: Davis Publications.

Garbarino, J. (1995). *Raising children in a socially toxic environment*. San Francisco: Jossey-Bass Publishers.

Fine, M., Weiss, L., Weseen, S. & Wong, L. (2000). For whom? Qualitative research, representations, and social responsibilities. In N. K. Denzin & Y. S. Lincoln (Eds.), *Handbook of qualitative research* (2nd ed., pp. 85–106). Thousand Oaks, CA: Sage.

Gildin, M. & Perlstein, S. (2004). Community connections: Living history arts. In A. M. La Porte (Ed.), *Community connections: Intergenerational links in art education* (pp. 83–92). Reston, VA: National Art Education Association.

Greenberg, P. (2004). Preface. In A. M. La Porte (Ed.), *Community connections: Intergenerational links in art education* (pp. vii–viii). Reston, VA: National Art Education Association.

Greenwood, D. J., & Levin, M. (2000). Reconstructing the relationships between universities and society through action research. In N. K. Denzin & Y. S. Lincoln (Eds.), *Handbook of qualitative research* (2nd ed., pp. 85–106). Thousand Oaks, CA: Sage.

Hicks, L. (1994). Social reconstruction and community. *Studies in Art Education. 35*(3), 135–148.

Hughey, J., Speer, P., & Peterson, A. (1999). Sense of community in community organizations: Structure and evidence of validity. *Journal of Community Psychology, 27*(1), 97–113.

Mbugua, T., Wadas, J., Casey, M., & Finnerty, J. (2004) Authentic learning: Intercultural, international, and intergenerational experiences in elementary classrooms. In *Childhood Education, 80*(5), 237–244.

Prince, S. R. (2004). The magic of mentoring. *Educational Leadership, 61*(8), 84–86.

Reese, S. (2006). The art of mentoring. *Techniques: Connecting Education & Careers, 8*(6), 14–19.

Richardson, L. (2000). Writing a method of inquiry. In N. Denzin & Y. Lincoln (Eds.), *Handbook of qualitative research* (2nd ed., pp. 923–948). Thousand Oaks, CA: Sage Publications, Inc.

Sickler-Voigt, D. C. (2003). Out of the woods and into the light. *Journal of cultural research in art education, 21*(1), 60–67.

Sickler-Voigt, D. C. (2006). Southern African American art: Chronicles of shared history, religious zeal, and personal expression. *Journal of Cultural Research in Art Education, 24,* 71–82.

Sommerfeld, M. (1995). Grants to enlist older citizens as school mentors. *Education Week, 15*(5), 5.

Stake, R. E. (1995). *The art of case study research.* Thousand Oaks, CA: Sage Publications, Inc.

The New London Group. (1996). A pedagogy of multiliteracies: Designing social futures. *Harvard Educational Review, 66*(1), 60–92.

Tucker, C. (1999). *African American children: A self-empowerment approach to modifying behavior problems and preventing academic failure.* Boston: Allyn and Bacon.

Vygotsky, L. (1962). *Thought and language.* Boston: M.I.T. Press.

Wachowiak, F., & Clements, R. D. (2006). *Emphasis art: A qualitative art program for elementary and middle schools.* Boston: Pearson Education, Inc.

Wakefield, M., & Ericson, C. B. (2003). Pathways to intergenerational understanding. *Academic Exchange Quarterly, 7,* 326–331.

Williams, A., & Nussbaum, J. F. (2000). *Intergenerational communication across the life span.* Mahwah, NJ: Lawrence Erlbaum Associates Publishers.

Creative Expression for Social Justice with Older Adults

Katy Barrington

Introduction

Older adults are often ignored or even mistreated. As we age, many people in society expect us to gradually decline and accept it. As such, aging is a social justice issue. The more we know about the aging process, the more we can understand it. With this knowledge and understanding, we as a society can address the challenges of aging by overcoming the stigma of aging and by bringing value to a well-lived life. In this context, one relevant issue in our society is that of aging and creativity. Creative expression is fundamental to each culture (Anderson & Milbrandt, 2005). The questions here are whether aging is a process of decline or a time for improvement—and whether as people age, does creativity decrease. In that context, what is the role of creativity in making a better quality of life for aging adults? Some researchers assert that the aging process does not decrease creative expression (Cohen, 2000; Erikson, 1988). How an individual uses creative expression tells a story about that individual and reveals values about that person's culture.

I am an art therapist interested in the role creativity plays across the lifespan. I conducted qualitative phenomenological research with older women in hospice and used grounded theory to analyze results. This research integrated life review and art as a way to highlight achievements each older adult made.

Each participant recalled a highlighted story of her life and created an artistic interpretation of that story. Grounded theory was used to analyze the data. These stories became the data; when the data were coded, the patterns that emerged became the cornerstone for the theory that I developed. Each individual confronted adversity and used creative expression to solve problems, enrich their quality of life, and strengthen their relationships.

This chapter focuses on four areas of the aging process within the lifespan development: biological, psychological, social, and spiritual. The discussion includes a brief explanation about phenomenology and existentialism and contributes to the theory that I developed, illustrating the cyclical process of creativity throughout a lifespan. The theory incorporates the idea that skills are taught by a person proficient in a particular ability, and then re-teaches this knowledge to another person who has an interest in learning the skill. The new learner then utilizes the skill incorporating his/her own modifications and/or improvements. Skills that were taught build on pre-existing skills, and are then combined with new information and the creative process to form new skills. By accessing and utilizing those skills while sharing them with others, an individual may then either repeat those skills or invent and refine new skills, forming new information, which in turn leads to new skills. When an individual faces adversity, the creative process becomes integrated into solving the problem. The skills that were learned influence and help promote solutions, which can then be taught to others. This study emphasized that the creative cycle continues proactively into the end-stage of life. This influence continues even after the death of the teacher.

KEY CONCEPTS

- Aging Process: Biological, Psychological, Social, and Spiritual
- Phenomenology and Existentialism
- Adversity and Personal Development
- Creativity as a Cyclical Process
- Aging as a Time for Improvement

In this chapter I have chosen to focus on one person who was part of the research. Her name has been changed to protect her privacy. Her story illustrates how creativity plays an important role throughout life as the created art portrays resourcefulness, improved resiliency, increased personal pride, and strengthened relationships, all of which demonstrate the benefits that creativity plays within a lifespan toward the ends of social justice. Creativity within the lifespan involves experiences that impact biological, psychological, social, and spiritual aspects of a person's life.

Biological Issues

Historically, many people have viewed aging as a process of decline (Cohen, 2000; Hooyman & Asuman-Kiyak, 2005). Cohen (2000) asserted that some biological systems may decline due to overall wear and tear as cells and organs weaken. Deterioration of brain cells can happen in the aging process, but it is not conclusive that deterioration is debilitating. Indeed, the fact that a person has achieved a degree of maturity signifies that they exhibit the ability to survive and adapt to the situations around them. The aging process has already created a number of brain cell pathways that the individual can tap into. "Advanced age, in any species, signifies an individual with the strength and smarts to survive" (Cohen, 2000, p. 43). Currently, individuals are generally living longer and their quality of life in most areas of life is progressively improving (Hooyman & Asuman-Kiyak, 2005).

Psychological Issues

Psychological changes over time "not only shape our emotions, thinking, behavior, and overall identity, but also influence our creative potential" (Cohen, 2000, p. 69). Csikszentmihalyi (1996) noted two basic types of mental abilities. The first is called "fluid intelligence," which is the ability to "respond rapidly [by] computing fast and accurately" (p. 213). The second type is called "crystallized intelligence" which "involves making sensible judgments, recognizing similarities across different categories [and] using induction and logical reasoning" (p. 213). Csikszentmihalyi asserted that fluid intelligence tends to decline with age, while crystallized intelligence increases with age: identity is linked to crystallized intelligence.

Social Issues

Through the aging process, relationships are formed (Hooyman & Asuman-Kiyak, 2005). These relationships shape our community and link us to ideas, values, and rituals within the community (Anderson & Milbrandt, 2005). In this context, the aging process connects us to our community. This collective perspective provides a structure where a sense of identity and belonging begin. From the personal perspective, the aging process is a time when individuals cultivate personal selfhood and identity by having the courage to take risks and making the choice to take that risk (Greenspan & Shanker, 2004).

Spiritual Issues

Individuals yearn to feel that they belong and are connected in some way to others, the earth, and/or to a higher power (Corr, Nabe, & Corr, 2006). This yearning leads to a belief system that transcends personal knowledge and experience by helping an individual create meaning about life. Though abstract, spirituality aids in defining purpose and meaning. As we age, it is not always clear what our meaning and purpose are, yet there is an order about being connected to self, others, and the world which helps us decipher the role we play in this life.

The Role of Adversity

When adversity challenges us, whether it is physical, psychological, social, and/or spiritual, we are prompted to find relief in some way (Cohen, 2000). The act of searching for resolution accesses creative abilities (Cohen, 2000; Frankl, 1984; May, 1975; Sartre, 1957). Cohen (2000) said "adversity holds the potential for creativity … whether we use our creative energy to produce tangible works of art, activism that changes our society or new perspectives that change our lives" (p. 183).

The aging process is a culmination of integrating that which we know with that which we do not know. In the continuum of life, everyone faces that similar task: integrating that which is known with something that is not known. This integration then becomes a building block to explore new ways of doing things. The adversity faced in each area challenges an individual to find personal meaning and resolution (Bayles & Orland, 1993; Sartre, 1957). It requires the individual to creatively confront adversity and proactively deal with its consequences.

Existentialism and Phenomenology

The theory that I have developed is based on existentialism and phenomenological inquiry. A central theme in existentialism is authenticity. Authenticity means one is open and honest with the self and others (Sartre,

1957), which allows the individual to be open to a full range of experiences. Understanding and interpreting experiences gives personal context. Sartre's existentialism asserts that when an individual is born, that individual exists before he/she has essence (Kamber, 2000). Sartre (in Kaufmann, 1975) wrote "man first of all exists, encounters himself, surges up in the world—and defines himself" (p. 349). The notion of defining oneself occurs through the action of making choices. These choices sculpt the essence of the human being as he/she exists (Kaufmann, 1975). The process of reminiscing life experiences, contributions, and highlighted events helps an individual solidify meaning.

Phenomenology has its origins with Husserl (Gubrium & Holstein, 2000; Scruton, 2002), who made two assertions. The first is that experience constitutes knowledge; and, the second is that meaning is derived from the experienced knowledge (Scruton, 2002). Relative to the aging process, accumulated experience and knowledge form context and structure to assess and derive meaning for an individual.

Spiegelberg (1965) noted three characteristics to phenomenology: intuiting, analyzing, and describing. Intuiting is recalling a phenomenon by becoming consciously aware of it—almost as if one relives the experience. This can be done through reminiscing. Analyzing is examining the experience and understanding the dynamics of how it relates to the self. This can be done by acknowledging the experience and exploring the specific characteristics that make the experience important. Describing is accomplished by communicating these understandings so that it is clear to the self and others, including the magnitude and meaning of the experience. This can be done by documenting these understandings through writing, and/or illustrations and/or through music.

Method

The participants in the study included women with varying backgrounds, all in hospice programs. Using the semi-structured interview format, each participant was asked to tell one highlighted story about her life and to create an illustration about that story, which could be either representational or abstract. Each participant was encouraged to use the medium of her choice. Their art generally incorporated multiple achievements from their lives. At the conclusion of the study, the participants and their loved ones collaboratively created a collage depicting their shared reminiscences. Each collage symbolized the joys, adversity, growth, and values that demonstrate their individual determination, creativity, and resiliency.

One participant, Ella, was 88 years old at the time, had heart problems, and lived in an assisted living facility. Ella grew up on a rural dairy farm without much money. She told a story about being an adolescent and admiring the embroidery work of an elderly neighbor. Ella has always been left-hand dominant, which made it difficult for the right-handed neighbor to teach her. After Ella learned how to embroider, she not only did it for enjoyment, but also to decorate her farmhouse.

Eventually, Ella would sell her work or donate it to her church to be used for fund-raising. She became well-known for her colorful and intricate design work. At age 85, Ella suffered a stroke that paralyzed her left side. Determined to continue embroidering, she taught herself how to embroider using her right hand with the help of an adaptive device that braced and framed the fabric. (Figure 1)

Figure 2 is an example of Ella's embroidery using her right (non-dominant) hand.

Figure 1. Ella demonstrating the adaptive device used after her stroke.

Figure 2. An example of Ella's post-stroke embroidery.

Ella and her family also included embroidery exhibits produced throughout her life in the collage that they collaboratively created as part of my study.

Figure 3. The collage Ella and her loved ones created. (Personally-identifying information has been deleted by the author.)

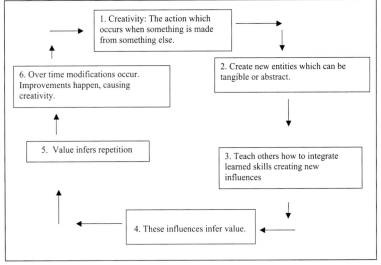

1. Creativity: The action which occurs when something is made from something else.

2. Create new entities which can be tangible or abstract.

3. Teach others how to integrate learned skills creating new influences

4. These influences infer value.

5. Value infers repetition

6. Over time modifications occur. Improvements happen, causing creativity.

Table 1. The Creative Process Over Time.

Results and Theory

The theory that emerged from this investigation is that creativity is inspirational, which fosters self-sufficiency and the nurturing of others. The tangible items that resulted from using a person's creative abilities have two purposes. The first is that they are functional, and the second is that they strengthen values.

The first step begins with the inspiration for someone to create something. The embroidery of the elderly neighbor inspired Ella to emulate her. Ella was so motivated, she believed that she might have the ability to embroider creatively. This belief was rooted in the social relationship that Ella had with her neighbor.

The second step of this process emphasizes the act of appreciating the entity's usefulness or potential. Ella not only admired the neighbor's work, she was genuinely interested in learning how to create herself. She possessed the psychological self-confidence and willingness to risk failure so that she could master the skills necessary to create her own work.

The third step is for the skill to be learned. Ella was taught how to embroider by the person whose work inspired her. Biological pathways were formed which allowed her not only to formulate an overall plan for her creation but also to develop the dexterity to accomplish her vision.

The fourth step is for others to recognize the value in what was created. Ella first used her work to decorate her farmhouse. Eventually, others came to admire her work and Ella was asked by parishioners to donate her work for fundraising.

The fifth step advocates repetition, which strengthens value. Ella enjoyed creating her embroidery and was supported in doing so. Others expressed the value of her work not only through their admiration for it, but also in a more tangible way. They were willing to exchange their money for her creations. These interactions were both social and spiritual. They helped Ella find her place in the greater order of her community and thus her world.

She has also taught others how to embroider. Teaching others creates a baseline and helps impart skills and information from one generation to the next, in a sense giving spiritual immortality to Ella's creativeness. Repetition occurred in two ways, first for herself when she continued making more items, and second in teaching others.

The sixth step asserts that over time, adjustments and modifications occur, oftentimes as the result of adversity. Ella's stroke paralyzed her dominant hand. Rather than abandon her passion for embroidering, she exhibited her ability to create new biological pathways demonstrating that the fluid intelligence could be learned even at an advanced age as referenced by Csikszentmihalyi (1996). Ella taught herself how to embroider with her non-dominant hand, overcoming the psychological and physical challenges of a stroke and demonstrating that aging can be a time for improvement rather than decline in spite of adversity.

Throughout her life, Ella expressed her values through her embroidery. Over time, the influences that shaped her values were passed on to loved ones. From an individual perspective, she first learned to embroider for her own enjoyment. This evolved into sharing her creations with her community, a community focus.

Implications for Social Justice

The implications for social justice occur on two different levels: individual and social. On the individual level, older adults, right up to life's end, can and frequently do maintain their faculties, including their creativity, spiritual development, and a drive to be productive. All her life, Ella nurtured her creative development by following her desire and passion to embroider. Her spiritual development flourished through her own satisfaction of her work as well as from the admiration and recognition of others. Ella took great pride in her work. Though the stroke caused a devastating loss of mobility to her dominant side, Ella's desire and passion to embroider did not diminish. At age 85, through her own tenacity and resiliency, and with the support of others, Ella adapted by teaching herself how to embroider using her non-dominant hand.

On the social level, those connected to the individual are impacted by the circumstances and decisions that the individual makes. Ella used her creativity and resiliency to continue to be productive, which added value to her life and to those around her. Ella's values, tenacity, and resiliency influenced and inspired others. One family member said that she was impressed with Ella's achievement and that Ella was an inspiration for her. We learn from others as we cultivate and nurture our own creativity, spiritual development, and the drive to be productive. We then have the opportunity to integrate what we have learned from others into our own lives.

Conclusion

Creative expression is fundamental to each culture (Anderson & Milbrandt, 2005). As we age, biological, psychological, social, and spiritual changes bring evolutionary changes to our creative process. Aging can be a process for improvement and not simply a time of decline. Creativity does not necessarily deteriorate with age. In fact the aging process can strengthen the desire to overcome challenges, even at the end-stage of life. As we face of adversity in the biological, psychological, social, and spiritual areas of life, we adapt by continuing to nurture and develop creativity and personal development. We are social beings and need the support of others. The dignity we have for ourselves and the respect that others have for us provide support. As we influence others, and others influence us, a bond occurs that may extend beyond what we will completely understand during our life. Our choices, actions, and creative energy can impact future generations. Creative expression is a vital component of a healthy aging process. The obvious implication for those who are invested both in facilitating the aged and social justice is to create and foster opportunities for creative expression. In this way the elderly can continue to be a vital part of society right up until death, contributing to and benefiting from society, rather than being sidelined, as sadly so many now are.

Anderson, T., & Milbrandt, M. (2005). *Art for life: Authentic instruction in art.* Boston: McGraw-Hill.

Bayles, D., & Orland, T. (1993). *Art and fear: Observations on the perils (and rewards) of artmaking.* Santa Cruz, CA: The Image Continuum.

Cohen, G. (2000). *The creative age: Awakening human potential in the second half of life.* New York: HarperCollins.

Corr, C. A., Nabe, C. M., & Corr, D. M. (2006). *Death and dying, life and living* (5th ed.). Belmont, CA: Wadsworth/Thomson Learning.

Csikszentmihalyi, M. (1996). *Creativity: Flow and the psychology of discovery and invention.* New York: Harper Perennial.

Erikson, J. (1988). *Wisdom and the senses: The way to creativity.* New York: W.W. Norton & Company.

Frankl, V. E. (1984). *Man's search for meaning.* New York: Pocket Books.

Greenspan, S. I., & Shanker, S. G. (2004). *The first idea: How symbols, language, and intelligence evolved from our primate ancestors to modern humans.* Cambridge, MA: Da Capo Press.

Gubrium, J. F., & Holstein, J. A. (2000). Analyzing interpretive practice. In N. K. Denzin & Y. S. Lincoln (Eds.), *Handbook of qualitative research* (2nd ed., pp. 487–508). Thousand Oaks, CA: Sage Publications.

Hooyman, N. R., & Asuman-Kiyak, H. (2005). *Social gerontology: A multidisciplinary perspective* (7th ed.). Boston: Pearson.

Kamber, R. (2000). *On Sartre.* Belmont, CA: Wadsworth/Thomson Learning.

Kaufmann, W. (Ed.). (1975). *Existentialism: From Dostoevsky to Sartre.* New York: Penguin.

May, R. (1975). *The courage to create.* New York: W.W. Norton & Company.

Sartre, J. P. (1957). *Existentialism and human emotions.* New York: The Wisdom Library.

Scruton, R. (2002). *A short history of modern philosophy.* New York: Routledge.

Spiegelberg, H. (1965). *The phenomenological movement.* The Hague, Netherlands: Martinus Nijhoff.

K-12
FOCUS

An Environmental Art Project for Children with At-Risk Tendencies: The *Eco-Wall of Hope*

Michelle Creel

Introduction

Presently, I teach at Oakland Terrace Elementary School for the Visual and Performing Arts. This school meets the federal guidelines for Title I eligibility. Due to poverty, low self-esteem, lack of social skills, and motivation, students are in danger of dropping out of school if their needs go unmet. Oakland Terrace has a 73% mobility rate and 85% free or reduced lunch. Most students live in "the projects," lack parental support, exhibit little interest in academic achievement, feel negatively toward school, have inadequate social skills, and experience very low self-esteem resulting in aggressive and impulsive behaviors. Some are in gangs and have been arrested; they generally have no faith in systems. Life is about survival. In order to cope they learned a different set of skills and behaviors than more privileged children. So how can they be helped?

In trying to answer this question, it struck me that perhaps on some level we are all at-risk, all endangered. These students are endangered in many of the same ways that creatures and habitats are endangered. Yet, how can a connection be made that these students and many creatures are deprived of living healthy, productive lives? How can they recognize that connection and their place in the larger scheme of things? If we assume that "survival" and "at-risk" are common concepts to all species, I decided an answer might lie in the development of empathy through an ecological theme-based curriculum. Potentially, learning about issues that confront the environment and threaten its very existence may lead to personal

> ## KEY CONCEPTS
> - Interdisciplinary Environmental Art Curriculum
> - Participatory Action Research
> - At-Risk Children
> - Empathetic Development
> - Endangered Species

understanding, empathy, and action. Creating art around ecology-related problems may be useful as a first step toward students taking responsible action in their personal lives and in the larger environment. In this context, the study presented in this chapter examined empathetic behaviors in the context of an environmentally centered art curriculum designed to foster caring behaviors, resulting in a product we called the *Eco-Wall of Hope*. An important intention of this project was to foster students' empathy for each other and for the animals they studied. The hope was that this kernel of empathy would grow to encompass students' personal and social growth both in and beyond school.

I hoped this study would stimulate students' empathetic behaviors toward each other and other species in the environment, rising from the aesthetically caring activities. Through the results I also hoped to encourage educators and inspire teachers to implement curriculum that would provide opportunities for children to show compassion and empathy toward each other, other species, and the environment. In this chapter I will first present the context for this study, the methods employed to conduct the study and project, the steps necessary to complete the Eco-Wall of Hope, the interactions and camaraderie that developed between the participants, and a discussion on its implications.

Setting

Oakland Terrace School for the Visual and Performing Arts is located in an older neighborhood in Panama City, Florida. The school's mission is to foster lifelong learning in all students by promoting creativity and excellence in academics, character education, and fine arts, to prepare them to be productive, ethical, and responsible citizens.

Population

Oakland Terrace has approximately 440 students, 46% of which comprises minorities, mainly African American, Hispanic, and Asian students. The group that worked on the *Eco-Wall of Hope* project included about 20 third-grade, 18 fourth-grade, and 22 fifth-grade students. These students worked with approximately 10 high school students and briefly interacted with kindergarten and preschool students who were not centrally involved in the project. To further explore the effectiveness of the project, I selected 4 fourth-grade students, who became known as the core group, to interview.

Curriculum

To focus on the goal of empathy development, a multidisciplinary, environmental art project, entitled *Eco-Wall of Hope*, was developed that addressed the issue of endangered species and challenged students to work on solutions to the problems that caused their endangerment. Students incorporated research, science, literacy, social responsibility, writing, and art in this project. There were several components of the project. After critiquing artworks by artists who focused on environmental issues, children chose an endangered animal to research and used this animal as the subject of ceramic tiles they created. Poems and prose were written to accompany each tile. In the writing, students were asked to vicariously become their selected animal so that they might imagine another perspective, that of the animal selected. With 10 at-risk high school students helping to guide them, the children combined the tiles to create the *Eco-Wall of Hope*. Students then reflected on the experience in their journals about their interactions with the high school students, with their groups, and in their art activities to document social and artistic processes. It was thought that such reflection may help students validate their experiences while providing important insight into students' reactions.

Method

Participatory action research was the primary, overarching strategy of this study (Kemmis & McTaggart, 2000). The end goal was insight that would improve my own teaching and programs. Because I was actively engaged with my students, I inevitably connected personal thoughts and experiences with the thoughts and experiences of students as they were involved in projects. In order to acquire knowledge and understanding of participants and establish a partnership between us as equal agents for social change, I took a discovery-oriented approach that placed no prior constraints on outcomes, while I simultaneously looked for layers of meaning and multiple perspectives from the processes and products we developed.

As a participant observer, I monitored verbal and nonverbal dynamics between participants, collected field notes, photographed the progress, looked at films of these interactions, and reflected on the results. Additionally, I interviewed 4 selected students, the so-called core group, in order to understand the participants' personal experiences and perspectives, allowing me to contextualize my observations. I chose 4 students from the fourth-grade group to study in depth, chosen because they seemed most excited and dedicated to the project. These students were Frankie, Alexis, Kyree, and Jeffery. Open-ended interviews were used in order for the intricacies of the situation to emerge as participant meanings. In using various methods to better understand multiple perceptions and meanings, or triangulating the collection of data (Stake, 2000), the possibility of misinterpreting the resultant information was diminished.

Ultimately, the goal of this study was to discover and understand the nature of experiences and the meanings attached to them by the participants, focusing on their empathetic understanding and actions; I wanted to understand if and how the *Eco-Wall of Hope* and subsequent interactions facilitated the development of empathy.

Point of View

Based on my personal experience as an art educator, and my involvement with children with at-risk tendencies, I believe there is much our children, particularly at-risk children, require. Centrally, many children who lack empathic awareness also feel devalued. At-risk youth and our environment, both injured, face similar problems and threats, and it seemed to me that it is possible that devaluing nature and each other have roots in the same alienation from empathy. So maybe students would benefit from the development of a vehicle to develop an ethical foundation, a personal moral consciousness, and empathy. I wanted to explore this connection to empathy through a communal, environmental art project for my at-risk students. I anticipated that implementing an environmental arts curriculum might inspire children to learn and practice empathy, and thus encourage their development into socially successful adults. I believe that an emphasis on ecology, which focuses on the needs of other sentient beings through art, might help to reach at-risk children so that they might begin to value themselves, each other, and the world. I hoped this study would help me understand, in part, how children can exhibit empathy through participating in art education for environmental consciousness and social justice.

Preliminary Tasks

I applied for two grants that might fund the project. I presented my project concepts to Dr. Stephanie Gall, the principal. Because she is a visionary and an incredible leader, and is always supportive of others' dreams, I was not surprised when she became excited about the project and gave it her full support. Within a few months we were notified the grants were awarded. I contacted Cyndee Smith, a high school art teacher, to collaborate and involve her students who displayed at-risk tendencies, to serve as mentors. I ordered materials, wrote lesson plans, and contacted district brick masons to build the safe wall.

Processes, Issues, and Personalities

The ideas and goals of the *Eco-Wall of Hope* project were explained to the students. They were asked to have their guardians complete and return the permission forms; those few students who did not return the forms were not included in the results of this study.

Portfolios and paper were distributed to the students; they were told that everything they did for the project should be kept inside this portfolio. The students were next shown images of art created by artists who engage environmental themes: Nancy Holt's *Sun Tunnels* (Matilsky, 1992), Andy Goldsworthy's *Soul of a Tree*, Mel Chin's *Passenger Pigeon* (Matilsky, 1992), and Joseph Beuys' *Coyote: I Like America and America Likes Me* (Matilsky, 1992). I asked students to write down their initial impressions, with the hope that students would identify with these artists who create art to promote awareness about ecological issues to prompt change in peoples' perception toward the environment and creatures.

Then using Anderson's (2000) art criticism methodology, a discussion was initiated on students' initial impressions, visual descriptions, internal description, and interpretations of what they saw. Offering students art criticism exercises often helps them discover that all art is available for interpretation. After the critiques, each fifth-grade student chose one endangered animal that they would represent on the *Eco-Wall of Hope*. Resources about animals were available, including books and calendars. The students were shown examples of tiles, received pencils and were told that 10 high school students would be coming to help them create clay tiles, so they needed a drawing to transfer to the tile. This motivated the students. This lesson was repeated with 17 fourth-grade students and 19 third-grade students.

Students quickly decided which creature they would represent on their tiles. They researched and documented facts about their chosen animals. As the students drew their chosen images, they were asked to consider the questions: "How do you want to portray your animal?" and "How might the meaning of an animal portrait differ from depicting an animal within a landscape?" Issues such as animals as beasts-of-burden, food sources, hunted animals, endangered species, and cultural differences were considered. The students seemed excited and seemed to have a sense of shared purpose and anticipation. Some of the animal portraits seemed to emphasize individual personalities. Other drawings, which depicted an animal frozen or in action within a detailed environment, seemed more illustrative.

After colored pencils were placed on tables, the outcome seemed to change. For example, Jeffery drew a baby elephant. The line was immediate, continuous, and direct, showing the elephant's tough, fragile beauty. He added water by the elephant's feet with soft, tall grass at the water's edge. In the corner was a smooth rock where a lizard happily dozed. He used a regular pencil to color the elephant, shading the belly. The sky was deep red with violet hues to create wind-clouds. Cerulean water and ochre grass enhanced the drawing. The students were highly complimentary of Jeffery's drawing. Although he is frequently bullied, Jeffery seems to gain recognition in the art room. But he had difficulty concentrating and was forgetful. He'd been held back twice and was tutored daily to help him pass the Florida Comprehensive Assessment Test. For 3 years, Jeffery had been a willing morning helper, and had enjoyed the art process. For 2 weeks, rather than going to tutoring, he came to the art room, unauthorized. After this was discovered, Jeffery was promised that he could stay after school and do extra projects after he completed his FCAT. Not surprisingly, Jeffery was involved in almost every aspect of the wall.

The High School Students' First Visit. Ten high school student mentors arrived early one morning with their teacher, Ms. Smith. They brought their own tiles they had made as examples and gifts for the wall. As they dragged in heavy boxes of clay already formed into slabs, they looked nervous and vulnerable. They would work with three classes that day.

It is always surprising to me how responsive my kids are to high school students. My students were polite and quiet as they intently (and seemingly adoringly) watched the high school students. The high school students paired up with the younger ones and immediately became their teachers, artists, and mentors. It did not take them long to become acquainted, and they all seemed to interact well as they created tiles together.

Deto, whose life is saturated with craziness and is at the mercy of his own restless storm, had cozied up to Vincent, a Latino high school student. As they talked, they worked steadily. Deto smiled several times, which is rare. Deto's drawing on his clay slab, a portrait of a tiger, was delightful, a bit frisky and adorably cartoonish, and he even added a rainbow on the tile. It seemed obvious that Vincent was a positive influence on Deto.

Despite the positive atmosphere, there were a few students who were frustrated. Kyree, a fourth-grade core student, could not seem to get the drawing on his tile just right, and appeared exasperated. Kyree was a talented young violinist with a strong bow arm, who was gentle, polite, helpful to teachers and students, and a perfectionist. This resulted in a general unwillingness to take chances. Eventually, with a bit of encouragement and several compliments from his peers, Kyree finally completed a delightful dragon-snake tile. Alexis, another core student, drew a manatee on her tile. She was smart, gregarious, artistic, quick-witted, and was sensitive of others' feelings. She was quick to help other students with disabilities.

All three classes that involved the high school students were successful, ending with much activity and chatter. The students were excited to see the completed pieces as they placed their tiles onto trays. I thanked the high school kids at the end of the third class. They would join the younger students again in 2 weeks to attach the finished tiles on the wall. In the meantime, the masons would erect the 5 x 10 ft. cement wall while the younger students would write poems and glaze their tiles and write about when they helped someone, or felt empathy. They discussed personal survival issues and compared them with endangered animals. They also glazed their tiles. Also during this period I tested the adhesive that would be used to affix the tile to the wall. All seemed well.

Overall, it seemed that the high school and elementary students benefited from the interactions. The older students became teachers, art coaches, and mentors as they collaborated with the younger students. Much of the meaning of the *Eco-Wall of Hope* was not only its focus on endangered species, but also the collaboration with peers and high school mentors. Ms. Smith, the high school art teacher, commented that her students' experiences had been beneficial for the at-risk students, particularly for Vincent, who "became more engaging. He came to class everyday, his demeanor more positive, and he was more polite and respectful to others." After the initial visit of high school students, Ms. Smith indicated that her students had an "earnest desire to return. They exhibited a real commitment to the project and moreover to the younger students."

The High School Students' Second Visit. Only 9 high school students arrived the second time. Despite Ms. Smith's previous positive reports about Vincent, he had been expelled. Deto was noticeably upset and at first refused to participate. Eventually, he was encouraged to participate. The high school students praised the children's completed tiles as they were carried outside to the erected wall. Together, the students categorized and arranged tiles on the ground. The younger students were less shy, chummier, but the high school students still maintained a mentorship role. They opened the bucket of adhesive and took charge. "Stand in line with a sea-tile," one girl said. "We'll put on the adhesive and you can put them on the wall." The students placed the sea-tiles on the bottom row and held them in place. Six students, crowded side-by-side, pressed their tiles on the wall. Adhesive squeezed out around tiles. After a few minutes some students let go and slowly their tiles slid down. "Whatever it is, it ain't magic," Kyree said as he watched his tile hit the ground. We tried to hold those tiles on that wall, but gravity was against us.

Eventually, the impatient and discouraged students lost their focus and began to run around. As I stubbornly kept trying to press on the uncooperative tiles and verbally redirect the progressively wilder children, I reminded

Students pressing tiles on the wall.

myself that play is the foundation of emotional and psychological development. Although I was relieved when class ended, the younger students were disappointed that the older ones would not be returning. It was sweet to see them shake hands and hug farewell. However, we would have to complete the wall by ourselves.

Technically and emotionally I felt the day had been a disaster. However, despite the technical failures, students had initially worked well together to design the wall's composition. They categorized, arranged, and attached the tiles to the wall. As the tiles slid down, most students tried to hold each other's in place by grabbing sticks to prop them in place or, with spread arms, pressing two tiles at once. Most students recognized they were a necessary part of a whole and their commitment and contribution to the project's success was important. Ms. Smith pointed out, "Everyone frantically banded together trying so desperately to remedy the situation. Hands, feet, and objects were used to secure the dripping tiles onto the vertical wall. Certainly," she concluded, "the crisis brought about cohesion."

Reevaluation and Changes. Later that day, Frankie, a core participant, came to the art room to help scrape adhesive off the tiles and wall. She was perceptibly quiet. An independent and fearless student, I could count on Frankie. Her parents, excellent role models, drive out of the area in which they are zoned so that Frankie could come to our school and associate with kids who are less fortunate. She helped me the remainder of the day. After school I spoke to a professional, and discovered I had the wrong kind of adhesive. After I purchased the new adhesive and arrived home, there was a message from Frankie's father. He wanted to help.

Student arranging tiles.

The next afternoon Frankie's father and Steve Penney, a wood-carver, came to the school. Mr. Penney, scheduled to come the following week to carve a bear for the school, suggested we put the tiles on wood boards and bolt them into the wall. He offered to prepare the wood and wall, which he accomplished quickly. After Mr. Penney delivered the boards, Frankie,

Alexis, Kyree, and Jeffery stayed after school to arrange and glue the tiles to the newly constructed boards. Working on the floor allowed gravity to help. The kids, particularly Frankie and Alexis, were serious and competitive about the strategic placement of the tiles.

The following week Mr. Penney returned to the school to bolt the completed boards to the wall. The next morning a kindergarten teacher exclaimed, "That tile wall is awesome!" Jeffery, who overheard this compliment, beamed with pride. A little later Frankie rushed through the door. "It's spectacular and not one (tile) fell down on the ground yet." She was half laughing and playful. Collectively, the tiles had evolved into a visual metaphor, poetry of parts and wholes, of rebirth and revival.

Eco-Wall of Hope.

Writings from the *Eco-Wall of Hope*

As I mentioned, the literary arts were also incorporated into the art curriculum whenever possible. Students wrote poems or stories about their endangered species. A few chose to pretend to be an animal penned in a box or cage and described their imagined experiences. Some choose to write haikus, while others wrote about how they felt about their creature, about a time when they had helped someone or experienced empathy. Students were encouraged to work together and read their writings aloud. Following are examples of students' works, each influenced by a different set of circumstances and complexities.

Sensory Tile-Poems

Tile of Dragon
By: Kyree
Me, watching the sun turn into the moon, dead silent.
Slowly the sun gets coal black.
What a nice sight it was.
Cricket! Cricket!
My house in the distance where
New grass is coming up.
This makes me feel like I have more patience.
Concentrating. Watching stuff.

Tile of a Manatee
By: Alexis
Manatees, so loving and gentle.
Boats scar and kill them.
Imagine swimming,
Baby manatees all around you,
Their gentle touch to you,
Your hand against their flipper.
Save manatees!
Let them be free!

Daylight
By: Erika
My first memory was where my happy
place in my mind was heaven,
pink like a heart.
Inside a closed box
Is too dark,
Like a time of war.
Too dark to have
A good heart.
It would be good to see daylight,
Because it was so night.

Haikus

Black Panther
By: Chyna
Black Panther stretches
Against white rough river rock
River flows to see.

Tree-Wolf
By: Ciara
Arms tickle gray.
Screaming through all hearts and souls.
Every bark like mans.'

A Student's Personal Empathy Story

Doug's Story
Once I saved a girl in a ditch. The water had almost sucked her into a tunnel. I was playing basketball with a friend. I heard someone scream, "Help!" My friend and I went over. A girl was trying to hang on to the bottom of the tunnel, but she couldn't hang on because the water was rushing. I climbed on the side of the ditch and me and my friend jumped into the ditch where there was a little stump-stick poking up. The girl stepped on the stump and we pulled her up. As we walked her home, she said, "Thank you." The mom gave us ten dollars each for saving her daughter. I bought a new skateboard.

To me, the writing was evident of the children's enormous capacity for empathy. Their words are sensitive and have layers of complex meaning. The intention of the writing was to motivate students to embrace their language and view writing as an extension of visual art and an important means of communication. I did note, in some of the writing, empathetic growth through their words as they were engaged in the project.

Reading to Kindergarten and Preschool Children with Disabilities

After the students finished their writings, they read them to the kindergarten and preschool children with disabilities. The students appeared more nurturing and mature as they interacted with the even younger children. This nurturing behavior in these students seemed to parallel the behavior of the high school students' caring behaviors described by Ms. Smith. I was proud of their sensitivity and compassion. As the students read to the younger children, they became involved. Providing such opportunities could help them to know what it feels like to be a good citizen and an important part of society. In this aspect of the study, social interaction and cooperative learning played a fundamental role in the students' learning process (Vygotsky, 1978). If one of the goals of education is to help our children become good citizens, the whole idea of belonging to a society is critical.

Conclusions

From the project to real life, it seems that most of the children who participated in this project benefited from environmental art curriculum for empathy, within that framework. They also had what I took to be a valuable experience in integrating arts and academics. This project seems to me to have been more relevant to the children's lives, more enjoyable and challenging, through the integration of the real world problem of endangered species to foster empathy than rote, pre-circumscribed curricula. In addition, incorporating community members and high school students into the learning process, and facilitating the older elementary students to read to the younger ones provided opportunities to enhance empathy and social skills, and seems to increase self-esteem across the board. Generally, there seemed to be more compassion and empathy exhibited by the students who participated in this project than they usually demonstrated in other art activities, although I didn't see much evidence of transfer to other activities and it is not clear if there is a long-term effect. A long-term study would need to be done to see any longitudinal results.

Art encourages creativity, emotional expression, appreciation of diversity, and social skills that enable alternative perceptions and multiple perspectives that enhance the awareness and acceptance of the differences in others (Gardner, 1994). In this context, art experiences seem to me to be a natural way to foster empathy, to allow students to imagine themselves from another perspective, in this case another at-risk sentient being. This may also extend to the group process in the sense that most participants were able to connect with one another meaningfully during the project. As students worked in close proximity with each other to reach common goals, the majority were cooperative; they shared responsibilities, voluntarily helped others, shared their knowledge, skills, and tools with one another, comforted each other, and listened attentively. In short, the students were caring and empathic.

Thus, as art teachers develop art curriculum and lessons, it may be useful and important to develop strategies for enhancing the capacity for children to experience and practice empathy as a way to prevent antisocial behaviors, as a way to counter some factors causing children to be at risk. In this schema it is important to remember that adults who work with children are the role models, and there are many ways for them to demonstrate compassion and empathy. Many at-risk children have become desensitized because of their challenging lives. So it is incumbent on teachers not only to develop curricula fostering empathy but also to act with and model empathy in the performance of those curricula. Such actions may create ripple effects in the pool of violence in which many of our children exist.

REFERENCES

Anderson, T. (2000). Using art criticism strategies in ethnographic research. *Visual Arts Research, 26,* 80–83.

Gardner, H. (1994). *The arts and human development.* New York: Basic Books.

Kemmis, S. & McTaggart, R. (2000). Participatory action research. *Handbook of qualitative research.* Thousand Oaks, CA: Sage Publications.

Matilsky, B. (1992). *Fragile ecologies; Contemporary artists' interpretations and solutions.* New York: Rizzoli International Publications.

Stake, R. E. (2000). Case studies. *Handbook of qualitative research.* Thousand Oaks, CA: Sage Publications.

Vygotsky, L. S. (1978). *Mind and Society: The development of higher psychological processes.* Cambridge, MA: Harvard University Press.

Catching Time: Documentary Photography and Social Reflection

Miriam Davidson

Introduction

The warm air of summer holidays permeated the atmosphere at Coronation Elementary School in the Côte-des-Neiges district of Montreal. As the year came to a close, I prepared for an exhibition of photographs and writing created by the children of Room 24. During our time together, I taught these fourth-grade students how to use their cameras to document their families and their community. They learned to print their own black-and-white photos, turned their images into stories, and created handmade books and mixed media self-portraits (Davidson, 2000). Additionally we spent countless hours reflecting on the images they produced by talking and writing about them. As we prepared to celebrate their work that late June afternoon, I asked the children to share their thoughts about photography and what they enjoyed most about taking pictures.

As many of these students struggled with writing, we composed a few standard beginnings to sentences to get them started, such as "I like photography because ..." or, "If you could see through my eyes, I'd show you ..." Armed with these simple openings the children wrote with far less fear and anxiety. Boris considered a series of photographs he made of his mother and wrote: "If you could see through my eyes, I'd show you a picture of my mom, because she gives me good lunches." Then Bryan, a thoughtful, energetic boy who struggled to focus his attention, wrote: "I like photography because we get to take our own pictures and we get to catch time." When Bryan proudly read these words aloud, I was struck

by the compelling metaphor he had created for the act of photography. With this phrase, Bryan had summed up what photography has always meant for me: a way to "catch time," to hold on to instances that so quickly pass out of experience, to freeze those moments for future consideration, for mental travel or memories held.

I borrow Bryan's words for the title of this chapter, as much to honor his insights as to give shape and meaning to an approach to art education where documentary practices are central. Over the years, I have invited many diverse and dynamic communities of learners to use their cameras to catch time in their homes, their neighborhoods, and their schools. I have continued to explore the ways that photography, in conjunction with creative writing and oral history collection, enables young people to bring their personal histories and real world experience into the classroom and the community. Catching time not only relates to the practice of photography, but is descriptive of many hours spent fostering relationships and constructing learning environments where documentary practices work in tandem with an approach to teaching that respects, values, and encourages student voices (Ashton-Warner, 1963; Fried, 2001; hooks, 1994; Noddings, 1992; Shor, 1992).

The accessibility of photography and its connection to the world outside the classroom through popular genres such as sports, journalism, and fashion make it a familiar and relevant medium, and to a greater extent than most other visual media photography carries with it the democratic potential to empower and represent the experience of everyday life (Buckingham

& Sefton-Green, 1994). The photographic process also allows beginners to make complex images with relatively little experience and instruction, and photographs are easily combined with other media and often experienced in connection with stories and other forms of written text. My love for photography as a means of contemplating the world, in conjunction with observing students' immediate excitement when working in a photographic medium, provided the impetus to employ the camera as an integral tool in much of my work in school and community settings.

The documentary projects I facilitate are designed to address a number of unique yet interrelated issues, including student disengagement, strengthening literacy skills, and building intergenerational or intercultural understanding. Although similar tools and approaches are explored with each new group of students, their unique interests and challenges drive the direction, rhythm, and specifics of each project. The images and stories created by project participants often provide a dramatic contrast to stereotypical representations of minority, immigrant, economically disadvantaged, or other marginalized communities. This approach is informed and inspired by teachers, artists, and scholars who have made explicit the value of asking young people to speak through images and words (Coles, 1995, 1998; Ewald, 1985, 1996, 2007; Hubbard, 1991, 1994). These individuals have created and supported grassroots documentary projects and encouraged learning opportunities that empower participants to become active researchers of their own experience.

The Roots of Documentary Photography as Social Activism

Children in North America commonly participate in the creation of photographic imagery at some point in their lives. They do so as consumers, as in the case of engaging with popular print and electronic media; as subjects, when they are included in family and school photographs; and increasingly in the role of the photographer, when using cell phones or other digital devices to make images. Notwithstanding this familiarity, few students are aware of the extensive history of photography and even fewer know anything about early documentarians whose photographs turned public attention toward the plight of those experiencing the ravages of war, poverty, and oppression. While it would be impossible to share the work of every artist whose photographs function as social commentary, it is important for project participants to gain some understanding of this rich history in order to contextualize their own documentary image-making

practices. To provide this foundation a number of key figures are introduced, including documentarians such as Civil War photographer Matthew Brady and early 20th-century artists like Jacob Riis and Lewis Hine, whose images of life in New York's urban tenements and of child laborers were instrumental in changing public perception and in some cases policy and laws. The force of this journalism of conscience continued into the 1930s with a new generation of photographers setting out to capture the plight of Americans during the Dust Bowl era.

Potent images by Arthur Rothstein, Dorothea Lange, Walker Evans, Marion Post Wolcott, Gordon Parks, and others provided tangible evidence of the struggles American families faced during the Depression (Stott, 1986). This body of work built a solid foundation on which contemporary documentary image-makers, such as Sabastião Salgado, Mary Ellen Mark, and Clare Richardson developed their unique approaches to visual storytelling. Learning of these photographic traditions, students begin to see the camera as a tool for expression and transformation, and they are inspired to tell their own stories and to view their work as connected to an enduring tradition of documentary photography as social action.

Documentary Photography: Truth or Propaganda?

Exploring this photographic history regularly includes the discussion of issues relating to representation, truth, and the role of the photographer in shaping the scene to his or her own purposes. For example, it is well known that Matthew Brady, Jacob Riis, Lewis Hine, and Depression-era Farm Securities Administration photographers, such as Walker Evans or Dorothea Lange, regularly took liberties in repositioning subjects, restaging scenes, and arranging lighting or composition so that each photograph was conducive to the social or political messages that they wanted to convey (Davis, 1989; Newhall, 1980; Trachtenberg, 1979).

Throughout their careers Roy Stryker (Director of the FSA photography project) and his team made every effort to insist that the photographs they took represented some real truth. However, even Stryker had to admit that the photographer's bias often entered into creating an image, making the photos part cultural record and part propaganda (Anderson, 1977). Susan Sontag (1977), in considering the veracity of photographs with a particular focus on the work of FSA photographers, indicated that:

…The immensely gifted members of the Farm Security Administration photographic project of the late 1930s … would take dozens of frontal pictures of one of their sharecropper subjects until satisfied that they had gotten just the right look on film—the precise expression on the subject's face that supported their own notions about poverty, light, dignity, texture, exploitation, and geometry. In deciding how a picture should look, in preferring one exposure to another, photographers are always imposing standards on their subjects. Although there is a sense in which the camera does indeed capture reality, not just interpret it, photographs are as much an interpretation of the world as paintings and drawings are. (p. 7)

Discussions with respect to the politics of representation, authenticity, and truth related to the photographic image lend additional credence to the argument for turning the camera over to the subject. When the camera is put into the hands of ordinary citizens, the accounts that emerge can be more genuine, multifaceted, and compelling than when outsiders try to record these same stories. By asking individuals to record, then to reflect on their lived experiences, they are empowered to tell their own stories their way. Point of view is a reality, perhaps even the point of all art forms. At least with first person documentary projects, the stories are their own.

The Growth of Photography as Pedagogy

By the 1970s, camera technology had advanced making inexpensive and user-friendly 35mm SLR cameras readily available. Despite the growing popularity of television news programming during this period, the still photograph continued to have a powerful impact on the public, especially through picture magazines such as *Look* (1936–1971) and *Life* (which remained popular in one form or another until as recently as 2000). These publications came of age in an era when photographic documentary traditions held an influential place in shaping the collective consciousness of Americans. A dramatic example of the relationship between photography and the social/political climate of this time is evident in the important role photojournalists played in supporting the peace movement.

A single photograph taken by Associated Press photographer Nick Ut, entitled *The Killing Fields*, published on the cover of *Time* magazine in 1972, became an iconic visual metaphor for the agony of war. This image embodies the suffering of the Vietnamese people through the wounded figure of a small girl. Images such as this fueled the peace movement of the 1970s and encouraged thousands to demand an end to the Vietnam War.

Nick Ut did everything in his power to make sure that the child he had photographed, Kim Phuc Phan Thi, obtained the medical care she required. Kim survived and eventually defected to Canada where she runs the *Kim Foundation International: Healing Children of War*. Nick Ut and Kim Phuc Phan Thi are still in contact today. To see a copy of this photograph and to learn more about this story, visit www.kimfoundation.com.

In keeping with this tradition of socially-minded documentary photography, a number of photographers, art educators, and community activists in Britain and the United States harnessed the potency of the photographic image and put it to work in a variety of educational and community contexts. Many of these early programs targeted segments of society who were disenfranchised due to economic downturns, racial, class, and social issues. One of the earliest and most successful community photography projects to emerge in Britain during this period was *Bootle—Art in Action*. Founded in 1978 in an effort to draw attention to the "dreadful social and environmental problems" of a North Liverpool neighborhood (Pinnington, 1986, p. 14), the mission of *Art in Action* was to encourage people of all ages to discover their own visual language and develop an awareness of their surroundings. These grassroots programs inform my approach to bringing the camera into the classroom and the community; in particular, the work of contemporary photo-educators Wendy Ewald and Jim Hubbard provide inspirational examples of what is possible.

An accomplished photographer and teacher, Wendy Ewald is currently Artist in Residence and Director of the Literacy through Photography Program at the Center for Documentary Studies at Duke University. In the early 1980s Ewald taught photography to a group of school children in Appalachia. Their work together culminated in a compelling book of images and stories entitled *Portraits and Dreams: Photographs and Stories by Children of the Appalachians* (Ewald, 1985). This book depicts, through visual and narrative means, the "complex and inspiring lives" (p. 5) of impoverished Appalachian children with an honesty and integrity that professional photographers would find difficult to match. Since the publication of this book and several others after it, Wendy Ewald continues to work with children from her local community in and around Durham, North Carolina, as well as throughout the world. Her projects entail asking children to create images that explore issues of class, race, work, and location, as well as more fictional works that are based on the children's dreams and imaginations.

Similarly Jim Hubbard, then a Washington, DC photojournalist, wondered what would happen if the homeless children he had photographed were provided with cameras and instruction and invited to tell their own stories. In 1989 he did just that by founding *Shooting Back, Inc.*, an education and media center bringing together volunteer professional photographers with homeless and other at-risk children. Using cameras on loan from the center, the children portrayed the world of the homeless shelter with great dignity, providing a more authentic and less marginalized picture of their lives. Notwithstanding the ongoing struggles of impoverished and homeless families throughout the world, these photographs effectively illustrate that life goes on with a sense of normalcy, even in these temporary and often inadequate living arrangements. For many of the children, their role as photographers gave them a new way to see themselves and to reflect on their own experiences and challenges. A collection of their work, entitled *Shooting Back: A Photographic View of Life by Homeless Children* (1991), has been used to lobby for improved programs and support for the homeless, and to educate school children and teachers about homelessness.

Jim Hubbard continues to develop new social-activist arts programs. He is currently Creative Director and Co-Founder of *Venice Arts in Neighborhoods*, an outstanding inner city arts enrichment organization featuring several grassroots photographic projects. In 2007 he was awarded the Lewis Hine Distinguished Service Award given by the National Child Labor Committee. On the *Venice Arts* website (www.venice-arts.org), Hubbard (2008) stresses, "When you give a child a camera, you give a child a voice."

Bringing History and Practice Together

In an era when young people are bombarded with fast-paced images, the still photograph continues to offer art educators a means to encourage students to slow down, observe, record, and reflect on their own experience. In my own work with young people, creating their photographic imagery is the starting point on a journey of social reflection through dialogue, writing, exhibition, and publication. Toward this end, I have developed several key activities to help guide the students' explorations. In the section that follows, I share one such example that resulted in the creation of a compelling series of portraits and oral histories.

Focus: Finding Oral Culture and Urban Stories

The following activities were designed and implemented from 2002 to 2005 while I was a faculty member in the Peck School of the Arts at the University of Wisconsin-Milwaukee (UWM). Milwaukee is a city challenged by a long history of racial segregation and contemporary poverty and violence. It is also a city with a vital and enduring tradition of grass-roots activism and community-based artistic practice. The many arts, cultural, and recreation centers around the city serve as sites where diverse individuals come together to build relationships and make positive contributions to their communities. It is in this complex and artistically rich context that the imagery and stories created by the young people who took part in *FOCUS (Finding Oral Culture and Urban Stories)* emerged and were shared with the public.

FOCUS, a title given to this project by the students themselves, spanned 2 years and involved students from Hartford University School for Urban Explorations, a K–8 public school in Milwaukee. At Hartford, African American students are in the majority; however there are also a significant number of Mexican American, Hmong, Asian American, and Caucasian students. The project participants ranged in age from 12–15 and were enrolled in grades 6–8. Preservice art education students from University of Wisconsin, Milwaukee (UWM) acted as assistant photography instructors, lab/darkroom technicians, curators, and mentors to the children.

Twelve to 16 students from Hartford School and their art teacher spent 2 to 3 hours at UWM each week. Hartford School is located directly beside the UWM campus, which made it possible for students to walk to our workshops and use the darkroom facilities in the photography area of the Fine Art school. We began by introducing project participants to the history of photography and asking them to identify and discuss the elements of design evident in compelling photographic imagery. They analyzed images in terms of composition, point of view and lighting, and learned how to develop and print photographs in the darkrooms. To hone their skills the students shot several introductory roles of film, producing self-portraits and photo essays of their families and neighborhoods (see Figures 1 & 2). The images and stories that follow are the result of an oral history activity the students completed toward the end of the project.

Figure 1. *Self-Portrait* by Crystal, age 13.

Fabled for their resourcefulness and valor, many Hmong became members of a secret CIA-backed militia that helped rescue downed U.S. pilots and disrupted North Vietnamese supplies and troop movements along the Ho Chi Minh Trail through Central Laos. The communist Pathet Lao movement…has never forgotten the Hmong's complicity with the Americans. Shortly after the Pathet Loa took power in 1975 … a communist newspaper declared the Party would hunt down the "American collaborators" and their families "to the last root." [Excerpt from http://www.time.com/time/magzine/article/0,9171,447253,00.html]

In preparing this oral history assignment each participant selected a mentor—an individual who they admired and who they had a positive relationship with, such as a parent, grandparent, teacher, aunt, or close family friend. As a group, the FOCUS team composed interview questions that each student then tailored to their individual subject. The students were curious about the childhood experiences of their mentors; thus, they composed interview questions about schooling, chores, clothing, play, parental expectations, discipline, and the role of girls and boys. These were questions both the young people and their adult mentors could relate to, which helped the students to collect rich data for their written histories. The moving portraits and stories that resulted from this project are a testament to the power of caring, supportive adult role models and to the sensitivity and thoughtfulness of these young people.

Sharing Their Stories

Crystal, a seventh-grade student at the time she created Figure 3, entered the US with her family, as a refugee because of Hmong support of American interests in Southeast Asia during the Vietnam War.

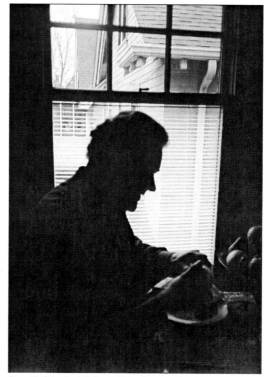

Figure 2. *Sebastion's Father* by Sebastion, age 12.

Figure 3. *My Grandparents* by Crystal, age 13.

For her oral history project, Crystal chose to interview her grandparents; however she found it difficult to convince them to sit for formal portraits. Instead Crystal opted for an environmental portrait, photographing her grandparents as they prepared the family dinner. Their story follows her photograph of domestic life in Milwaukee.

My Grandparents by Crystal, age 13

This is a history of my grandparents' childhood.

My grandpa's name is Kia Chue Yang and my grandma's name is Mao Yang.

My grandparents were both farmers in Laos. They lived in a village called Kieng Khouang, Laos (Northwest).

My grandpa is a wise man and became a respected leader of his village. Everyday after eating breakfast, he would go farming. A lot of Hmong people who lived in this area farmed. They would work all day on the land.

The boys would feed the animals and go to school only two days a week or so. The girls would make food, go farming, and stay home making clothes and doing needlework.

"It is a very poor country, but it holds a lot of memories for us," said my grandma. "There was nothing special back there, except being with my wife," said my grandpa. "It was beautiful and peaceful there until the war with Vietnam started," said my grandpa. "Yes indeed, we had to walk across a great river and travel to Thailand to a safe land," said my grandma.

This is all I can ask for now because it seems like they have tears in their eyes.

Melody chose to document a day in the life of one of her favorite teachers. She created a narrative of Ms. C's busy workday with great honesty and a sense of composition rivaling many professional photojournalists. Melody managed to infuse her photographs with a deep respect and admiration for Ms. C.; her reportage-like series capture the warmth, energy and commitment this teacher brings to her practice. Figure 4 accompanies Melody's playful story.

Figure 4. *Ms. C at Work* by Melody, age 12.

Ms. C. by Melody, age 13

She may seem like an ordinary woman, but she has more adventure and drama in her life than you might think. Her name is Karen, Karen C. She is a baby boomer. The exact date of her birth is unknown.

During her childhood years she went to a Catholic school from 1st–12th grade. Because of her school situation she was required to wear a black and green uniform, which she didn't much like. In those days the style was mini-skirts.

Karen said her school was not as privileged as the schools are today. The only special subjects she had were gym and art. She said, "We had art, but it was only with wimpy things like macaroni."

Karen has quite a love for music. She names several bands and groups like the Temptations, Smokey Robinson, The Beatles, Sly and the Family Stone, Al Green and Marvin Gaye that she still enjoys listening to. Her favorite shows on TV were things like *The Twilight Zone* and other science fiction programs.

At 17 years of age she told her mom she was leaving home. Karen traveled the world. She went to places like London and France.

Now you know that Karen C. had a lot of adventure in her life and she still does today.

Angellica was a sixth-grade student when she wrote this detailed story of her grandfather's life. She spent many hours shaping her oral history interview data into a cohesive narrative that she and her family were proud of when it was complete. Her story reflects the experience of many African American people who left family homes in the Southern US to move to booming industrial cities in the North, such as Milwaukee, after WWII.

My Grandfather—Edward A. by Angellica, age 12

My Granddad was born on October 30, 1927. He was born in Holly Spring, Mississippi. He grew up in a small, quiet neighborhood with five brothers and sisters. It was really hot in Holly Spring in the summer and icy in the winter. The nearby falls were very beautiful. When my Grandpa was a boy he spent time babysitting

Figure 5. *Edward A. After Church* by Angellica, age 12.

his sisters and brothers, playing jacks and marbles, singing and dancing, and jumping rope. My Grandpa was the eldest child, so he had many chores to do, like washing dishes, cleaning his room, taking out garbage, and sweeping the porch. The rules he had to follow were to do his chores, do his schoolwork, get good grades, and respect elders. If he broke the rules, he would get spanked with a paddle.

My Grandfather was in the army for 2 years. When he got out he went to college at Mississippi Industrial. Then he moved to Chicago where he went to engineering school and found a job in South Milwaukee at the Everbrite Electric Sign Company. My Grandpa was the head project engineer at Everbrite, designing menu signs, lighting and other outdoor signs for businesses like McDonalds. He also designed the largest and tallest Burger King sign in Milwaukee, which is located on Capital Drive and Green Bay Road. He worked on projects for the Jolly Green Giant, beer companies, and other well-known businesses. He has shown us lots of pictures of himself with these great works.

Even though he got married in 1955 and had one child (my mother), he spent three years commuting from Chicago to

Milwaukee before he could convince my Grandmother to move here with him. She finally agreed and they have lived here ever since. In 1992 my Grandfather retired when he found out that his first grandchild (that's me) would soon be born. He chose to be home with my Grandma to help take care of me. My Grandma died in 1999. My Grandpa was really thrilled when he found out my sister would be born that same year.

My Grandfather is now 76 and every year we visit his mother (my Great Grandmother), who is almost 100 years old, in Mississippi for a family reunion. I love my Grandpa because he is filled with candy and hugs. I'm glad that he is here.

Conclusion: Bringing their Voices into the Community

Integral to the design and implementation of all the educational documentary projects I facilitate, is the component of presenting the finished photographs and stories to the public through exhibition in art galleries, schools, or other community and public venues or through "zine," journal, school newspaper, or website publications. While preparing their work to be presented to local, national, and international audiences, young documentarians gain experience organizing, formatting, and setting up their exhibitions. Once the work is matted and displayed, or laid out for desktop publishing, students are often surprised by its professional look and are proud of their accomplishments. At the exhibitions we invite viewers to respond to the students' work in writing or by recording their voice. Both modes of response are then collected and transcribed and segments of that feedback become part of the next exhibition or publication. The understandings, inspiration, admiration, and questions generated by viewers help to frame the work and to direct future projects. This process is a circle with voices ringing out and voices returning.

FOCUS participants displayed their oral history projects along with mixed media self-portraits they created as an introduction to their work, at the University of Wisconsin-Milwaukee Student Union, the Beverley Art Center in Chicago, and the School of Education at Trent University in Peterborough Canada. In all three venues the children's work was well-received and many individuals wrote thoughtful responses.

From the exhibition at UWM viewers wrote:
The photos show a vibrant energy, caring compassionate leaders and a new side of America. The youth seem strong and grounded.—T.W.O.

These images haunt me. I keep coming back to see them. I'm already mourning the fact that they will be gone next week. You have taught me so much.—Marc

It's so nice to see young African Americans doing something constructive! It's great that you give African Americans as a whole a positive name, instead of the media portraying us as animals.—Tara

At the exhibition at Trent University in Canada viewers wrote:
... I was able to connect with many of your pictures as I thought of what it was like for me growing up, and considered the people who mattered in my own life.—R.C.

Wow! It is a rare gift to be shown the beauty and strength in people through someone else's eyes. You have taught me much about how to see. Thank you for sharing your photos and your lives with us.—Karen

The students' oral history projects and the comments they elicit from viewers are potent reminders of the enduring power of the still image. It is clear that when photography is employed as a form of social reflection it has the potential to enhance intergenerational and intercultural understanding, to reduce stereotypical attitudes and to celebrate the dreams and ingenuity of youth and other groups whose stories are often lost in the din of our popular media. It is reassuring to know that despite the extremely fast paced visual culture that seems to engulf young people today, art educators have the means to provide students with simple tools and techniques the can enable them to, as Bryan so eloquently put it, "catch time"— to slow down, record, reflect, and then speak thoughtfully and intelligently about the world they live in, a world that is theirs to inherit.

Anderson, J. C. (Ed). (1977). *Roy Stryker: The humane propagandist.* Louisville: University of Louisville.

Ashton-Warner, S. (1963/1986). *Teacher.* New York: Touchstone.

Buckingham, D., & Sefton-Green, J. (1994). *Cultural studies goes to school: Reading and teaching popular media.* London: Taylor & Francis.

Coles, R. (1995). *Listening to children: A moral journey.* (Video recording) Virginia: PBS Video/Social Media Productions.

Coles, R. (1998). *Doing documentary work.* New York: Oxford University Press.

Coles, R. (1992). *Their eyes meeting the world: The drawings and paintings of children.* Margaret Sartor (Ed.). Boston: Houghton Mifflin.

Davidson, M. (2000). *Catching time: Pathways to engagement in the elementary classroom through the visual arts.* Unpublished doctoral dissertation, Concordia University, Montreal, CA.

Davis, Allen F. (1989). *Mind's eye, mind's truth: FSA photography reconsidered.* Philadelphia: Temple University.

Ewald, W. (1985). *Portraits and dreams: Photographs and stories by children of the Appalachians.* New York: Writers & Readers.

Ewald, W. (1996). *I dreamed I had a girl in my pocket.* New York: Umbra.

Ewald, W. (2007). *Literacy through photography.* Retrieved February 28, 2008, from http://cds.aas.duke.edu/ltp/index.html

Fried, Robert L. (2001). *The passionate teacher: A practical guide* (2nd ed). Boston: Beacon Press.

hooks, b. (1994). *Teaching to transgress: Education as the practice of freedom.* New York: Routledge.

Hubbard, J. (1991). *Shooting back: A photographic view of life by homeless children.* Washington DC: Chronicle Books.

Hubbard, J. (1994). Shooting back from the reservation: *A photographic view of life by Native American youth.* New York: The New Press.

Hubbard, J., & Warshafsky, L. (2008). *Venice Arts in neighborhoods.* Retrieved February 28, 2008, from http://www.venice-arts.org/studentWork/socialart.html

Johnson, B. (2004). *Photography speaks: 150 photographers on their art.* Virginia: Aperture.

Newhall, B. (1980). *Photography, essays and images: Illustrated readings in the history of photography.* New York: Graphic Society & University of Michigan Press.

Noddings, N. (1992). *The challenge to care in schools: An Alternative approach to education.* New York: Teachers College.

Pinnington, M. (1986). Art in action. *Ten: 8,* 21, 14–20.

Shor, I. (1992). *Empowering education: Critical teaching for social change.* Chicago & London: University of Chicago.

Sontag, S. (1977). *On photography.* New York: Picador.

Stott, W. (1986). *Documentary expression and thirties America.* Chicago: The University of Chicago Research Press.

Trachtenberg, A. (1979). *The American image: Photographs from the National Archives, 1860–1960.* New York: Pantheon Books.

Take Me on a Journey: Self-Identity Through the Arts

Terry Galloway, Talicia Scriven, and Isabelle Potts

Introduction

Isabelle: In 2003, I was in charge of a research project funded by the United States Department of Education. We were to develop an arts-in-education curriculum and implement it in a poor rural district in the Florida Panhandle. The plan—derived from the work of Terry Galloway—was for middle-school students to write about their lives and use their writing as the basis for staged performances. To enrich their presentations, the children would also experience dance, music, and the visual arts. Enter Talicia Scriven, a doctoral student in the Florida State University Art Education Department. Her original role: to provide this supportive visual arts instruction. Little did I know that Talicia was developing her own curriculum—one that fit perfectly with the issues of identity raised by our project.

In this chapter, we learn from the separate, but parallel, stories of Terry and Talicia's lives how they struggled with their own sense of identify in their school years, and the salvational role of the arts. Their personal narratives preface and help explain parts of our three-year curriculum.

Year One at the Middle School

Terry Galloway
My Personal History as a Disabled Child and Adult

At age 9-1/2, my life changed. Not because of my deafness, which had been coming on gradually for a long time, but because, with my diagnosis and treatment (the box hearing aids and coke bottle glasses of the era) I had been suddenly branded. I was now, in the lexicon of the time, handicapped

> ## KEY CONCEPTS
> - Performance
> - Autobiography
> - Multi-Media
> - Personal Voice

and "special." Special, then, was not a good thing to be. In the Texas elementary school I attended, I was put in a class for special students where nothing much was expected of me or the other students. By the time I was 13, I still did not know how to diagram a sentence or add a column of figures. I was on my way to living the life society then thought I deserved: the warehoused life, the place over in the corner where the rejects are swept.

How Art Saved Me

A few good, passionate teachers and art, which in my case was writing and performance, saved me. What saved me was the unique ability of art, as a form of self expression, to awaken in me a sense of worth and a defiant yearning to matter.

In the classes of a few exceptional teachers during my crucial middle and high school years, I learned to perform in class, on stage, or in speech and poetry competitions. If it had not been for those few teachers who loved me, who understood that everything people do is a form of self-expression, the life I live now would be very different.

With her help of one speech teacher, Suzanne Woods, I learned to make myself understood precisely enough that I won a scholarship to the University of Texas in Austin to study theater. With scholarship in hand, I marched right up the steps to the University of Texas Drama Department and asked to be advised. The advisor took a long look at my hearing aids and said, "You're deaf." Then he said, "Costuming."

I hate being told no but the word in itself never had the power to crush me. I was a good enough actor to get myself out of my advisor's office, smiling, even nodding as if I agreed. Inside I was crackling with fury, both at him and at myself, for my shuffling, grinning exit, but I was again making up my mind. I would show him; even if I did not yet know how.

A Yearning to Matter

That fury became one of the driving forces of my life. I was going to do theater with a vengeance. And I did. I worked hard, got a few miraculous breaks, and over the years managed to carve out a place for myself. I co-founded two theaters, performed Shakespeare, German experimentalism, one-woman shows, performance art, new vaudeville, and old vaudeville all over the world. I wrote, directed, and performed for TV, radio, film, and stage. I was never rich, famous, or even modestly well known. But I had a happier life than I had ever envisioned.

Over time I found myself working quite a lot with other groups of imperfect people—disabled, poor, or living in the boondocks—listening to stories about their lives and helping them shape their stories into theater. I brought these stories and my own experiences with me when I went to teach writing and performance in one of the poorest schools in the Florida Panhandle.

What We Came to Do That First Year

I hope this project will give these kids some self-esteem because they have none. —Sixth-grade teacher at the middle school

The day our arts education team walked into the middle school and saw the leaking roof, the dank hallways, the battered desks, the peeling paint of the schoolrooms, we knew that the goals of our project would have to become much more far-reaching than we had envisioned. On paper, our project's primary goal was to improve the students' scores on the Florida Comprehensive Assessment Test (FCAT). We believed we could do this by engaging these low performing middle school students in an autobiographical approach to the arts, most particularly the language arts, but also performance, visual arts, dance, music, computer graphics, video, and film.

But our first goal had to be to awaken in them a yearning to matter. Although our students were aware that literacy can equal an enhanced quality of life, they also knew on some level that they had been shortchanged in that regard. Many of our students had less than rudimentary writing skills (at best), and a deep suspicion, even a hatred of writing itself; some of these sixth-graders could not spell the word "dog."

Students Writing About Themselves

Our goal that first year was to address the students' hatred of writing directly. Our initial step was to make them do what they hated (write) but on a topic they found endlessly fascinating (themselves). Throughout that first year the subject matter of everything they wrote was always themselves: who they were, where they came from, their earliest childhood memories, how they had changed from one year to the next, what they liked or disliked about their lives, and why they did or did not like to write.

What we kept emphasizing throughout the workshops was that it did not matter if they could not spell. It did not matter if they did not know how to write. We would take dictation or sit by their side and help spell the words, or just brainstorm with them about the words they wanted to use. Writing was the tool. What mattered is that they had something to say and that it was accepted seriously.

Using Media as a Focusing Method

We also brought in media to emphasize the importance of the work students were doing. In our media-saturated society video is equated with fame, status, importance, and meaning. We used that belief to our advantage, bringing in video production college students who trained the camera on the children as they worked. We then we played the images of them back to them. They loved it.

The Poetic Ethic

For these students writing was the ogre. They imagined they had to write hundreds of words in order to express themselves. However, we demonstrated that meaning and even eloquence can exist in the smallest increments. We told the kids that we would examine their work to find meaning in the smallest of details—the single word, the short phrase, the two-sentence allusion. Like most people who write about their own lives, they were constantly overlooking their own dropped hints. They seldom gave what they had written (or what they had lived) the weight it deserved. We took everything they wrote as a hint to meanings that they themselves might have overlooked and told them what we were doing as we were doing it.

Performance as Integral to Meaning

We read what the students had written out loud. This helped them to find meaning in their words. If they wanted their name attached to their writing we named the author; if not, their anonymity was respected.

The workshop leaders not only read what had been written, but they performed it as well. This was done to make the words in even the briefest phrase resonate with meaning. Thus, performance became a way of underlining the seriousness of the writing students had done.

When the students read their work, we provided them impromptu lessons in public speaking in the form of play; stand up straight, breath deep as you can, imagine every word you are saying as you are saying it. One interesting benefit to this exercise was that, as they read their own writing, they discovered the misspellings and grammatical errors. These they were eager to correct to improve the flow of their readings.

A Celebratory Ending

We ended our first year with an art and pizza party. We bought scores of pizzas, decorated the cafeteria at the school, and displayed the framed artwork and writing. In a formal performance, the students read the work they had written and presented their dance and music performances. It was a way for the children to share with the other students and teachers at the school as well as their families. It was a huge success. One teacher told me I shouldn't be disappointed if very few people attended, "We've had PTA meetings when only one or two parents came." So it was deeply satisfying to open up the door to the auditorium to the waiting crowd of 200 people.

Year One: Lessons Learned

We discovered that although some of the students were shy about talking or reading what they had written about themselves, most were forthcoming. One young sixth-grade girl who was failing her other courses wrote a powerful six-page missive—misspelled and grammatically incorrect—detailing how she, with the help of her brother, tried to get her mother to stop smoking and drinking by flushing her cigarettes and beer down the toilet. A young boy who was chronically absent from school wrote eloquently about his love of his mother who had rescued him and his brothers from the Department of Family Services after ending her drug habit and working two full-time jobs. Another young boy wrote about football, how he loved the feel of the ball in his hand, but how most of all he loved the company of his friends when they played together. One young woman wrote about having lupus and how the pain that was her constant companion translated to the sorrow for the pain she felt for the world.

Through this exercise the students learned that they had stories that mattered. By enacting these stories, they found that they not only knew how to use language, but also could actually enjoy doing so. Just as importantly, our own beliefs were confirmed: the goals for the students—sharing themselves, their talents, stories, and songs through live performance or recorded video in a community setting—provided incentive to their willingness to work, think, plan, and create. In keeping with our mission of listening to the students, we took some of our cues from them, and began to rethink what we would ask of them in the second year of our program. Fortunately, by that time Talicia Scriven had joined our project.

Year Two at the Middle School

Unrestricted Visions: Finding the Power to Become Through Art

Talicia: My life as a child was hard. My parents divorced before I was 3 years old and although my mother was a hard-working special education teacher, for a large portion of my childhood we were very poor. We lived for many years in a shoddy, tiny house in the backyard of my unloving, abusive grandparents. Yet, from a young age, art served as a safe haven for me, so much so that my self-worth became tied to my personal identity as an artist.

When I was young, I had no friends, and as I got older, I was made fun of every day for being too poor, too ugly, or too dumb. I was often taunted by students, and even a few teachers. The only thing I was respected for was my ability to draw.

Over the course of my elementary and secondary school years, I found myself shut off from this special avenue for achievement. As art fell out of the school curriculum, my dominant art voice, along with my sense of worth, slowly diminished. By the time I entered high school, the art classes had vanished. In my senior year, I gave up on my artistic ambitions, and decided to major in business. Certain people found out about this and warned me not to throw my talent away. It was life-changing advice, and I am glad I followed it. When I entered college I decided to major in art.

Art as Life

The predominately African American university I attended had a profound impact on me, fostering a sense of personal power. During freshman year in college I created a drawing entitled *Cover Girl*. Fragmented pieces of a woman's face peeked and peered through massive lipsticks, make-up brushes, and so-forth. *Cover Girl* was essentially my way of stating my deep concern about cultural standards of beauty and the primacy of appearance. I won "Best in Show" for this piece at the university's annual student art exhibit. I also received the "Most Promising Design Student" award and, as one of the top 25 freshmen at the university, a silver medallion as a Presidential Scholar. One year as an art major at a historically African American university had provided more for me than my entire K–12 education. I was finding out who I was and what I was capable of, and for the first time in my life, I felt that art had given me a sense of real accomplishment, even in academic areas.

Unrestricted Visions: Personal Empowerment through the Arts

As a graduate student at Florida State University, I came to the notion of art as a means of unrestricted visions, meaning that art allows people to express the depth and breadth of their imagination and feeling in an indirect, safe way. During the summer of 2004, project manager Isabelle Potts asked me to write a curriculum for the students at Howard Middle School. Isabelle and Terry Galloway, along with others working on the Arts-in-Education project, would later add valuable input and suggestions for my part of the project.

Year Two: What We Did

Talicia: Initially, my struggles with self acceptance and concepts of beauty lead me to formulate the idea of exploring with the students at the Middle School notions of intrinsic versus extrinsic worth. I thought that exploring popular culture and the culture of materialism would help students to address concerns that are very central to what they may have to face in school and in society in general.

With the invaluable help of co-workers, I devised lessons that dealt with the symbolic languages of the arts. I used my own artwork as an example so students could see first-hand how I symbolically depicted my own struggles with self-acceptance and peer pressure. Terry also contributed to the class by discussing the personal struggles engendered by her deafness. I believe our stories and our art helped to humanize us in the eyes of the students. I think they were impressed with the fact that we were willing to make ourselves vulnerable simply for the purpose of helping them to learn.

Terry: In our second year, with Talicia's curriculum, we began to demystify the act of writing and intensify our examination of self in the context of cultural symbols. We concentrated on reinforcing the link between the visual arts and the language arts. Most of the children loved to draw, loved to create collages from images they cut from magazines, especially since the images they were choosing for their artworks represented who they were, who they believed themselves to be. When they were creating these collages our one stipulation was that they had to use words as well as pictures.

Inner Self Versus Cultural Self

The second year was devoted to encouraging the students to examine questions about self and to look at symbols with a new understanding, most particularly how to distinguish the symbolism of the inner self from the symbolism of the cultural self. They were again asked to think about the symbols they were expressing through their images and words, and their power as individuals to use these symbols to create a "self." To motivate their thinking they were asked a series of questions: Where does your power as an individual lie in the shaping of the culture that shapes you? What power do you have over your culture and over self-image? How much of that power comes from symbols?

We tried to awaken in the students an awareness of how their expression and presentation of themselves could change other people's perceptions about them. We tried to show them that the skill with which they used symbols—language, picture, body, voice, presence—did represent power. We hoped to awaken in them the desire to use that power well and at will.

Creating a Historical Record of Their Work

The artwork the students created eventually became the cover of their own individual compact disc (CD), which featured them performing their own writings. Once again, performance was added to the curriculum as an impetus to inspire the students to do what they hated (writing) by pairing it with something they loved to do (hearing themselves talk, having an audience, being appreciated). As they worked on their CD covers they were encouraged to think about what the art they were creating was saying about each of them, and to use what they were thinking as the basis for a short written piece that could be recorded, even if their contribution was two short lines. Two sentences of spoken words were treated with the same seriousness as a 14-stanza poem.

We also continued to use technology to great effect. When we presented the CDs the students had recorded, we often accompanied the recorded word with PowerPoint to add a visual representation. For instance, in the case of a Spanish-speaking child from a migrant working family, we played the CD of him reciting the poem he had written in Spanish while simultaneously showing a PowerPoint of the poem's English translation. We presented a number of videos featuring the students themselves: videos of them dancing, in the style of an MTV rap video. We also presented a video collage of the artwork they had created, including images of the murals they had painted on the school walls. The children were enthralled by their own images represented through these media. Again, they saw themselves played back in a way that was both objective (the media themselves) and subjective (they were the focus of the media attention) which gave them a perceived status they might not otherwise have had.

Interpreting Symbols

Even when they knew there was meaning in the visual symbols and single words they had used on their covers, they did not always know how to recognize them for what they were. It was imperative for the workshop leaders to help the children interpret those symbols and always do it in the best, most positive, light. For example, one of the boys (like most of the boys) made a collage of football players, basketball players, cars, motorcycles, and money when asked to focus on personal images. In the middle of all of the imagery he had fastened a picture of a colonial-traditional house. I wondered aloud if this was his way of telling me that home was at the heart of his life. He agreed. Another example was when one young girl made a collage featuring six different rappers, all of them tough in their chains, headgear, and tattoos. But all of six of them were smiling sweetly. It was as if she was saying that there's a soul behind the 'tude.

End-of-the-Year Presentation

At the end of the second year we again presented the students' work in a public performance. This time it was during school hours and was primarily a presentation for their classmates, their teachers, and the students in the sixth and eighth grades. Again, the walls of the auditorium were decorated with original art around the theme of "Who Do You Think You Are." But this time there were papier maché symbols—letters, stars, and animals—hanging from the rafters of the stage to create a set for their presentation. More of the students were interested in performing than the first year. They presented their poetry, rap, spoken word, dance, and songs.

The presentation at the end of the second year had many high points, but a hand-full stand out: A student who is legally blind and has learning disabilities performed a live rap about Christmas and all the gifts he had received, including an X-Box. We had been a bit apprehensive about his performance, fearing that the other students might be lukewarm despite all his efforts. After

his performance—which was flawless despite its mistakes—all of the students gave him a standing ovation. Another student had begrudgingly written a stanza of a song to his mother, called Candy. He just as reluctantly recorded it. As it played during the final performance the audience was still; they were listening and enjoying what he had written. He sat there as it played with his head in his hands, the picture of despair. But when it finished he leapt up from his seat, danced in place, and pumped his hands in the air.

A student with a long history of disengagement had written a piece called Censored. This boy was part of a mixed group of kids who had interests that were considered less mainstream; they were Goths or agnostics or simply those who could not be or would not be compartmentalized. When his piece was played, which was quite witty, featuring every foul four-letter word masked by a beep, the small knot of cynics with whom he was sitting erupted in hoots of disbelief and a kind of triumph. They were taken by surprise. An MTV-style video of a rap written and starring a young man named Ross was one of the hits of the show. As we came to discover, it conferred upon this seventh grader a newfound status. Ross-ified became the new word among his classmates. Ross-ified epitomized intelligence, self-possession, and cool.

At the end of the show the seventh graders spontaneously broke into long, heartfelt, and well-deserved cheers for themselves. After the performance, students from the sixth and eighth grades came up to help us dismantle the sets. They talked to and praised the seventh graders, and asked if they too could put on a show like that.

Year Two: Lessons Learned

It seemed imperative not to censor anything the students wrote, even when it was about violence and guns and "ho's and pimps." Sometimes they had good reasons to write about guns, for example a story about an uncle who died at the card table, or a cousin who was killed in a drive-by. They had good reasons to use the word "fuck" or "asshole": against the father who hit them, or the mother who left them. But we tried to get them to understand when they did or did not have the moral authority to express these images or use these negative words. They had the authority, we told them, when they were talking about their lives, the real life culture that surrounded them. They lost that authority, the authenticity when they were referring to what we took to calling the media-ized culture which was not necessarily true to them but which they had absorbed. What we tried to do was make them go back and refer to their own lives, for better and for worse.

Year Three at the Middle School

Terry: The third, our last, year we returned to the primary focus of writing. Writing was still hated by the students, but this year the students knew from the beginning that our goal and their reward was the final performance. For most of the students the threat of being banned from the final performance was regarded as a punishment, especially because the nature of the projects we would be doing that year had changed.

Upping the Ante

In the third year, we wanted to increase the students' stake in the final outcome by involving them in the mechanics of production as well as in the performance. To this end we showed them how to write a video script, choose locations, perform for the camera, direct the shots, and help with the editing. Five different videos were created, one a very funny exploration of how to cheat on the FCAT. We did the same with the CDs; this time the students recorded, critiqued, and coached their classmates. Each one then edited and mixed his or her own piece. In the same vein, the students were also involved in directing live performances, correcting enunciation, and helping with appropriate posture, gestures, and movement.

Year Three: Lessons Learned

Isabelle: As the students had matured over the 2-plus years that we worked with them, in the third year we witnessed their exploration of broader cultural issues. They commented on the dreaded FCAT, the high-stakes test that students must pass every year to be promoted to the next grade; also the test that ascribes a grade to the school. They parodied the iconic *American Idol*, focusing on the quirkiness of contestants and panelists. Our Mexican students presented their country of origin and their journey to the United States. A group of rebellious jocks gave us a glimpse into their collective identity as "Backward Boys."

Still, our project did not seem to engage *all* students. A small number of boys, in particular, seemed reluctant to participate in any artistic activities. It was only at our third annual performance that I saw these boys' potential as "techies." Although they had probably not written more than a dozen lines between them, and did not perform, they were hooked when we gave them photo cameras and instructions on how to focus on images that mattered to them. In that moment we learned not to give up on any child too quickly.

A Few Conclusions

Terry: Both Talicia and I grew up struggling to believe in ourselves and in our right to matter. We both came to find meaning and purpose in our lives through art. But art alone was not enough to save us. So we went looking for communities of people who believed in us. Talicia found hers in a university where she could explore the philosophical underpinnings of her artwork. I found mine in an alternative theater where I was able to work unimpeded by classical theater mores. When we came to the middle school we identified with the children there, recognized that they were engaged in a struggle much like ours: to matter. Many of them had only the flimsiest emotional investment in their continued existence. They did not much care how they lived and, in some cases, *if* they lived.

Awakening in those children a love for themselves had to be the true, if not the highest goal of our project. We were enthusiastic about their slightest creations, anything they wrote or drew. Many had so little sense of self-worth and self-regard that we were simply trying to find something, anything in which they could excel. When we found excellent things in them—and we always did—we worked with them to make something compelling out of even the slightest of ideas, the simplest of stories, the shortest of paragraphs, and the briefest of dialogues. When they saw what could be made out of those small things they felt somehow freer. We could see it happening. That freedom from pressure, censorship, and criticism awoke in them a real desire to create, to lift their heads, and to make themselves known.

After we had awakened that desire, we rewarded them and ourselves each year with our end-of-the-year performances, when the whole school came together in an assembly to bolster and applaud the work those students had struggled so hard to create. The assemblies affirmed their self-belief and the hard work it took for them to believe. And every year there was a huge crowd doing the affirming: those of us involved in the art project (the dancers, visual artists, musicians, *and* recording and video artists), the teachers, school and district administrators, local dignitaries, children from the other classes, and family members. We were all there to support them by acting as audience and witness, and to give them a sense of meaningful community.

We believe our Art in the Schools project helped foster in these young people a belief in the worth of their own lives. We hope that the skills we were able to teach them will enable them to share that passion with the wider world and enter communities of meaning.

Animated Sitcoms as Social Justice: Preadolescents Critique the Morality of *The Simpsons*

Mary Stokrocki

S ince Aristotle, it seems that the elite have valued tragedy over comedy and regarded popularity with contempt. *The New York Times*, for example, still refuses to print a comic, but a caricature is acceptable (Coleman, 1994). Schools, similarly, regard frivolity as a deviation from the serious business of education. But some educators argue that schools should be teaching children about social issues by guiding them to examine stereotypes in the children's environment, namely by having them look at cartoons (Pang, 1991). Until recently, art teachers focused on developing technical skills when teaching cartooning or animation and rarely guided students to examine these powerful cultural images and stories behind them. Keifer-Boyd, Amburgy, and Knight (2003) discovered a dearth of practical materials and lessons that examine the "power of comic book and cartoon images as cultural narratives" (p. 48). However, Freedman (2003) examined the roles of television as a developmental and representational process, including building a consumer culture, constructing self-identity, and exploiting such stereotypes as violence and sex. She found that television operates as a national curriculum more powerfully than any single school curriculum. She argued that students remember visual texts, such as television, more accurately than written texts. They seek information through TV that enables their adult development, such as that which is real, right and wrong, important, and **demonstrating** how to relate to other people. Tackling another aspect of television entertainment, Taylor and Ballangee-Morris (2003) reported on the situational comedies (sitcoms), such as *Everybody Loves Raymond*, as

KEY CONCEPTS
- Reflexivity
- Intertextuality
- Subliminal Pleasures
- Critical Pedagogy
- Power Relations
- Morality

parodies of contemporary values and society. Such shows present reflections on food tastes, fads, and social situations. Taylor and Ballangee-Morris (2003) noted that people today seem more accepting of controversial matters and they argue for exploring the issues behind sitcoms. The purpose of this article is to discuss one animated sitcom, *The Simpsons*, for what it teaches, what kinds of social justice or morality it communicates, and how art educators can use it to help students critique television.

Sitcoms as a Platform for Discussing Social Justice and Morals

What is social justice? What are good morals? On the one hand, justice is equated with moral rightness and also can deal with liberty or fairness. On the other hand, libertarian justice focuses on self-interest and the pursuit of happiness, which is often in conflict with fairness, the social allocation of benefits in an equitable way (Shapiro, 2000; Irwin, Conrad & Skoble, 2001). In light of conflicting ideas about what is just and true, "understanding and appreciation for the relationship between justice and fairness, as well as an increased ability to apply the principles of justice for themselves" (Irwin, Conrad, & Skoble, 2001, p. 18) is an issue to be addressed in education.

"Now in our society more so now than ever before, attention is being focused on the standards and behavior of professionals and officials working in society's institutions, especially on issues of excesses" (Burgh, 2004). Excesses are a pressure in everyday life. Discussion and clarification of excess are important. In addition, what is good behavior is debatable; what is good for one person may be bad for another. For example, in assessing *The Simpsons* some dads may identify with Homer due to his continuing failures, not for his love of family. The sitcom can be used to inspire moral contemplation, consideration of behavioral issues concerning what is right and wrong, as shown in the Shakespearean parody play called *MacHomer* and a Scottish church course on the gospels as seen through the eyes of the family (McGuire, 2003). Sitcoms can provide opportunities to address moral issues and social justice.

Moral Learning as Multi-Relational

According to Tuan (1993) culture is a moral aesthetic venture to be judged ultimately by its moral beauty. Moral beauty is "a spontaneous act of generosity performed with unselfish conscious grace" and also acts of average genuine modesty (Tuan, 1993, p. 240). Moral beauty flourishes in societies that nurture moral learning. Purpel (1989) pointed out that our culture teaches us to be responsible for ourselves and not others and not to feel guilty when others fail. Schools, therefore, tend to reflect the cultural indifference toward cooperation, emphasizing individual success or failure and focusing on individualism, competition, achievement, and personal success and not collective responsibility. Learning is the pursuit of knowledge; the problem is, what kind of knowledge are we pursuing? Is it crucial, trivial, or relational? Noddings (2002) explained moral learning as "multi-relational, a kind of moral learning based on a teacher's caring willingness to assist students and for students to care for each other" (p. 69). So what does this have to do with *The Simpsons*? Seen one way, *The Simpsons* may teach morals: lessons about how we can live together and why life is worth living. But should art education even be considering the task of interpreting these lessons in terms of social justice? I believe so because through the vehicle of popular culture children can tell us who and what they care about. Art education should care not only about things and ideas, but also about people and their relationships.

Critical Pedagogy Method

Critical pedagogy is the reflective theory that supports this study. "It problematizes epistemology and social concerns to empower students" (Tavin, 2003). Critiquing sitcoms invites reflexivity through multiple interpretations, imitative behavior from younger male students, astute comments from rebellious students, and fresh insights from foreign students. Reflexivity

is "the process of making one self-aware of one's immersion in everyday and popular culture in order to examine one's own position, sometimes through intertextuality" (Sturken & Cartwright, 2001, p. 269). Intertextuality is "the introduction of another text and its meaning inside the present text with the assumption that viewers understand the inserted text" (p. 265). For example, *The Simpsons* often refers to storylines of old films, such as *Dracula* (e.g., Bram Stoker's 1992 version) or the rock culture of the Rolling Stones (Stam, 1989). Engagement with popular culture not only entertains, but also can invite viewers to the meta or reflexive level that captures their attention in a different way. In this context, teachers should promote students' reflection about hidden texts and behaviors.

In critically examining *The Simpsons* with the children in this study, I borrowed discussion questions from educator Pang (1991) who examined cultural stereotypes in cartoons by asking children their opinions. I found her leading questions limited, thus I reworded some questions to solicit stronger explanations. Later, I held a class discussion that was audio-taped, transcribed, and analyzed for frequent themes. The participating teacher added reflections and findings were compared to other testimonies on *The Simpsons* and related literature.

Context and Participants

The large public middle school (1,200 students) in which this study was conducted is in a working class suburb of Mesa, Arizona. I chose this school because the teacher loved *The Simpsons* and was excited about developing a moral education curriculum for use in her classroom. The cooperating art teacher has been teaching for over 30 years and was very concerned with updating the content of her curriculum. Two of my former student teachers recommended her as "a super-motivating teacher." The students involved in this study were 24 eighth- and ninth-graders in the teacher's first-period Advanced Art class that lasted about 55 minutes.

Lesson, Standards, Assessment, Motivation

This lesson explores social justice issues related to the animated sitcom, *The Simpsons*, directed by Matt Groening. *The Simpsons* has been notoriously popular for more than 20 years on Fox TV. The longest running animated sitcom, the show seems to lampoon everything sacred, from gender issues to religion, politics, and sexuality (Lewis, 2002). Even John Ashcroft, former Attorney General of the United States, is fond of

Homer Simpson, but finds him irreverent and appreciates Marge as "pure" (*CBS Sunday Morning News*, June 29, 2003).

I invited students to review one episode of *The Simpsons* on video and examine its theme and morals. Later we discussed other episodes and issues. I announced our purpose, "You benefit by learning to critique popular culture, exchange your views, and becoming tolerant of other views." The lesson addressed NAEA Visual Arts Content Standard 6: Making connections between visual arts and other disciplines, in this case, philosophy. In this lesson, the moral and ethnical value of contemporary comic animation in United States was explored. Also Content Standard 3 was addressed: Choosing and evaluating a range of subject matter, symbols, and ideas (ArtsEdge, 1994). Assessment of this lesson was based on a simple rubric: inadequate, acceptable, and exceptional ability to understand art and debate cultural ideas.

Overview of The Simpsons *Episode*

Students watched the November 10, 2002 episode, *How I Spent My Strummer Vacation*, as a catalyst for discussion (Wikipedia, 2008). Homer works at the power plant in Springfield and he is bored with his job and his family. The episode opens with Homer hurting his family's feelings by rejecting them as boring. Marge chastises him as incredibly thoughtless, even though he works a job that he doesn't like so she can be at home with the kids. To pacify Homer, the family decides to send Homer to rock and roll camp, a place that he has wanted to go, instead of going on their own family vacation. I selected this episode because it was the United States Poet Laureate Robert Pinsky's (2002) selection to review. The following includes the students' responses to the questions that I posed to them about this and other favorite episodes.

Critical Questions and Students' Discussion

What are your first impressions of the show? Most of the students (20 out of 24 students) acknowledged that they watched the show regularly because it was funny. Several students reported that it is the only show they watch because of its satire of life today. Four students admitted that they had never seen the show before and two students considered it "stupid." Females seemed more sensitive to Homer's condition. They said Homer needs excitement and time away from his family.

What is the show's purpose? All students said that the animated sitcom was meant primarily to entertain. Students also admitted that the sitcom,

"Tells about reality; It's educational;" and "reveals society." One Nigerian student confessed, "They mirror everyday family life. They are not perfect." "Homer is too impulsive," a girl from India noted.

What form of art is it? Most students regarded *The Simpsons* as a cartoon. Other students labeled it as graphic art, animation, and even contour drawing. One sophisticated answer was "It's surreal—distorted reality."

What was the best episode? Why? Students mentioned the Halloween episode—*Tree House of Horror*—because it was the day when Lisa found the angel skeleton. Another favorite episode was when Maggie shot Homer with a staple gun onto the wall. A third favorite episode was when Bart's class was snowed in and Principal Skinner ran the school like a military camp, "because it was make-believe." Each episode mentioned featured some personal or social problem engaging some moral dilemma.

Who was your favorite character? Why? Ten students regarded Homer as their preferred character "because he was stupid, crazy, but irresponsible." Ten students also identified with Bart because he was "cool, rebellious, rude, and gets into trouble, and doesn't worry." They also realized that in real life, kids don't always get away with pranks. Males also admired Bart because he breaks the rules, which is something they wished they could do. We also discussed Bart's clowning as an art form. Students felt that a clown should be clever. In contrast, five students thought Lisa was "nerdy; humorless, too normal." Several students had no dislikes and found all characters unique. The range of responses indicates that the class found the show to have a good balance of characters, again focused on social issues.

What type of family are they? Several students remarked that the family was "dysfunctional." Other comments included "chaotic," "twisted," "weird-messed up," and "exotic." One male stated, "They are angry one moment and happy the next." One female found similarities with her family. Three females found the family as "kind and caring" in this segment. One comment was that "most families are divorced and this family is still together." Two other students found that the family "fights but love each other." Finally, another student summarized the cartoon as "a caricature of life."

Who has the most power? Students discussed the meaning of power as the ability to influence others. Some students found Homer powerful, mainly because he was the central character. Others mentioned that Mr. Burns, the owner or the power plant, had economic power. Additionally, students expressed that the rock stars had power to influence kids. One female regarded Marge as the strongest character because "she was the pillar of the family" and regarded Maggie, the baby, as the weakest character. Students, therefore, realized that power comes in different forms and has social consequences.

What does the animator exaggerate? Students suggested that the characters' eyes are enlarged, skin color is bright for contrast, and facial expressions and emotions are inflated. The females regarded Marge's hairdo as weird and hated her voice. Students realized that the characters' behaviors were "inflated—such as Homer's stupidity."

What is the moral of this episode about Homer going to Rock and Roll camp? Three students found that the episode explores values, conveys messages, and cheers up people. Specific comments were: "People need to grow up; no matter how old you are, you can still make mistakes; love your family, no matter what; ignorance plus compassion for family; life is not perfect: appreciate what you have; and life is hard, be real." One male student said, "The rock stars taught Homer about life—you can't always get what you want and family is more important."

How is The Simpsons bad? Students do not generally regard the sitcom as bad. Males identified with Bart who has limited appreciation for school, is obsessed with chalk, and fights a lot. They laughed at examples of violence such as Homer's strangling of Bart. One male reflected, "My dad gets like that sometimes," meaning that his father gets angry with him. They find the show mainly directed to adults but agree that kids watch it too. One female summarized their bad behaviors, "They [Homer and Bart mostly] swear [what the hell are you doing here?], make fun of people, stereotype people, and are destructive [e. g; burning a guitar]. Rock stars are bad examples for children." The class did not mention the sexual undertones, such as the term "crotch-stuffing" and STDs. We avoided this issue because the school principal felt that discussing The Simpsons was "too controversial" as a lesson. Students surmised that The Simpsons series reflects middle class moral behaviors or values. Instead of discussing issues of sexuality, students noted issues of anger and aggression.

Furthermore, while many people regard violence in such animated sitcoms as harmless entertainment, others find it symptomatic of a culture gone astray. The act of strangling, especially, is an unacceptable punishment type. Green (2004) reported that The Simpsons archive listed 130 examples of violent acts in its programs. She contended, "This example demonstrates how consideration of images and societal contexts provides valuable data when evaluating societal images" (p. 9).

What is the role of humor? Students realized that humor "releases stress" and "helps people not to regard life so seriously," and "it's controversial." A few students mentioned as an example, an earlier episode, *Bible Stories*, which elicited condemnation from a local Mormon church. The producers of *The Simpsons* have become accustomed to strong reactions. Similar to carnival, Halloween festivities can be regarded as a culture of laughter, a result of popular custom, as opposed to official culture, a class distinction. Jokes, puns, satirical comments are all part of behaviors that can evoke laughter. When deprived of power, Bakhtin (1981) explained, folk people appropriated humor and satire as a powerful, liberating, generative force.

What were differences in students' reactions? Mrs. Tabor also noted different perspectives in her students' reactions, "Younger kids are more entertainment-oriented, inclined toward silliness due to unfamiliarity or novelty of such social situations. They also seem more physical, they loved the part about beating up the cardboard paparazzi." She noted that some of the best insights came from the more rebellious students who identify with deviant behavior.

Other notable responses came from multicultural students. Foreign students bring fresh outsider viewpoints. For example a female from India mentioned that Homer is too impulsive. One student remarked that *The Simpsons* can "conform you—make you like everyone else." She disliked the contagious cynicism that the show evoked. Not all students believed that "school was hell" as Bart Simpson complained. Reeves (1999) advocated for students to learn with and from The Simpsons; thus discussing an episode around the theme of schooling helps students to review what is worthwhile/worthless about school.

What dysfunctions do students reveal in their own lives? Students revealed similarities in their middle class backgrounds in family conditions, problems, and pastimes. Mrs. Tabor assigned a follow-up lesson "to create their own moral cartoon prints in Styrofoam about their family to include strengths, sorrows, weaknesses, fun and future and to write about their families." Students wrote about their family in conjunction with this format. For example, one male wrote, "My dad throws fits; my mom works too hard; my dog tears up the house, my brother and I fight too much. We like to water ski, go out to dinner. Sorrow—my brother will be moving out soon. My dad had a couple of strokes and heart attack." Mrs. Tabor confessed, "Now that I know my students' ideas, I find they think this kind of family life is normal. Morals in America may be dysfunctional, but at least students are aware of problems and they are not hidden. Since this was the students' first exercise in critical pedagogy reflection, we did not formally assess each student's understanding of the visual culture lesson, although we were amazed at the class's insightful comments.

What is the nature of television? Some students conflated television's nature with its purpose to entertain (6 of 24), specifically as a comedy (4 of 24). Some felt television also conveys information about different ways of life (5 of 24). At this point, I took the opportunity to tell students what Pinsky (2002) had to say about *The Simpsons* and the nature of television as an art form. He praised this sitcom and its ability to portray fakery as reality. He explained,

> It deals with life in the 20th century American culture and how it reflects the moral times and in the case of *The Simpsons*—poke fun at it. The characters capture life's play between the literal and the imagined, the fake and the genuine that is central vibration in life and in television. It's based on historical context of previous shows. *The Simpsons*' aesthetic nature deals with representation (exaggeration) and expression (social satire) issues. (p. 2)

Excellence in expression depends on skill in dealing with the medium's nature and its past. Television's greatest moments deal with such characteristics as "presence, immediacy, and unpredictability" and TV's quintessential art form is situational comedy" that is something that is "cartoonish or closer to life" (Pinsky, 2002). Presence is the ability to be self confident or influential. Immediacy is a good sense of timing, nearness, and familiarity. Unpredictability is the ability to surprise or shock. Teachers can discuss these characteristics in relation to electronic media as well.

Conclusions and Implications

As reflected in this study, animated sitcoms, such as *The Simpsons*, can provide students with opportunities for social justice critique and discussion. Critique heightens awareness of the complexity of life situations and enables different views through parody. Parody is a cultural production that satirizes other works or aspects of life, for example, in this case, the idolization of the Rolling Stones lifestyle, involving forms of rebellion and moral ambiguity. Also in this case, students realized Homer's adult "rebellion

against the social drudgery of a blue-collar job," and preadolescent sarcasm, as a legitimate form of rebellion for the deviant, providing a platform for discussing what is truly moral and just. They did understand the sitcom episode's main point that family is more important than selfishness, and realized that other issues are involved, making individual rights and collective responsibilities a balancing act. Thus students paid attention to "the art form [animation], style [distorted, caricature of life], genre [comedy] and conventions [e.g., parody on stupidity] rather than the story itself" (Sturken & Cartwright, 2001, p. 269) as carriers of moral and immoral content and social justice issues. This suggests that teachers also can invite students to examine other forms of rhetoric, such as documentary fiction (Stokrocki, 2004). They also can delve deeper for hidden social justice concerns, such as gender concerns, generational differences, middle class values, and political agenda, in everyday contexts through the vehicles of popular culture, such as *The Simpsons*.

Gender issues. When discussing the bad behavior of the father and son, many of the males seemed to tolerate physical aggression, as in Bart's fighting at school, Homer's strangling of Bart, and Homer's smashing guitars. The father role [Homer] imitates the rock star as role model and gets away with negative behaviors initially. "It's a male thing," according to various male students. Female students, similar to Marge Simpson, are somewhat understanding of the male desire to escape, but are more critical of such behaviors. Tuman (1999) finds that females tend to react to "feminine content of social experience, care and concern, and domestic life, while males tend to choose traditional 'masculine content, including danger, power, aggression, violence, heroism, sports, mechanical objects and humor" (p. 57). Tuman (1999) suggested, "Uncovering the hidden, untapped meanings of artistic intentions might help children to break out of the gendered stereotypes that currently inform their drawings" (p. 57). Teachers must encourage students to reconsider their cultural gendered mores. For additional information on feminist resistance pedagogy, see Luke and Gore (1992).

Generational differences and middle class values. *The Simpsons* presents conflicts in values between ages and classes. The boomers' (people born between 1946–1960) throwaway income, in *The Simpsons*, enables the older folks to continue their brand of youth culture of escapist fun (ponytails, rock, motorcycles). Dad is featured as a big kid at heart who just wants to have fun. The busters (people from age 11–35 years old), in contrast, grab the fifties values of love, garish colors, and swing. Much of the contentiousness is white, heterosexual, and middle class, as seen in an exaggerated heroic view of a fictional America (jagodzinski, 1997). Thus boredom and apathy are by-products of the spoiled middle class as shown by life in the fast lane that features drugs, sex, and fast cars. *The Simpsons* sitcom, in a sense, questions various meanings and stages of adolescence and its values and even critiques itself in relation to class values; for example, an analysis of the family TV viewing (jagodzinski, 1997) pointed out that people watch "all the popular shows … the highest rated ones," but the boss pointed out that "They also watch the lowest … these people watch everything!" *The Simpsons* reveals such reality bites as the imperfect family and realistic personalities, such as knucklehead Homer and demon seed Bart, and family problems and platitudes. Educators need to offer quality programs rather than censorship to decrease symbolic and physical violence.

Sitcoms also are a kind of carnival [street party or charade] that bring out the devilish, the critical, and subversive pleasures in people (Stam, 1989). Subversive pleasures are those delights or amusements that are hidden or rebellious. With postmodernism comes change in values that occur as people criticize traditional norms and market economy shifts. The nineteenth century writer and cultural critic Bakhtin (1981) suggested that, "every community brings a distinct dialogical angle, each conveys its own cultural orientation and political aspirations to bear on the event" (p. 43).

Political agenda. What students do not see in *The Simpsons*, what is hidden, is the critique of right-wing power and the manipulation of capitalism—a "let them have rock and roll" attitude. It's one thing to laugh at the boomers for their faults, but baby busters need to realize how they are being misled as well. Educators need to discuss what power and economic issues are embedded in aesthetic forms such as sitcoms and to ask students to offer their solutions as well.[1]

Whereas other television shows may seem apolitical, *The Simpsons* is superficially conservative but full of subversion (McKenna, 2001). It tries to awaken our political and ethical consciousness. Groening explained, "Hidden in plain view are indictments of consumerism, jabs at bureaucracy and pokes at pretension" (Anthony, 2003). *The Simpsons* reveals the darker strains of satire as a celebration of America and the American family in its exuberance and absurdity. People seek happiness and settle for less. People may laugh at the everyday issues that evolve during the episodes, but they ultimately find relief when the stories conclude in a humanistic resolution. Visual culture reveals a hyper-reality characterized by the need to escape but then to face reality. Inane humor might be entertaining but moral training that considers several relationships and viewpoints is educationally memorable.

Discussing issues about outrageous television families, like *The Simpsons* with middle school students, in relation to their own families, empowers them possibly to do something about their problems (Polaniecki, 2006), or at least to understand them. Whereas, some people may find *The Simpsons* immoral (Sterle, 2001), the social justice aim of the sitcom is to find the fool in each of us. Ultimately, the teacher's role is to facilitate discussion to broaden students' understanding of diverse opinions, deeper issues, and maximization of collective benefits and penalties in the social justice system.

AUTHOR'S NOTE
Special thank you to Art Teacher, Karen Tabor and her students from Fremont Middle School, Mesa, Arizona, for participating in this lesson.

Anthony, T. (2003). Simpsons' creator Matt Groening talks comedy. Associated Press. Retrieved on April 21, 1999, from http://www.canoe.ca/TelevisionShowsS/simpsons_groening.html

ArtsEdge. (1994). *The National Standards for Arts Education.* Sponsored by The Kennedy Center. Retrieved January 27, 2008, from http://artsedge.kennedy-center.org/teach/standards.cfm

Bakhtin, M. (1981). *The dialogic imagination* (C. Emerson & M. Holquist, Trans.). Austin, TX: University of Texas Press.

Burgh, G. (2004). Seeking justice as a strategy for teaching and learning in SOSE. *The Social Educator, 22*(3), 25–33. [SOSE means Studies of Society and Environment.]

Coleman, E. (1994). The funnies, the movies, and aesthetics. *Journal of Popular Culture,* 89–95.

Freedman, K. (2003). The importance of student artistic production to teaching visual culture. *Art Education, 56*(2), 38–43.

Green, G. (2004, March). Reading violent images. *Art Education, 57*(2), 6–13.

Irwin, W., Conrad, M., & Skoble, A. (2001). *The Simpsons and philosophy.* Chicago: Open Court Pub.

jagodzinski, j. (1997). Pun(K) *Deconstruction: Experifigural writings in art & art education.* Mahwah, NJ: Lawrence Erlbaum.

Keifer-Boyd, K., Amburgy, P., & Knight, W. (2003). Three approaches to teaching visual culture in K–12 school contexts. *Art Education, 56*(2), 44–51.

Lewis, T. (2002). Religious rhetoric and the comic frame in *The Simpsons. Journal of Media and Religion, 1*(3), 1153–165.

Luke, C. & Gore, J. (1992). *Feminisms and critical pedagogy.* New York. Routledge.

McGuire, M. (2003, Nov. 2). The immortal Simpsons: From counter culture to pop culture. *The Tribune,* D12.

McKenna, K. (2001, May–June). Matt Groening interview. *My generation, AARP,* 52–54.

Noddings, N. (2002). *Educating moral people: A caring alternative to character education.* New York: Teachers College Press.

Pang, V. O. (1991). Teaching children about social issues: Kidpower. In C. Sleeter (Ed.), *Empowerment through multicultural education* (pp. 179–197). Albany, NY: SUNY Press.

Pinsky, R. (2002, Nov. 5). Creating the 'real,' in bright yellow and blue. *The New York Times,* 1–2.

Polaniecki, S. (2006). Teaching through TV: Transformative encounters with constructed reality, In P. Duncum (Ed.), *Visual culture in the art class: Case studies* (pp. 39–46). Reston, VA: National Art Education Association.

Purpel, D. (1989). *The moral & spiritual crisis in education: A curriculum for justice & compassion in education.* New York: Bergin & Garvey.

Reeves, M. (1999). School is hell: Learning with (and from) *The Simpsons.* In T. Daspit, & J. Weaver (Eds.), *Popular culture and critical pedagogy.* New York: Garland.

Shapiro, D. A. (2000). Some active alternatives to reading in philosophy for children, *Analytic Teaching, 21*(1), 15–20.

Stam, R. (1989). *Subversive pleasures.* Baltimore, MD: Johns Hopkins University Press.

Sterle, F .G. (2001). Simpsons: Morality from the 'Immoral'. Retrieved September 30, 2006, from http://www.snpp.com/other/papers/fs.paper.html

Stokrocki, M. (2004). Documentary rhetoric or fiction? University students react to *Bowling for Columbine. Journal of Social Theory in Art Education, 24,* 46–61.

Sturken, M., & Cartwright, L. (2001). Postmodernism and popular culture. *Practices of looking: Introduction to visual culture.* New York: Oxford University Press.

Tavin, K. (2003). Wrestling with angels, searching for ghosts: Toward a critical pedagogy of visual culture. *Studies in Art Education, 44*(3), 197–213.

Taylor, P., & Ballengee-Morris, C. (2003). Using visual culture to put a contemporary "fizz" on the study of pop art. *Art Education, 56*(2), 20–24.

Tuan, Yi-Fu. (1993). *Passing strange and wonderful: Aesthetics, nature, and culture.* New York: Kodansha International.

Tuman, D. (1999). Gender style as form and content: An examination of gender stereotypes in the subject preference of children's drawings. *Studies in Art Education, 41*(1), 40–69.

Wikipedia. (2008). How I spent my summer vacation. *The Simpsons,* 2, fourteenth season [2002]. Retrieved January 30, 2008, from http://en.wikipedia.org/wiki/How_I_Spent_My_Strummer_Vacation

ENDNOTE

[1] For cross-cultural comparison, a Turkish professor asked these same questions to students in Turkey and they pointed out that life is more democratic in America and students have freedom to say what they want. He pointed out that in Ottoman Turkey, Marge Simpson's hairdo [status] couldn't be higher than the Sultan's turban.

Engaging Students' Social Imagination Without Telling Them What to Think: Two Curriculum Projects

Mary Hafeli and Linda McConaughy

Introduction

Teaching students to become socially responsible people who are curious about and active participants in issues and events in their worlds is an essential goal for many art educators. Yet, at times, fostering dialogue and encouraging students to produce artwork around socially relevant issues can be daunting for teachers. The challenge, for some, is how to encourage students to develop informed views and individual voices instead of teachers simply presenting their own personal social and political beliefs. What are effective ways to invite students—who bring their own ideas, artistic concerns, and age-based cultural perspectives—to engage social issues as source material for their studio work? What kinds of classroom strategies help them to form personal insights about things they might otherwise consider of no real consequence to their lives? And how do we in turn teach kids that their art can both resonate with and have relevance in worlds beyond their immediate ones?

In this chapter, we describe two middle school curriculum projects, developed by art teacher Linda McConaughy, which address these questions. Our focus is on what we consider an enabling component of social justice art education—students' development of a "social imagination" (Greene, 1995).[1] In the account of the lessons themselves and samples of student artwork and writing that follow, we examine how young adolescents' ideas about war, justice, and the seemingly private and at times isolating experience of being human were invited, developed, transformed, and made

KEY CONCEPTS

- Empowering Students as Creators of Meaningful Art/Culture
- Encouraging Independent Views and Voices
- Envisioning World and Social Issues
- Developing Empathy
- Building Community Through Collaborative Artmaking

public. In tracing some of the pedagogical decisions made and actions taken, we also describe how the circumstances were set up for the students to develop their own socially engaged views and voices—not as a result of indoctrination or through adopting their teacher's ideological leanings but through open-ended, learner-centered inquiry. Education is a place where a "common world … may come into being in the course of a continuing dialogue, which we ourselves can provoke and nurture in the midst of change" (Greene, 1995, p. 196). With this in mind, we portray not only what the experience was like for students but also the related issues for the teacher who wishes to engage in this kind of pedagogy.

Fallen Heroes

Encouraging students' social imagination as artists can be accomplished by locating entry points for incorporating issues-based content into the ongoing teaching of formal and media-based concepts and skills. For McConaughy, who has been teaching at Parkville Middle School[2] for 14 years, this opportunity emerged 3 years ago in an eighth-grade portraiture unit. Every year McConaughy's students, like many teens, want to be able to make images that look "real," and they welcome studio experiences that teach representational skills while focusing on subjects and themes that are interesting and meaningful to them. At the start of the unit, the students explored the structures and proportions of the human face, directly observing each other and examining the visual qualities of their own faces with mirrors. Typically, after guided and independent sketching, exploration of value and color, and examination of artists' works, the students' studio work would culminate with drawing or painting self-portraits.

During the winter of 2005, McConaughy began teaching the unit as she had in previous years, helping students learn the proportions of their faces through observation and sketching. However, as she recalls:

… my ideas about how to proceed changed while watching the evening news. I learned of a university project honoring soldiers who had been killed in the Iraq war. University students and teachers worked together to paint portraits of soldiers that were displayed in a campus gallery. I was moved by the exhibit and by the impact it had on the university community. I began thinking about ways I could modify my portraiture unit to include a similar response to the Iraq war. The following day, I showed my students the videotape of the news report and we discussed their thoughts. I presented my ideas for a new way to culminate our portraiture unit: would they be interested in painting portraits of soldiers from Maryland who had died in combat?

The students initially hesitated. Many had family members in active military service, and thus supported the war, whereas some were against the war and did not want to participate in a project that might be seen as endorsing it. The students were also concerned about the level of difficulty the assignment presented and doubted their ability to paint the portraits with the high degree of accuracy they felt would be necessary. "What if our paintings don't look enough like the soldiers?" These worries seemed to go beyond the developmental need for realistic representation, evidenced by the comments of several students who, in class discussion, voiced the concern to "get it right" in order to honor the memory of the soldiers who had died. After they were promised they would receive one-on-one help if needed, they agreed to do it. Internet searches identified Maryland soldiers who had died in the war and students found and recorded their names, ages, hometowns, and circumstances of their deaths. After much consideration and discussion, and an agreement that the project would remain politically neutral, each student selected a soldier to adopt as the subject of their portraits.

One student, Carlyn, wanted to paint a woman so she chose Army Pfc. Leslie D. Jackson, of Richmond, Virginia. The only photograph Carlyn could find was her soldier's graduation photo—Jackson was only 18 years old at the time of her death. Lauren, another student, chose Army

Staff Sgt. James L. Pettaway, Jr. of Glen Burnie, Maryland—after learning about a young son he left behind—and based her painting on a photo of the sergeant in uniform. Lauren wanted to make something that would help Sgt. Pettaway's son know about his father's heroic service and his life. Students selected and printed the photos and created sketches of their subjects, concentrating on proportion, light, and shadow. They then experimented with color mixing and practiced painting techniques to build the confidence they needed to begin painting their soldiers' portraits.

Soldier Portraits.

The paintings were hung around the classroom several times for students to share their ideas and talk about their work. It was during one of these informal critiques that the personal impact of the studio process on the students emerged. For Kelly, as for many of the students, the project had turned into something more powerful than a typical unit on portraiture had. In a mid-critique debate about the war in which various viewpoints were shared she indicated, "I used to support it. I thought it would prevent terrorists. Since we started doing this, I changed my mind. It's not fair that people have to die, and it's so many."

Fallen Heroes Installation.

*The process of creating and displaying the nameplates was time-consuming and tedious; I questioned the merit of spending so much valuable class time on an activity that didn't encourage students to explore art skills. We needed to cover many more concepts and skills before the year was through, and I wondered if we should cut the project short. When students had completed 300-plus nameplates, I thought they were tiring of the process and might need me to give them a reason to bring the project to a close. I asked them if they wanted to stop: the answer was a resolute **no**.*

As the display continued to expand, more students questioned involvement in the war. One student, Alyssa, wrote in an artist's statement, "I believe this war has united America, but I also believe America could have been united in a way that wouldn't harm these soldiers." Raven wrote, "I think this war will impact America against terrorists, but I don't think it's fair that we have to put all of the government's money into war for more people to die, when it could be saving others." Students still did not want to leave a single soldier out. As Hannah put it, "Everyone deserves to have something." The more than 500 nameplates forced the exhibit to extend beyond the display space and into the hallways. The overwhelming volume and visual impact moved some viewers to tears, as witnessed by students, teachers, and school administrators.

The visual, social, and emotional impact of the Fallen Heroes project was obvious to the artists and to the school community at large. It was evidenced in the students' push to continue the production of nameplates, and it prompted a new understanding of how expressive, practiced, and skilled representation, relentless repetition, and overwhelming visual volume can be combined to create an arresting and evocative work.

Hopes, Wishes, and Regrets

In another eighth-grade community art initiative 2 years later, McConaughy again sought to develop a project that would allow her students to see the power of art and the power of their own ideas beyond the classroom. It was during her research that she came across My Secret (Warren, 2006), part of a series of books that chronicle the anonymous contributions to PostSecret, an ongoing community art project by Frank Warren.

Begun in 2004 with 3,000 postcards distributed on the streets of Washington, DC, Warren invited people to anonymously contribute

The 40 finished paintings with accompanying nameplates were hung in the school. Although this exhibition was in and of itself a moving tribute, the students asked to continue the project so that they could pay tribute to more of the fallen. After one brainstorming session, they decided to create and post nameplates (with name, age, hometown, and circumstances of death) for every American soldier killed in Iraq and Afghanistan. At the time, the number of the war casualties was nearing 2,000. Students formed teams and assigned jobs to research, design, and create the nameplates. One group researched the soldiers' stories, several groups formatted and typed the information, and the remaining groups worked in an assembly-line style to organize the finished nameplates and attach them to banners that would be added to the display.

The students' decision to expand the project seemed to indicate that they valued the newly realized social and political potential of their artwork. However, at the same time, their drive to continue the project posed a pedagogical dilemma. As McConaughy observed:

personal secrets—hopes, regrets, fears, betrayals, desires—in the form of handmade postcards mailed to his home address. Although he no longer solicits secrets on the streets, he continues to receive postcards by the thousands. The postcards are often elaborate and artful, and visually powerful. They combine text and images to divulge intimate admissions and confessions, the messages of which often transcend the individual who created them. To date, the PostSecret project has produced four books, been featured in exhibitions across the United States, and grown into a global community through Warren's website, postsecretcommunity.com. *My Secret* is a collection of postcards from teens and college students that carry the same visual power and emotional immediacy that have made Warren's project an international phenomenon.

McConaughy wondered if the PostSecret project could lead to a meaningful art experience for middle school students. She saw the potential, and after talking with students, colleagues, and school administrators, began to develop a plan. The project, called "Hopes, Wishes, and Regrets" by the students, was adjusted to not only address the varied maturity levels of middle school students but to encourage the involvement of the entire school. As McConaughy explained:

> *Rather than asking my students to share their secrets, my students asked the school community to share theirs—their hopes, wishes, and regrets—and my students made art in response to what was shared with them. In class, students brainstormed ways they could encourage others to share their secrets in a way that was not threatening and would remain anonymous. What would get the attention of kids at Parkville Middle School? What could we do to encourage kids to write down their thoughts without making it seem like just another school assignment?*

The solution was to promote the project with an underground advertising campaign. Students created flyers that they secretly left in desks, slid inside lockers, and even attached to snacks in cafeteria vending machines. One team's flyers looked like handwritten notes passed between friends that had been carelessly left behind in classrooms. Other students slipped flyers in between the pages of textbooks for their classmates to find. All of the advertisements contained this message:

> *Do you have a secret? Is there something you wish other people knew about you but you were too afraid to tell? What's your secret? Hope?*

> *Regret? Drop it in the box in the back of room 112. It's anonymous. VGA 8 students will make art out of your words. And maybe we'll all understand each other a little better.*

While they waited for the box to fill the class examined the qualities of *PostSecret* postcards, exploring ways the artists created relationships between images and text. They also looked at works by Kurt Schwitters, Robert Rauschenberg, and Jaune Quick-To-See Smith. These artists' works exemplified for the students the use of mixed media in the narrative juxtaposition and layering of image, formal elements and composition, and written text. McConaughy introduced materials for creating text and images, and students experimented with collage techniques incorporating image transfer, monoprints, letter stamps, gel medium, and digital photography. The notes that began to accumulate in the box were posted on a bulletin board each afternoon. When the students came to class the next morning they congregated around the display to read the new postings and make personal selections. Each student then evaluated which hope, wish, or regret he or she would choose as inspiration for his or her work that day.

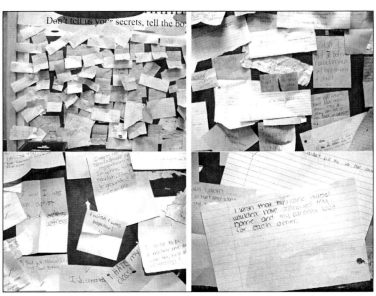

Secrets Wall.

When creating artworks that re-presented the statements, students considered the relationship of image and text as well as the expressive potential of formal elements and relationships like color, contrast, scale, and juxtaposition. They also chose materials whose sensory qualities aided in furthering particular visual messages. Hoping for a compelling impact, they opted to work in a format larger than the original PostSecret postcards. As artworks were completed, they were linked together to form panels that began to fill the school.

Topical themes emerged as the box continued to fill. Many of the hopes, wishes, and regrets dealt with relationships within families, between friends, and among classmates. While some notes were amusing and even silly, many of the messages expressed difficult and often painful emotions concerning self-image, loneliness, fitting in, and family security.

Students sometimes struggled to find ways to illustrate the messages in ways that would honor their writers' words. As Eva wrote:

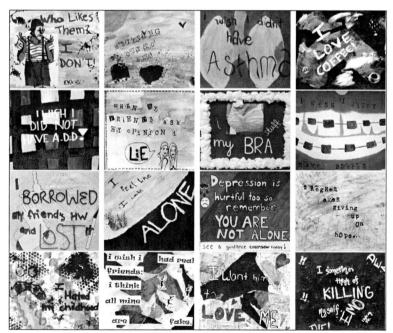

Hopes, Wishes, Regrets Panels.

Anybody can put hopes, secrets, anything in the box. We make art out of what people write, and we try to express the ideas as best we can, so we can try to connect everybody and help people understand each other. When we make a piece of art out of someone's secret, we have to try to figure out what the person was feeling so we can express it through the artwork. I also tried to put my own personal feelings into the artwork to help me connect with the person that wrote the secret.

Moreover, they came to understand that they had more connections to other students than they had ever realized. This was startling to many, such as Jessica, who said: "They really surprise me because I can relate to a lot of the secrets, and I'm sure a lot of other kids can too." As Orret indicated:

Some people may think that their lives are different, but this project shows that there are other kids out there who have some of the same problems. For kids who thought that they were the only ones who felt a certain way or had to deal with a certain problem, they found out other kids were going through the same things.

As the project progressed, the students talked about controversial content that sometimes appeared in the message box. How should a note that expressed racist attitudes be handled? In one case, the students decided to turn a submission that read, "I hate black people" into an art piece with the message "I think I'm a racist" because they felt that racism was an issue that needed to be addressed. Similarly, when several messages about family violence appeared a group of three students responded by working with the school guidance department to start a peer counseling group.

Because of the project, the art students also began sharing more of their own secrets with each other, including their experiences with homelessness, illness, and self-image. The exhibition inspired other teachers at Parkville to use the project as a way to start dialogue in their classrooms about race, religion, family, and violence. When Frank Warren included photos and writing about McConaughy's project on the *PostSecret* website, teachers from as far away as Australia responded, asking about how they might develop similar art experiences for their students.

Teaching Art With the Social Imagination in Mind

Designing studio art experiences for the development of young people's social imagination requires teachers to carefully consider their instructional goals and philosophical values. To plan instruction such as what was

Hopes, Wishes, Regrets Panels.

Too often, teachers seem to believe that teaching for socially based art requires a replacement, or trade off, of one instructional focus for another. These perceived tradeoffs include skills with materials and techniques for concept, a concern for formal issues and compositional relationships for an attention to message, open-ended questions for predetermined ways of thinking and doing, or kids' own beliefs and attitudes for those of teachers or other adults. While we recognize that socially engaged studio work, indeed any meaningful studio practice, demands transformative thinking and a building within the process of new insights about an issue or problem, we also think such tradeoffs are unnecessary. Kids do not need to mimic their teachers' step-by-step directions toward uniform visual outcomes, nor do they need to be told what to think about issues in order to become socially engaged as artists. Instead, they need opportunities to research, debate, and form their own ideas about issues, and time to learn the art concepts and develop the technical, representational, and expressive skills that will enable them to communicate their socially imaginative ideas to the world.

done for these two projects—with the explicit aims of furthering students' command of technical, formal, and representational skills and concepts, meeting kids where they were at conceptually, and inviting *their* artistic, political, and social ideas without imposing the teacher's views—can be a complex pedagogical undertaking. As Greene (2007) wrote:

> There are not only the meanings implicit in the surrounding culture; there are the meanings that develop in children's and adolescents' cultures. It may be possible to help students trans-form information into knowledge if teaching were to take place in a context of open questions, questions finding differing kinds of expression depending on the questioner's age and life situation. (¶ 7)

REFERENCES

Greene, M. (1995). *Releasing the imagination: Essays on education, the arts, and social change.* San Francisco: Jossey-Bass.

Greene, M. (2007). *Beyond incomprehensibility.* Retrieved May 30, 2008, from http://www.maxinegreene.org/articles.php

Warren, F. (2006). *My secret: A PostSecret book.* New York: William Morrow.

ENDNOTES

[1] For Greene, "social imagination" is "the capacity to invent visions of what should be and what might be in our deficient society, on the streets where we live, in our schools" (1995, p. 5).

[2] Parkville Middle School is located outside Baltimore, MD in an economically and culturally diverse community. The school, with 1200 students, hosts both a magnet program for technology and a well-supported art program.

We Begin Again After the Tabula Rasa

Anne Thulson

Concentration is not one's friend, but is treacherous.
(Charles Garoian & Yvonne M. Gaudelius, 2006)

I teach social justice through interruption. Through an Expeditionary Learning Design, my school's kindergarten through eighth-grade students explore our curriculum deeply, uncovering, rather than simply covering, the content (Hawkins, 2000). A culture of inquiry is expected, including in the art studio where the students work on long-term projects integrated with their classroom studies.

The three projects presented in this chapter demonstrate how my fourth- and fifth-grade students and I disrupt the continuous narratives of power. My students and I stop and think about these narratives and develop other ways these stories can be told. One opportunity for this to happen is through the making of things. A cue can be taken from the Dadaists, who *lost confidence* in their own culture's continuous narratives. Their disgust and anger over WWI led them to dismantle the norms of the institutions that brought them the war by shocking the bourgeois, demolishing <u>their</u> idea of art, attacking common sense, public opinion, education, institutions, museums, good taste, and in short, the whole prevailing order (Tzara, 1918).

Through demonstrations, performances, and journals, Dadaists spread new theories and contexts for understanding art throughout Europe that included the poetic role of the subconscious, non-sequential narrative, text-image interaction, juxtaposition, and play (Hofmann, 2001). We used these

KEY CONCEPTS

- Continuous Narratives of Power
- Dada Collage as Deconstruction of Power Narratives
- Deconstructing 20th-Century Child Labor
- Deconstructing Spanish Colonialism
- Deconstructing School Culture

patterns of disruption to challenge prevailing historical narratives in three projects.

The following three projects addressed the narratives of early 20th-century child labor, the Spanish colonization of Mesoamerica, and our own school's culture. These narratives seem to defy questioning, prohibit trespassing, and deny multiple perspectives (Dimitriadis & McCarthy, 2001; Garoian & Gaudelius, 2006). They are formidable and therefore it was necessary to develop a wily plan to crack the system (Sullivan, 2008). This plan relied on the intelligence of young children, a classroom culture of inquiry, 21st-century art practices, an integrated arts curriculum, and the medium of collage (Marshall, 2008).

We attacked the continuous narratives in the art studio using integrated projects that spring from the school's science and humanities content. When other disciplines are integrated into the art curriculum, opportunities are developed in our classroom for students to critique and enchant the world. Responding poetically to the world through many media deepens our understandings and makes us smarter (Daniels, Hyde, & Zemelman, 1998; Duckworth, 1987; Expeditionary Learning, 2003; Marshall, 2008; Pink, 2005). "Creativity requires that the school of knowing finds connections with the school of expressing, opening the doors to the hundred languages of children ... The spirit of play can pervade also the formation and construction of thought" (Malaguzzi, 1998, p. 79).

The first act is to take things apart: to deconstruct the dominant narrative. "Everything had to be demolished" (Janco as cited in Lippard, 1971, p. 36). Through practices of inquiry we conceptually deconstruct images and text. Then we pick the pieces up and imagine new constructions. I want my students to be harsh cynics, but also sanguine reformers. Thus, I seek projects where irony and earnestness go hand in hand.

I base instruction on Gablik's (1991) idea that:

It is precisely at this crossover between the reactive mode of deconstruction and the more active mode of reconstruction, in which we are no longer merely the observers of our social fate but are participating co-creators … the shapers of new frameworks, the orchestrators of culture and consciousness. (p. 26)

Or, as Janco put it, "We begin again after the 'tabula rasa'" (Lippard, 1971, p. 36).

I scaffold carefully what I want my students to experience and learn. We build background knowledge (Duckworth, 1987), use artist models (Expeditionary Learning, 2003; Stiggins, 2004), apply 21st-century art practices (Gude, 2004), use a limited palate of images (Garoian & Gaudelius, 2006), and assess for learning in the midst of the artmaking (Bennett, 2007; Stiggins, 2004).

I create opportunities for the students to construct knowledge and projects, and students interrupt my own continuous narrative as the authoritative voice in the classroom. As I observe my students' words and work, they change my teaching process and my thinking. I hold my own narrative lightly as I adjust my lesson plans and expectations accordingly (Bennett, 2007; Duckworth, 1987; Stiggins, 2004). What becomes clear is that "there is great destructive … work to be done" (Tzara, 1918, p. 1).

Recontextualizing the Child in Child Labor (Rights of Childhood Collage)

My students studied simple machines and robotics in science through the question, "Does technology bring us progress?" In the art studio, we looked at artistic responses to that question.

The Italian Futurists madly loved the machine (Marinetti, 1909). When I presented The Futurists to the students, they marveled at their enthusiasm for speed and smokestacks. The students made a futurist-type photomontage using repetition and pattern to show mechanization, and wire sculptures representing human machine hybrids. As they worked on this project, they pondered the question "Does technology bring us progress?" They believed that "maybe so."

The students then watched Charlie Chaplin's *Modern Times* (1936) and noticed a different view on mechanization. Through the film, Chaplin asked the question: What do machines do to people? The discussion ensued about how artists use humor to critique society. Once again the students wondered, does technology bring us progress? Well, maybe not so much.

The concept of the artist as critic of culture led straight to the early American photographer, Lewis Hine, who used his camera as a research tool and for social reform. The students pondered the question "What did [Hine] think of machines back in the 1910s? Did [Hine] believe that technology brings us progress?" (Freedman, 1994).

The students used Hine as a bridge to consider early photography, and used his photos and primary source texts to explore the topic. To further understand the concepts, the students explored contrasting images of hand-looms and textile factories and a mill town before and during the industrial revolution. Their differences were discussed.

Next, the class read together a one-page document of the National Child Labor Committee's Declaration of Dependence (NCLC, 1913). At first the students were offended by the title. They said, "It's supposed to be Declaration of Independence!" "Yeah! Kids should have freedom!" However, after we read the document together, the students were uncharacteristically solemn. The document asserts that all children are born with four rights: the right to play and dream, the right to a normal sleep of the night season, the right to an education, and the right to freedom from toil for daily bread. Children have the right to be dependent on adults for their basic needs. What became clear to them was that the document is not about freedom for fun; it is about freedom from tyranny.

The final collage emulated in art what Lewis Hine and the National Child Labor Committee did in life—they disrupted those institutions of child labor. Through the art piece, I wanted the students to remove the children from the context of abuse and put them into the context of the four rights of childhood.

Before the students began the collage, two 21st-century concepts were introduced: indexing and re-contextualization. The students practiced both through two mini projects: a shoe installation mimicking Antin's *100 Boots*, and recontextualizing animals from nature photos.

They were now ready to interrupt the contexts of Hine's documentary photographs. Each student chose one of the four declared rights of childhood to illustrate through indexing and re-contextualization. They then selected one Hine photo to interrupt the narrative of child labor. Students cut out the children from the factory in the photographs and placed them on a blank piece of paper. On the paper they recreated a new context, of their childhood rights, with paint, colored pencil, and colored papers. There created soccer fields (the right to play and dream), classrooms (the right to an education), cozy beds (the right to the proper sleep of the night season), and abundant feasts (the right to freedom from toil for daily bread). Hine's children suddenly found safer and happier contexts. The barefooted bobbin boy went after a soccer pass across a grassy playing field. The mill girl staring out of a factory window now stared at a table of gifts and cake with a colorful banner overhead that read, "Happy Birthday Sophie!" Although she still looked just as dazed as before, it now seemed out of delight instead of despair. The coal breaker boys played video games and someone had gently tucked the glass factory children into bed.

The students then returned to the photographs and attached black paper on the back, behind the missing children's spaces. These eerie images seemed to serve as dark witnesses to the continuous narrative of oppression of the powerless. We displayed the two images side by side. The hopeful images seemed to celebrate the work of Lewis Hine and the National Child Labor Committee, while the ghost silhouettes seemed to remind the viewer to keep vigilant and to remember children who still labor throughout the world.

Primary Source Collage (Spain and Mesoamerica)

With their classroom teachers, the students studied the 16th-century collision between Spain and Mesoamerica. They developed an understanding about both cultures through a guided study of primary sources. In the art studio, students learned that the dominant narrative is just content they learn, not necessarily truth. But as they learn the content they are building a scaffold of knowledge where they can then place more new knowledge into a context. In this context they learned the art of Spain, Mesoamerica, and Latin America in order to make a primary source collage.

The Primary Source Collage project required students to respond poetically to the conflict between Spain and Mesoamerica. Each student thought of an event or idea that represented one consequence of the collision of these cultures. They then reconstructed and arranged images from Mesoamerica, Spain, and Latin America to represent this consequence.

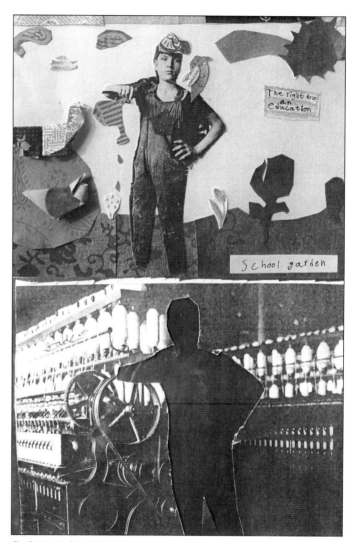

The Right to an Education, Jade Walker (Rights of Childhood Collage).

Students used collage to represent and deepen their thinking (Malaguzzi, 1998), and it also became an emotional processing tool for students. They were bewildered and troubled by both cultures' acts concerning religion and death. The collages provided a place to work through and reflect on this provocative content. In collage, anything can be selected, edited, and joined together. Until you glue, there are no commitments, which allows for risk-taking and exploration even among the most reticent students. Because the focus is not on image rendering, creative energy is spent on creating meaning through the joining of images. This fluid and forgiving medium of play offers a safe place to reflect and discover through a dialogue of images.

I used the book *Codex Espagliensis*, a result of a collaboration between Enrique Chagoya, Guillermo Gomez-Pena, and Felicia Rice (1998) as the project's model. The focus was primarily on Chagoya, who took history apart and threw it back together to show the unofficial stories that lie beneath textbook history and popular media. By appropriating traditional North, Meso, and Latin American imagery, he interrupted the grand continuous narratives that silence and eclipse the experience of those who did not win the wars. As Chagoya (2007) put it:

> History, it has been said, is written by those who win the wars. Yet, there is always the other's History. In this context, history is an ideological construction, more than a science. In my codex book concept, I have decided that I am entitled to my own ideological construction. I tell the stories of cultural hybrids, of political collisions, of universal consequences. (p. 1)

Chagoya offered a fantastic feast for the eyes and heart, for the fourth and fifth graders. His humor and playfulness seemed contagious and prompted them to make some ideological constructions of their own.

However, first my students had to learn about imagery from Spain, Mesoamerica, and Latin America, as the students were not familiar with the images that Chagoya appropriated, and they did not know the difference between an Aztec deity and the Virgin of Guadalupe. In order to interrupt something, you need to know what you are interrupting.

Through mini studio projects, the students investigated Pre-Columbian pictographs, sculpture, codices, textiles, and calendars. I used *Leonardo's Window* (Boston Museum of Science), a child-friendly, linear perspective curriculum to explain the pictorial structure of Spanish Colonial Art. We also looked at its patronage and iconography, explored the hybridization of Catholic and Pre-Columbian art and the use of Retablos and Ex-Votos as vehicles of prayer. We also made a visit to the Denver Art Museum's collection of Pre-Columbian, Spanish, and Santos art.

Finally, the students were ready to view the *Codex* for the first time. The students explored the *Codex* pages, for the art they had studied and that Chagoya had appropriated. Then we interpreted the meanings behind his provocative juxtapositions. Because of how they prepared to learn the contexts of the art, the students were able to appreciate much of his iconoclasm and symbolism.

While they learned Chagoya's irony and messages, students started to create their own ideological constructions of universal consequences of the collision of Spain and Mesoamerica. These consequences included smallpox, appropriating Mesoamerican gold by Spain, replacing Aztec royalty with Spanish royalty, layering Catholicism over Aztec religion, war, and eclipsing one identity by another.

The students used the images of the art from Spain and Latin and Meso-America to hybridize, re-contextualize, layer, and juxtapose through collage (Gude, 2004). An open-mouthed Aztec stone sculpture screamed "Nooooooo!" The bent-over posture of Itzcuintli represented a dying posture

Shouted, Matt Biggs (Primary Source Collage).

of a smallpox victim. An Aztec temple became a throne for a European man. The Aztec stone calendar represented Spanish gold coins, think bubbles, and a wrestling platform for two opposing sides. A burning village became a cart on wheels pulled around frantically by a mounted Cortes.

The collages mirrored the complexity of the narrative; their work did not read as bad guys versus good guys. The range of images evoked diverse interpretations of conquest from furious violence to contemplative musings. Regardless of the interpretations, the continuous narrative of conquest was questioned and mourned.

This project has raised questions about how appropriate it was to make art with another culture's sacred forms, and for years I kept this practice out of my curriculum. However, when I started using 21st-century art as models for projects, the practice of appropriation became an integral, conceptual tool. The students learned to check their work and ask, "Do you think this is disrespectful or is it OK?"

Voice and Power in Text and Image (Broadside Collages)

The fourth and fifth graders studied the American Revolution with their teachers, and asked, "Who has a voice?" and "Who has power?" They studied Broadsides, the protest street literature of the Patriots. In the art, voice, power, protest, and public contexts were addressed through mentor artist Barbara Kruger (Art:21, 2001). Kruger's photo-text collages placed in public streets challenge 21st-century American narratives of power with questions, rebuttals, and taunts. As a side benefit, my students liked her sassy cleverness.

Their final project was creating and posting their own protest broadsides. One question considered was if the public space for the American patriots were their streets, what was our public space as fourth and fifth graders? The school space became the answer. Students voiced concern about the school they felt they had no power to change—they interrupted the school's physical and psychological space (Sullivan, 2008).

Before Kruger was introduced, text-image interactions were explored. The students examined picture book pages with and without the texts and noticed how the meanings of the pictures were influenced by the text. Different texts words were applied to the images to try to shift their meanings. The students were then ready to examine Kruger's work about the discussion focused on contexts for art and why a piece of art seems different on a billboard than in an art gallery. Questions such as "How does art get seen?" and "Can art interrupt ordinary public life?" were debated (Gablik, 1995).

Kruger's ideas about voice and power also were discussed. After looking at *Your Gaze Hits the Side of My Face*, the students discussed how women sometimes do not like to be stared at like an object and that a gaze can feel like a slap. My students related this to their own culture:

"It's like when someone gives you a dirty look!"

"Yeah! And you can't prove it!"

"They get away with it and you can't prove it to the teacher."

"A look can hurt as much as words."

The students then illustrated a personal experience of when they stood up for what was right. This idea came from the book they read aloud in class, *Johnny Tremaine* (Forbes, 1999), a book about a young man in Revolutionary America who stood up for what he believed in. They recreated the place where they stood up for what was right, using colored paper collage. Their vivid memories helped them to make detailed environments of this place (Gude, 2007).

Next, they added the words they spoke in the situation: "I broke it!" "I'm her friend!" "Leave him alone!" "It was my fault!" Next to these words, the students added a cropped black-and-white photograph of the part of their body that acted. Most of the photos were of mouths (speaking the truth), but a few were of feet (walking away from a situation) or hands (not hitting or shoving). A discussion ensued about how our bodies and words can interrupt a bad situation and change it to good. Standing up for what is right is an interruption—it interrupts the continuous narrative of unreflective impulses and habits.

The students then made their own protest broadsides to post anonymously in the school; they protested anything within the context of the school. These protests addressed their feelings of powerlessness in an adult world, which included loss of play, meaningless rules, and feeling claustrophobic and trapped in a school day. They photographed images around the school that illustrated their protests (Gude, 2007).

They then added text to the images. Kruger's texts were meant as protests, but their meanings were not totally clear. As the students chose their words, we discussed the difference between protest art and literal protest. We were protesting, but we were doing it through art. White's (Strunk & White, 1959) quote, "Be obscure clearly" (p. 79), helped us craft our text. Students critiqued their texts to see if they were too obvious

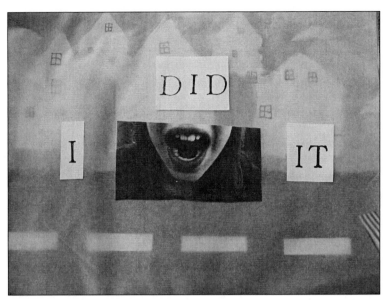

I Did It, Shannon Wilson (Standing Up Collage).

or too obscure (Hugo, 1979). Oftentimes, this led to revision. One girl's text "I don't like camping!" protested the school's camping trips. Her words accompanied an image of a tent. After she was challenged to be less literal, she changed her words from a direct statement to a wish. "I'd rather sleep in a hotel!" contrasted nicely with the tent image, and seemed to make a more powerful statement.

Students left the art studio in small groups and posted their broadsides within our building—they enthusiastically interrupted the walls with their voice. "I'd rather sleep in a hotel!" found a home on our camping supply closet. "It's not a crime!" which included a photograph of a pack of gum, was hung above a teacher's desk. "Homework kills trees!" was stuck above the faculty copier. A photograph of kids trapped behind bars with the words, "Work Contains Us!" was posted next to a math display. The broadsides were successful in interrupting the continuous narrative of the school, provoking conversation among staff, and giving students a chance to speak.

Conclusion

My intention through these projects was to join *the school of knowing with the school of expressing.* Compelling topics of social justice gave us a reason to make art. We needed the skills and knowledge from the art standards in order to represent this content in our art. Child labor, Meso-American conflict, and political protest were the horses pulling the art standards and not the other way around. Art standards are not an end in themselves but are used as a means to inquire into and create art about fairness and truth. This does not belittle the standards, but rather elevates them. The standards become indispensable tools for my students to poetically visualize fairness and truth. They want to master them because they need them, not because they need an A in art. My students' desire and demand for art standards increased greatly because they cared deeply about what they were visualizing (Duckworth, 1987; Expeditionary Learning, 2003; Hawkins, 2000). We *uncovered* continuous narratives by *covering* art curriculum: art history, criticism, design, art media, 21st-century art practices (Gude, 2004), visual culture (Li, 2007), and right brain strategies (Pink, 2005). This would be impossible without the firm belief that children can work competently with simultaneous concerns, justice and poetry. As I watch my students do this, I have no doubt that, *"we can begin again after the tabula rasa."*

Art:21 (2001). *Season One: Consumption: Barbara Kruger*. http://www.pbs.org/art21/artists/kruger/index.html

Bennett, S. (2007). *That workshop book.* Portsmouth, NH: Heinneman.

Boston Museum of Science (1997). *Classroom activity: Using Leonardo's window.* http://www.mos.org/sln/Leonardo/UsingLeosWindow.html

Chagoya, E., Gomez-Pena, G., & Rice, F. (1998). *Codex Espagliensis: From Columbus to border control.* Santa Cruz, CA: Moving Parts Press.

Chagoya, E. (2007). *Collage imagery.* http://www.movingpartspress.com/Text/enrique.html

Chaplin, C. (Producer and Director) (1936). *Modern Times* [Motion picture], Los Angeles, CA: United Artists.

Daniels, H. (2005, March). *Keynote speech.* Lecture delivered at Expeditionary Learning National, Denver, CO.

Daniels, H., Hyde, A., & Zemelman, S. (1998). *Best practice new standards for teaching and learning in America's schools.* Portsmouth, NH: Heinemann.

Dimitriadis, G., & McCarthy, C. (2001). *Reading and teaching the postcolonial.* New York: Teachers College Press.

Duckworth, E. (1987). *The having of wonderful ideas and other essays on teaching and learning.* New York: Teachers College Press.

Expeditionary Learning. (2003). *Core Practice Benchmarks.* Garrison, NY: Expeditionary Learning Outward Bound.

Expeditionary Learning National Conference (2004). *Mystery Text Protocol* Denver, CO.

Freedman, R. (1994) *Kids at work: Lewis Hine and the crusade against child labor.* Chicago: Carus.

Forbes, E. (1999). *Johnny Tremaine.* New York: Random House.

Gablik, S. (1991). *The re-enchantment of art.* New York: Thames and Hudson Inc.

Gablik, S. (1995). *Conversations before the end of time.* New York: Thames and Hudson.

Garoian, C., & Gaudelius, Y. (2006, April). *A critical conjuring process.* Lecture delivered at National Art Education Association National Conference, Chicago, IL.

Gude, O. (2004). Postmodern principles: In search of a 21st century art education. *Art Education, 57*(1), 6–13.

Gude, O. (2007). Principles of possibility: Considerations for a 21st century art and culture curriculum. *Art Education, 60*(1), 6–17.

Hawkins, D. (2000) *The roots of literacy,* Boulder, CO: University Press

Hofmann, I. (2001). Documents of *Dada and Surrealism: Dada and Surrealist Journals in the Mary Reynolds Collection,* Ryerson and Burnham Libraries, the Art Institute of Chicago, 1 (Electronic Version).

Hugo, R. (1979). *The triggering town.* New York: W. W. Norton.

Li, Y. (2007). Teaching visual culture in the 21st Century art classroom, *Translations, 16*(2), n.p.

Lippard, L. (1971). *Marcel Janco, "Dada at Two Speeds,"* trans. Margaret I. Lippard in Dadas on Art, ed. Lucy R. Lippard, Englewood Cliffs, NY: Prentice-Hall, 1971, 36.

Malaguzzi, L. (1998). History, ideas, and basic philosophy: An interview with Lella Gandini, *The Hundred Languages of Children* (2nd ed.). Greenwich, CT: Ablex Publishing Corporation, 79.

Marinetti, F. (1909). *The Founding and Manifesto of Futurism*, Paris, Le Figaro.

Marshall, J. (2008). Visible thinking: Using contemporary art to teach conceptual skills. *Art Education, 61*(2), 38–46.

National Child Labor Committee. (1913). *Declaration of dependence by the children of American mines and factories and workshops assembled*, National Child Labor Committee Publication, 1907–1967. Kheel Center for Labor-Management Documentation and Archives, Cornell University Library.

Pink, D. (2005). *A whole new mind.* New York: Riverhead Books.

Stiggins, R. (2004). *Classroom assessment for student learning.* Portland, OR: Assessment Training Institute.

Strunk, W., & White, E.B. (1959). *The elements of style.* New York: Macmillan.

Sullivan, G. (2008, February). *Art practice and research.* Lecture delivered at Museum of Contemporary Art-Denver, Denver, CO.

Tzara, T. (1918). *Dada manifesto* trans. Robert Motherwell, Dada Painters and Poets Robert Motherwell. New York: George Wittenborn, Inc.

Considering Personal Context for Authentic Problem Solving

Alexandria W. Zettler

Gallery Opening at Studio 1

I walked up the wide steps onto a wooden wraparound porch. The open double doors seemed inviting as I stepped into a simple portico. Shuttered, double French doors blocked further entry. I was confused, and I looked around. There was a collection of red phones along the sidewalls. It seemed that I must pick one up in order to be admitted inside. A quiet, pained voice echoed through the mouthpiece:

> In a white supremacist patriarchy, that relationship which most threatened to disrupt, challenge, and dismantle white power and its concomitant social order was the legalized union between a white man and a black women. Slave testimony, as well as the dairies of southern white women, record incidents of jealously, rivalry, and sexual competitions between white mistresses and enslaved black women. Court records document that individual white men did try to gain public recognition of their bonds with black women either through attempts to marry or through efforts to leave property and money in wills. Most cases were contested by white family members. Importantly, white females were protecting their fragile social positions and power within patriarchal culture by asserting their superiority over black women. They were not necessarily trying to prevent white men from engaging in sexual relations with black women, for this was not in their power—such is the nature of patriarchy. So long as sexual unions with black women and white men took place in a non-legalized context, within a framework of subjugation, coercion, and degradation, the split between white female's status as "ladies" and black women's representations as "whores" could be maintained. Thus to some extent, white women's class and race privilege was reinforced by the maintenance of a system where black women were the objects of white male sexual subjugation and abuse. (hooks, 1995, p. 96)

I put the phone down, feeling a little sick.

Suddenly, the cloistered glass doors began to swing open. A long hallway stretched before me, decorated with dozens of eleven-by-fourteen-inch picture frames. Each frame displayed one or two figures, drawn with black ink on white paper. From a distance, the figures looked like little tribal cartoon characters from Africa or Australia. Were these story panels, each framing a single scene in a comic strip? As I drew near, I was both fascinated and horrified by the tiny, physically deformed characters, each adorned with intricate aboriginal designs. The androgynous figures had flat features and open mouths full of white teeth, white or black faces, and clothing drawn in elaborate designs, including soaring headdresses. The implied story lines seemed macabre, even gruesome; figures lay helplessly on the ground, and they lacked arms and feet. Malformed babies were strapped to armless adults. Figures appeared spider-like, with multiple sneaker-shod legs and feet and twisted limbs. The figures seemed to be reeling in the midst of violent action, in an apparently suspended moment of violent fusion. Sharp objects protruded from bellies of figures that writhed on the baselines of the drawings. Were the objects growing from the people? Or had the objects pierced them? I did not know.

KEY CONCEPTS

- Layla Ali
- bell hooks
- Kara Walker
- Contextual Considerations in Creating Art
- Authentic Problem Solving in Art Education

Holding my breath, I walked slowly into the interior chamber. Blue, red, purple, and yellow lights revolve in front of me, yet I am attracted to a small note card tacked to a wall. "Dear Cruel and malevolent Master, what irks me, you know this, is that I am and forever shall be a slave to that which brung me here" (Walker, 2001). The walls were covered with 19th-century-style black silhouettes of presumably southern, antebellum, black and white children, adolescents, and adults, displayed against white walls in grotesque, sexually violent, victimized, or compromised positions. Did these figures represent slaves and their owners, going about their business amongst copulation, murder, and mayhem? Silhouettes of towering oak trees and a variety of flora and fauna completed the scenes. The beauty and the attention to detail were fascinating. I saw my own black silhouette, cast amongst garish colors and chaos. I felt disgusted and confused. What was my part in these scenes?

Suddenly, I woke up; it had all been a dream, a dream about a collaborative installation of bell hooks' (1995) book, *Art on My Mind*, Laylah Ali's pen and ink drawings from her *Typology Series*, and Kara Walker's paper cutouts and commentary from her art instillation, *Darkytown Rebellion*. Why was I drawn to these women in my dreams? What did they share? And, more specifically, in what framework did the artwork interrelate?

Initial Thoughts

While considering relationships between artists and their respective frameworks, I have realized that I am not interested in thinking and reflecting about art history as an independent concept; rather, I am interested in placing art into the socio-cultural and political context of my own experience. What fascinates me is how critical analysis and authentic problem solving relate to the here and now. When I was a high school art teacher, I encouraged my students to consider specific problems related to their personal socio-cultural, political, or emotional issues. The question I would often ask was, "What problem are you trying to address in your work? Does this issue relate to racism, identity, violence, or personal and/or human suffering? Do these issues pertain to you, as an individual?" The objective was to use personal context as a source of power in their works. I believed that by studying the *who, when, where, how,* and *why* (Anderson & Milbrandt, 2005) of ourselves first, we could bring art history forward in an authentic way. In order to teach this process properly, though, I first needed to understand the conceptual relationship between hooks, Ali, Walker, and myself. I began with a contextual examination of our shared history.

Our Shared Cultural Context

bell hooks, Laylah Ali, and Kara Walker are all African American women. I am a woman, but I am not African American, so why do I feel such a connection with these women? Perhaps growing up with one foot in the North and one foot in the South helped me understand racism as a fundamental issue of egalitarianism.

I was born in the summer of 1962 in Chicago, Illinois, where I grew up in the midst of the nationwide Civil Rights Movement and the turmoil of the Vietnam War. Presidents Eisenhower, Kennedy, and Johnson (respectively) signed the Civil Rights Act of 1957, 1960, 1964, 1968, and the Voting Rights Act of 1965. In 1963, President Kennedy was assassinated in Dallas, Texas. In 1965, Malcolm X, a black minister and activist, was assassinated in New York City. Dr. Martin Luther King organized sit-ins and mobilized a range of other nonviolent protests. On April 4, 1968, King was assassinated in Memphis. On June 5, 1968, Bobby Kennedy was assassinated in Los Angeles, and from August 26 through August 29, demonstrators and police officers clashed in violent confrontations during the Democratic National Convention in Chicago.

All of this occurred against the backdrop of the Tet Offensive in Vietnam, which effectually forced President Johnson to announce that he would not seek reelection in 1968. Many southern blacks who registered to vote were evicted from their homes; shop owners refused to sell them basic goods; professionals withheld services from them. Despite legislation, "desegregated" schools and universities barred blacks from entering. Black and white civil-rights activists, called *Freedom Riders*, challenged segregation by riding interstate buses into the south in order to test the Interstate Commerce Act of 1887. Some activists disappeared or were executed and thrown into rivers. When my parents and I drove from Illinois to Natchez, Mississippi, to visit my maternal grandparents for Christmas, we needed to obtain a special letter from the Natchez Sheriff that assured any reader that we were not "causing trouble."

My grandfather was one of the few town physicians who treated *black folks*, even though the Grand Dragon of the Ku Klux Klan was a family friend. My grandparents employed blacks to do menial labor around their large antebellum home and paid them comparatively well. One of these employees was Lena, a black cook who was as old as my grandparents. She could neither read nor write, and she lived with several generations of relatives in a shanty house near the Mississippi Bayou. The buildings that had once been slave quarters still remained on my grandparents' property.

In Chicago, my mother taught at a progressive inner-city public magnet school called *Metro*. Many very intelligent black children attended the school. I remember riding high on my father's shoulles in Freedom Marches <u>in</u> the midst <u>of</u> people singing, "We Shall Overcome." Once a year, my parents hosted a huge pig roast in our suburban backyard. The guest list frequently included black high-school students, their families, and my parents' colleagues and peers from the University of Illinois and the School of the Art Institute of Chicago. We also rented our carriage house to a black elementary-school teacher and rented our sunroom apartment to a black sociology student from Northwestern University. According to my mother, our neighbors suggested that we were "bringing down our elite Evanston neighborhood with those people."

Ten years before me, bell hooks was known by the name of Gloria Watkins in Hopkinsville, Kentucky. Prior to integration, her teachers recognized her as a gifted child with an outstanding ability in critical thinking. hooks loved attending school because she knew she was the black community's hope for the future (hooks, 1994). She attended high school in the late 1960s, during desegregation. hooks wrote about this experience in *Teaching to Transgress* (1994).

> School changed utterly with racial integration. Gone was the messianic zeal to transform our minds and beings that has characterized teachers and their pedagogical practices in our all-black schools. Knowledge was suddenly about information only. It had no relation to how one lived, behaved. It was no longer connected to antiracist struggle. Bussed to white school, we soon learned that obedience, not a zealous will to learn, was what was expected of us. Too much eagerness to learn could easily be seen as a threat to white authority. (p. 3)

When she was treated like a second-class citizen, hooks (1994) lost her love of the school experience. Nevertheless, she continued in school and earned a doctorate in 1983 from the University of California, Santa Cruz, with a dissertation on the writer Toni Morrison.

Laylah Ali and Kara Walker are both closer to my age. Ali was born in 1968 in Buffalo, New York, and Walker was born in 1969 in Stockton, California. In several interviews, Ali commented on her experience as the only black student in an all-white school. Specifically, in an interview with inNIVA (2007) Ali explained,

> I think that a brown person who has lived amongst a white majority—and this could apply to any visible minority, though I think it is intensified in those groups that have a long historical track record of being despised—has often been looked at, singled out, noticed, because of the visual spectacle that is inherent in being visually different. (¶ 12)

In contrast, Walker grew up in the "multicultural" environment of California in the 1970s. Her father was first a university art professor at the University of the Pacific but accepted a chair position at Georgia State University when she was 13. In an interview with Sheets (2002), Walker described the culture shock she experienced when moving to the suburbs of Atlanta:

> Going to Georgia was a little bit like going back in time, with the social mores, the dos and don'ts, the very conservative Christian things (most of which were racially based), the divisions of who's a good person to talk to and who's a bad person to talk to, black and white. All in all, it was like being a Martian! (¶ 10)

In the early 1990s, around the time when hooks published her book *Teaching to Transgress: Education as the Practice of Freedom*, Ali earned her Master of Fine Arts (MFA) from Washington University, Walker received her MFA in Painting and Printmaking from the Rhode Island School of Design, and I worked on my Master's degree in Teaching at City University in Seattle. This is where I took my first class in cultural diversity and multiculturalism, which was required by the state.

The Here and Now

When my husband settled in Cedar Key, Florida, in 1983, he hired professional movers who were black. A resident pointedly told these men to make sure that they left town by sunset. Until a few years ago, a local restaurant there still refused to serve people of color. Has America, as a society, really changed much from the 1960s?

Social justice appeared to have been served in Rosewood, Florida, when, on May 4, 2004, Governor Jeb Bush dedicated a Florida Heritage Landmark roadside marker. The cast-aluminum sign memorializes those who died in and those whose lives were forever altered by the racially motivated violence that decimated the town in 1923. "This marker will ensure that Rosewood is remembered," Bush told the hundreds of people who attended the event, which was held about 40 miles southwest of Gainesville. Bush stated that the marker was one more way to insure that "the tragedy of Rosewood will be remembered, not repeated" (Finger, 2007, p. 2). Only 10 years earlier, however, my husband had driven through Rosewood and encountered Klansmen in full regalia, protesting Governor Lawton Chiles' action on behalf of the former residents of Rosewood whose homes and businesses were burned to the ground during the week of violence that occurred after a white woman accused a black man of assaulting her. To this day, if you were to travel through some of the rural counties of West Florida and find a westernized nativity scene, you might see, as I did, that the traditionally black Moorish King, has been replaced by a Bozo the Clown.

When I lived in Seattle, Washington, some of my acquaintances used to complain bitterly that blacks in this country often "played the racism card" as an excuse for laziness. I pointed out that since they lived in the Northwest, a generally multicultural region, they may not have encountered the atrocities of racism that occurred, and still occur, in some communities. Confederate flags are still proudly displayed in public parks and on bumper stickers throughout North Florida.

In 2001, I moved to a Floridian rural town and was confronted by overt discrimination based on race, gender, and class. Criticism was directed toward anyone who dared to rise above his or her "station" or edify himself or herself. The high school where I taught art was a microcosm of the local culture. Like hooks, my students had to overcome incredible socio-cultural and political obstacles. It seemed that these children, 40 years later, still lived in the same oppressive circumstances as hooks' integrated Kentucky classroom. hooks (1995) wrote,

My art teacher, a white man whom we called Mr. Harold, always promoted and encouraged my work … And even though Mr. Harold told me I was an artist, I really could not believe him. I had been taught to believe that no white person in this newly desegregated high school could know anything about what black people's real lives were all about. After all, they did not even want to teach us. How then could we trust what they taught? It did not matter that Mr. Harold was different. It did not matter to grown folks that in his art classes he treated black students like we had a right to be there, deserved his attention and his affirmation. It did

not matter to them, but it began to matter to us: We ran to his classes. We escaped there. We entered the world of color, the free world of art. And in that world we were, momentarily, whatever we wanted to be. (p. 1)

Although I expected my students to face reality in my classroom and to use this reality to lift themselves up, hooks' narrative resonated with me, but left me with questions.

Questions of Race

What does it mean to be racist?

My favorite reflection on racism is the question Ali raised in her *ART: 21* (PBS, 2005) interview:

I'm fascinated, how a different facial color directs you. Green absorbs you into it. Pink or red comes out at you … I sometimes wonder if that is what it is about? Dark-skinned people—their faces absorb more light so you have to look at them more. They're more mysterious? What is that? Could racism just be attributed to bizarre visual phenomena? There's a question. (¶ 15)

Ali's reflection raised the same issues that artist Adrian Piper discussed in Bowles' 2001 article, *Blinded by the White: Art and History at the Limits of Whiteness*. Piper challenged the notion of words used to describe skin color, specifically, those who use the word *white* to describe themselves. She explained that Caucasians are not white any more than Negroes are black. She argued that white people are delusional in being attached to their whiteness, which they somehow cannot surrender even though no other traditional culture actually considers them to be white. White is an identity we hang onto for fear of losing our "companionship, approval, money, status, [and] power" (p. 65).

As a teacher, I challenged my students to reframe their concepts of "color." I told them that I was really a black person; I just had a lot of white freckles. Why not? After all, the skin cells of my freckles are the same as those of a black person.

Recently, in the midst of the racial issues surrounding Senator Barack Obama's Democratic presidential nomination and his subsequent election, a university research team conducted a study on the perceived "American-ness" of the presidential nominees. New York Times columnist Nicholas Kristof (2008) wrote:

Race is a controversial, emotional subject in America, particularly in the context of this campaign. Many Obama supporters believe that their candidate would be further ahead if it were not for racism, while many McCain supporters resent the insinuations and believe that if Mr. Obama were white, he would not even be considered for the presidency. (¶ 7)

I could not understand why the American people did not consider that if Senator McCain were not white, then perhaps he would not have been considered for the presidency.

In the first line of *Blinded by the White*, Bowles (2001) wrote, Unquestioned, whiteness provides the models by which the Western subject judges culture. As the norm, whiteness passes unremarked, perpetuating the canonical conventions and traditions that sustain its privilege; whiteness is assumed white. Only otherness is pronounced. (p. 39)

In fact two adjunct professors, one white and one black, who taught the Cultural Diversity and Multiculturalism class at City University, told me, "Simply being white makes you racist." I was completely insulted because I never considered myself racist. In this regard, hooks (1994) wrote, "Many folks found that as they tried to respect 'cultural diversity' they had to confront the limitations of their training and knowledge, as well as a possible loss of 'authority'" (p. 30). Could this have been me? I never felt that I struggled with issues of authority; rather, I hypothesized, perhaps simply being human made me racist.

Kristof (2008) discussed experiments on implicit racial bias that had been conducted by a team of university psychologists:

Some scholars link racial attitudes to a benefit in evolutionary times from an ability to form snap judgments about who is a likely friend and foe. There may have been an evolutionary advantage in recognizing instantaneously whether a stranger was from one's own tribe or from an enemy tribe. There's some evidence that the amygdale, a center in the brain for emotions, flashes a threat warning when it perceives people who look "different." Yet our biases are probably largely cultural. One reason to think so is that many African Americans themselves have an unconscious pro-white bias. All told, considerable evidence suggests that while the vast majority of Americans truly believe in equality and aspire to equal opportunity for all, our minds aren't as egalitarian as we think they are. (¶ 9–10)

I am not sure whether a person is racist because of skin color, humanness, or simply biological instinct. But I do know that race, by definition, is an artificial construct in which humans are classified by physical characteristics such as skin or hair color.

Framing the Work

"Art history—like the making of art—is a social construct, and as such is continually changing. Art history is not written in stone. Human meanings and human experiences, including aesthetics representations and art history are constructed daily" (Anderson & Milbrandt, 2005). Perhaps this idea comprises the framework around these three women and their work; an artificial construction of extrinsic meaning attached to their work as African American women. Is their work valued because of the commentary on the reorganization of history, as written by white men? Is racism the problem they are trying to solve? Or do their works represent personal or intrinsic meanings? Or does their work accomplish both simultaneously?

Barnwell and Buick (1999), in an article they wrote for the Art Institute of Chicago, stated, "On the threshold of the new millennium, how should we proceed with the dialogue about art made by African Americans? … [An] examination of African American art is double-edged" (p. 181). By singling out the work of African Americans, the historical suppression of such works "fosters the recognition (and often the rediscovery) of under-researched artists and their work" (p. 183). Nevertheless, "the term 'African American art' is an artificial construct; we would never consider linking art by Benjamin West, Fredrick Remington, and Cindy Sherman because of their race" (p. 183). The double edge seems to be the idea that such works may be recognized based solely because they were previously obscured or undervalued aspects of American art history, rather than because of the inherent qualities of the works themselves. For example, one of my photographs from the series *After the Wedding* (see Figure 1) is an image of a young white man sitting on a bench in front of a window in an empty room. The intention of this photography series was to communicate the emotional separation that had taken place early in a marriage, but I wonder how the meaning would change if this were a young black man. Or would it? Does stereotype trump our deeper human concerns?

Figure 1. How would the meaning of this photograph change if the young man was black? From the series *After the Wedding*. Sepia-toned photograph by Alexandria Zettler (1983).

Anderson and Milbrandt (2005) argued that, in making and studying art, "It is important to understand that (1) art and visual culture are visual communication between human beings, (2) art has both an intrinsic value and an extrinsic value and meaning, and (3) in making and studying art, humans express themselves and through this process discover meaning, value, and [a] way of living" (p. 7). Presumably, hooks, Ali, and Walker all work within this paradigm. But rather than clumping these artists together based on some artificial grouping such as race or gender, even if that construct does serve the purpose of social justice, it is important to note that each artist has an individual and separate identity. Each artist communicates a unique point of view that contributes to solving a problem in a larger global context and that constructs personal meaning.

All three women seem to address issues of racism, identity, violence, personal suffering, and human suffering—issues regarding being the *other*—in their works. hooks has dedicated many years to writing about the role of critical thinking in social justice in order to improve the lives of her students. She wrote, "My own sense is that the most enabling resource that I can offer as a critic or an intellectual professor is the capacity to think critically about our lives" (2005, ¶ 4).

Likewise, in talking about her *Typology Series*, Ali said, "I have become interested in exploring types and blurring the distinction between the obvious and the absurd way in which people are categorized" (inNIVA, 2007, ¶ 13). Ali's work may appear humorous at first, but, upon closer inspection, it is clear that the series was a visual expression of the powerlessness and even *otherness* felt by individuals or groups who may have been outside of and discriminated against by the dominating culture in their societies. In Ali's early work, the *Greenheads*, she readily admitted that she fueled her work with rage over socio-cultural and political issues such as racism and violence (PBS, 2005); she labored, however, to distance her presence from the pieces. In an interview with *Believer* magazine (Bryant, 2008), Ali stated, "I really wanted to resist any easy connection to the artist—people always want to go there, to the pathology of the artist, rather than examining themselves. I think I need to disappear a bit in order for the viewer to engage more fully" (¶ 7).

In discussing her work, Walker (Museum of Modern Art, 1999) said,

I knew that if I was going to make work that had to deal with race issues, they were going to be full of contradictions. Because I always felt that it's really a love affair that we've got going in this country, a love affair with the idea of it [race issues], with the notion of major conflict that needs to be overcome and maybe a fear of what happens when that thing is overcome. And, of course, these issues also translate into [the] very personal: Who am I beyond this skin I'm in. (¶ 3)

Walker further discussed how she used her medium, the silhouette, as an avoidance technique. She explained, "The silhouette lends itself to avoidance of the subject. Of not being able to look at it directly, yet there it is, all the time, staring you in the face" (¶ 3). But at the end of the interview, she admitted that her work was also a way of "avoiding who she is in the here and now" (¶ 12).

Bowles (2001) wrote, "Kara Walker's cut paper silhouettes … represent, on some level, who white viewers fear they might be … It seems the debate surrounding her art demonstrates the difficulty we have with work that implicates viewers in the perpetuation of whiteness's claim to privilege" (p. 39). Is Walker's intention to keep the American past and present in the minds of the white, elite, and well educated? In his digital video, John Thornton (n.d.) told his students that these are the type of peoplethe white, elite, and well educated—who often visit Kara Walker's exhibits, buy her books, and listen to her interviews.

Apparently, the black community has ostracized Walker's work. Blacks felt they were already underrepresented and misrepresented. It seemed that Walker was contributing to the negative stereotype of black people (Sheets, 2002). hooks (1995) spoke to this issue regarding Romare Beardon, an African American artist, writer, and spokesman born in 1911: "When Bearden painted images reflecting aspects of black life that emerged from underclass experience, some black viewers were disturbed.... They wanted art to be a vehicle for displaying the race at its best" (p. 5-6). Some of hooks' (1995) essays roundly criticized black men and women for perpetuating racism in art.

But, what is the point of having art about racism, if such work does not spread awareness about the social injustice of the people in question? Consider that the elements of beauty and artisanship as tempting the viewer in Walker's or Ali's work or even hooks'; once the viewer has been attracted, the horrific or accusatory subject matter throws the viewer immediately into discord. hooks' masterful writing style, Ali's and Walker's formalistic skills, and the paradoxical sense of the absurd have challenged socio-cultural and political biases. While working out who they are in the here and now, hooks, Ali, and Walker, though artificially grouped together as African American women, lend authentic voices to the oppressed and the marginalized *other* in modern culture. To make sense of their work, we must deconstruct the fairytale of history that is represented by the dominant culture, and we must reconstruct the story of America from their point of view. This collective voice fuels the quest for social justice.

But what about intrinsic, personal meanings in the work? How can we know? The truth about why these artists create their work is between them and their therapists! I can only listen, observe, and filter meaning through my own lens, my own social paradigm. In spite of my general disinterest in history, my connection to hooks', Ali's, and Walker's work is not based solely on the artificial construct of race. Rather, I strongly identify with their *larger socio-cultural and political contexts and the deeper human identities*. Thus, their complete histories are important to me, not just their histories as black people.

Figure 2. Represents this high school student's shattered dreams of being a professional athlete. *Shattered* by Leslie "CJ" Edwards, mixed media collage, 2007.

Hope for the Future

When I taught students how to approach the artmaking process authentically, I encouraged exploration of the artists' writings and works within the students' own socio-political contexts. Like hooks, Ali, and Walker, I believed in the value of drawing upon personal history, of looking within oneself as a point of reference. In other words, we should create art about what we know, about who we essentially are. We should address our own social, cultural, political, and emotional points of view (see Figure 2).

Like hooks, Ali, and Walker, my students faced similar sociocultural and political struggles nevertheless; I believed that by becoming visually literate they could join these three artists in interpreting and negotiating their issues in the real world outside of the educational setting.

That is what I expected of my students. I expected them to demonstrate technical skills, such as an understanding of the elements of art and the principles of design. But, more importantly, I expected them to use these skills to develop personal visual vocabularies and to use them for unadulterated self-expression, critical analysis, and problem solving. I expected every contour line drawing, every Matisse-style shape collage, every mandala, illustration, portrait, landscape, or photograph to communicate each individual student's point-of-view. My final evaluative question always was,

"Did you communicate the idea you intended to? Why or why not? And if not, did something better evolve?"

Through this process—the creation, publication, and critical analysis of personal work—my hope was for my students to deconstruct their histories and to reconstruct new meanings in their lives. My hope was for them to develop a strong sense of self and to earn a place in the global community, based on their own extrinsic and intrinsic analyses of their lives. This is authentic problem solving, in the tradition of hooks, Ali, and Walker, beyond stereotype, beyond merely extrinsic definitions based on race or gender or economic status, reflecting the deeper and more genuine qualities of their shared human lives.

REFERENCES

Anderson, T., & Milbrandt, M. (2005). *Art for life: Authentic instruction in art.* New York: McGraw-Hill.

Barnwell, A., Buick, K., Denny, M., Fox, M., Jankauskas, J., Narowcki, D., et al. (1999). African Americans in art: Selections from the Art Institute of Chicago. A portfolio of works by African American artists continuing the dialogue: A work in progress. *Art Institute of Chicago Museum Studies, 24*(2), 180–219, 265–267.

Bowles, J. (2001). Blinded by the white: Art and history at the limits of whiteness (J. Bowles, Ed.). *Art Journal, 60*(4), 39–67.

Bryant, T. (Nov./Dec. 2008). Laylah Ali. *Believer Magazine.* Retrieved from http://www.believermag.com/issues/200512/?read=interview_ali

hooks, B. (1994). *Teaching to transgress: Education as the practice of freedom.* New York: Routledge.

hooks, B. (1995). *Art on my mind: Visual politics.* New York: The New Press.

inNIVA. (2007). *Laylah Ali: The kiss and other warriors* [Exhibition Brochure]. London: Simonds, C. Retrieved from http://www.iniva.net/laylah/Resources/Layla_Brochure.pdf

Kristof, N. D. (2008, October 30). What? Me biased? *The New York Times*, A39.

Museum of Modern Art (MOMA). (1999). *Conversations with Kara Walker.* New York: Author. Retrieved from http://www.moma.org/onlineprojects/conversations/kw_f.html

PBS. (2005). Laylah Ali. *Meaning & influences* [interview]. *Art: 21, season 3, episode "power."* [Television broadcast]. Retrieved from http://www.pbs.org/art21/artists/ali/index.html

Sheets, H. M. (2002). Cut it out! *ARTnews, 101*(4), 126–129.

Thornton, J. (n.d.) *Color theory 8, a shocking negress* [digital video]. YouTube.com. Retrieved from http://www.youtube.com/watch?v=VM0zQd1Uoz8

Walker, K. (2001). *Darkytown Rebellion* [Installation]. New York. Collection of Foundation Musée d'Art Moderne Grand-Duc Jean, Luxembourg.

RESOURCES

Baker, A. (2007). *Laylah Ali: Typology.* Philadelphia: Pennsylvania Academy of the Fine Arts.

Finger, D. (2007). *Marking rosewood history.* Archer, Florida: The Real Rosewood. Retrieved from http://rosewoodflorida.com/2007/07/04/marking-rosewood-history/

Stanley, S. K. (1998). *Other sisterhoods: Literary theory and U.S. women of color.* Chicago: University of Illinois Press.

DISCUSSION QUESTIONS FOR FIGURES

Figure 1. How would the meaning of this photograph change if the young man were black? Or would it?

Figure 2. How has the sociocultural political environment "shattered" the dreams of this high school student?

Higher Education
and Teacher
PREPARATION

Walls and Bridges: Metaphor as a Tool and Lens for Cross-Cultural Art Education

Miwon Choe

Without bridges, we would all be islands. Mankind has always had a deep desire to build bridges, both figuratively and literally. We want to meet the people who live on the other side of the water. We want to know what they look like, sound like, and most importantly, think like.
(*The Economist*, 2006, May 13, p.10)

Knowing and Understanding through Metaphor

In this chapter, I examine the pedagogical merit of metaphor for cross-cultural understanding, a key component of social justice. I also address its effect on personal transformation as exemplified in an interdisciplinary art curriculum entitled *Walls and Bridges: A Metaphor for Humanity*. This literature-based, intercultural art curriculum reflects my personal interest in art and visual metaphor as an orientation to thinking and understanding. Art enables me to create personal metaphors to help me understand my life and the lives of others. Metaphor has been my third eye to understand my world and the world around me. My fascination for art as visual metaphor took on another dimension as I had been confronted with cultural differences teaching in a rural Indiana community. Juggling the two cultures, Korean and American, forced me to readjust and negotiate my personal boundaries, and I began to see my struggle metaphorically as walls and bridges. This personal struggle of cultural negotiation became a "feedback system" (Anderson, 1989, p. 43) and conceptual framework to process my cultural encounter. In other words, metaphorical thinking served as mind's eye and senses with which to understand, construct meaning, and communicate my experiences as an art educator.

Scholars (Feinstein, 1982; Lakoff & Johnson, 1980; Langer, 1957; Davis, Hicks, Pugh, & Venstra, 1992) have argued that metaphor crosses traditional boundaries of linguistic expression and can expand its meaning in and through the visual arts. Metaphor, therefore, may be a shared domain across modes of expressive forms in the visual and language arts. As one interacts with and learns from one's experiences, the meaning assigned to a certain metaphor becomes a foundation for an additional layer of interpretation. Therefore, the heart of metaphor lies in reciprocal and continuous interactions between oneself and one's reflection on experience. In this sense, I propose that metaphorical thinking may be incorporated in teaching and learning art as personal meaning making through the conceptualizing metaphor as a tool (accessibility), metaphor as a lens (viewpoint), metaphor as a negotiation (metamorphosis), and using all three perspectives together, as an instrument for social justice.

Meaning Making through Metaphor

What does it mean to think metaphorically? How does metaphorical thinking manifest in artistic forms and images? To what extent does metaphor facilitate and transform one's experience into meaning? The quest to understand the unknown and make sense of it is a collective affinity for all humanity (Dissanayake, 1995). In this quest, metaphor has been a torch

KEY CONCEPTS

- Metaphor as Reflective Tool and Lens
- Metaphor as Metamorphosis
- Metaphor for Social Justice
- Inter-Cultural Art Education
- Personal Transformation
- Walls and Bridges

that lights the way toward understanding the world around us. The use of metaphor originated with the ancient Greeks as a trope of classical rhetoric (Lakoff, 1993; Tilley 1999). The word *metaphor* came from the Greek term *meta* (involving change) and *pherein* (to bear or carry). Lakoff and Johnson (1980) explained *metaphor* as "understanding and experiencing one thing in terms of another" (p.55). According to Davis, Hicks, Pugh, and Venstra (1992), metaphorical forms provide a bridge that connects the known to the unknown and constitutes meaning by "drawing parallels between apparently unrelated phenomena and building bridges from the known to the new" (p. 2). Winner (1988) stated that metaphor is one of the earliest intellectual skills apparent in humans. It is critical to language acquisition and as such, very young children may be more facile in their understanding and use of metaphor than are older children and adults. Egan (1997) also described metaphor as one of the earliest tools of meaning making. Metaphor permits visualization and narration of our lives in ways that allow meaning to be made of amorphous forms and phenomena.

Tilley (1999) suggested that human communication would be almost impossible without metaphor, because metaphors provide the basis for an interpretative understanding of the world. In addition to Tilley's view on the interpretative nature of metaphor, Lakoff and Johnson (1980) advocated the conceptual nature of metaphor. They explained that, "our ordinary system, in terms of which we both think and act, is fundamentally metaphorical in nature ... Metaphor is pervasive in everyday life, [and] the way we think, what we experience, and what we do everyday is a very much a matter of metaphor" (p. 3). Feinstein (1982a) took this perspective further:

> Metaphor, once regarded solely as an ornamental linguistic device, is now considered to be an essential process and product of thought. The power of metaphor lies in its potential to further our understanding of the meaning of experience, which in turn defines reality. In art and in language, metaphor urges us to look beyond the literal, to generate associations and to tap new, different, or deeper levels of meaning. (p. 45)

In her analysis of linguistic and visual metaphors, Feinstein cited Langer's view (1957) that "metaphor is an essential process and product of thought and therefore art, as a developed product of thought, is metaphor" (p. 45). Metaphor crosses traditional boundaries of linguistic expression and can expand its meaning in and through the visual arts; therefore, metaphor

may be a shared domain across modes of expression including the visual and language arts. Thus, it could be argued that metaphor may be used as an additional tool for teaching art appreciation and understanding art by relating to metaphorical meaning represented in the visual arts.

At the crossroads of art and metaphor lies a door leading toward empathy and renewed understanding through aesthetic and cultural symbols that contribute to visual metaphor. In this sense, metaphor serves as a scaffolding device for students. *Scaffolding* is a term coined by Vygotsky (1978), who indicated that the vital connection between children's actual development level and the level of potential development is established by and guided through the hands of educators. This is called the zone of proximal development. He used the term *scaffolding* to explain the instructional process by which the teacher modifies pedagogical support to suit the level of a child's development. I adopted the metaphor of scaffolding to be a series of stepping-stones that facilitate student learning in art education. Metaphor as a scaffolding strategy allows students to develop holistic and comparative perspectives as well as to draw their own conclusions from visual evidence. Thus, metaphorical thinking is heuristic and places the learner as an integral part of the meaning making process.

Metaphor is not a blueprint, archetype, or template. As one interacts with and learns from one's experiences, the meaning assigned to a certain metaphor becomes a foundation for an additional layer of interpretation. The heart of metaphor lies in reciprocal and continuous interactions between oneself and one's reflection on experience. Art activities and methods that integrate metaphorical thinking engage students in understanding the relationship between art, culture, and self. In this sense, metaphorical thinking may be regarded as a reflection of understanding based on one's own personal experiences. Therefore, students need to be given a personal space to learn and develop on their own terms and in their own ways, to make sense of their personal explorations.

Nadaner (1983) stated that the visual arts communicate inner images that define one's subjective experiences and the reconstructions of meaning in the visual arts helps us understand perspectives of others. We live in a value-laden culture and society and art forms created in a particular context of culture are considered as "cultural containers reflecting the life force of their places and times" (Anderson, 1989, p. 51). Art promotes cultural experiences because of its inherent cultural point of view represented in aesthetic content, subject matter, and technical styles. In relating art to

Chinese Dragon as a Flying Bridge in the Sky by 1st-grade student.

Monet's Bridge by 4th-grade student.

culture, the concept of metaphor is a valuable instrument because metaphor accommodates multitudes of explanations and interpretations that might be grounded on cultural assumptions, beliefs, and experiences.

The pedagogy of one's teaching frequently manifests as a personal domain. It is not about a systematic application of a curriculum theory, but rather a personalized implementation of one's sincere and truthful convictions exhibited in a daily practice of instructional interactions with students. My interest in metaphor as a conceptual process motivated me to expand the use of metaphor in a broad-based thematic art curriculum. In the next sections, I will describe how the concept of metaphor was used as a strategy for teaching art in an elementary setting and how this brought the students to a more empathetic understanding of themselves and those of other cultures, a root concern of social justice. In addition, I will describe the use of metaphor to assist graduate preservice and in-service art teachers experience the power of metaphor as a model and strategy for self-understanding that can be conceptualized as a tool and a lens for personal transformation.

Walls and Bridges: A Metaphor for Humanity

As an elementary specialist in a rural Indiana town, I developed a school-wide, yearlong thematic curriculum unit entitled *Walls and Bridges: A Metaphor for Humanity*. The wall that separated my students in a rural community in Indiana from diverse cultural experiences was its rural location that created distance from various cultural resources including arts programs and services. Studying about walls and bridges around the world provided excellent opportunities to learn the unique features and different ways of life of many cultures, hence the walls theme, but also to draw attention to shared humanity and common artistic heritage, which captured the bridges theme. Walls and bridges, however, are not always structural. They may also reside in our perceptions and experiences. As I searched for ideas for literature-based curriculum connection, I serendipitously discovered the children's book entitled *Talking Walls* (Knight, 1992). The book illustrated stories of distinctive walls around the world: a wall to tell a story (cave painting), a wall to worship (Wailing Wall), walls to keep an enemy out and protect people (The Great Wall of China, a medieval fortress), a wall to separate people and ideas (the Berlin Wall), and a wall to bring people together (The Vietnam Memorial Wall). The more I thought about it, the more fascinated I became with the conceptual richness of what walls mean to various people.

One of the challenges for implementing the walls and bridges program was to accommodate the theme to be developmentally appropriate and relevant for levels of students' artistic and cognitive understanding of the select themes. For primary-grade students, I introduced walls and bridges as concrete and tangible objects such as a mirror wall for symmetry, walls in the house, a flower garden as friendly bridge to walk through, a peek-a-boo wall for play, and a dragon as a flying bridge in the sky. Third- and fourth-grade students created actual walls and bridges found in their own communities as well as the world at large. Upon completion of their artmaking, I asked them to explain their choice of walls or bridges in writing. Following are excerpts of third-and fourth-grade student reflections.

This bridge is strong and takes my family to our home to Mexico.
The milky-way bridge is a magic bridge that goes from the earth to the moon.
Love and friendship are bridges between two people.
The Underground Railroad is a great secret bridge!
This wall is called atmosphere. It keeps us from floating away.
A petroglyph is a wall of a rock and it has ancient drawing on it.
Blanket wall is my secret place to hide.
Museum walls have great art like Vincent Van Gogh's painting.
The Great Wall of China is like a dragon sitting on top of a mountain.
The walls in this house hold in love and keep out hate.

Initially, this unit focused on physical architecture as found in walls and bridges worldwide. Emphasis soon shifted, however, toward human architecture in the cultural, psychological, and political walls and bridges that define, separate, and connect disparate social groups. From this focus, Internet and e-mail capabilities were used by the art students in order to access information and learn about people in places far from their rural community. An electronic pen pal program encouraged students to improve their communication skills through written exchanges with people from England, Germany, India, South Africa, Saudi Arabia, Singapore, Ukraine, as well as other states within the United States. Throughout this unit, the metaphor of walls and bridges signified a unifying theme to hold ideas together as well as an entity to express interpretations of the students' art experiences.

The Vietnam Wall by 5th-grade student.

Yin and Yang as a Metaphor for Walls and Bridges by 5th-grade student.

Fifth- and sixth-grade students were engaged in reading, research, and small group discussions to examine what inspired humans to build walls and bridges and how those walls and bridges affected human relations throughout history. Literature selections for the walls and bridges curriculum provided a common ground for a beginning journey into an exploration of the physical and spiritual power of the curriculum. As students first used books to research actual walls and bridges found in the community and throughout the world, they began to develop a concrete link. Many books guided students' thinking toward a symbolic understanding of the concept of walls and bridges. Through the readings and discussions of these books, students began to grasp how countries, social conditions, and economics may create walls to divide people. They also related to the idea that bridges can be built to provide passage round these walls when people work together. Students also began to recognize the symbolic walls and bridges in their personal lives and the need to keep some but let go of others. Most importantly, they understood that bridges were a way of reaching out and moving forward. Below are a few examples from student reflections.

To me, art is like a bridge that can connect feelings by paintings and drawings. Art can also be a wall by showing how everyone is different so it sort of separates them. So I feel good when I show my artwork because I can show people how I am the same and different from other people. (Craig D., 5th grade)

Art is a bridge like Miss Choe is talking to us. Art is like a classroom bridge. It has bars to hold it up. Drawing, writing, and even learning can be a bridge. Bridges in art are colorful, neat, and sometimes move. Bridges are like moving to another place. So go make, see, and build one. (Devin K., 4th grade)

Art is a bridge because after you cross a bridge that you've never crossed before you learn what it's like to cross that bridge. It is like that when you draw, you learn what it's like to draw it and you know how. (Chelsea A., 3rd grade)

Art means love. Art means people. Art means Hi. Art means drug free. Art means good-bye. But most of all, art means to make the right choice. (Elizabeth B., 3rd grade)

A bridge doesn't move! You have to take a step up to get on the bridge. When you are having troubles and you don't want to try anymore, that's where the wall stops you. So, that's why I keep trying. I don't want to be stopped. (Megan F., 6th grade)

Art means doing your projects well, and respecting what you do. It also means working hard and being proud. Learning about art will never stop because there are no walls to your imagination. There are just bridges to new experiences and activities. (Bryan K., 5th grade)

1000 Cranes as a Symbol of World Peace by 4th-, 5th-, and 6th-grade students.

The depth and quality of student reflections exceeded my expectations. Through the course of teaching children about art, culture, and metaphor, the relationship with my students deepened as we became a cooperating team to nurture and encourage each other. This was an unexpected, affective gain that I consider as one of the most important outcomes of my unit. The walls and bridges were not only an interdisciplinary theme to study various architectural structures worldwide, but also a metaphor to create and express meaning as my students reflected upon their art experiences. Many students enjoyed a process of free association as they viewed art in light of their personal experiences, past events, familiar places, memories, and feelings. Various metaphorical comparisons and contextual information helped them recognize multiple purposes and meanings of artworks.

Therefore, walls and bridges theme as metaphor helped them gain an ownership of their learning as they continuously added layers of new insight onto old understandings. Reflecting on the process and outcomes of the walls and bridges unit, I was convinced that metaphor could be an effective pedagogical instrument for a meaning-making process toward personal transformation.

Think Metaphor: Metaphor as a Tool and Lens

My fascination with art as visual metaphor, the conceptual richness and pedagogical merit of metaphor led me to incorporate metaphor while I was teaching a graduate course called Non-Studio Approach to Art Education, to preservice and in-service art teachers at a large state university in the south central Kentucky. One of the course assignments was to relate oneself to aspects of specific art image through metaphor. For example, I asked students to begin with "I am … " as a figure, objects, symbols, or specific art elements in the painting. This project was inspired by the fascinating idea presented in the article by James (2000) entitled, "I am the Dark Forest: Personal Analogy as a Way to Understand Metaphor." I found the personal analogy James incorporated in the understanding of art highly engaging and useful. At first, I observed most teachers feeling awkward about the process, but they began to understand art images as visual metaphor and related these to their own personal lives as well as professional role as teachers. Drawing an analogy through metaphoric expression increased the potential to enhance the teachers' imaginations to construct personal meaning and "a living relationship" (Jeffers, 1996, p. 10) with art. In this sense, I was interested in the ways metaphor might work in negotiating and constructing cultural and personal meaning (Nadaner, 1985) and providing an avenue to communicate, understand, and transform. This is a conceptualization, I propose of metaphor, as a tool. Metaphor as a tool provides a personal strategy and framework to understand one's aesthetic preferences, appreciation, and interpretation of art experiences.

Of particular importance for social justice, metaphor also helps us to "think dialectically rather than judgmentally, not only for seeing another point of view, but for seeing from that point of view" (Davis, Hicks, Pugh, & Venstra, 1992, p.130). I propose that this second conceptualization is a lens. Metaphor as a tool helps us categorize, organize, and sort out experiential information for construction of meaning. Metaphorical thinking also can be used as an analytical set of lenses through which to form a persistent

perspective grounded on a particular experience. Wolcott (1991) argued that culture is manifested through an individual's expressions, perspectives, and ideas. Within collective aspects of a culture shared by members of a particular culture, each individual creates a unique version of culture from his or her personal experiences. He referred to this individual version of culture as "propriospect." I believe the use of metaphor as a lens constructs and frames the unique individual version of cultural expression, propriospect. Specifically, teachers' views of art as metaphor, for example, were expressions of understanding at that particular time of their lives. Their experiences of art and culture, if persuaded by a single viewpoint in an exclusive manner, became a lens.

Metamorphosis of Metaphor: Negotiation

The concepts of metaphors as tools and lenses are not independent of each other as they interact in constructing meaning. When a tool is being utilized in a definitive manner and with finality, it would likely be considered as a framing lens. A tool becomes a lens when the use of it grows saturated. A retooling process occurs to accommodate a newly discovered demand. The tool improves in its utility and application until another saturation occurs. The pattern of metamorphosis infinitely expands each time it completes as an expanding cycle. Therefore, the tool and lens metaphors are guiding forces toward each other to enlarge the boundary of understanding and interpretation of art forms. A tool metaphor connotes fluidity and flexibility. On the other hand, a lens metaphor implies permanence and exclusiveness. Flexibility is needed for growth and permanence is important for stability. Therefore, metaphorical thinking with working relationships between a tool and a lens encourage fluidity and flexibility in terms of one's intuitive understanding of experiential information. According to Lakoff and Johnson (1980), the intuitive understanding through metaphor is not necessarily an antithesis of rational objectivism. They called for imaginative rationality to explain how metaphorical imagination is not devoid of rationality. In their words:

> We have seen that truth is relative to understanding, which means there is no absolute standpoint from which to obtain absolute objective truths about the world. This does not mean that there are no truths; it means only that truth is relative to our conceptual system, which is grounded in, and constantly tested by, our experiences and those of other member of our culture in our daily

interactions with other people and without physical and cultural environments. (p. 193)

Some in-service teachers responded that their metaphorical thinking was not static. It evolved into deeper meanings and sensibilities as they spent more time in creating their own personal metaphors from art. Their metaphors were not only vehicles with which to explore their art experiences, but also lenses through which to generate new insights into their own thinking processes. Thus, metamorphosis of metaphor has taken place. Metaphor as a tool organized, condensed, and vivified the teachers' experiences, and thus subsequently reframed them from a particular vantage point for deeper levels of meaning. This process helped them make connections between new and old information, and arrive at a more thoughtful and mature understanding than before. Feinstein (1985) explained fluidity and flexibility by using the analogy between water and metaphor. In her words, "Like water, metaphor is fluid. Just as water can take the forms of ice and steam, so metaphor can take different forms, linguistic and visual. As water is essential to physical life, metaphor is essential to cognitive life" (p. 29).

Metaphor as a Tool for Social Justice

Anderson (1989) and Anderson and Milbrandt (2005) strongly argued that art is about something beyond itself, a particular social practice, and inseparable from life. They also pointed out that art is culturally embedded with collective consciousness of societal values and beliefs, therefore, art forms and their meanings are intrinsically connected to an unavoidable socio-cultural context. Most of us may hold a view that culture is a foreign and obscure concept, foreign in a sense that it is not our own, obscure that it was far away from our realities. The predominant themes of culture seem to be around the key term *different and obscurity*. The concept of obscurity connotes that a *different* culture is about *other* people, but not about *us*.

The walls and bridges metaphor was a tool to explore questions and socio-cultural issues, to attempt to negate the concepts of *different* and *other* when thinking about people. Students engaged their knowledge, emotions, and creative imagination in understanding the viewpoints, ideas, and beliefs of the other as well as us. Students also questioned established assumptions and belief systems as they interacted with pertinent culture-based art forms. It is important to note that on one hand, art forms and contextual meanings reflect the experiences of the creators. On the other hand the art forms tend to mirror the viewers' fears and hopes rather than what might exist in some objective reality. The heart of understanding the other in a critical manner is intimately associated with one's personal experiences within a particular socio-cultural context. It is easier to exploit or dehumanize people of other cultures if we believe that they are radically different from us. Metaphor as a reflective tool, critical lens, and metamorphosis of cultural negotiation helps bridge these superficial differences, provides an access to a deeper empathy, and humanizes the obscure notion of the other. In this way, metaphor, I believe, may serve as a critical bedrock instrument toward establishing equity and social justice.

It is my hope that the walls and bridges program inspired my students to learn not only about the content of art, but also moral, affective, and critical viewpoints of tolerance and empathy that may endure beyond their formal education. As we extended our bridges through art and metaphor, the walls that once defined our world became flexible, safer, and a more inviting place to visit. So the best part of the walls and bridges curriculum was the intangible bridges of acceptance and understanding. Fennes and Hapgood (1997) stated that "It is not possible to understand other cultures without understanding one's own; it is also not possible to understand fully one's own culture until the encounter with another culture has put it in perspective" (p. 49). In order for one to become an informed interpreter of cultural information represented in art, Feinstein (1982b) argued, education is necessary. She stated:

> The eye and mind must be taught; for what the eye sees is determined by what the mind knows. Students who learn to decipher visual forms can uncover the value embodied in them and can critically examine them for their merit, utility, and relevance. (p. 15)

We live in a world of confusion, misinformation, and hatred that grew from selfishness and greed, and they are manifested in all forms of cultural, economic, and political realities. I believe that metaphorical thinking of tools and lens, and the metamorphosis of cultural negotiation will help students appreciate and value common experiences that bind us. As we attempt to put ourselves in someone else's shoes and walk around through a personal narrative of metaphor, we may be able to understand those concerns and viewpoints of the other. Equity and social justice will be achievable when this compassionate cross-cultural understanding through art and metaphor connects all of us in a circle of global humanity.

AUTHOR'S NOTE

I dedicate this chapter in memory of my dear friend Ms. Jane Major. Jane was a media specialist at Lena Dunn Elementary School, Washington, Indiana. Her gentle soul, kind heart, and her unfailing faith in art education empowered and nurtured me through my public school teaching years as an elementary art specialist. Jane passed away in December 2005.

REFERENCES

Anderson, T. (1989). Interpreting works of art as social metaphor. *Visual Arts Research, 15*(2), 42–51.

Anderson, T., & Milbrandt, M. (2005). *Art for Life: Authentic Instruction in Art.* New York: McGraw-Hill.

Davis, M., Hicks, J. W., Pugh, S. L., & Venstra, T. (1992). *Bridging.* Urbana, IL: National Council of Teachers of English.

Dissanayake, E. (1995). *Homo aestheticus: Where art comes from and why.* Seattle: University of Washington Press.

Egan, K. (1997). *The educated mind: How cognitive tools shape our understanding.* Chicago: Chicago University Press.

Feinstein, H. (1982a). Meaning and visual metaphor. *Studies in Art Education, 23*(2), 45–55.

Feinstein, H. (1982b). Art means values. *Art Education, 35*(2), 13–15.

Feinstein, H. (1985). Art as visual metaphor. *Art Education, 38*(4), 26–29.

James, P. (2000). I am the dark forest: Personal analogy as a way to understand metaphor. *Art Education, 53*(5), 6–11.

Fennes, H., & Hapgood, K. (1997). *Intercultural learning in the classroom.* London: Cassell.

Jeffers, C. (1996). Experiencing art through metaphor. *Art Education, 49*(3), 6–11.

Knight, M. B. (1992). *Talking walls.* Gardiner, ME: Tilbury House.

Lakoff, G. (1993). *The contemporary theory of metaphor.* In A. Orthony (Ed.), *Metaphor and thought* (2nd ed.) (pp. 202–251). New York: Press Syndicate of the Cambridge University Press.

Lakoff, G., & Johnson, M. (1980). *Metaphors we live by.* Chicago and London: University of Chicago Press.

Langer, S. (1957). *Problems of art.* New York: Charles Scribner's Sons.

Nadaner, D. (1983). On art and social understanding: Lessons from Alfred Schultz. *Journal of Multicultural and Cross-cultural Research in Art Education, 11*(1), 15–22.

Nadaner, D. (1985). The art teacher as cultural mediator. *Journal of Multicultural and Cross-cultural Research in Art Education, 3*(1), 51–55.

The Economist (2006, May 13). Without bridges, we would all be islands. p.10.

Tilley, C. (1999). *Metaphor and material culture.* Malden, MA: Blackwell.

Vygotsky, L. S. (1978). *Mind in society: The development of higher order psychological processes.* Cambridge: Harvard University Press.

Winner, E. (1988). *Point of words: Children's understanding of metaphor and irony.* Cambridge, MA: Harvard University Press.

Wolcott, H. F. (1991). Propriospect and the acquisition of culture. *Anthropology and Education Quarterly, 22*(3), 251–273.

Telling Stories: Feminist Lessons Through Art

Future Akins-Tillett

M y art has been called the art of a storyteller. It resides somewhere between the world of defined fine arts and traditional craft, in a territory blended from a respect for process, impatience with the status quo, and the love of a good story. Autobiographically romantic, each work allows memories, daydreams, and reality to meander, like the ramblings of a diary, sentimentally seeking absolution for situations long past. Often, there is humor, sometimes there is only the sly smile of a survivor. One motivation for my storytelling comes from resurrecting a sense of fairness for the combined voices of struggling feminist artists of the 1970s. I feel society has taken away their voices. Another motivation stems from remembrances about my father and grandfather and their good-hearted parables loaded with advice, and the whopper stories told by my aunt and sister.

A room from thousands of hours
of sketches and drafts,
of doubts and decisions,
of tears and smiles,
of whys and why nots,
of work by hand,
of work with heart,
swirling around a lifetime of stories. (Akins-Tillett, 2006)

KEY CONCEPTS

- Classroom Environment Preparation
- Techniques to Initiate Dialogue
- Voices Heard Through Stories
- Social Justice Issues/ Feminist Lessons
- Outcomes Revealed by Artwork

My Background and Beliefs

I am a Visual Studies professor preparing students to become public and private art education teachers. I am also actively engaged in ongoing dialogue about the difficulties, complexities, and values of a continuing, constant creation of art while experiencing the sometimes overwhelming demands placed on art educators transitioning through leadership roles which require realistic and creative guidance to art students.

In the 1970s and 1980s, I held various offices in local and regional feminist organizations, and the National Women's Caucus for the Arts. Although the term "feminism" conjures up many things for different people, I was particularly drawn to the idea of fairness as fundamentally proposed by Section I of the Equal Rights Amendment. Thirty-five years ago, as an undergraduate and graduate student at a conservative university, I, along with the other women, was subject to policies that now, in hindsight, are considered discriminatory, gender-biased, and unfair. For example, we were not allowed to use the welding torches in sculpture class with the premise that it was too dangerous for females. The limitations that imposed on creativity are self-evident.

As an educator subscribing to social theory and education practices, I have been influenced by the likes of Parker Palmer and bell hooks, colleague Ed Check and friend Helen Klebesadel, Director of Women's Studies for the University of Wisconsin system. My philosophy subscribes to the notion that certain classroom techniques may be used at appropriate times to ensure a systematic and practical application of learning, leading to storytelling through art which in turn introduces social justice issues to art students. The process may take place within a single semester classroom, but more than likely will come to fruition over several years as art education students pass through their undergraduate and graduate courses.

For me, the best environment for social theory and education practices takes place in an emotionally safe classroom. Emotional comfort with the teacher and other art students will set the stage for members to share vast stories of interesting and useful knowledge in and out of class. To help develop such an environment, I start out by discussing the dignity inherent in each student and asking the class to respect differences of opinion, approach, and philosophy. I want to establish the belief that everyone counts. Tolerance and compassion are brought to the forefront along with concepts of equity, acceptance of diversity, and the value of non-biased, unprejudiced reason. I do not dictate boundaries, but the outlining of what is most positive in academe and human nature implies a laudable classroom environment. Sometimes the ideal is not achieved, but when this happens it helps reinforce previous understandings about respect and dignity.

Safe classrooms are hospitable; such hospitality begins with simply asking students how they are doing again and again when seeing them on the sidewalks, in the classroom, hallways, and school offices. An emotionally safe learning environment charges the teacher to be the most approachable of the group. Students are encouraged to show up at my office with or without an appointment. I believe that learning does not take place in a void, nor is it limited to classroom lessons. Each student and teacher brings to the table their own set of stories, dreams, opinions, curiosities, and fears. Good educators know this; great education celebrates it. The voice of learning speaks that all involved should have the chance to seek a sense of self in relation to their discipline. I try to give all students this voice and opportunity. Acceptance and enthusiasm, not exclusion and judgment, are methods I practice.

Listening is essential to hearing what the heart is really saying amidst student insecurities, which can be disguised as giggles, denials, dismissals, or bragging. It takes self-assurance and knowledge of oneself to have patience to be silent long enough to hear another's voice, especially the voice of a student who may feel inferior or anxious in the classroom. I listen to my students attentively. I want to know them well and to gain their respect. Once an open, mutual respect-based conversation has begun, the exchange can produce a remarkable environment for learning, allowing my students to find their identity within art. In many ways, the fairness of an equitable dialogue parallels the goals of 1970s feminist consciousness-raising.

I always try to bring an inquisitive mind and enthusiasm to the classroom because I want my students to get excited about art and art education. I tell stories about myself in an enthusiastic and open manner. I talk about what I am comfortable with, but I am direct and honest to earn authenticity with the listeners. Some of my stories are about relationships, spirituality, and life changes. Regardless of the theme, I work with the proviso that students understand substantial learning can come from previous experiences, good or bad. Concurrently, I may show my autobiographical art, which reflects my research including its feminist manifesto nature. Post story, it is question and answer time. I have found that if all has proceeded neatly, and the classroom dynamics are right, few questions are asked. Rather, the students are anxious to let others know how they relate to the stories I have told. This signals a great start and lets me know that I can now bring techniques I use into the classroom.

Respect

One exercise to elicit storytelling and open up communication is the "They call me … " lesson. This lesson was developed spontaneously about 5 years ago in the classroom after realizing that students sometimes casually issue and then disregard prejudicial, hurtful words spoken about others. When questioned as to what they said, many respond with "I didn't mean it …," "It's just a joke …," or "Everyone says it …" After such responses, I explain that negative generalizations used to justify thought rationale during our discussions of assigned reading material will not work. I apprise the students that opinions based on fact might be the best way to express individual differences, and that it is important to understand that wrong words can hurt and haunt. To get the lesson started, I relate to the class words that I have been called and that have hurt me in the past. I write these on the board. Then the students are asked if they would reveal words that they have been called and have hurt them, someone else, or a group. The response rate is incredible with multiple examples from each of the students. When these ideas are put on the board, it isn't long before someone points out that they are not truisms. After this it is my experience that blanket negative generalizations decline while thoughtful "I believe …" and "It is my opinion …" expressions predominate. Not only have we learned to appropriately express ourselves without hurting others, but we have set up a condition of fairness to all in the classroom while essentially gathering total group participation and communication.

Collages in the Classroom

Another technique relies on creating a collage. Magazines, scissors, 8 ½ x 11 in. paper, and glue sticks are used. As an in-class assignment, it results in students creating a visual image centering on who they want to be, a remembrance, or where they are from (in either the conceptual or literal sense). I want my students to learn to be comfortable with themselves and what they seek. It is a feminist lesson of the highest magnitude. Students are told that in the next session they will have an opportunity to tell a short story about their creation. Students receive a brief lesson on creating a collage, are shown several of mine as examples, and I tell them my own stories. Magazines are given out with instructions to share them. Students are also encouraged to call out to the others what they are looking for in case someone has seen it in their magazine. This makes for a more efficient search, but it also opens up little side conversations between people who heretofore have not known each other. I relish this. The students are told that they may tear whole pages from magazines before they cut their chosen images out. They are also cautioned that they may not glue images to the paper until they have arranged them in a fashion so that no white of the paper is showing; this may result in 20 small or 5 large images on a single page.

Before the next class, I reduce the collages on a color copier and then glue them individually onto magnet sheets. These are handed back at our next meeting. I ask the students to tell a brief story about their collage with assurances that students only have to reveal what is comfortable. They are also assured that explanations are not required and any student may skip this part of the exercise without penalty. Over the years, it seems that 99% of my students tell a story. Many of the themes are about home and hope. Before class is over I ask the students to place their magnets in their dorm rooms, apartments, or homes in a place they are viewed easily. I tell them that when things get a little too hard in their lives, to take a look at their creation as an assistance in getting past the difficulty. Invariably, students describe the collage class as their most enjoyable of the year and I have noticed afterward they are more comfortable, open, and settled in the classroom. Some have told me years later that the magnet was still up on their refrigerator.

Food Stories

My next technique was developed from exit interviews from my Visual Studies Seminar course. Initially, the seminar students loathe the intense reading assignments they were given to help prepare them for the world they were about to enter. Later, when they become art teachers, they reveal that they highly value the information contained in the reading list. This includes books such as *Art on My Mind: Visual Politics* (hooks, 1995), *The Heart of Learning: Spirituality in Education* (Glazer, 1999), and *The New Teacher Book: Finding Purpose, Balance and Hope During Your First Year in the Classroom* (Salas, Tenorio, Walters, & Weiss, 2004). These books question the motivations of my art students' desires to be teachers and realistically depict changes and emotions they will undergo in the classroom. The readings lead to energetic classroom discussions among the group of students who are anxious and scared of their upcoming student teaching assignments.

I know the students by mid-semester are tired and need a break from our constant reading and discussion. Therefore, I announce a class food assignment. I believe that the best classrooms are similar to a small and cheerful dinner among friends where all are respected and accepted. They are asked to bring their favorite food to class to share with others, and tell a story about this food choice. The intention is for them to relax, have some fun, and, experience a basic feminist lesson of honoring chores traditionally given to women. The food choices are wide-ranging. In some cases, the food choice is an exotic dessert or some unusual family fare barely edible by others. We all laugh heartily at some of the dishes. The food stories turn into a loud, open, and outrageous group conversation, reminiscent of a happy family gathering. I think the food story break helps my students experience a cheerful dinner atmosphere and gives them another positive consideration in the future regarding peoples' choices and lifestyles.

A Space for their Lives

Probably the best technique I use to get stories told comes directly from Linda Christensen's article in *Rethinking Our Classrooms, Teaching for Equality and Justice, Volume 2* (2001). She calls her lesson "Where I'm From: Inviting Students' Lives into the Classroom." Christensen's lesson advances six points of teaching strategies she has developed and ends with students writing "Where I'm From" poems using an "I am from …" refrain to describe memories and details of their lives. The lesson generates very intimate poems. Christensen's goal is for her high school students to feel "significant and cared about … to find space for their lives to become part of the curriculum" (pp. 6–10).

In a different vein, I present this lesson to graduate students who are expected to have more knowledge and life experience. The intention is for them to step beyond their roles as teachers and reconnect with their self in order to adapt to a high level of reading and artwork required for their post-baccalaureate degrees. Their poems, one of which is presented in this chapter, can be intensely personal, intuitive, and revealing. Christensen's lesson, outstanding for almost any education level, assists me in understanding my graduate students better and gives me insight to guide and motivate them to examine new methods of teaching, and to work with them to expand their artwork.

Sooner or Later

Earlier it was pointed out that results from introducing storytelling at many junctures in art students' academic journeys can be noticeable within a single semester, but it is more likely that any discernable changes gradually creep into their work. During the past several years, I have been pleasantly surprised at the number of social justice issues finding their way into the artwork, stories, poems, and conversations of my students. In many cases, I have come to see this as a natural evolution from telling stories, particularly as macro social justice is not paramount to the curriculum I teach. I can only hope to improve the human condition with the actions I take in my classroom with a realization that social justice, like all human rights, can be an intense personal issue. That an intense personal issue find its way into art is not surprising; this art may serve as a window on the past, as creator of present and future culture and knowledge (Ayers, 2003), and as therapy for social justice issues. It is often difficult to arrive at a consensus on what social justice means, but issues will be revealed when art is done and stories are told. That is the only guarantee. Art professors are not personal counselors, psychiatrists, psychologists, or lawyers. However, consciousness-raising through storytelling can evoke a few students to come forth with problems that need professional assistance. Cultivation of close relations with on-campus counseling services, a center for addiction and recovery (if part of the university's organization), and ombudsmen is vital for every professor espousing the tenet of open and honest communication. Recommending referrals at times may be necessary.

Three Stories

Three former students have allowed me to present their stories; I thank them for letting me mention them by name, give their background, and reproduce their work to illustrate the substance of intertwining stories with feminist lessons within the classroom, especially when their artwork reflects social justice issues. One, Chad Farris, earned both a Master of Art Education (MAE) degree and a Master of Fine Arts (MFA). He is now a tenure track associate professor at a southern Texas university. The next, Pamela Sprangler, graduated with a Bachelor of Fine Arts (BFA) in Visual Studies with an all-level teaching certificate and teaches art at a middle school in the Fort Worth, Texas, area. The third, Marisa Mejia, obtained her MAE directly after she graduated with a Bachelor of Science (BS) in Architecture and teaches high school art in west Texas.

Chad

A self-described contemporary Lowbrow artist with a social theory and education teaching style, Chad grew up in west Texas. He left at one point and supported his art by working at different jobs in Las Vegas and San Francisco. Returning to Texas, Chad taught art at a Boys and Girls Club and soon decided he loved this work. He enrolled at Texas Tech University in the MAE program to obtain his teaching credentials. During studio courses, Chad's artwork lead to rumors being spread about him by other graduate students, all females. Chad used tattoo imagery in his work, including pinups. Based on assumptions, and forgetting that feminism honors, at its core, the equality of the sexes, the female graduate students branded Chad a misogynist, generally treated him poorly, and felt his art promoted a form of abuse.

When Chad started taking MAE classes, he was still the subject of this discrimination. I did not know this at first, but it soon came out in the stories elicited from him in class. During a Visual Studies Seminar course held in the summer at Texas Tech University's Junction campus, Chad completed the "Where I'm From…" lesson. The poem Chad wrote is called "No Apologies."

I am from the dusty fields of West Texas.
I am from a three-year-old's feverish nightmares.
I am from a family that loves me the best way they know how.
I am from Murmur A's pecan and apricot fried pies.
I am from Murmur P's cherry icebox pie.

I am from the class that never stopped working.
I am from broken and tortured eyes that never saw what they
were suppose to.
I am from a place where I never grew up or needed or wanted to,
but had to.
I am from small town I have never been able to wash off.
I am sinew and suet.
I am from burnt out Texas nights infused by Hank's "I'm So
Lonely I Could Cry."
I am from a collection of ink colored scares.
I am from nightmares walkin', psychopaths talkin' and blues
killers.
I am from a loneliness I have never been able to shake.
I am part monkey on a weekend bender that never ended.
I am from broken hearts only healed by too much time.
I am from the heavy side of memories that are harder to get rid
of than tattoos.
I am from nothing and that is something.

When discussing this poem, Chad shared that he cherished his grandmothers, was partially blind, and had been in a few romances that did not
work out. Far from the stereotype he had been labeled, Chad supports
feminist causes and honors women in his art. Chad became more open
in class, and the female graduate students listened to what he said. Their
perceptions changed and they began to understand, appreciate, and support
the stories underlining his art imagery.

Pamela

Because I come from a studio background, I am always asking my
students about how their art is going, and encourage them to show it to me
at any time. I consider this the visual equivalent of listening to my students'
stories. In the case of Pamela, a BFA student in Visual Studies, this approach
yielded superb dividends especially in a social justice context with feminist
underpinnings. It evidenced that one of the grandest outcomes of social
justice is a citizen giving back to society for the good of others. I had taught
Pamela in several courses prior to her participating in a student exhibition
show. The students asked me to consult on selecting pieces to be shown.

Pamela included color photos taken at the 2006 Albuquerque Balloon
Festival. They were her choice, but for some reason she also offered to show
me ten black-and-white photos rarely seen. The titles for these images
included hurtful and demeaning words. She explained that the titles for
these photos were all interchangeable, as the hurtful words of the titles
could be placed under any of the photographs and still make sense. The
photos were her story as a beautiful, plus-sized woman. Pamela told me
that these would be hard to show as some of the well-intended, but hurtful
words in the titles had been spoken by members of her own family. She
further indicated that hardly a day went by when somebody, ostensibly to
be kind, offered a comment to her that was in reality harsh. We talked
about what feminists described as the false body image, such as a *Playboy*
model, and the feminist goal of being seen as a whole person and not just a
body. With some trepidation but demonstrated courage, Pamela hung the
powerful black-and-white photos. At the show, they touched a chord in
the hearts of the students, faculty, and visitors viewing them. Their praise
of Pamela's talent and her willingness to shock them into recognition by
telling her story was gratifying. Her photos were subsequently shown at
Texas Tech University's Women's Studies office for 6 months. From this
event, Pamela gained self-confidence and acceptance as a knowledgeable,
gregarious woman with vision. Figure 1 is titled "I was told if I lost weight
I would be beautiful. Until then I never thought I was ugly."

Figure 1. *I was told if I lost weight I would be beautiful. Until then I never
thought I was ugly.* B/W Photography, 16" x 20", 2006.

Marisa

Marisa came to Texas Tech University's MAE program after earning her BS in Architecture. She felt her heart was leading her to teach art. Much like feminists working to establish non-traditional roles for women, Marisa was drawn to teaching art in non-traditional, non-western world ways. She knew that traditional curriculum has yet to be influenced by types of outsider art (Mahir, 2004). A quiet, highly intelligent woman of Mexican-American heritage, Marisa grew up in a single parent household where her mother worked several jobs to raise her family. During Marisa's undergraduate and graduate days, she worked full-time to pay for her education.

Marisa encountered opposition by some faculty members who either felt she was not a good enough artist in studio classes, or was too quiet during discussion sessions. There were also possible philosophical differences with some questioning her rationale for leaving what they saw as a burgeoning, lucrative career in architecture.

Marisa's stories were presented in my class and soon she began frequenting my office. She was confused particularly because she felt academe by nature should be fair, equitable, and motivating. I explained that this wasn't always the case, but that successful feminists overcame by perseverance and by believing in themselves. I told her I was impressed by the passion I heard in her stories and she was encouraged to keep making her non-traditional art.

A unique opportunity presented itself to Marisa. A Texas Tech University professor was conducting an architectural studio workshop in Panama City, Panama, during the summer of 2006. The subject of *chivas*, the painted buses of Panama City, came up. Marisa felt that with her Mexican-American background and knowledge of low-rider cars and airbrushing she could travel to Panama and capture the chivas' unnoticed beauty, recognize the apprenticeships that take place, and conduct research about the transportation system in Panama City (Mejia, 2006). The project would help satisfy her MAE degree requirements. In order to fund her trip, Marisa put in overtime at her full-time job while maintaining her course load. She returned and wrote a beautiful, highly regarded project paper, and, during her MAE art exhibition, Marisa's art earned superb accolades. The following poem was inspired by her experiences riding the chivas of Panama City. The poem is called "Congested Beauty."

    I lay in this colored filled dream, while bachata and salsa music
    whisper in my ear and to my body

Figure 2. *The Price of a Soul.* Linocut, 25" x 14", 2007.

As I close my eyes and let the music of my ancestors begin to sway my hips.
I enter a world full of English lessons, and a thirty-five cent loaf of bread.
As I look for a seat on a bus full of congested beauty and almond colored skin.
I open my eyes to see a young mother and let her baby boy fall asleep on my shoulder.
As I walk through the roughest town I've ever seen and admire the beauty of twenty-five story buildings with no elevators,
School girls walk across "the median" in catholic uniforms with looks that could kill.
As I attempt not to stare at a young mother breastfeeding her baby during the World Cup,
I struggle to remember a home that feels foreign.
As I sit on a bus nicknamed Diablos Rojos in honor of death certificates.
I watch the day drift by in a flood of water, and walk away with rain soaked shoulders,
As I have a conversation that can only happen in the privacy of strangers,
I walk through a city where the color of my skin keeps me from getting mugged,

As I look at no one in particular because it is forbidden,
I enter a place full of people I do not know; despite the warnings,
I drop my quarter into the cashier's styrofoam cup and walk away.

Conclusion

I am an avid proponent of art teachers developing art continually as I believe it is therapeutic and helps them guide their students to find their identity as artists. Many burn out from the demands of their profession and personal lives and they delay or stop making art altogether. Over the years, my art has been mainly autobiographical primarily focusing on feminist themes. Recently I have been drawn to new themes, particularly after hearing the stories and seeing the social justice issues contained in my students' work. In the past year I have had the opportunity to submit three social justice pieces to an international show called "Human Trafficking." One piece, *The Price of a Soul*, is shown here. It was an experimental piece, differently constructed than usual.

There are diverse ways for teachers to create positive classroom dynamics and elicit storytelling in different forms from their students. I have given several here that work for me, and I have shared outcomes that had social justice as the theme and feminist lessons at the heart of the issue. What has become significant is that regardless of the techniques used, the rewards of letting student voices take center stage in the learning process are worth the effort invested.

REFERENCES

Akins-Tillett, F. (2006). Meditations on my art. *Visual Culture and Gender*, (1) 79–80.

Ayers, W. (2003). *On the side of the child.* New York: Teachers College Press.

Christensen, L. (2001). Teaching for equity and justice. In B. Bigelow, B. Harvey, S. Karp, & L. Miller (Eds.), *Rethinking our classroom: Teaching for equity and justice, 2* (pp. 5–10). Rethinking Schools.

Glazer, S. (Ed.). (1999). *The heart of learning.* New York: Tarcher.

hooks, b. (1995). *Art on my mind: Visual Politics.* New York: The New Press.

Mahir, J. (Ed) (2004). *What they don't learn in school.* New York: Peter Lang Publishing.

Mejia, M. (2006). *Congested Beauty.* Unpublished manuscript, Texas Tech University.

Salas, K., Tenorio, R., Walters, S., & Weiss, D. (Eds.). (2004). *The new teacher book: Finding purpose, balance, and hope during your first year in the classroom.* Milwaukee, WI: Rethinking Schools.

Art Teachers as Change Makers

Kimberly Cosier and Jeanne Nemeth

T eaching for social justice lives at the very core of our work at the University of Wisconsin-Milwaukee (UWM). As art educators in an urban university, we believe we have a moral imperative to guide our students toward a philosophy and practice of teaching that is not only inclusive of all children and young people, but also focused on working toward anti-biased schools and society (Ayers, 2004). We believe that affirming diversity and teaching tolerance is just the first step in answering the moral implications of teaching. Teaching for social justice means going beyond teaching tolerance to engage in the difficult personal and cultural work necessary to help create a brighter future for all (Kildegaard, 2008).

In order to effect change, teacher educators must prepare preservice teachers to go beyond their roles as artists/ researchers who plan multicultural curricula and celebrate diversity and guide students to understand how to draw on their creativity and imagination to actively work toward justice (Greene, 1995). We understand that this is a challenge, particularly at a time when there is a backlash against multiculturalism, affirmative action, and tolerance of difference. On many college campuses today academic freedom is being hijacked by right-wing extremists who put pressure on professors to give equal time to exclusionary and hateful ideas (O'Regan, 2007).

As well, the standards and accountability reform movement, including the No Child Left Behind Act, are edging out the arts in many schools

KEY CONCEPTS

- Become Reflective Practitioners
- Utilize Visual Means to Evaluate Power, Language, and Difference
- Understand Institutional Racism and White Privilege
- Cultivate New Personal Constructs and Attitudes
- Investigate Artists Who Promote Critical Ways of Viewing Race and Identity

(Chapman, 2004; Wood, 2004). Finally, budgets are shrinking; funding for the arts is often among the first items on the administrators' chopping blocks. Art teachers in many schools work hard to keep their programs afloat. Despite these challenges, we believe we should not be swayed from the important work of teaching for social justice.

Situating our Story

UWM is situated in the largest urban center in Wisconsin. Fifty percent (50%) of the state's students of color and 71% of the state's African American students live in Milwaukee (Kailin, 2002). In Milwaukee Public Schools (MPS), due to desegregation, the number of white students in the district has continued to fall since the 1970s, whereas the number of African American students has remained stable over the past decade, and the number of Hispanic students is on the rise. There are also a small, but significant, number of Asian (primarily Hmong) and Native American students in MPS schools.

According to Skiba (2005), "41.3% of all the children in the city live in poverty, ranking the city fourth in the nation." As the percentage of students of color rose in MPS, "funding per pupil plummeted compared to funding in overwhelmingly white suburban districts. From 1980 to 1998, the gap between school funding for urban students (students of color) and that for suburban students in Wisconsin had increased by 400 percent" (Kailin, 2002, p. 45). The district has recently been named a "Level 2 District Identified for Improvement" under the rules of the No Child Left Behind Act. As a result, art programs in MPS have been eroding for as long as the district has been under-funded and overburdened.

Although UWM is an urban university, our own student population looks different from the MPS student population. UWM art education students are predominantly white, middle- or working-class women who primarily come from suburbs and small towns outside the City of Milwaukee. They usually come to us with limited understandings of the city and its inhabitants, often conflating race and poverty as one and the same.

Our program is housed in the Department of Visual Art, and the students have the advantage of a strong studio preparation. Art history and general education classes are offered in other schools within the university. Our students are introduced to art education theories through a three-credit introductory class. Following that, we team-teach our elementary and secondary methods courses. Each is six credits and includes integrated urban field experience components. This allows us to address theory through practice and provides a shared foundation upon which to engage students in the challenge of developing an art teaching praxis that attends to social justice issues.

Growing an Anti-Racist/Anti-Biased Teacher Education Practice

Although the mission of the university and the art teacher-preparation program focuses on urban issues, many students must be convinced of the importance of the urban mission in relation to teaching. They often come to the program with fond memories of an art room in their former schools, and they want to reproduce what they know. They also believe that if they do not plan to stay in the city after graduation they should not have to deal directly with racism and other biases. With the shortage of jobs in art in MPS, it is almost guaranteed that they will leave; however, we believe that it is important that they be advocates for social justice, and to understand the dynamics of race, social class, and other issues of identity, regardless of where they will teach in the future. Our students want the art room simply to be a safe haven, as it was for many of them when they were in school. However, "the classroom is not a space outside of society, and students and teachers do not check their histories at the door when they enter it" (Kandaswamy, 2008, p. 7). Therefore, we believe it is necessary to convince them that all schooling is political and that teachers have a moral imperative to work for social justice (Ayers, 2004; Cochran-Smith, 2004).

As well, most of our students have come of age in a supposedly post-hate, "colorblind" society (Agid & Rand, 2003; Jay, 2007.) Therefore, they may be resistant to critically examining their evolving teacher identities in relation to otherness, bias, and institutionalized racism in schools. Additionally, like most white Americans, they believe in the "bootstrap" mentality of the American Dream. This myth of meritocracy, in which anyone who works hard can make it, can inhibit some students' abilities to empathize with the people of Milwaukee who have been barred from moving out of poverty because of institutionalized racism and the related dynamics of capitalism.

Finally, many of the students come from home environments that have taught them to be suspicious of difference, thus, they see themselves and their outlooks on life as normative. They can be resistant to the challenge to interrogate their relationships to class, gender identities, sexuality, and physical and mental ability. All of these factors make dealing with the biases inherent in our society particularly difficult. Yet, we muddle through, each year building upon knowledge gained through experience and finding new and more interesting and engaging ways to do this important work.

Because our students are not yet practicing teachers, we find that the first thing to do is get them to connect with a group of urban students. The students begin with elementary settings to ease them into the experience. Despite the youth of the elementary pupils, however, our preservice teachers are usually quite apprehensive about going into an "inner city" school. They have grown up fearing the city and its inhabitants; even 5-year-olds can have some of them shaking in their boots. Most often, they enter our partner schools a bit nervous and hesitant, but by the time they go home at the end of the first day, they have already begun to make connections with the children and come out of the building with big smiles on their faces.

We visit the schools with the art education students twice per week. The students develop integrated art lessons that they then teach in the classroom. Thus, they get to know the children well, while they learn about classroom management and elementary curricula from their cooperating teachers. In exchange, the classroom teachers enjoy learning ways to integrate art into their lessons. By the end of the 8- to 10-week experience, many of our students are misty-eyed at the thought of saying goodbye to children they once thought of only as "other."

In the next semester, the group works with secondary school settings. In their UWM classes, the students focus on developing their teacher identities by having them process their experiences and evaluating themselves in regard to power, language, and differences (Keifer-Boyd & Maitland-Gholson, 2007). We address the formation of teacher identities through various means, including art-based assignments such as sketchbook journals. These experiences are then informed and processed through feminist, queer, critical race, and whiteness theoretical perspectives (Crenshaw, Gotanda, Peller, & Thomas, 1995; hooks, 1994).

In-Class Preparation: Confronting Personal Constructs

Preparing these preservice students to teach in urban, multiracial schools is not an easy task. Initially the work begins with teaching students how to become reflective practitioners, ones that are aware and sensitive to their own assumptions about race and schooling. Such frames of reference often guide perceptions and actions. It is essential that the students understand issues of race on interpersonal levels as well as in a broader context. Thus, it is necessary to teach them how they might begin to reflect about and confront cultural bias and stereotypical constructs that are part of their personal belief systems. Learning to critically examine stereotypes that are prevalent in our society and global communities is another significant step in deconstructing and reconstructing race and identity.

Most importantly, students need to figure out how to situate themselves in an urban classroom and learn to cultivate new personal constructs and attitudes. As noted earlier, our students are fearful when they enter the elementary preservice practicum. Although they learn much through the elementary experience, and substantially develop in their relationship to difference, the secondary school placement presents new challenges and can initiate further feelings of fear and anxiety, as they are often unsure about how to interact in a classroom filled with students unlike themselves. Therefore, preventive reflective practice outside of the classroom is highly recommended.

Anticipating this scenario, we introduce activities in the methods courses that foster open dialogue and risk taking. These activities challenge attitudes, beliefs, and opinions. In order to encourage critical awareness, reflection, and dialogue students are assigned weekly readings related to the complex issues of identity, race, power, and politics in our society. They are expected to respond in visual journals by formulating critical questions for class discussions and visually interpreting concepts that they find relevant. In class, students participate in small and large group discussions about readings in relation to classroom situations that they have encountered in their assigned schools. These conversations routinely provoke intense class discussions concerning beliefs and concerns about cultural differences that they are experiencing in their teaching practice.

Investigating and presenting social issues of race, identity, and power through the eyes of contemporary artists is another component of our art methods classes and a necessary priority. We specifically choose artists for the students to research and present to the class who promote ideas that engage their audience in critical ways of viewing race and other markers of identity. Such artists include Kerry James Marshall, Michael Ray Charles, Carrie Mae Weems, Lorna Simpson, Kara Walker, and Ellen Gallagher. Students are expected to present questions for class discussions about an artist of their choosing. These class assignments and discussions encourage students to move from silence, denial, and guilt about race to awareness of differences in an open dialogue comparing discourses about race and stereotypes in a larger context.

Classroom Dialogue: What is Whiteness?

As instructors of future teachers, we are particularly interested in how students perceive, adjust, and adapt to their new roles as teachers. What are the implications for our teaching when students are raised in primarily white communities and may be unaware of the richness of other cultures? Do students believe the concept of sameness, that one-size-fits-all "color-blindness" that is often portrayed in media and other venues of popular culture with respect to white and black America?

Our students work toward becoming mindful of their own situated place in society. We work with students to problematize the "colorblind" view of society and intentionally construct and model classroom art lessons to address critical social issues. One of the classroom activities initiated one semester in the methods course addressed perceived notions and definitions of race, in particular, whiteness. In this activity, we use the critical tools of Whiteness Studies to reveal problems with colorblindness (McIntosh, 1990).

Whiteness Studies is an expanding multidisciplinary field which focuses on whiteness as a political and cultural position. It is the study of the social construction of race and privilege and is defined in more detail as follows:

Whiteness Studies traces the economic and political history behind the invention of "whiteness," challenges the privileges given to so-called "whites," and analyzes the cultural practices (in art, music, literature, and popular media) that perpetuate the color. Instead, Whiteness Studies thinks critically about how white skin preference has operated systematically, structurally, and sometimes unconsciously as a dominant force in American and indeed in global society and culture. (Jay, 2005)

The purpose of the activity about whiteness is to stimulate students' thinking so they begin to analyze their own biases and constructions of race. An important objective of this lesson is to help our students achieve a new awareness and understanding of race and whiteness. Our goal is for our students to move from a *rhetoric of dysfunctional silence to a rhetoric of listening*. The *rhetoric of dysfunctional silence* is demonstrated by a state of denial, defensiveness, guilt, or blame. Whereas, the Rhetoric of listening is the stage in which recognition, critique, and accountability are possible (Ratliffe, 1999).

To begin the lesson in a recent semester, we presented an image of a slice of white bread with the word "homemade" typed underneath (Figure 1). This visual metaphor was created in response to the following poem:

A WHITELIST
White race
White house
White wash
White bread
White collar
White supremacy
White lies
White trash
White elephant
White guilt

Figure 1. *Homemade.*

Figure 1. *Homemade,* Nemeth, 2002. The image was created by one of the authors of this chapter Jeanne Nemeth; the poem, *A Whitelist,* was adapted from the text written by Ware (1997).

After reading the poem to the class, students were asked to respond to the question "What is whiteness?" and create a visual metaphor for their written response. The results proved to be interesting. We discovered that a few of our students interpreted the term whiteness literally and scientifically. Some responses referenced color theory, such as prisms or color wheels, with written responses such as "whiteness is the absence of color" or "whiteness is overabundance of light." One student drew skin cells (Figure 2) and wrote, "whiteness is a skin pigment." Responses such as these do not address the political nature of whiteness and could reflect denial or defensiveness. According to Jay (2005), such responses might represent a person who has chosen to ignore any connection between whiteness and racial connotations; their response would fit within the category "Rhetoric of Dysfunctional Silence" (Ratliffe, 1999).

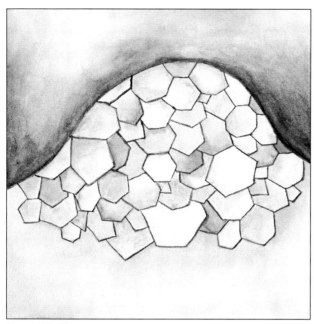

Figure 2. *Skin Pigment.*

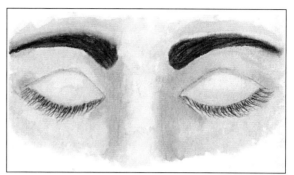

Figure 3. *Oblivious.*

Figure 4. *White Wig.*

Encouragingly, the majority of the 30 students wrote comments and created metaphors that were complex, insightful, and critical. Such responses would fall into the category "Rhetoric of Listening" (Ratliffe, 1999). Responses in this category would reflect a level of acceptance or recognition of issues associated with race, critical interpretations, and a sense of responsibility or accountability. For example, one student addressed the ways white people shirk responsibility for racial inequities; she wrote, "whiteness is being oblivious," accompanied by a metaphorical drawing of closed eyes (Figure 3).

Making a critical point about stereotypical ideas, style, and accepted norms, another student wrote, "Whiteness is the need to conform to the stereotypical American standard by extinguishing all racial identities" (Figure 4). In the discussion that ensued, this student connected her visual metaphor to the work of Lorna Simpson. This response is a critique of the pressures of the "colorblind" society; she is wrestling with this problem, through a discourse, which she recognizes can be a strategy that deflects challenges to white privilege (Kandaswamy, 2008).

Figure 5. *White Wash.*

Figure 6. *A Walk in the Park.*

Figure 5 represents another interpretation of whiteness. The accompanying reflection describes a phenomenon in which "whiteness is caused by diminishing the details of culture and history." For this student, dominant cultural forces detract from the richness that could be shared among us in our culture, that then "whitewashes" or sanitizes history.

To accompany the drawing in Figure 6, our student wrote:

Whiteness is a walk in the Park…

Watching out for booby traps along the way.

Whiteness in this country means privilege, opportunity, and power. It also means taking blame for all of the white people's historical faults and having to watch out for everything said and done, so as to not be labeled as a racist just because you are white.

This student is clearly acknowledging white privilege, while at the same time bristling at her accompanying guilt and blame. Her honesty and openness about this difficult topic came only after prolonged in-class dialogue and self-reflection. As she and the class learned, images can be read in multiple ways. During the discussions it was noted that there was a visual reference to lynching with the blacksmith's anvil hanging from the tree; this made the image an even more powerful metaphor.

This exercise provided valuable insights into students' perceptions and attitudes toward race. After students participated in this introductory lesson and discussed personal responses to the term *whiteness,* we went on to examine academic discourses on whiteness and other identity markers. For example, Thompson (2003) argued that it is important for educators to understand that schools are structured around white cultural norms. She asserted that a teacher who can deconstruct his or her own prejudices is more likely to understand why prevailing pedagogical and curricular patterns might not work for students. "Even white teachers who are fully committed to multiculturalism often fail to see how their own investments in white culture as a universal culture get in the way of their good intentions vis-à-vis students of color" (http://www/pauahtun.org/6624-7624.F03.html).

Other anti-racist/anti-bias teaching advocates have written about pedagogical strategies that have worked for them. For example, Kailin (2002) outlined four methods to examine racism for teachers:

1. Examine characteristics and definitions of race and racism and related terminology.
2. Become aware of how our own personal socializations have been affected by racism, particularly in the social construction of whiteness.
3. Relate this personal experience to the institutional or systemic and historical features of racism, as manifested in political economy, ideology, and cultural and social institutions.
4. Examine the possibilities—and the responsibility—teachers have to become agents of anti-racist change. (p. 122)

Conclusion

Our approach to art teacher education for social justice follows a rhythm similar to Kailin's (2002) anti-racist teaching. We believe it is our obligation to educate students about identity and expose them to ideas that challenge their preconceptions about white cultural norms. These discourses give relevant and essential background knowledge providing valuable tools for teaching, not only in urban schools, but also in all schools. Through such experiences, such as the whiteness metaphor project, school field experiences, reflective journaling, research projects on contemporary artists who deal with issues of identity, and difficult in-class dialogues, we endeavor to offer future teachers an artful and productive way to become effective guides for their own students. We want art teachers who leave this program to be agents of change and to teach with the goal to make the world a better place for all.

REFERENCES

Agid, S., & Rand, E. (2003). Introduction: Teaching beyond tolerance. *Radical teacher, 80*, 2–5.

Ayers, W. (2004). *Teaching toward freedom: Moral commitment and ethical action in the classroom.* Boston: Beacon Press.

Chapman, L. (2004). No Child Left Behind in art? *Arts Education Policy Review, 106*(2), 3–17.

Crenshaw, K., Gotanda, N., Peller, G., & Thomas K. (Eds.). (1995). *Critical race theory: The key writings that formed the movement.* New York: New Press.

Cochran-Smith, M. (2004). *Walking the road: Race, diversity, and social justice in teacher education.* New York: Teachers College Press.

Greene, M. (1995). *Releasing the imagination: Essays on education, the arts, and social change.* San Francisco: Jossey-Bass.

hooks, b. (1994). *Teaching to transgress: Education as the practice of freedom.* New York: Routledge.

Jay, G. (2007). Who invented white people? In R. P. Yagleski (Ed.), *The Thompson reader: Conversations in context* (pp. 96–102). Boston: Thompson/Heinle.

Jay, G. (with Jones, S. E.) (2005). Whiteness studies and the multicultural literature classroom. *MELUS, special issue on "Pedagogy, Praxis, Politics, and Multiethnic Literatures, 30*(2), 99–121.

Kailin, J. (2002). *Anti-racist education: From theory to practice.* Lanham MD: Rowman & Littlefield.

Kandaswamy, P. (2008). Beyond colorblindness and multiculturalism: Rethinking anti-racist pedagogy in the university classroom. *Radical Teacher, 80*, 6–11.

Keifer-Boyd, K., & Maitland-Gholson, J. (2007). *Engaging visual culture.* Worcester, MA: Davis Publications.

Kildegaard, L. (2008). Constructive intersections: White students meet Black history in August Wilson's *The Piano Lesson. Radical Teacher, 80*, 19–23.

McIntosh, P. (1990). White privilege: Unpacking the invisible knapsack. *Independent School, 49*(2), 31–36.

O'Regan, M. (2007). Censoring our educators, *Utne.com.* Retrieved April 26, 2008, from http://www.utne.com/2007-03-01/CensoringOurEducators.aspx

Ratliffe, K. (1999). Rhetorical listening: A trope for interpretive invention and a "code of cross-cultural conduct" CCC, 51(2), 195–224.

Skiba, K. M. (2005, October 12). Housing experts work to address city poverty. *JSOnline/Milwaukee Journal Sentinel.* Retrieved April 28, 2008, from http://www.jsonline.com/news/metro/oct05/362728.asp

Thompson, A. (2003). *Whiteness theory and education.* Retrieved May 9, 2008, from http://www.pauahtun.org/6624--7624.F03.html

Ware, V. (1997). The white issue. In S. Golding (Ed.), *The eight technologies of otherness* (pp. 244–252). New York and London: Routledge.

Wood, G. (2004). A view from the field: NCLB's effects on classrooms and schools. In D. Meier & G. Wood (Eds.), *Many children left behind: How the No Child Left Behind Act is damaging our children and our schools,* (pp. 33–50). Boston: Beacon Press.

Reflections on Social Justice Art Teacher Education

Dipti Desai

Teacher education needs to be conceptualized as both a learning problem and a political problem aimed at social justice. (Marilyn Cochran-Smith, 2004)

A decade ago, teacher education caught the attention of policymakers, media, private interest groups, and the public. One of the reasons for the failed public education system cited by various education and media pundits was the lack of qualified teachers. How teachers are trained became the focus of much debate. Nine years ago, in an attempt to raise the quality of teachers in public schools, the New York State Board of Education required all teacher education programs, including the arts, to redesign and register their programs based on certain guidelines in an attempt to ensure rigor and accountability. This directive by the State was an attempt to change the way we prepare teachers, still conceptualized as a problem of training and testing, rather than as a problem of politically situated learning (Cochran-Smith, 2004). The primary focus of teacher education programs in New York was to ensure that "all teachers have basic subject matter knowledge and the technical skills to work in schools devoted to bringing pupils' test scores to certain minimum thresholds" (p. 1). New York's call to action created an opportunity for the faculty involved in teacher preparation at New York University (NYU) to re-conceptualize what was meant by teacher education. In this essay, I explore the journey that was undertaken to design a social justice based art education program that embodied NYU's teacher education mission. I also reflect on the questions, issues, and challenges that have emerged as this program grows and

KEY CONCEPTS

- Social Justice
- Critical Pedagogy
- Contemporary Art
- Teacher Education
- Critical Race Theory

our teachers begin their teaching careers in schools, museums, and other alternative educational environs.

Rethinking Teacher Education

For a year (1998–1999), the faculty involved in teacher education and faculty from various departments at NYU's Steinhardt School of Culture, Education, and Human Development met to discuss and debate what teacher education meant. These discussions led to the creation of a Vision Statement that provided the framework for all curriculum revisions—a framework that conceptualized teacher education as a process that is simultaneously a political problem as well as a learning problem that involves "intellectual, cultural, and contextually local activity" (Cochran-Smith, 2004, p. 2). NYU's commitment is to train teachers "whose practice is informed by broad and deep understanding of their disciplines and specializations, and by a moral commitment to equity and social justice" (Taub, Tobias, & Mayher, 2006, p. 4). Thus, education is understood to be a moral and political endeavor rather than a neutral, value-free process. Grounded in this understanding, the complexity of teaching and learning is viewed as a series of dynamic tensions that our students learn to mediate (Table 1). The five tensions in the NYU/Steinhardt vision statement will be briefly outlined to set the stage for how the art education program is currently conceptualized.

The Five Tensions

The first tension that periodically may emerge is the divide between those who argue that pedagogy should focus on transmitting subject knowledge and those who believe that pedagogy should focus on how students learn. Our position is that NYU teachers need to simultaneously acknowledge their content area and understand the way their students learn (Taub et al., 2006). Teaching and learning are inseparable, as two sides of the same coin.

The second tension suggests that teaching and learning is not a neutral act that takes place in insular classrooms. Rather it is influenced, shaped, and responsive to social, cultural, political, and economic contexts. The notion that teacher education is simply a technical problem that can be solved using a set of methods, techniques, and evaluative measures is a pervasive viewpoint in society. Instead, our teachers strive to explore their classroom in a wider context (school, community, society, nation, and world).

The third tension addresses the need for teachers to "function in the real world of urban and suburban classrooms while simultaneously being committed to striving to improve them, to bring them closer to their potential as democratic learning communities" (Taub et al., 2006, p. 6). Tension four is based on the understanding that teaching and learning are collaborative social activities that require working with both the needs of individual learners and the classroom community to ensure fairness and social justice for all learners. It is necessary to respect "diversity of ideas as well as backgrounds ... Such mutual respectful democratic classrooms must be exemplary learning communities that both enact and are explicitly committed to anti-bias education" (p. 6).

The fifth and final tension requires teachers to mediate between caring for their students and caring for themselves so that "all aspects of the learning transaction can be mutually beneficial" (Taub et al., 2006, p. 7). This final tension is based on the ethic of caring advocated by Noddings (1992); our teachers "create caring learning environments where each participant can reach their full intellectual, moral, and human potential" (Taub et al., 2006, p. 7).

Envisioning the Art Education Program

Keeping the NYU mission for teacher education at the forefront, the challenge faced was to design a master's program that allowed prospective art teachers to *embody a social justice perspective* in an *integrated manner across the entire program*. Forever mindful that embodiment and commitment to a social justice perspective is a lifelong endeavor, we first had to be clear about how we understood social justice art education. Similar to

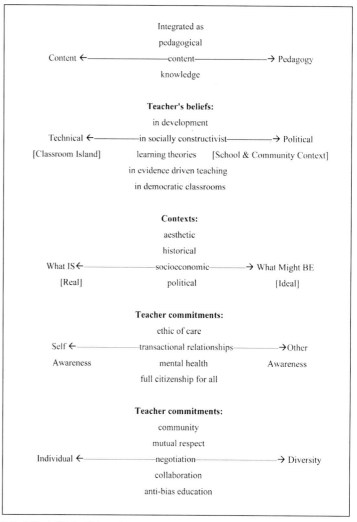

Table 1. Chart of Vision Statement.

Bell (1997), social justice art education was to be viewed as a process and a goal that involves working in a collaborative, participatory, and democratic way to change the unequal distribution and access of resources that hamper equal participation of all social groups in society. It "involves social actors who have a sense of their own agency as well as a sense of social responsibility toward and with others and the society as a whole" (p. 3). It follows that a social justice perspective requires a fundamental personal transformation in the ways that teachers understand their own world, their place in it, and their relationship to others in an unequal society.

As many educators have noted, this personal transformation cannot be achieved by one or more courses, or over a few years, but takes place over a lifetime of active, conscious, critical, reflective, and mindful teaching and learning (Cochran-Smith, 2004; Darling-Hammond et al., 2002; Ladson-Billings, 2001; Nieto, 2000). Thus, the challenge was creating an educational experience rooted in social justice over a 2-year period (the length of our program) that teachers can internalize and make their own.

First, it was necessary to understand that social justice education requires self-actualization to take place in order for students to commit to it for the long haul. Research in social justice programs has shown that prospective secondary teachers revert back to their own high school teaching experiences in their first year of teaching because it is familiar among the unfamiliar multiple facets of teaching that they have to consider. This meant not only thinking about the theoretical framework, but the dispositions art teachers would require in order to pursue social justice art education in schools that remain, for the most part, focused on skill-based art education. The program had to be coherent, which meant weaving key ideas of social justice pedagogy together and across each of the courses, field experiences, seminars, and readings. Two aspects immediately became clear. First we had to interview students applying to this program to make sure they understood what they would be signing up for if admitted, and to assess their disposition toward working for social change. Unlike Kohl (2002), who pounded the pavement to recruit new teachers with a social activist agenda to enroll in the new social justice teacher education program at San Francisco State College, we had to accept a range of students, many who chose the program simply because of the NYU credential and had no prior experience or commitment to social activism.

Second, it was necessary to create a cohort of students who entered the program together and took many of the same courses collectively in order to create a community of learners who could support each other while at NYU and during their first few years teaching in urban schools. The challenges of balancing the wide spectrum of students in our program will be presented in a later section as it raises pressing questions regarding the ability to embody and practice social justice art education.

The preservice curriculum required by state guidelines and developed by many art education programs is based on art education methods, aesthetics, child and adolescent developmental, and art history. These curriculums provide little room for socially relevant content and remain virtually unchanged. Too often in art teacher education programs multiculturalism is associated with social justice and included in a single course to fulfill the state requirement of acknowledging diversity in the classroom. A social justice approach to art education departs from this one-course deficit model of cultural diversity and pluralism and instead is informed by critical or social reconstructivist multiculturalism.

Social reconstructivist multiculturalism encourages a "critical understanding of how race, class, gender and culture structure the life chances and school experiences of both individual school children and large groups of people who are not part of the cultural, racial, language, and socio-economic mainstream" (Cochran-Smith, 2004, p. 17). This critical lens challenges students to look at their own biases and the ways oppression gets internalized and embodied. Eventually the goal is that these notions will become common sense. Thus, it is important, as Boler (1999) stressed, to conceive of "how structures and experiences of race, class and gender … are shaped by the social control of emotions" (p. 5). Emotions are collaboratively constructed and historically situated; therefore, a pedagogy of emotion is "not confession, not therapy or spectating and voyeurism, but witnessing" (Boler, 1999, p. 18). Witnessing requires both students and teachers to be aware of and express our feelings and emotions—those that might be uncomfortable, horrifying, disquieting, fearful, contradictory—regarding the complexity of race, gender, sexuality, and social class that for the most part are deliberately kept from entering the classroom. Teaching for social justice requires witnessing in order to work toward social change.

Art pedagogy is "a form of cultural politics and not a science of knowledge transmission" (Goldfarb, 2002, p.2). Critical pedagogy is one of the foundations of the program that encourages students to not only care about the "savage inequalities" (Kozol, 1991) that exist in urban schools and society, but to understand how society is structured in a hierarchical manner that impacts our daily social relations. This understanding is essential in order for students to imagine social change in their classrooms and communities. Freire's (1990) problem-posing approach to education makes the participants in the learning process responsible for each other's development. This is crucial to creating a community of learners.

The other foundation of the program is contemporary art and its relationship to critical theory. Contemporary art is understood as a social practice that shapes an understanding of the world and also serves as a site for the production of new knowledge. As the NYU Art Education website indicates:

> The Art Education program is designed for students who wish to pursue graduate-level professional training as artist-teachers in public and private schools, museums, community-based programs, and other alternative educational sites. It also prepares students to be innovative researchers and strong advocates of the arts in schools. NYU's program in art education combines a foundation in critical theory with a solid grounding in practice. With special focus on contemporary art and its social context, the program conceptualizes the artist-teacher as cultural producer, intellectual, and activist. Through a sequence of core courses that incorporate a critical multicultural approach, students examine the making and teaching of art as a social act, considering it within philosophical, historical, political, and sociological contexts. (www.nyu.edu/education/art)

It is through a sequence of courses that the students learn how to use critical inquiry, dialogue, and reflection. These courses may also prompt the development of moral and social responsibility that allows students to work toward changing art education practices in schools. The following section presents two interconnected ideas: teachers' socio-political consciousness and contemporary art as a pedagogical process that shapes the art education program. Then I discuss the challenges they pose.

Teachers' Socio-Political Consciousness

In order for teachers to foster the socio-political consciousness of their students, prospective teachers need to explore how their own social position shapes their understanding of the world and their relationship to society. It is beneficial to respect graduate students' experiences and use that knowledge in dialogues, readings, observations in schools, and discussions that move toward a critical perspective of how oppression functions in our daily experiences and within social institution. Such understandings need to lead to social responsibility, to a commitment to the welfare of others (Berman, 1997). As Freire (1990) argued, it is only through praxis, what he defines as "action and reflection of men [and women] upon the world in order to transform it" (p. 66), that students will develop the critical skills necessary to become thoughtful citizens willing to engage in social action.

"Learning to teach social justice then requires not only learning about and struggling with issues of racism, sexism, class and homophobia but, rather 'unlearning' racism and other problematic stances that are often buried in teacher education courses and curricula" (Cochran-Smith, 2004, p. 13). This means critically reflecting on the assumptions and biases we have about teaching and learning art that are shaped by social positions. For a majority of the students who are typical of the teacher education demographics—white, female, and middle class—the ideology of color-blindness (Bonilla-Silva, 2003; Frankenberg, 1993; Winant, 2004) informs their worldview. This ideology asserts that racism is a condition of the past, that the struggles of the Civil Rights movement have lead to racial equality, and that society is now witnessing "reverse racism" (Bell, 2003; Bonilla-Silva, 2003). The common claims to color-blindness, that "I do not see race, I just see individuals," by many of my white students is an assertion of "a race-neutral social context," that "stigmatizes attempts to raise questions about redressing racial equality in daily life through accusations such as 'playing the race card' or 'identity politics' which imply that someone is trying to bring race in where it does not belong" (Lewis, 2003, p. 33). This colorblind notion of race hinders students' ability to see how the content and methods in schools, including art curricula, textbooks, lessons, and disciplinary practices may be based in race, gender, and social-class. Moving students to deconstruct such biases in school practices and texts cannot be accomplished if students do not first acknowledge how white privilege functions in their lives, schools, and society and how a color-blind ideology might support racism. Educating for socio-political consciousness in art education means getting student to ask: How does my race, class, and gender privilege impact the lives of others? How is my daily life connected to the lives of others in our nation and the world? What can I do to create a more just society and world through art?

Teachers support or challenge injustices through their daily action in schools (Zeichner, 1993). The challenge is to move the students from the state of paralysis and guilt that often follows the realization that despite the abolishment of legalized racism in this country that race still matters, toward a non-essentialist understanding of race and racism. It is only through this process of self-actualization that prospective teachers can design art practices and curricula that will allow their students to examine their lives through multiple and critical lens in order to imagine other ways of being. This socio-political awakening of the complexity of social relations is necessary for prospective teachers to think about ways they can engage children and youth in their classrooms to address issues that affect their lives through art practices to develop their emerging sense of empathy and social responsibility. "Social consciousness and social responsibility are not behaviors we need to instill in young people but rather behaviors we need to recognize as emerging in them" (Berman, 2004, p. 110). Children and youth are constantly trying to negotiate their relationship to society. Engaging youth through the arts to take social action requires thinking about the role of art in today's society. This process often requires questioning notions of art that prospective art teachers bring with them from their own art educational experiences.

Contemporary Art as a Pedagogical Site

Understanding the interconnectedness of the world and our relationship to it requires us to think about art and its role in society in a different way. By highlighting the relational process of contemporary art and pedagogy, art education "shifts in focus from teaching 'about' contemporary art to an understanding of contemporary art 'in the making'" that produces "new ways of understanding experience" (Springgay, 2008, p. 23). We learn about ourselves always in relation to others. It is through embodied experiences that we learn about our world.

The first step for prospective art teachers is to examine how their past educational experiences and current relationship to artmaking has shaped their ideas about art. In other words, students are encouraged to explore how they embody art practices. This self-reflection lays the groundwork for examining the ways art practices are contextual and fluid, and connect to society in particular ways. For the majority of the students who come from undergraduate art programs, art is described as a universal language that requires exploring a set of formal skills, manipulating different materials and mediums, and a form of self-expression. Art is considered a solitary act and the autonomy of art is taken for granted. This view of art shapes their view of art education. Therefore, teaching and learning is considered an individual endeavor that is unconnected to society and is not a relational process. School art is more about illustrating or analyzing existing knowledge rather than a practice that sparks new forms of knowledge about our world (Desai & Chalmers, 2007). Most of the students do not think about art as a space where meaning is constructed about the world. The notion that one of the roles of the artist is to ask critical questions that can "unframe" both personal and social, cultural, political issues of our times (Rogoff, 2005) is rarely considered by many of our prospective art teachers. Contemporary art practices embody "knowledge in the making" (Ellsworth, 2005, p. 2) and can be pedagogical pivots that provide the opportunity to rethink how we teach art in schools.

Contemporary artists use a wide range of tools, materials, and sources of inspiration to critique, explore, and comment on pertinent issues from the personal to the global. Some artists envision new possibilities designed to generate dialogue and engage people to imagine "new forms of civic engagement constituted with, in, and through the body" (Springgay, 2008, p. 22). Often, contemporary artists "create social spaces—temporary and permanent opportunities for people to connect and interact" (Gude, 2007, p. 13). Some artists deliberately work as part of collectives, thus challenging the process of how we make art and the notion of authorship. Socially engaged artists, such as Suzanne Lacy, Krzysztof Wodiczko, and Peggy Diggs seek to involve broader audiences thus taking their artwork out of galleries and museums into public spaces in order to create strategic interventions (Thompson, 2004) that are pedagogical in their intent.

It is through various courses that build on each other that we explore the relationship between art practices, critical theory, and critical pedagogy. Through this sequence students are encouraged to consider contemporary art as a pedagogical site that can inform their teaching practice. This exploration of contemporary art requires moving beyond the development of prescriptive art lessons and curricula that simply re-present the work of an artist, such as creating a silhouette after learning about the work of Kara Walker. Instead, the goal is to explore a topic or theme and then find the most appropriate medium and range of artists' work and methods to realize it. Although much is written in art education about including contemporary art (the March 2008 issue of *Art Education* is devoted to this topic), the reality is that most art schools still teach from a modernist perspective and little contemporary art is part of art history courses. Thus for our students, a majority who come to our program with a BFA from various schools, the initiation into contemporary art can be intimidating, challenging, and unsettling.

Looking Ahead: Challenges and Possibilities

The art education program at NYU is a work in progress. We continually try to address the challenges of conducting social justice based art education. Many of the students choose to enroll in our master's program because it is NYU and not because of its social justice perspective. The majority of prospective students have no prior background in this kind of work and the immersion in this philosophy can be overwhelming. Often the students' entire worldview is challenged, often resulting in defensive attitudes. Several years of implementing this social justice art education program at NYU it is not clear whether or not we can encourage students who come with no socio-political consciousness and no knowledge of contemporary art to embody a social justice perspective in art education and integrate these ideas in their teaching practices in 2 years, which is the length of time of the program. What we have witnessed is that we are more successful with those students who enter our program with an existing socio-political consciousness. For those students who come directly from art schools with little consciousness of the politics of art and education, the challenges at times seem un-surmountable. These students often learn to use the terminology and may even understand the ideas intellectually, but may not embody the social justice perspective.

Another challenge faced has been breaking the theory and practice divide that shapes the students' common-sense understanding of teacher education. The pervasive notion is that learning to teach requires obtaining a set of skills and techniques (Cochran-Smith, 2004). To begin to address this chasm, several courses require students to go into the field (schools, museums, community centers) and place their practical experience in dialogue with the theory that they read in class. For instance, when they read Paulo Freire's (1990) work or *Critical Race Theory* (Dixon & Rousseau, 2006) the intention is that they observe how race, class, gender, and sexuality is presented in schools, museums, and other educational spaces. These works question how location and social position shape their understanding of the world in particular ways and how that might be different for the

students they will teach in inner city schools. Yet, a majority of our students complain that there is too much theory in the first year of the program that is unconnected to real, observable, examples. This, in turn, encourages the students to see the student teaching that is accomplished in the second year of the program as practice devoid of the theory they struggled with the first year. The understanding that theory and practice are interconnected, that theory informs practice and practice needs to be theorized, seems hard to grasp despite readings, discussions, and assignments. It is these notions of teaching that have to be dismantled in order for students to envision new possibilities for educational change and their place in that change.

A comment we often hear from the students is that they want to see some models of social justice art education in practice. The lack of these models in both public and private schools makes it hard for students to imagine what teaching from this perspective might look like. Lessons from Olivia Gude's Spiral Workshop (http://www.uic.edu/classes/ad/ad382/sites/SpiralWorkshop/SW_index.html), books such as *Art for Life: Authentic Instruction in Art* (Anderson & Milbrandt 2005) and *Finding Art's Place: Experiments in Contemporary Education and Culture* (Paley, 1995), socially engaged art projects done by contemporary artists in schools, examples from local and national art educators, and some examples from NYU alumni seem to be the only social justice based art education models available. Although we use many written resources, the lack of classroom experience or a social activist background makes it difficult for many of the students to translate these ideas from other subjects into art lessons. It has become clear that the students need more opportunities to practice social justice art education. To this end we are currently planning a Saturday program that will offer thematic art classes to high school students from around the city and simultaneously provide a chance for the graduate students to conceptualize and implement curricula.

Final Thoughts

Much like an art project, the social justice perspective of our program requires us to engage in our own learning—it is a transformative process. We are constantly thinking and rethinking the program. I still view art education as a radical place of transgressive possibility—one that takes risks. In moment of doubts and despondence, I remind myself "to open our minds and hearts so that we can know beyond the boundaries of what is acceptable, so that we can think and rethink, so that we can create new vision, I celebrate teaching that enables transgressions—a movement against and beyond boundaries. It is that movement which makes education the practice of freedom" (hooks, 1994, p. 12). Reading the newspaper everyday, spending time in inner city schools, and witnessing the power of art to prompt dialogue reminds me of not only the need for socially engaged educational practices but its possibilities to move us beyond apathy and imagine other possibilities for living together.

REFERENCES

Anderson, T., & Milbrandt, M. (2005). *Art for life: Authentic instruction in art.* New York: McGraw-Hill.

Bell, L. A. (2003). Telling tales: What stories can teach us about racism. *Race, Ethnicity, and Education, 6*(1), 3–28.

Bell, L. A. (1997). Theoretical foundations for social justice education. In M. Adams, L. Bell, & P. Griffin (Eds.), *Teaching for diversity and social justice* (pp. 3–15). New York & London: Routledge.

Berman, S. (1997). *Children's social consciousness and the development of social responsibility.* Albany, NY: SUNY Press.

Berman, S. (2004). The bridges to civility: Empathy, ethics, civics and service. In M. Seymour (Ed.), *Educating for humanity: Rethinking the purposes of education*, pp. 108–121. Boulder, Colorado: Paradigm Publishers.

Boler, M. (1999). *Feeling power: Emotions and education.* New York: Routledge.

Bonilla-Silva, E. (2003). *Racism without racists: Color-blind racism and the persistence of racial inequality in the United States.* Lanham: Rowman & Littlefield.

Cochran-Smith, M. (2004). *Walking the road: Race, diversity and social justice in teacher education.* New York and London: Teachers College Press.

Darling-Hammond, L. (2002). *Learning to teach for social justice. New York and London*: Teachers College Press.

Desai, D., & Chalmers, G. (2007). Notes for a dialogue on art education in critical times. *Art Education, 60*(5), 6–12.

Dixon, A. Rousseau. (2006). *Critical race theory in education: All God's children got a song.* New York & London: Routledge.

Ellsworth, E. (2005). *Places of learning: Media, architecture, pedagogy.* New York, London: RoutledgeFalmer.

Frankenberg, R. (1993). *White women, race matters: The social construction of whiteness.* Minneapolis: University of Minnesota Press.

Freire, P. (1990). *Pedagogy of the oppressed.* New York: The Continuum Publishing Company.

Goldfarb, B. (2002) *Visual pedagogy.* Durham & London: Duke University Press.

Gude, O. (2007). Principles of possibility: Considerations for 21st century art and culture curriculum. *Art Education, 60*(1), 6–15.

hooks, b. (1994). *Teaching to transgress.* New York: Routledge.

Kohl, H (2002). Developing teachers for social justice. Retrieved on September 18, 2008, from http://findarticles.com/p/articles/mi_m0JVP/is_2002_Winter/ai_97483139

Ladson-Billings, G. (2001). *Crossing over to Canaan: The journey of new teachers in diverse classrooms.* San Francisco, California: Jossey Bass.

Lewis, A. E. (2003). *Race in the Schoolyard: Negotiating the color line in classrooms and communities.* New Brunswick, NJ: Rutgers University Press.

Kozol, J.(1991). *Savage inequalities: Children in America's schools.* New York: HarperCollins.

Nieto, S. (2000). Placing equity front and center: Some thoughts on transforming teacher education for a new century. *Journal of Teacher Education, 51*(3), 180–87.

New York University Art Education. http://steinhardt.nyu.edu/art/education retrieved on May 13, 2009.

Noddings, N. (1992). *The challenge to care in schools: An alternative approach to education.* New York: Teachers College Press.

Paley, N. (1995). *Finding art's place: Experiments in contemporary education and culture.* New York: Routledge.

Rogoff, I. (2005). *Engendering terror,* retrieved November 7, 2006, from http://mediageographies.blogspot.com/2005/08/irit-rogoff-engendering-terror.html

Springgay, S. (2008). Corporeal pedagogy and contemporary video art. *Art Education, 61*(2), 18–24.

Taub, A., Tobias, R., & Mayher, J. (2006) *TEAC Inquiry Brief. Steinhardt School of Culture, Education and Human Development*, New York University. Submitted to the Teacher Education Accreditation Council.

Thompson, N. (2004). Trespassing relevance. In N. Thompson & G. Sholette (Eds.), *The Interventionist: Users' manual for the creative disruption of everyday life*, (pp. 13–22). North Adams, MA: MASS MoCA Publications.

Winant, H. (2004). *New politics of race: Globalism, difference, justice.* Minneapolis: University of Minnesota Press.

Zeichner, K. M (1993). Connecting genuine teacher development into the struggle for social justice. *Journal of Education for Teaching, 17*(1), 5–20.

Art Education that is "For Something": Action Research and the Pedagogy of Listening to Our Students

Lisa Hochtritt, Robin Houdek, and Therese Quinn[1]

The arts will help disrupt the walls that obscure ... spheres of freedom. (Maxine Greene, 1988, p. 133)

KEY CONCEPTS
- Art as Social Change
- Critical Pedagogy
- Student Teaching as Action Research
- Urban Education
- Transformative Photography Curricula

Education is always *for* something and *against* something else. The Department of Art Education of the School of the Art Institute of Chicago (SAIC ARTED) promotes an education through and about the arts that is for *social justice*. As used, the term is broad, and as a goal, it is decidedly distant. In fact, teaching for social justice is always more possibility than accomplishment but it usually includes versions of the following themes: democracy, activism, history, public space, self-awareness, social literacy, and imagination (Ayers & Quinn, 2005). Lipman (2004) described four social justice imperatives: equity, agency, cultural relevance, and critical literacy. Cochran-Smith (2004) pointed to a lineage of social justice education linked to critical theoretical and social movements for justice. She claimed that while "teachers cannot substitute for social movements aimed at the transformation of society's fundamental inequities, their work has the potential to contribute to those movements in essential ways by being part of collective projects and larger communities for social justice" (p. 19). All of these definitions emphasize education focused on analysis and action (Quinn, 2006) and the role teachers can play in fostering critical understandings that contribute to social movements. This is the vision of art education that SAIC ARTED supports through its teacher education coursework at both the graduate and undergraduate levels.

The SAIC Master of Arts in Teaching (MAT) program prepares art and visual culture educators as critical citizens. This term means people who are self-reflective, have a deep concern for the lives of others, and actively question and challenge the social, political, and cultural structures and discourses that comprise everyday life. Through coursework, thesis research, fieldwork, apprentice teaching experiences, and the writing of a thesis that documents their action research project, the MAT candidates have the opportunity to experience praxis within a K–12 art educational context and to try out the theories they learn at SAIC while practice teaching in their final semester. Leadership and critical transformation in the program are also stressed as we encourage students to incorporate contemporary issues and highlight contemporary artists in their lesson plans. As Urbanski (2003) suggested, "when teachers consider themselves to be researchers, not just consumers of research, they are exercising leadership" (p. v). Providing apprentice teachers the opportunity to lead change in schools, while meshing their theoretical questions with ideas related to art and social justice, can allow for meaningful transformation in K–12 classrooms.

This chapter explores in detail one such action research thesis project undertaken by a Master of Arts in Teaching (MAT) graduate student. We—two art education professors at SAIC during the project, and the then-graduate student, now-art teacher, who conducted this research—have co-written the chapter to offer our colleagues in the field an example of how social justice-focused art education looks in practice.

Robin's Choice to Teach Art for Social Justice

When I decided to go to SAIC I knew I wanted to teach art. I did not know what social justice-focused art education was, let alone how I might someday practice it in the classroom. After going through the SAIC coursework and specifically choosing to research injustices that disproportionately affect students of color I felt that I was left with a choice: I could ignore the injustices that exist and are perpetuated in schools, or I could try to address them by starting a dialogue in the classroom through art. In the following pages I describe my action research project and first attempt at teaching art for social justice. I begin with a quote from Ernest Morrell (2004), an educator whose work helped inform my project.

> Inquiry that aspires to be called critical must be connected to an attempt to confront the injustice of a particular society or sphere within a society. Research thus becomes a transformative endeavor unembarrassed by the label "political" and unafraid to consummate a relationship with an emancipatory consciousness. (p. 42)

How I Started

As I observed art classes at a College Prep Magnet High School in Chicago to fulfill preservice teaching requirements, I was reminded of my privilege in the context of a public school system—I was a former magnet school student. My notes from the day described the amazing facilities, the endless shelves of supplies and equipment, and the impressive productivity of the classes from bell to bell. As I sat in on classes from freshman art to advanced placement metals, I began to wonder about those not privileged, those students who would not be able to attend a school such as this.

As I have grown more aware of systemic influences that dominate and oppress groups of people in our society, and specifically in our public schools, I have felt that it is my role as an educator to understand why these inequities exist and work toward creating educational spaces that serve all children equally. One inspiration was the work of Ernest Morrell (2004), whose book about critical action research conducted by urban youth I read during my graduate studies. My reflections on this and other writing by activist scholars and observations in schools led me to my action research thesis project.

In preparing my thesis that accompanies the apprentice teaching action project, I explored existing youth programs geared toward critical action research, investigated many studies and theories related to racism and social justice in schools, and talked to adults who were already working with youth to address these types of issues. I talked to teachers, artists, and community workers and was inspired by the powerful messages kids were already producing through poetry slams, independent magazines, and artwork. It was my hope that by introducing my students to artwork and spoken word by young activists that they would feel supported in knowing that young people are addressing important issues and that they too can use the arts as a powerful voice.

The Action Research Begins

I had 7 weeks to do my project, which is the standard length of time for one student-teaching placement in my graduate program. I knew that I would be teaching a high school photography class and that I was going to show the students work by other young artists. The lessons were based on the concept behind Augusto Boal's Theater of the Oppressed and involved students creating three photographic images: the first would represent the problem they wanted to address, the second would represent the solution to the problem, and the third would represent the steps it would take to get from the problem to the solution. I was unsure about how the project would develop; I genuinely wanted the students to guide the direction of the work.

I chose to focus on the students in my beginning photo class. Students were working with black-and-white film and digital cameras, and used the computers as their digital enlargers. Students who shot black-and-white film scanned in their negatives and students with digital cameras imported their images, and they all printed their work from the computers. There were 28 students in the class, 4 of whom never came, 2 that attended a handful of times, and 2 more that were present only 50% of the time. Most often, I worked with around 20 students in the class who focused on this project. The class was composed mostly of black students; only 2 were white. Their grade levels ranged from freshmen to seniors. Following, I will present the lessons completed in class, frustrations encountered, and conclusions.

The Project

The students and I began class with a discussion about the journals I hoped they would use throughout the project, and then I showed a portion of a video—*Echoes of Brown: Youth Documenting and Performing the Legacy of Brown v. Board of Education* (Fine, et al., 2004). This documentary highlights a social justice writing and dance workshop in which New York City high school students participated. I was anxious to read my students' reactions to the movie because I knew it would determine how I might proceed with the rest of the unit. With a few minutes left in class, I asked them to respond to the following questions in their journals:

1. What were some of the issues or topics that came up in the movie?
2. Do you think these are important issues to talk about?
3. How can you relate (or not) to one or more of the topics discussed?

The students' responses revealed their concerns about racism, segregation, color and class conflicts, and sexual orientation. One wrote poignantly about loneliness. Others related that few in the school spoke up about problems, and said that these important topics were rarely addressed, and in fact, were "suppressed."

The next class began with a discussion about the movie. Many students mentioned the discussions about segregation and racism; some believed that segregation still existed, while others did not. The term 'modern day segregation' was raised by one of my students in an attempt to explain to another that although segregation does not look the same as it did 60 years ago, it still exists. The students also talked about how people of the same culture or race may stick together because it is within their comfort zone to do so. However, many believed being unfamiliar with others' differences caused misconceptions and unfair stereotypes of others.

There were many times when I felt unsure about what questions to ask next, and there was no way to prepare for some of the things that were said. This type of conversation is one that I had never had with a group of students, let alone as a minority in the room, and I felt unprepared. However, I knew that these conversations would serve as a catalyst for their artwork.

Next, the students were shown four examples of billboard art created by elementary-age students in Indiana. Each image dealt with free speech and addressed issues of discrimination due to gender, ability, and race. They were asked to pick one image and write about it. In addition to the issues described above, the students were also interested in knowing how the elementary students got their artwork onto billboards.

Many students began to feel overwhelmed by the amount of writing, discussion, and work that I was asking them to do. "Man, this isn't English class, why do we have to write so much?" one said. "Are we going to watch a movie every day? Ugh, we have to write AGAIN?"

Despite these complaints, my cooperating teacher told me that he had never seen so many of his students engaged in activities and discussion at one time. The informal journal entries also seemed to allow the students to feel comfortable expressing their ideas, regardless of their writing abilities.

Moving into Making

After a quick inventory of what the students knew about Photoshop and cameras, I asked them to get into their groups and brainstorm topics that they felt were important as youth in their community. Student groups used large sheets of newsprint and markers to brainstorm various topics. Along with the paper and markers, the students were given reference materials, such as reports on racism, segregation, and educational justice issues created by Generation Y, a youth organization on the southwest side of Chicago. I thought that these would help the students make connections between the artwork and our conversations about racism and segregation and relate those issues to their own lived experiences.

The students seemed to really struggle with this process. Very few read through or even looked at the reference materials and many seemed lost and unsure about what they were supposed to do. The transition from looking at artwork and spoken word to generating their own ideas for making artwork wasn't as obvious to my students as it was to me. I learned that it is better to be explicit than to assume that everyone is on the same page. In order to make a better connection, we talked about how they were able to relate, or not, to the issues raised in the other artwork and referred back to prior conversations where they established that they felt it was important to make art for the purpose of speaking out about something. Then, I asked them questions about life at home, in their neighborhoods, and at school to help them recognize issues they could address in their own work. Once they had at least five topics (e.g., segregation in schools, police brutality, stereotyping) I encouraged them to explain further. What was the issue? And, what did they want to say about it as a group? As an example, the following is one group's list of negative stereotypes:

• According to *some* people, black people can only survive life only if they are in the music industry or doing drugs.

- White people are of higher power.
- Hispanics play soccer.
- Europeans are alcoholics.
- All Asians are smart.

The responses to the brainstorming session made me realize that in order for students to be invested in their projects they need the freedom to talk about their issues, meaning that I had to let go of issues I wanted them address, such as educational inequities and segregation in schools. I wanted the students to begin working with visual images and decided to use the youth billboard images as part of their first project.

We spent the next few days looking at and gathering images. They looked at several artists' works related to a variety of social issues, including billboard art by Keith Haring, Gran Fury, and Elizabeth Sisco. We discussed composition and narrative, and students began thinking about

Robin's example of the assignment.

how to address their topics with visual imagery. I then led them through a Photoshop lesson and showed them how to take an image of a billboard, erase the original illustration and insert their own images and text. They collected images from the Internet related to their topics and created new billboards that addressed their concerns. While students were working on these, I gave them a photo assignment for homework and showed them an example of what I wanted them to do for their final project.

Their assignment was to create an original photographic narrative, combine it with text, and use Photoshop to alter the picture they took of the billboard by replacing its content with their new narrative. This final project differed from the previous assignment because the students had to create and photograph their own original content, not use the Internet for images. They had a week to shoot the film. I thought that with the in-class practice and my example, the assignment was clear. But on the day their images were due none of the students came to class with their photographs.

A Low Point

I was discouraged that no one brought in their homework and felt like I was losing my students' attention. We started off strong, with engaging conversations and great student ideas, and I thought we were getting to a point where the students were on top of it—the work, their topics, everything. But somewhere in my lesson there must have been a disconnection. I did not know what the problem was. Regardless, I needed to quickly figure out what to do next.

I decided to show the students how to role-play to create narrative in a photograph. I began by asking the students what a common stereotype was of white people and rhythm. They responded without hesitation, "They don't have any." Then I asked for a couple of volunteers that would be willing to dance and we acted out the stereotype together. The point of the assignment was to actually raise a question or cause the audience to think differently about the topic. We then acted out the idea that this was a stereotype by demonstrating that some white people do have rhythm, which thankfully I was able to display. Visually, they could see how to act out an issue using people and props. Students worked with their groups to act out their topics and presented them to the class. After this exercise, students moved easily into the project.

At the end of the project students were asked to explain, critique, and reflect on their artwork. Here's an example from Group One:

Art Education for Social Justice

This billboard consists of a fist. It's straight and to the point. You can really understand it at first glance. But it was made in a creative way. We had an African American and a Russian put their fist together. Then in another shot they shook hands.

Most of the students were not able to make images as complex as their ideas; however, their writing showed how thoughtful and passionate they were about their topics. Although the students rarely responded in the ways that I expected, or sometimes hoped, I realized that the project needed to go in the direction they were taking in order for this experience to be meaningful for them. "The problem-posing educator constantly re-forms his reflections in the reflection of the students. The students—no longer docile listeners—are now critical co-investigators in dialogue with the teacher" (Freire, 1970, p. 81). I realized that the students had figured out their own agenda for what I initially thought of as my project.

This thesis topic grew from a desire to understand and challenge the injustices that exist within the system. Young voices are often left out of the dialogue regarding school reform; however, their lives are most affected by the faults of the system. Through my research and action project in the classroom, I gained a better understanding of myself as a teacher and discovered ways teachers and students could collaborate toward a common goal. Together my students and I addressed how we could become active, critical participants in our own lives and communities, as opposed to passive recipients of the circumstances in which we live. This is, I think, teaching art for social justice.

Reflecting on the Apprentice Teacher Model

Robin had the opportunity to explore issues of race and funding inequities through an action research project she conducted while completing her 7 weeks of student teaching in a Chicago area public high school. As she stated, she went into her research with some assumptions that were quickly dispelled by the young people with whom she worked through their daily conversations, the students' journal entries, and artmaking. In the weekly seminar classes held at SAIC, Robin admitted to being discouraged by daily administrative elements such as student tardiness, absences, class disruptions, and dress code enforcements. She realized that teaching art was much more about helping students find their voice through exploring critically relevant topics of their own choosing, than by specific topics imposed by the teacher. Robin also stated that developing trust between the students

Group One explored issues of race.

Group Two explored ideas about poverty and housing.

and the teacher, as well as adjusting for unexpected events in the research, was imperative to the project's success.

Projects such as the one Robin conducted support critical research and student voice through the exploration of topics related to social justice and students' lived experiences. Although she had well-documented lesson plans and a general idea of the flow of the lessons going into the project, she had to listen to her students and alter the lessons based on their needs and understandings of the complex issues she was presenting. This teaching experience was Robin's first attempt at discussing such intense and complicated issues. In her own words, she looked at the students' involvement, their artwork, and their comments to her in class such as, "Our teacher doesn't ever talk to us about things like this," to show that young people enjoy opportunities to discuss critical issues.

(Re)Searching for a More Just Public Education

The action research and thesis components are important parts of the MAT program in that they reflect the culturally relevant ideas, social justice theories, and critical lens that the students have acquired while at SAIC. The SAIC ARTED program shares the vision of the editors of *Rethinking Our Classrooms* (Au, Bigelow, & Karp, 2007) when they stated, "schools and classrooms should be laboratories for a more just society than the one we now live in" (p. x). By encouraging and supporting new teachers who strive for social justice and activism, we hope that this type of teaching will continue on in their own classrooms. Too often teachers are worried about being "too political" in their lessons. As Shor (1992) stated, "education is politics (and is) an agenda for empowerment" (p. 11). Keeping issues out of the classroom is a political act, as well. No curriculum is neutral and teachers always have important choices to make in deciding what is allowed in and what is kept out. When initially assessing our project ideas, we can begin by asking: Whose voices are heard and whose are left out? As Robin and her high school students have shown us in this chapter, putting student voice and activism at the center of an art curriculum is teaching art for social justice, or, teaching art, as Greene (1988) said, to reveal "spheres of freedom" (p. 133) and the possibility of a more just world.

REFERENCES

Au, W., Bigelow, B., & Karp, S. (Eds.). (2007). *Rethinking our classrooms: Teaching for equity and justice*, Vol. 1 (2nd ed.). Milwaukee, WI: Rethinking Schools.

Ayers, W., & Quinn, T. (2005). Series foreword. In G. Michie, *See you when we get there: Teaching for change in urban schools* (pp. vii–ix). New York: Teachers College Press.

Cochran-Smith, M. (2004). *Walking the road: Race, diversity, and social justice in teacher education*. New York: Teachers College Press.

Fine, M., Roberts, R. A., Torre, M. E., Boom, J., Burns, A., Chajet, L., Guishard, M., & Payne, Y. A. (2004). *Echoes of Brown: Youth documenting and performing the legacy of Brown v. Board of Education*. New York: Teachers College Press.

Freire, P. (1970). *Pedagogy of the oppressed*. New York: The Continuum International Publishing Group.

Greene, M. (1988). *The dialectic of freedom*. New York: Teachers College Press.

Lipman, P. (2004). *High stakes education: Inequality, globalization, and urban school reform*. New York: RoutledgeFalmer.

Morrell, E. (2004). *Becoming critical researchers: Literacy and empowerment for urban youth*. New York: Peter Lang.

Quinn, T. (2006). Out of cite, out of mind: Social justice and art education. *The Journal of Social Theory in Art Education, 26*, 282–301.

Shor, I. (1992). *Empowering education: Critical teaching for social change*. Chicago: The University of Chicago Press.

Urbanski, A. (2003). Foreword. In E. Meyers & F. Rust (Eds.), *Taking action with teacher research* (pp. v–ix). Portsmouth, NH: Heinemann.

ENDNOTE

[1] This is a co-authored work with equal contributions from each of us and has no first author. We are listed alphabetically.

International
PERSPECTIVES

Animation Education in an Indigenous Context

Melanie Davenport and Karin Gunn

Introduction

During a recent conference on Indigenous People in Digital Culture[1], videographer Caimi Waiassé, a member of the indigenous Xavante population of central Brazil, explained that his first encounter with visual media was watching cartoons on television as a child during a visit to the city. The idea that animation can open doors to a world of visual media can inspire the work of art educators, not only because animated images are pervasive on the Internet, as well as in television programming and advertising, but also because it is within the scope of possibility for many art teachers and students to produce their own, regardless of their access to computers or cameras. Animation seems intrinsically engaging to watch and to create, perhaps because it plays to the imagination, making possible the telling of stories that may not be filmable with real actors and sets (Laybourne, 1998). Teaching animation involves students in interdisciplinary learning opportunities, reinforcing language arts and mathematics, as well as teamwork and problem-solving skills, while introducing fundamental concepts and techniques of media production.

Many media educators are concerned that young people should become more critical consumers and producers of media. Although literature in the fields of visual culture art education and media literacy typically focuses on youth in developed nations or urban areas whose lives are saturated with various technologies, young people in more rural or isolated areas likewise need opportunities to develop media literacy, as the consumption of tech-

nological media becomes increasingly accessible and influential in their lives and communities.

As art teachers, we feel that learning to decode and employ visual language is as important to living in contemporary globalized society as gaining literacy in written languages, especially for those whose voices are less commonly heard in the dominant media discourse. One of the most fulfilling and exciting projects that we have developed was a series of workshops held from January 22 to February 2, 2007, for students enrolled in high school and in college-level teacher preparation programs

Figure 1. Workshop participants work together to create a mural of their school as the backdrop to a cut-paper animated short about *A Day in the Life of CRES Estipac*.

in Estipac, Mexico. A large number of these students were Huichol, an indigenous group from central Mexico. Like many indigenous cultural groups, even isolated Huichol communities are gaining greater access to mainstream media, but typically lack access to means of production. Our workshops were designed to provide equipment and instruction for this school population to produce their own animated stories as well as develop skills for teaching others. In this sense, we are aligned with the larger indigenous media movement that seeks to empower indigenous populations to have a greater voice in the larger media discourse.

Following, we describe processes and outcomes of these workshops, after grounding our project in a brief discussion of the indigenous media movement.

Indigenous Media Movement

Over the past 30 years, anthropologists, videographers, filmmakers, and journalists have been working with diverse indigenous groups around the world to provide training and technology for video production so that these groups might create their own media representations, in support of their struggle not only for cultural maintenance, but also for political empowerment.[2] Vincent Carelli, a video producer with the Centro de Trabalho Indigenista in Sao Paulo, for example, initiated the *Video in the Villages* project in the late 1980s to provide individuals like Caimi Waiassé with the technical support necessary to begin documenting traditions and activities of his community on video. Organizations in Mexico, such as Ojo de Agua Communicacion and the Chiapas Media Project, also provide video equipment and training to individuals from indigenous communities and promote indigenous media as a means to gain political clout.

Empowering indigenous people to produce media representations from their own perspectives in their own languages supports their efforts to challenge inaccurate representations of themselves typical of the media from the dominant culture, to assert their own voices and visions as cultural producers, to find new modes to express new conceptions of indigenous identity, and to participate more fully in public discursive space. Faye Ginsburg (1991), who works with Aboriginal Australians, explained that for indigenous people, media such as film and video are increasingly serving as important means for both internal and external communication, as well as supporting efforts for self-determination and resistance to cultural domination from outside groups. Claudia Magallanes-Blanco (2007) agreed that

video has become vital in the struggle for justice of indigenous people, not only as a means to combat misrepresentation, but also as a means to self-define and self-represent.

Introducing new media to indigenous populations may be seen by some as an inappropriate imposition of Western modes of communication that might threaten more traditional practices, but such views depend upon a notion of authentic indigenous identity that would deny adaptability as the key to cultural survival. Turner explained that the indigenous media movement supports the construction of hybrid representations that give traditional elements new vitality through technologies for mass communication.

Animation with Indigenous Youth

Within the larger indigenous media movement are individuals who work with indigenous youth; in particular, there are a few who make animation with indigenous students. Black Gum Mountain Productions in Oklahoma (www.blackgummountain.com) has produced a series of claymation shorts with students of Cherokee and Muscogee Creek heritage, presenting traditional stories in their original languages. Mike Vermette, art teacher at the Penobscot Indian Island School in Maine, has produced longer animated works with his students, recording tales from the Penobscot tradition. Another animator involved with indigenous youth is Dominique Jonard, a French filmmaker who has worked in Mexico for the past 15 years. Among the projects he has developed are several cut-paper animation shorts created with groups of school children from different indigenous groups in Mexico, including the Raramuri of Chihuahua and the Purepecha of Michoacan.[3]

In selecting the location of our workshop, we were aided by a colleague and collaborator at the University of Guadalajara: Sarah Corona. Learning of our interest in presenting an animation and technology workshop for indigenous youth and their teachers, Corona recommended that we contact the director of Centro Rural de Educación Superior (CRES) in Estipac, Jalisco, Mexico, for permission to conduct our project with students enrolled there. In November 2006, we visited CRES Estipac and met with the Director, Madre Maria Dolores Morales Perez, to discuss our proposal for a series of workshops on animation and technology for intercultural education. Originally, we sought permission to offer only one workshop to one group of students, but after assessing the facilities and needs of the community and soliciting input from the Director, we expanded our plans to conduct four workshops at the school. In this way, we could better meet the needs of different participants and provide more training for the school faculty as well. I submitted our plans to the Institutional Review Board for ethical research with human subjects at Florida State University and obtained their permission to proceed with this educational project. We were able to return to the school and conduct our workshops early in 2007, thanks to support provided by the Florida State University Foundation, for our travel and planning expenses, and the Fundacion Alejandro Diáz Guerra, for the supplies and equipment needed for the workshops. Among the materials that we were able to acquire and donate to the school with this funding were a new iMac computer, iStopmotion and Final Cut Express software, a video camera, a still camera, a tripod, and a wide assortment of art supplies. We also brought along two each of our own video and still digital cameras, an extra tripod, and a Macintosh laptop to facilitate the workshops.

The School

Madre Maria Dolores Morales Perez founded CRES Estipac in 1980 with the goal of educating rural students to become self-sufficient through entrepreneurial and vocational programs, in addition to providing a rigorous academic curriculum. About 8 years ago, the school began focusing on the needs of indigenous students, in part by adding coursework to reinforce native languages and customs, and additionally, by emphasizing study of policies, opportunities, and practices that impact indigenous people in Mexico.

In 2007, there were approximately 150 students enrolled at the high school level. Of these, almost 98% were indigenous, representing nine different groups in Mexico, but the vast majority of these were Huichol. High school students, because they typically come from distant communities, live on campus in gender-segregated dormitories or other housing provided by the school, as do many of the faculty members. We learned that all of the indigenous students receive scholarships that covered their educational expenses, with much of the funding provided by donors from the Basque region of Spain.

The school also has approximately 150 students enrolled in the *Licenciatura*, or college-level, program in teacher training for elementary and primary teachers. Although these students are primarily local townspeople, mostly *mestizo*, some of the indigenous graduates of the high school go on to attend the Licenciatura as well. For many of these students, their teaching credentials will lead to opportunities to work in schools that serve indigenous children. Toward our goal of reaching indigenous youth, we wanted to help prepare these future teachers to utilize animation in interdisciplinary curricula with their future students as well.

The campus of CRES Estipac covers many acres of a scenic hillside and valley outside the main village of Estipac, about an hour south of Guadalajara by bus. Two buildings house classrooms for the college-level students and two others consist of high school classrooms, workrooms, an office for faculty, a science laboratory, and a computer center. A well-stocked library on the grounds serves not only the school but also the public. In addition to gardens, orchards, and livestock, there are greenhouses, a woodshop, a bakery, and a cafeteria. Students actively participate in running all of the productive activities that take place in these facilities, as part of their vocational education, but only in the early morning hours, leaving the rest of the day and evening for academic pursuits and other enrichment activities.

CRES often hosts educators from other parts of Mexico who come to investigate this curriculum model for application elsewhere. But, according to the assistant director of the school, we were the first outsiders ever to come to CRES as teachers offering workshops and insights into a different curriculum model for their own application.

Animation and Technology for Intercultural Education

In any media production project, it takes a team of dedicated people to make it happen. For this series of workshops, Davenport acted as the producer, identifying sources of funding, developing the project proposal, dealing with logistical arrangements, co-teaching, and otherwise facilitating as needed. Gunn took on the primary responsibility of the director, providing leadership and training on technical processes, guiding the participants through the creation of their work, and working side-by-side with them in the post-production process. Gunn used Final Cut Express to edit most of the projects, except as noted below, and simultaneously trained several teachers and students on the fundamentals of using this program. Although she wielded the technical expertise, workshop participants were the ones making the editorial decisions and suggestions that resulted in the final products. Two CRES faculty members worked very closely with us throughout the workshops: technology instructor Mahite Acuña and art teacher Alvaro Lopez, both of whom were relatively new to the school and enthusiastic about developing new skills in order to continue similar projects after our departure.

Workshops

During the 2 weeks we lived and taught at CRES in January 2007, we worked with approximately 28 participants in four different workshops: one on video documentation, one on cut-paper animation, one on 3-D animation, and one specifically designed for preservice teachers to learn lower-technology approaches for integrating animation into their future teaching practices. We met with each group for 2 to 3 hours each day over 8 or 9 days, saving the last day for post-production and a public screening. The following brief descriptions of each of the four workshops provide overviews of the processes undertaken and the products that resulted.

Trabajo Productivo Workshop. This workshop focused on training high school students in documentary video and photography so that they could utilize these skills in future school activities and home communities.

Figure 2. CRES student learns how to use the video camera to document productive activities on campus.

For 2 hours each morning, participants recorded the various school projects that provide vocational training and help the school toward achieving self-sufficiency. Students wrote their reflections about their participation in the school's entrepreneurial and vocational programs, and then used three video and three still digital cameras to record themselves, each other, and their peers engaged in various activities. First, we explained how to use each piece of equipment and demonstrated the recording process by shooting brief interviews with a couple of students. Then we sent teams of students out with equipment to record the myriad entrepreneurial activities and facilities throughout their campus. With assistance from the students, Gunn edited their footage and stills into a 13-minute documentary film that the Director of CRES has shared with funders and government officials both for accountability purposes and for promotion of their expanding mission.

The eight students who worked on this project enjoyed seeing their school through the camera lens, and took great pride in their participation. This workshop fostered a certain level of knowledge and confidence in a core group of students who were able to support continued use of the video and camera equipment after our departure. We learned that one of these enthusiastic students who graduated from the high school is now studying communications at the university level and continues working with visual media.

Cut-Paper Animation Workshop. This workshop, held from 1 to 3 p.m. every afternoon, allowed students and teachers from both the secondary and collegiate levels to work together to tell an animated story about a day in the life of their school community. First, we engaged the group in watching and discussing examples of cut-paper animation. Then, the participants painted a large mural on paper depicting the school grounds and facilities. After a demonstration by Davenport, several individuals focused on producing small paper figures with jointed limbs, representing distinct personalities within the school community, including Madre Maria Dolores.

To film the animation, participants hung the mural on a classroom wall and used tape to attach and position the paper figures in various places. They then took turns animating the figures, using a video camera, laptop computer, and iStopmotion software to record them frame by frame. Students and teachers enjoyed recording sound effects and commentary for each short scene, which was then edited together using iMovie software into a 3-minute-long humorous portrait of their school. Throughout the process of producing the cut-paper short, students also took turns documenting each other working on the project, with both video and still cameras. The images and footage collected were then edited into a 3-minute "making of" short film to help other audiences appreciate the effort that was required to create the animation.

Animating Traditions Workshop. Every evening from 4 to 7 p.m., a group of six Huichol student volunteers, from both high school and college level, worked on a project specifically intended to promote the use of animation in recording stories from their traditional culture in their traditional language. Prior to our arrival, we wrote to the school and asked these students to meet and discuss which story they would like to bring to life. For their project, they selected a traditional story that explains "Why Corn Has Many Colors" (see Figure 4), first written down and published in a Huichol language textbook produced by Martinez and Corona (2002).

Interestingly, even though the students had agreed upon this story, at first they couldn't agree upon the ending. Because participants came from different communities within the Zona Huichola, they had learned several different versions of this oral tradition. Gunn resolved this minor crisis by giving each student a blank storyboard sheet and asking them to sketch out their own versions to share with each other the next day. This proved to

Figure 4. Huichol student captures frames on computer while others animate plasticine figures for *Como Apareció el Maíz.*

Figure 3. Student manipulates cut-paper figures on the mural of the school grounds for cut-paper animation.

be a successful strategy, because all of the storyboards they brought in had different strengths and presented different perspectives on each important scene. For the first hour of the workshop the following day, each student shared his or her storyboard and then we made copies of all of them to cut apart and piece back together. The students enjoyed this exercise, and actively engaged in negotiating whose depiction would become the key frame for each scene. When it came to the ending, students discussed each option and then combined aspects of a couple of different versions to create a final scene that satisfied all participants.

After negotiating their storyboard, the students set about building sets, props, and figures, using plasticine, cardboard, natural objects, paper, wire, beads, and other materials. We set up two stations with lights, video cameras, and computers so that two groups could work simultaneously on different scenes. They used iStopmotion software installed onto the

Macintosh computers to record frame-by-frame their stop-motion animation. Each of the six students took a turn at animating the main figure for one scene, and each had an opportunity to use the software, capturing the images and directing the action. As in the cut-paper project, participants also gathered video and photo documentation of the process, which was compiled into a "making of" video that reveals much about the decision-making that goes on behind the scenes in media production.

Sound for this short included passages spoken in the Huichol language; one student, Adela Chivarras Lopez, provided the voiceover for the title sequence, and another, Marcelo Salvador Martinez, narrated the story. Two other Huichol students, from outside the workshop, performed original music on traditional instruments for the soundtrack. Students worked closely with Gunn to learn the editing process, insert the sound clips in the proper places, assist with subtitles, and make other creative decisions about the final piece. In the end, these Huichol students produced a four-minute short that shares their own vision of a traditional story in their own language.

As both facilitators and observers of the process, Gunn and Davenport learned much from this experience. We understood that Huichol spiritual practices utilize few objects or images. Drums, arrows, God's eyes, and corn are used in ceremonies, and traditional clothing is elaborately embroidered with symbolic figures, but sacred sites contain no pictures or representations of spiritual figures. Colorful yarn paintings have emerged over the past several decades as an art form for tourist consumption, but the production of these images is limited to a few individuals in one or two Huichol communities. We weren't sure how the students would choose to represent the main figure in the story, ancestral grandmother figure Tatutsi Nakawe, since there seems to be no standard iconography. It was interesting to note that the students made her twice the size of the other figures, and gave her more elaborate beadwork decoration on her clothing. They also used brown for the flesh color of the ancestor, but chose a gray-colored plasticine when modeling the figures that represented the human beings, perhaps representing the distance between the human experience and the spirit world.

We gained insight into Huichol culture not only from learning this traditional story of the corn, but also by working closely with these students and getting to know them as individuals. Personal characteristics, which contributed to the success of group efforts, included great patience, attention to detail, and collaborative working styles. Their creative decisions regarding shots and characters helped us to understand better the story being told, and ensured an utterly unique result.

Teacher Training Workshop. Besides the workshops described here, we also designed and presented an animation pedagogy workshop specifically for teachers. This workshop, held each morning from 10 a.m. to noon, was a pilot project to implement and assess a series of activities designed to train preservice and in-service teachers in ways to utilize lower-technology animation for interdisciplinary lessons in their classrooms. The participants in this workshop included both mestizo and indigenous educators, many of whom may eventually teach in small rural or remote village schools.

In this workshop, we presented the participants with a structured series of activities to complete, which incorporated diverse teaching strategies for classroom applications, including small group work, peer tutoring, and hands-on activities. It also included production of three different optical

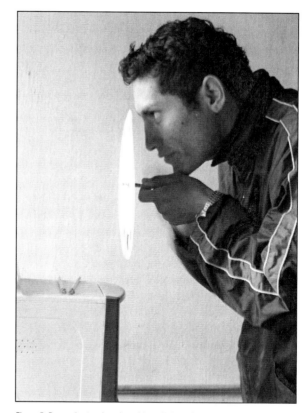

Figure 5. Preservice teacher views his optical mechanism in mirror.

mechanisms—thaumatropes, flipbooks, and phenakistoscopes. Participants also learned the basic stop-motion camera technique of pixilation, and engaged in critical viewings of such classic works as Norman McLaren's (1952) Neighbours. At the end of the workshop, participants paired off to develop interdisciplinary lesson plans for preschool and elementary students, using animation as both a teaching tool and lesson content. Lessons addressed topics such as grammar, history, science, and sex education, showing the wide range of possibilities of incorporating animation into lessons for children.

In order to evaluate and refine the materials and processes of this workshop for future presentations to other teachers, we administered pre- and post-evaluations and gathered reflective responses, written documents such as lesson plans, and other qualitative data for analysis. We also encouraged students to document their work, and each other working, with video and still cameras to have a record of the workshop activities. These photos and clips were compiled into a 13-minute video to share with the school community. Preliminary analysis of findings indicates that participants felt they had successfully gained useful new teaching skills and understandings. This was a very worthwhile outcome from our perspective because we hope to empower more teachers, and through them, more students, who might otherwise have few opportunities to engage with media education and learn any skills of production whatsoever.

Workshop Outcomes

Among the immediate outcomes of our 2 weeks of intensive work at CRES are the completed video shorts that were created during our stay and shown to the community on our last Friday afternoon. Over 400 people attended the final viewing, including guest professional animators from Guadalajara, Tonatiuh Moreno and Ruy Fernando Estrada, who spoke to the students afterwards about their own professional work.

In all, during our 2 weeks in CRES Estipac in 2007, we facilitated the production of six short works: two animated stories, two "making of" shorts about the animation process—both cut-paper and claymation— as well as two 15-minute short video documents: the Trabajo Productivo and the Teacher Training workshop. Several faculty members and a core group of students became very proficient at using the technology and have continued to work and practice with the equipment and software since our departure.

The Maiz story has garnered much attention, having been shown at three conferences, three college campuses and one film festival so far. The faculty, administrators, and students at CRES were so pleased with the results of this effort that they invited us to return in 2008 to facilitate the production of another Huichol story, the *Fiesta del Tambor* (Festival of the Drum).

Implications

We were thrilled to have the opportunity to work on video and animation with the students and teachers of this school, and in particular, to bring visual communications technologies into the hands of indigenous and rural people. As we pursue opportunities to expand upon this strong beginning, we are encouraged by the positive impact that this quick introductory round of workshops had on the school population at CRES. Based upon participant reflections and other viewers' responses, we would like to suggest that this project and others like it may have positive implications for indigenous education, media literacy, and art education as well.

Indigenous Education

Around the world, indigenous peoples are engaged in efforts to establish rights to an education that honors their own languages and knowledges, in a challenge to official curricula that has often destroyed or undermined their traditions (see May & Aikman, 2003; Tuhiwai, 2005). In documentation of recent meetings of the United Nations Permanent Forum on Indigenous Issues (2003), participants asserted that school systems internationally should develop curricula to respect the interests of indigenous peoples, including promotion of literacy in oral traditions. Members of the Forum also stressed that indigenous people would benefit from education that addresses modern technologies and promotes innovative means for placing indigenous knowledge systems on equal footing with Western systems.

Others concerned with indigenous education, such as Aikman (1997), have promoted intercultural approaches to education that attempt to preserve and revitalize indigenous cultures while also providing access to useful knowledge from the wider society. Such approaches regard indigenous knowledges as important content for the dominant culture to appreciate and learn from as well.

In our animation workshop with the Huichol students in particular, we attempted to provide these individuals with the skills and technology to preserve and creatively present their own knowledges and to challenge inaccurate representations of their traditions in the media of the dominant culture. We feel that greater opportunities for indigenous youth to develop skills in visual communication and technology will ultimately lead to a greater presence of indigenous perspectives in public discursive space.

Media Literacy

With the rise of the Internet and other visual communications technologies has come concern over the consumption of media messages by young people. Buckingham (2003, 2006) suggested that engaging in critical analysis is one strategy for fostering media-savvy youth able to engage on a more sophisticated level with the pleasures and problems of representation. However, Buckingham (2006), Willett (2003), and others have also recommended that involving young people in the production of media may be even more effective at creating critical consumers of media, turning passive knowledge into active engagement. Buckingham (2006) reiterated, "the experience of media production is valuable both in its own right, as a means of promoting self-expression and communication skills, and also as a way of developing a more in-depth critical understanding" (p. 44).

Concern for media literacy draws attention to the 'digital divide' or technology gap between those who have easy access to communications media and those who do not. "The simple fact is that poor communities are entering the Information Age far behind their wealthier neighbors" (Goslee, 1998, para. 3), which can negatively impact the economic development of those areas and limit the opportunities for education and civic engagement of the individuals within them. Buckingham (2006) asserted that access is not simply a factor of affording a computer, but is also a question of the "quality of access" (p. 41) in terms of how it is utilized and to what ends.

Formal education is an important factor in leveling this playing field; therefore teacher preparation and the development of new pedagogical strategies take on increased significance in media education. Goslee (1998) noted that inadequate teacher training often results in the underutilization of technological resources even when they are available in school settings. Buckingham (2006) noted that "the capacities of the new technologies often exceed teachers' abilities to exploit them" (p. 41).

To encourage media literacy among participants in our workshops, we included both critical analysis and production of media, so that students and teachers might gain insights into every step of the process. Even lower-technology historical mechanisms for animation, such as optical toys, can introduce important media literacy concepts, and since many of the schools in which these participants may find themselves will lack computers, we deliberately emphasized this content in our teacher training workshop. As we reflect upon the outcomes of this series of workshops, we hope to identify more ways to bring more effective media education to populations on the periphery of global communications networks.

Art Education

As art educators, we are enthusiastic about emerging paradigms in our field that promote the study of visual culture (see, for example, Freedman, 2003) and draw attention to social justice issues (see Garber, 2004, for example). We feel that our project and others like it highlight a key point of intersection between these two trends: the development of models for teaching creative media production that bring to less privileged populations the means of asserting their identities and perspectives to a wider audience while gaining critical insights into the media that increasingly inundates their lives. The production aspect of media education dovetails smoothly with the content and pedagogy of art education; likewise, developing a critical and analytical stance toward visual images is foundational to our practice. We feel that art teachers are well-positioned to empower youth of all backgrounds to express their stories, concerns, and potentials through media projects. However, many art teachers may not feel adequately equipped or prepared to engage their students in the production of animation or video.

We feel that it is important for art educators to be aware of the indigenous media movement. The work produced by indigenous groups offers a rich resource for teachers who wish to promote intercultural education as well as understanding of indigenous rights and the politics of representation. Recognizing indigenous populations as producers of cultural media and incorporating exemplars of indigenous video and animation into curricula are steps that art teachers can take to promote consideration of social justice issues in a visual culture art education curriculum.

To see clips and images from our workshops at CRES, please visit www.teachanimation.org/estipacmenu.html, a site created and maintained by Karin Gunn. Resources for teaching critical viewing and production of different types of animation are also available at this site.

ARTISTS' NOTES

We would like to thank The Florida State University Foundation, the Fundacion Alejandro Diáz Guerra, Dr. Sarah Corona, Patricia Diaz Romo, Madre Maria Dolores Morales Perez, and the students and faculty at CRES Estipac for their support of this project.

Photos in this chapter courtesy of Melanie Davenport and Karin Gunn.

REFERENCES

Aikman, S. (1997). Interculturality and intercultural education: A challenge for democracy. *International Review of Education/Internationale Zeitschrift für Erziehungswissenschaft/Revue Internationale de l'Education, 43*(5/6), 463–479.

Buckingham, D. (2003). Media education and the end of the critical consumer. *Harvard Educational Review, 73*(3), 309–328.

Buckingham, D. (2006). *The media literacy of children and young people: A review of the research literature on behalf of Ofcom.* London: Centre for the Study of Children Youth and Media Institute of Education, University of London.

Freedman, K. (2003). *Teaching visual culture: Curriculum, aesthetics, and the social life of art.* New York: Teachers College Press.

Garber, E. (2004). Social justice and art education. *Visual Arts Research, 30*(2), 4–22.

Ginsburg, F. (1991). Indigenous media: Faustian contract or global village? *Cultural Anthropology, 6*(1), 92–112.

Goslee, S. (1998). *Losing ground bit by bit: Low income communities in the information age.* Washington, DC: Benton Foundation. Retrieved April 10, 2007, from http://www.benton.org/ PUBLIBRARY/losing-ground/one.html

Laybourne, K. (1998). *The animation book.* New York: Three Rivers Press.

Magallanes-Blanco, C. (2007, February). *Video and identity: Community self-determination amongst indigenous peoples and peasants from Mexico.* Paper presented at the 56th Annual Conference of the Center for Latin American Studies, University of Florida, and Gainesville, FL.

Martinez, A., & Corona, S. (2002). *Nuestro libro de la memoria y la escritura: Apuntes para la ensenanza de la cultura wixarika.* Guadalajara: Universidad de Guadalajara.

May, S., & Aikman, S. (2003). Indigenous education: Addressing current issues and developments. *Comparative Education, 39*(2), 139-145.

McLaren, N. (1952). *Neighbours* [Motion picture]. Canada: National Film Board of Canada.

Tuhiwai, L. (2005). Building a research agenda for indigenous epistemologies and education. *Anthropology and Education Quarterly, 36*(1), 93-95.

Turner, T. (1992). Defiant images: The Kayapo appropriation of video. *Anthropology Today, 8*(6), 5-16.

United Nations (2003). Press Release HR/4674. Permanent Forum on Indigenous Issues, Third Session. 21/05/2003. Retrieved April 8, 2007, from http://www.un.org/news/Press/ docs/2003/hr4674.doc.htm

Willett, R. (2003). New models of learning for new media: Observations of young people learning digital design. *Jahrbuch Medienpädagogik, 4*, 127-144.

ENDNOTES

[1] 56th Annual Conference, Center for Latin American Studies, University of Florida, Gainesville, FL, February 14–16, 2007.

[2] More information on the indigenous media movement is available through organizations such as CLACPI, La Coordinadora Latinoamericano de Cine y Comunicación de Pueblos Indígenas (an umbrella organization for indigenous populations involved in filmmaking and communication in Latin America) online at: www.clacpi.org

[3] Further information about Dominique Jonard and others involved with indigenous media is available through the National Museum of the American Indian, part of the Smithsonian Institution, at: www.nativenetworks.si.edu/Eng/rose/jonard_d.htm

The Kids' Guernica Peace Mural Project: A Vehicle for Social Justice

Takuya Kaneda and Hatto Fischer

Is it Possible for Art Education to Contribute to Social Justice?

Art education and the arts can be linked to a search for and expression of human values, but attempts to change or to impose values on others, warns the Greek philosopher Cornelius Castoriadis, can lead to conflict, if not to war (Curtis, 1997). However, art gives cultures a way to recognize and express values that can be understood by all individuals. To avoid misunderstandings and mediate violence between different values, a prerequisite for social justice, human values can be negotiated through art without them being taken as if self-understood (Adorno, 1997). Accordingly social justice entails three important aspects: (1) being just to both individual and social needs, (2) mutual recognition that all are human beings, and (3) public spaces to clarify common assumptions about public truths.

Because too many injustices burden the world today, every human community should give space and time not only to formal clarification processes; but daily life requires as well an informal learning process capable of addressing the three aspects of social justice described above. In that sense, Kids' Guernica, as a collaborative work process, allows people of all ages to address in public not only the issue of war, but also violation of human rights and especially abuse of children, and alternatively to construct positive options to these issues by transforming cultural into community actions.

KEY CONCEPTS
- Informal Learning Processes
- Collaborative Work Processes
- Peace Process
- Community Action for Social Justice
- Using Imagination
- Developing Empathy

Art takes various forms not always related to the issue of social justice, but when they do, we have found that informal learning processes are an excellent way to address social issues through art education. For instance, the coordinator of Kids' Guernica International, Takuya Kaneda, complements his formal teaching at his university by involving his college students in Kids' Guernica. Through this outreach, students gain practical insights into how to animate children to paint and to play together cooperatively toward a larger goal of peace. At the same time, the exhibition of peace murals involves the creation of a larger audience making a bottom-up cultural action become a community action. That is important for culture has to be perceived by art education in a much wider sense if a just society is to be brought about by means of the arts.

If social justice is a direct outcome of a society capable of making peace, then art education must address the causes of war by showing how aesthetic means of the arts can contribute to peace. However, there is the famous question by George Steiner (1967), who asked whether someone playing the piano, one day, would be dissuaded from entering a concentration camp the next with the intention of exterminating Jews. That question underlies the deeper question, whether participation in the arts allows people to retain their human self-consciousness despite all kinds of challenges and thereby find just solutions with non-violent artistic means.

No one has a definite answer to the question Steiner posed, especially not after what happened during the Second World War and the unabated violations of human values since 1945. The Kid's Guernica Peace Mural Project, founded in Japan 50 years after 1945, has attempted to further the impulse to work for peace by furthering collaborative learning processes through art. Painting a huge mural together involves freeing the imagination. And by taking place outside school, within the community, it involves others in the decision-making processes. As such it can become a bottom-up process to what traditional diplomacy would sideline but which is understood in terms of intercultural dialogue as a need for friendship, trust, and openness if peace efforts are to be successful. In this context, art education, grounded in the humanities and philosophy may have the potential to complement appreciation of the arts by including lessons taken from an informal learning process like Kids' Guernica, in and outside the context of schools.

If the gaps created by mistrust are not bridged by communities capable of mediating different values and outlooks, people will find it hard to work and live together. Work and life become only easier once social inclusion is made possible by all participating in a creative learning process. Many schools, as formal institutions, do not deal in these issues in their curricula, instead aiming solely to enhance the cognitive development of a child. Desiring to draw on the imagination and on alternative social possibilities—in particular how to remain spontaneous, sense-orientated, and outgoing to stay in touch with reality—pose the serious question of what can be a corrective as to the formalist learning that takes place in schools.

The Polish Journalist Ryszard Kapuscinski (2000) concluded after re-visiting the former Soviet Union following its break up that the people could not cope with changes due to a lack of cultural tools. It is our belief that art education can provide these tools by facilitating perception of things from multiple perspectives. This presupposes freedom in the imagination. Only then is the reality that exists not taken as a given, but viewed from the perspective of many possibilities. Because children inherit a world beset with many problems not resolved, they face many obstacles. The ability of artistic vision to correct mistakes and to give shape to something that is more compatible with the needs of everyone can give reason for optimism, and the much needed motivation to go forward.

In this context, The Kids' Guernica Project emphasizes that creative contributions to peace can come from not only individuals, but from the whole community, through painting ideas of peace together. The idea of painting for peace was demonstrated at an exhibition in Paris 1929 by Picasso's *Les Demoiselles d' Avignon* (www.moma.org/collection/conservation/demoilles). Drawing stylistically from African masks carved by anonymous artists of a village, Picasso juxtaposed individual creativity with a collective creative process handed on from generation to generation, giving us something collective to think about both in the content and style of the work. Likewise, by letting children and adults paint peace murals together, Kids' Guernica stands for a collaborative work process which can help clarify conditions for living together in peace.

From Picasso's *Guernica* to Kids' Guernica

Pablo Picasso created Guernica after the city by the same name had been bombed during the Spanish Civil War. The painting can be interpreted as a highly artistic response to something profoundly inhumane, namely the bombing from the air of innocent civilians. It was until then an unknown brutality and consequently evokes a question: Can an artistic response restore a sense of social justice despite such an event?

It is important that Picasso painted *Guernica* without taking sides with any of the political fractions of the day. While Communists condemned the painting as not depicting workers heroically fighting Fascism, the Fascists could not come to terms with such a poignant depiction of human pain (www.poieinkaiprattein.org/kids-guernica/picasso-s-guernica-beyond-politics). Up until today, Picasso is a source of a language in painting that can talk about human pain without getting engulfed in political ideology. By responding to the atrocities incurred in Guernica in such a way, Picasso sets an example of art going beyond politics and underlines that people belong to the much wider movement of humanity. By expressing human pain while not furthering hatred, he goes beyond the usual blame game.

Sadly enough new atrocities and new pain have come to overlay the old, including Hiroshima, which was the inspiration for the first two murals that grounded this project (Anderson, 1997). Also, significantly one of the Kids' Guernica murals painted in Nagasaki in 2007 has the title, *After the Bomb! Building a New Life!*

After the Bomb! Building a New Life! Nagasaki, 2007.

Unfortunately given the state of affairs in this world, whether in Baghdad or London, people continue to mistreat others or worse are prepared to kill. Many do so out of rage over real or imagined losses. It seems revenge frequently dominates over a peaceful settlement of disputes. A world without mediation lets violence rule. That lawlessness has brought modern slavery in forms of human trafficking luring young women into prostitution while in areas of conflict children soldiers learn from an early age on to kill (Bernstein, 2008). We believe that no human being should be treated as means to other ends, yet many are used for illicit and degrading purposes, and in this context it is children who are most vulnerable. It would seem by now the world could have learned from figures like Martin Luther King on how to overcome discrimination and all kinds of inequalities so that everyone can have a dream of justice. However, worldwide, it is still difficult to ensure social justice prevails between all people regardless of sex, religion, age, or race. One value of Kids' Guernica is that it brings together not only children, but everyone. There is, for example, the beautiful Japanese peace mural honoring the cherry blossoms done in Higashikurume, Japan, in 2003 (www.kids-guernica.org/MuralPage/No67.html). It was painted by 80 people, ranging in age from two to eighty.

Higashikurume, Japan, 2003.

Kids' Guernica Worldwide

Kids' Guernica has become since 1995 a series of bottom-up success stories not just in terms of art processes and products, but also for communities and political authorities who support this effort by providing space for workshops, exhibitions, accommodation, publicity, and so on. The exhibitions of the murals are always exceptional due their size (7.8 x 3.5 m) and they astonish everyone (www.productivityofculture/symposium/kid-s-guernica.eccm). And both the completed projects and the process itself affect adults as well as children. Once adults are touched by the imagination of children, they open up. When a woman on her way to work walked across the public square in Chios, Greece, where a Kids' Guernica exhibition of 18 murals was shown in May 2007, she saw one from Lebanon with the title *Enough: We Want to Live!* Suddenly, she stopped to look again and then started to cry. This illustrates that the Kids' Guernica Project can help adults open like children. It can bring about a special kind of empathy for others. In a world limited and inhibited by self-centered interests, it matters if the pains of others can be felt.

But war is not the only conflict addressed in the project. There is the peace mural brought about by the Blind Boys Academy in India. Blind children used threads and gums to make an outline of the form and the knots on the threads tell them what color to use: e.g., eight knots for red, six for blue, and so on. This alters the common epistemology used in art about how visual images are communicated beyond visual references and challenges our stereotypes about blindness and differing abilities. It changes our assumptions about common knowledge.

Blind boys using threads with knots to know what color to use.

Although the Kids' Guernica Project is an example of informal art education, that is, outside the bounds of formal schooling, it can be a valuable complementary action, and evidence is mounting that participants grow up with a different notion of the world, than they might have had. A young French girl who attended a workshop in Nepal at the age of 12 has since then become an advocate for the right to education for girls in central Asia. The next generations of Kids' Guernica participants are already leaving their marks. They have learned something invaluable, namely the ability to speak in public and to stand up for the rights of others.

Most of the murals send strong peace messages to the world. For instance, Greek-Turkish delegates sitting at the negotiation table, negotiating about Cypress can be reminded that there exists the Chios-Izmir peace mural (www.productivityofculture.org/symposium/kid-s-guernica.eccm). This mural project that brought together Greek and Turkish children shows how important intercultural dialogue is to let children enter at an early age a peace process based on friendship, trust, and openness. This also suggests one key constraint of the peace murals of Kids' Guernica: namely avoiding the depiction of "enemy pictures" (See for example the mural painted in Kabul, Afghanistan, in which a plane dropping bombs has no flag to indicate its origin at www.kids-guernica.org/workshopPage/No115Afghanistan.html). To always assign blame on the other is not the way to peace. Rather to go beyond borders drawn and depicted by national symbols signifying the enemy's territory and values, is an important prerequisite for any peace

Never again war. Kabul, Afghanistan, 2005.

process. Therefore, the setting of a constraint, already an art on how to start a creative process, is taken by Kids' Guernica a step further. By letting children respond to violence and war, while discussing with them prospects of peace, the amazing thing is that they end up not painting an enemy picture but expressing optimism that a solution can be found. That process should become, as well, a matter of formal art education. Simply put, the Kids' Guernica project has the potential to open up people, including children and adults, by letting them learn through art to work together, and thereby realize a creative and cooperative human community.

A part of the learning process in this project entails responding constructively and cooperatively to what others paint. The overall composition is composed of its constituent parts and everything matters. For instance, in *The War is Over* mural of Poiein Kai Prattein (www.poiein kaiprattein.org/kids-guernica/the-war-is-over) a figure floats down to bring to the sad figure sitting in the corner of the painting the message in a letter that the "war is over." The children simply equated war with sadness and thought a solution would be to convey that sad figure sitting in the corner such a message, one really meant!

Moreover, mistakes do not matter because everything can be painted over or corrected by the others responding during the group process. For example, on the first day, the Izmir-Chios/Turkish-Greek painting was dominated by only flags as symbols of nationalism. But by the second day, after many more joint experiences, including eating together and also playing games, this tendency had all but disappeared from the children. Instead of national symbols more emphasis was given to the tree of life. It reflected a common understanding was nourished by a growing friendship between the children (www.kids-guernica.org/kids-guernica). Consequently, murals take on different shapes as the children progress in their collaborative work. This demands ongoing appraisal not only in terms of what has been painted so far, but also what is just and fair; that is, not only if the colors go together, but if the younger and smaller ones have been given sufficient space and if everyone's ideas are represented.

Completion of such a huge mural is a success by itself. Everyone, participants and onlookers, end up being surprised by the outcome. Experiences through Kids' Guernica convince people as to what is possible once they allow themselves to trust the process. Fantastic to look at, every peace mural convinces even the skeptics who believed beforehand that would never be possible. To let so many paint together, and despite the number and ages

Ramallah, Palestine, 2007.

involved, to come up with significant solutions, aesthetically and substantively speaking, makes these peace murals into a testimony that human cooperation, needed to found peace, is possible.

Peace and Social Justice

How then are Kids' Guernica peace paintings related to the issue of social justice? If we think of 'war' as an extreme situation of social injustice, then peace would mean restoring social justice in a way that human relationships are no longer antagonistic but are brought about by democratic practice. People know then how to resolve conflicts peacefully. Still, the term 'social justice' is as evasive as the concept of 'peace' especially in times when politicians justify war as bringing democracy while still others believe they are doing something righteous when they declare a so-called holy war. Some cultural prisms may illustrate what is important to Kids' Guernica.

Traumas of War—Regaining Optimism and Stepping Out of Silence

War at a personal level involves many tragedies and manifests itself most directly in death. Above all, children suffer the most under all forms of dehumanization and abuse. If they survive as witnesses, they are marked for life. With no prospect of having any positive future, traumatized children imprison themselves in silence. Where they should laugh they shout out of fear that they cannot protect themselves. Kids' Guernica as collaborative work process allows them to step carefully out of their own silences by just watching at first what the others do. Joining in the collaborative work

process is possible when children are no longer lost in a sea of feelings and a real self can be felt. These traumatized children, if given an outlet to express themselves safely, can smile and let the paint dance again. Invaluable is that they feel basic human optimism cannot be defeated. These kinds of experiences are needed if a sense of social justice is to guide all in their interactions with others. Once children and adults trust themselves, they are no longer afraid to speak about what is needed to protect themselves and others against all kinds of injustices. It begins by saying 'no' to war and does not end by using 'enemy pictures' of others to justify one's own actions.

Spiral of Violence—Victims and Victimization

Kids' Guernica works toward ending the spiral of violence by discussing, imaging, and releasing people's fears, for example about their inability to protect themselves. Often victims end up victimizing others. The spiral of violence leaves children as most vulnerable, helpless and exposed to all kinds of abuse. It is important to alter the narratives of victims in order to show a way out. This goes hand-in-hand with being free in the imagination to show alternative ways to exist in this world.

Staying Free from Defining Moments Leading to Revenge

Steering away from the revenge motive is an ongoing learning process how to remain just according to human law. It requires freedom of the imagination and a life embedded in a peace process based on friendship, trust, and openness. Crucial are here the stories which underline each of the murals as they illustrate what is possible as peace process in a concrete context e.g. Belfast, Lebanon, Afghanistan, and so on. Investment in peace as a step toward collaborative work process defines the content of the project. Instead of retribution and blame, a positive culture of redemption and mediation is encouraged. Already in Kids' Guernica workshops children learn to pose critical but non-aggressive questions in order to bring out the ideas of others. Altogether peaceful dialogues should motivate the children and adults to see challenges to their own identities not as insults or threats but as positive challenges.

Vulnerability—Human Weakness as Strength

Child labor and sexual abuse are linked phenomenally speaking to the child still trusting and requiring the love of the adults (Fischer, 2000). Because of this they are most vulnerable. At times they are even over-eager not to disappoint the adults expecting them to perform in a certain way. By painting people as being vulnerable they show what they feel in their souls. In acknowledging our need to cooperate and please each other, a human weakness becomes a human strength.

The Possibility of an Honest Life

Children have a sense of social justice but they must be allowed and facilitated to speak up whenever they see unfair practices and negative treatment of others. Children must be enabled to share their sense of justice. Here good practices in communities at large have to be a part of an ongoing learning process. Children who grow up in negative circumstances discard very quickly the sense of fair play and sharing of resources but only because they see themselves as permanently disadvantaged. Painting together and working together toward a common goal in this project reaffirms what is possible when everyone is given a fair chance.

Overcoming Social Isolation—from Cultural to Community Actions

Children of war, abuse, and domestic violence feel left alone, unprotected, at risk at any time, and exposed to cruelty and unjust treatment.

There is apparently no one there to protect them against injustices. In the Kids' Guernica project, by bringing not only children, but also adults, including parents and friends, into the painting process, that feeling of isolation can be overcome.

Conclusion

The Kids' Guernica peace project is a way for children to come to terms with what they otherwise might miss in their lives: a real sense of peace, and a deeper understanding of what that means, namely a respect of life through the imagination of others and one's self. That can be learned by entering a process of working together for a common goal, namely to strengthen and to develop a sense for social justice when seeking to define for themselves conditions of peace. Using the language of color, line, and space can help children find important keys for their understanding of peaceful solutions to human problems. The Kids' Guernica peace murals entail stories that let people imagine peaceful solutions for a world marked by war and violence and limited by the perpetuation of all kinds of social injustices.

REFERENCES

Adorno, T. (1997). *Aesthetic theory*, trans. R. Hullot-Kentor. Minneapolis: University of Minnesota Press.

Anderson, T. (1997). Art, education, and the bomb: Reflections on an International Children's Peace Mural Project. *Journal of Social Theory in Art Education, 17,* 71–97.

Becker, C. (1994). *The subversive imagination.* New York: Routledge.

Bernstein , R. (2008). *New antislavery law in U.S. may be wrongheaded.* Retrieved April 9, 2008, from http://www.iht.com/articles/2008/04/09/america/letter.php

Curtis, D. (Ed.). (1997). *The Castoriadis reader.* Oxford, UK: Blackwell.

ECCM Symposium, Productivity of Culture' and Kids' Guernica exhibition: www.productivityofculture.org

Enzensberger, H. M. (2006). *Schreckens Maenner–Versuch ueber den radikalen Verlierer.* Frankfurt a. Main: Suhrkamp.

Fischer, H. (2000) "Child abuse in sex trafficking cases: the double morale." Paper for the Greens of the European Parliament (unpublished).

Gombrich, E. (1950). *The story of the art.* London: Phaidon Publishers.

International Kids' Guernica: www.kids-guernica.org

Kapuscinski, R. (2000) . *Sowjetische Streifzuege–Imperium* (Soviet impressions – Empire), Frankfurt am Main: Eichborn.

Kennelly, B. (1993). *Poetry and violence.* Essay posted on http://poieinkaiprattein.org/beyond-images/poetry/poetry-and-violence/

Poiein Kai Prattein in Greece: www.poieinkaiprattein.org/kids-guernica/

Steiner, G. (1967). *Language and silence: Essays 1958–1966.* Yale University Press.

Art Education Projects in Action: Kang's *Amazed World* and *Happy World* Community Arts Projects

Esther Kho

Ik-Joong Kang's *Amazed World* and *Happy World* projects addressed communities' longing for peace and collaboration. They were collaborative art projects completed for the United Nations building and the Princeton public library, respectively. For the *Amazed World* project, children's artwork from all over the world was displayed together at the UN building in New York; the images somehow created an experience of spiritual togetherness. For the *Happy World* project, Kang created a collaborative art project for and with the Princeton, New Jersey, community on their public library. Kang received children's paintings and drawings in a 3 x 3 in. size, a convenient size to make artwork. All the pieces of art contributed were hung together, balanced, composed, and attached in a way that enabled the participants and viewers to realize the concept of community. Such projects are about the relationship between the individual and the collective whole. Kang has demonstrated his role as an artist-connector in his works, for the individual and the collective whole, which reaches both global and local communities.

Kang's art is a kind of art education, revealing how art and art functions create communities and how art demands people to be aware of others, to maintain a sense of responsibility for their wellbeing. Under Kang's coordination, children and communities made art together in response to certain intrinsic human properties, such as empathy, sharing, and understanding. In this sense, art both teaches and encourages awareness and empathetic contemplation of others.

A rich quality of Kang's work is his passionate inclination to engage in the local particularities of his environment; improvisation seems to stimulate

KEY CONCEPTS
- Community-Based Art
- Collaborative Art Projects
- Art Education
- Global Community
- Cross-Cultural Art Education Project

and challenge his creativity and border-consciousness. *Amazed World* speaks to the notion of being a global citizen. As a cross-cultural art education project, Kang's *Amazed World* teaches how to engage in an empathetic dialogue and curriculum. Kang is an activist artist and a philanthropist sympathetic to national and global problems. Kang indicated that "living in this world as a piece of the whole, how a person contributes and connects to the world is very important. To be aware of the world is important for artists" (personal communication, December 19, 2005). This visual project by Kang represents what many countries have experienced through war and separation. Kang noted, "Now when I make my artwork, I think about the global community, since I collect children's or communities' paintings from all over the world and arrange them with my themes" (personal communication, December 19, 2005).

As a global citizen, Kang successfully incorporates local awareness and global empathy. Thus, his work becomes significant in the international community, and specifically in the multicultural New York art world. As an activist artist and a philanthropist, Kang is sympathetic to national and global problems. Combining painting, architectural design, and cultural figures with paintings made by children from around the world, Kang's artwork, *Amazed World*, teaches all of us about cooperation, collaboration, and unification through art.

Ik-Joong Kang's *Amazed World* (2001)

The project, *Amazed World* (2001), is a multimedia installation made of 38,000 children's drawings from 135 countries. It was installed at the

United Nations building in New York, in 2001. The opening of *Amazed World*, which was exhibited on three walls, was scheduled for September 11, 2001, but because of the World Trade Center attack, the opening was delayed by one month. Subsequently, as a response, Kang added one column, which was made by the children who created paintings based on their experiences of the September 11 attack.

Kang focused on the theme "Dream" for this project; to elicit art pieces from the children, Kang wrote this letter: "Hello, I would like to gather all of your dreams for the future and show them in one place so everyone can see! What is your dream? I am very curious about how you imagine your future,

Ik-Joong Kang. (2001–2002). *Amazed World.*

the future of the world." They were not asked to conform to any stylistic conventions; they were completely free to obey their own creativity and autonomy. The only rule they were asked to comply with was the painting was 3 x 3 in. size.

This letters were received at Kang's studio from the children's schools by e-mail, letter, and fax to the artist's studio. Kang worked on the project with 25 assistants. They sent 2,000 pieces. Art pieces were contributed by children from South Korea, Uganda, Cuba, Kenya, Swaziland, Mongolia, Australia, Bolivia, India, Tunisia, Sweden, China, and many other countries. The children's dream themes varied. One of the first images received was from a child in Cuba, whose dream was to become a doctor helping other children. "I have six sisters and want one brother," wrote one 12 year-old Uzbekistan girl. She depicted this by drawing herself pushing a little brother in a stroller. A young student from Switzerland designed a beautiful house walking with robot legs. A 10-year-old Italian boy made a painting of an overhead kick on a soccer field. One girl from Mexico drew an image of a Palestinian child and an Israeli child shaking hands.

Although Kang indicated that 98% of the drawings appeared bright in mood and topic, there were also images that depicted bad or dark messages such as images associated with suicide or cursing the world. Some images

focused on unhappy messages, such as an Afghanistan girl's drawing that said, "UN ignored Afghanistan women and children." Chico of the Congo wrote, "Les tois sages d'Afrique-Sourd, Avengle, Muet (the way to survive in Africa—never see, never hear, and never talk). Despite these negatively focused images, Kang did not censor the paintings; he accepted each of them as they were, because of their honesty (Russell, 2005). He explained that the children's drawings from all over the world were displayed next to each other, and although the children did not know each other, they somehow created an experience of spiritual togetherness. As Kang said, "We are all connected. I am relieved that I am not alone. I am a part of these children, and they are a part of me" (http://www.amazedworld.com). In *Amazed World*, dreams for the future come from children of diverse ethnic and religious backgrounds (Peyser, 2002).

The finished version of *Amazed World* consists of three-tiered walls supported by five traditional beams. Each beam is silk-screened with the five sacred colors. The five colors are known as danchung colors in Korean philosophy, and symbolize harmony and the universe. The engraved Korean patterns look like the sun rising against the mountains. The traditional Korean architecture, silk-screened engravings, and multicultural paintings also make for an interesting composition, and the temple design makes the wall seem like a ritual monument. The three windows in the three walls create an illusion. Together, with the tiny mirrors interspersed throughout the mosaic, they create the illusion of reflection, of both yourself and the images. The cylinder shaped-wall column, which was added after September 11, 2001, is composed of 3 x 3 in. blocks. The surface of the column is painted with eight colors: cerulean blue, cobalt blue, vermillion (red), yellow, orange, viridian (green), chocolate brown, and coral pink. The seven background colors were from the flags displayed at the UN building; these colors matched the various paintings. The final effect is vivid and bright.

Each painting is attached to a 3 x 3 in. piece of wood and each one has a small

Ik-Joong Kang. (2001–2002). *Amazed World.*

Ik-Joong Kang. (2001–2002). *Amazed World.*

space between it and the adjacent paintings. The wood is cut and unvarnished. Some of the content is personal, whereas some is more global such as the world or the children's nation of origin. The dominant images are naïve, childish, and frail. The children's drawings and paintings are rough, since the contents, colors, and skill levels differ. But their figures and languages evoke a nostalgic feeling. The children's names, countries, and ages are on the paintings. They are not organized by culture, language, or content; the paintings are freely arranged in rows and lines. There are so many things going on at once—the colors, content, languages, sounds, mirror reflections, and architecture—yet, they all work in harmony. Thus, Kang used the Amazed World project as an opportunity to provide new ways to address children's longing for peace and collaboration.

Kang's *Happy World* (2005)

Kang continued his other project, *Happy World*, with a New Jersey community, in the town of Princeton. Kang's *Happy World* (2005) is a 10 by 30 ft. mural installed in the lobby of that town's public library. It was completed through collaboration between artist and community.

When Kang was asked to coordinate the Princeton Public Library project, he visited the site many times. He realized that the area in which the public library is located is distinctive; the east side is a wealthy white

Ik-Joong Kang. (2005). *Happy World.*

college town, whereas the west side is poor and predominantly African American (personal communication, December 19, 2005). Kang was also impressed by the extent of Princeton's cultural and linguistic diversity. He gave a lecture in the library that explained his idea and asked the people to bring 3 x 3 in. paintings or precious personal mementos. Mr. Kang

Ik-Joong Kang. (2005). *Happy World.*

invited Princeton K–12 students—kindergarten through grade 12 who are native speakers of one of the 54 world languages spoken in households in the Princeton Regional School District—to write the word "library" in their native language and the name of their native language in English on a 3-inch-square paper using ink, crayon, marker, or paint. An accompanying sheet of paper would also include the name of the student and his or her school and grade.

Kang received thousands of personal objects from Princeton local residents; they included the young, old, famous, poor, and rich. There were historical mementos, poems, sculptures, doorknobs, photos, toys, crafts, decorations and symbolic objects, and items found in nature. There was even an old Einstein placard among the children's 5,000 3 x 3 in. paintings and drawings. Many items were specific to Princeton history: a picture of Paul Robeson, a piece of copper gutter from a Princeton house built in 1948, many family photographs and letters. Among the more whimsical pieces included a librarian action figure, a South Indian mask, seashells, a library card, a wiffle ball, a clock from the old library on Witherspoon Street, cards from the old paper library catalog and a Rubik's cube (Kalonick, 2004). "I had to capture my 7-year-old daughter's sprit," said one Princeton resident as she handed over a pencil drawing of a cocker spaniel in a hula skirt, drawn by her daughter Miranda. She also brought beaded artwork made by her son, an ink drawing made by her children's great grandmother and one of her own photographs, a television collage. Kang used the donated objects and adhered either the whole form or pieces of the object to 3-inch-square pine blocks. He encased larger objects in clear plastic or attached them to the blocks with sealants. He said, "I hope this mural and installation can be like crossing different cultures and ethnicities." (Karmoil, 2004).

The Three Themes in *Amazed World* (2001) and *Happy World* (2005)

The artist's biography and his responses to an interview were used to better understand and interpret his work. Kang was born in South Korea and moved to New York when he was 24 years old. His creative inspiration comes from his Korean origin and his experience of immigrating to New York. He has always favored the small 3 x 3 in. size to create his images because it was easy for him to make art while working for a living at the grocery store or subway station. In this context, three themes emerged in his community projects, *Amazed World* (2001) and *Happy World* (2005). These included unification and division, collective and individual, and collaboration with children.

Many of Kang's projects, including *Amazed World* and *Happy World*, address the themes of unification and division in the world. The title *Amazed World* has a double meaning: the promise of the future world that these children make, and the ironic world, which exists in the space between the children's innocent dreams and the horrible reality of terror and war. The title *Happy World* provides mutual understanding of a community who nevertheless has different backgrounds. These themes maintain universal relevance in the contemporary era in light of such conflicts as the U.S. war in Iraq, the terrorism of September 11, and the cold war between North and South Korea. As a connector and contributor, Kang (2005) commented that:

There are a lot of walls between neighbors and cultures, and even countries. By making a wall of art [in *Amazed World* (2001) and *Happy World* (2005)], I believe we can break down walls between each other ... A wall of dreams can break down the wall of hatred and ignorance that separated us for a long time ... This means I want to break the walls of class and hierarchical status in society through my art. Relationship and participation are important in this artwork. (Kang, personal communication, December 19, 2005)

Of Korean origin, Kang felt sympathy for the suffering and pain of South and North Koreans who still live within the DMZ border, separated from family and friends. On Kang's *Amazed World* website, one of the voices that most resonates from the piece is that of a Korean child who says, "My hope is everyone in this world live without war." This small phrase hints at what Kang's projects, conducted in cooperation with many communities, seem to say. His works reach out and personally touch both global and local communities.

This visual portrayal represents the many countries that have experienced war and separation. His work expands beyond borders to include the suffering and problems of the world, as shown through the innocent eyes and paintings of children worldwide. It seems to show that, he claims himself as a member of the global community and a border-crossing artist. Such art is obviously about the relationship between the individual and the collective whole. His beliefs lead him to find his material and his collaborators and projects.

Another characteristic in *Amazed World* (2001) and *Happy World* (2005) that one can draw many insights about the collective and the individual. Kang stated that his role as an artist is as "a connector between Korean culture and Western culture" (personal communication, December 19, 2005). Kang explained that is why he used the traditional Korean art and concept such as the *ranching* colors and the harmony symbol.

Kang believes that the children and their drawings of dreams represent the vision of our future while displaying the cultural knowledge as the past. He says "children's vision is very clear, simple: they want peace" (Kalonick, J., 2004, p. 123). He said of his choice of 3 x 3 in. canvases from the children:

It is small, but if you try to see and get close to it, you can see the world. The 3 x 3-inch small size is like a child; if you want to listen, you can hear the world through children's paintings. If the small child's painting is collected by one million, they can change the world. What matters is where you put value, meaning, and your distance. (personal communication, December 19, 2005)

In reacting to Kang's work, Castronovo (2001) stated, "The clean and pure dreams of our children are also our own dreams in our youth. A lump comes into my throat when I look at those immaculate dreams of children" (http://amazedworld.com/eamazed/eend/eend.htm).

Kang also cited a Korean and East Asian philosophy:
When I meditate, I'm part of this world, the entire universe. The entire universe is part of me ... Like my body our bodies, part of this example, small metaphor of universe... When I receive

drawings from children, they are tiny ... drawings from children we sometimes think they are small, that their ideas are small and we don't care but trying to kneel down myself, I make myself the same height and see their dream ... If I change my way of understanding, whether big or small doesn't matter ... we can find even bigger world. So it really connects. (http://www.amazedworld.com)

Ultimately the work finds a balance between small details and a larger meaningful whole. It also speaks to the relationship between the individual and the collective whole.

Art Education for the Global Community

Kang noted, "Now when I make my artwork, I think about the global community, since I collect children's or communities' paintings from all over the world and arrange them with my themes" (personal communication, December 19, 2005). In *Amazed World* and *Happy World* his dreams for the unification of the two Koreas and world peace between different cultures and backgrounds are realized with children's and local residents' artworks. As a global citizen, Kang successfully incorporated local awareness and global empathy. Thus, his work becomes significant in the international and local communities, and specifically in the multicultural New York art world.

Kang's art can be considered a kind of art education, about which Eaton (2002) wrote:

How does art function to create focused groups of the sort that are or might become communities? How might art turn [people] into a focused group and ultimately into a community? My character-ization of community demands awareness of others and a sense of responsibility for their well-being ... If a member of a collection of individuals creates something with an awareness of other members of the collection [then he or she] concentrates on exposing what is made in a way that will infuse the experience of others and produce feelings of pleasure or generate solidarity. (p. 252)

Eaton (2002) stated the collaborative art education project generated "relatedness, psychic closeness, and mutual respect" (p. 253). Under Kang's coordination, communities made art together in response to certain intrinsic properties, such as empathy, sharing, and understanding. In this sense, art can both teach and encourage the awareness and empathetic contemplation of others.

Amazed World speaks to the notion of being a global citizen. As a cross-cultural art education project, Kang's *Amazed World* teaches how to engage in an empathic dialogue and curriculum. Kang tries to create a balance between the Korean national mission and the world mission. It is a sympa-thetic political statement from Kang and 38,000 children from around the world. Kang is an activist artist and a philanthropist sympathetic to national and global problems. Combining painting, architectural design, and cultural figures with paintings made by international children, Kang's *Amazed World* teaches all of us about cooperation, collaboration, and unifi-cation through art. Community-based artwork and collaborative work with local residents and the global community allow the audience to interact with the artwork which ultimately will function as a bridge connecting many different cultures and backgrounds in the community. This, in turn, enables the public to envision the future and communicate between members of the community. Kang has successfully assumed the role of artist-connector as presented in both of these works *Amazed World* and *Happy World*.

REFERENCES

Castronovo, V. (2001). United Nations Secretariat news. *Amazed World*. Retrieved August 17, 2005, from http://amazedworld.com/eamazed/eend/eend.htm

Eaton, M. M. (2002). The role of art in sustaining communities. In P. Alperson (Ed.), *Diversity and community: An interdisciplinary reader* (pp. 249–264). Maiden, MA: Blackwell Publishers Ltd.

Kalonick, J. (2004, March 12). Portrait of the artist. *Princeton Packet*.

Karmoil, C. (2004, January 18). Artwork by donation Bits, pieces arrive for library mural. *The Trenton Times*.

Kee J. (1998). Living on the edge: Borders and cultures in the work of Ik-Joong Kang. *Art Asia Pacific*, 19.

Peyser, J. (2002, September). Ik-joong king in the United Nations. *Sculpture Magazine*.

Russell, N. (2005). Would like to build a wall of peace? In Press Release. *Happy World* at Princeton Public Library. Retrieved August 17, 2005, from http://www.amazedworld.com///AmazedWorld

Developing Contemporary Art-Based Curriculum Practices for Diversity and Social Justice

Montserrat Rifà-Valls

Multicultural Art Education and Curriculum Practices for Social Justice

In this chapter, I combine multicultural art education and curriculum development with social reconstructionist practices for teaching and learning identity and diversity. The art educational project I present here started 3 years ago with the aim of reflecting on and promoting a dialogic curriculum to focus on identity and diversity through understanding contemporary art. Principally, I narrate an educational collaborative project based on contemporary art through which diverse identity narratives were produced with ninth through twelfth grade students in an urban school in Barcelona.[1] In doing so, I interpret the role of visual arts for multicultural and social justice education (Sleeter, 2005; Apple & Buras, 2006) in teaching cultural, gender, ethnicity, and social class opportunities. Finally, a selection of diverse identity narratives based on contemporary art by immigrant boys and girls—who visually represent themselves as Latino, Muslim, heterosexual, immigrant, black, Mestiza, pre-adolescent, poor, daughter, or student—is reconstructed.

Specifically, I present data from an arts-based educational research project through which I interpret students' understandings on contemporary art and how the students' visual narratives engaged in dialogue with different contemporary art pieces. As Barone and Eisner (2006) indicated, arts-based research in education provides a variety of aesthetic elements, including evocative, contextual, communicative, and generative features. In this project, the contribution of arts-based educational research implies the need to reconceptualize knowledge and subjectivity through the idea of curriculum as aesthetic

> **KEY CONCEPTS**
> - Contemporary Art
> - Curriculum
> - Identity
> - Diversity
> - Arts-Based Educational Research

text. By developing visual ethnographic research using film narrative inquiry methodologies I rethought curriculum as discourse based on identity, autobiography, cultural diversity, gender, and sexuality. According to Cahnmann-Taylor (2008), the definition of arts-based research in education carried out by Barone and Eisner empowers qualitative research, both theoretically and methodologically, and consequently, innovative strategies can be implemented, such as "the creation of a virtual reality and a degree of textual ambiguity; the presence of the expressive, contextualized, and vernacular forms of language; the promotion of the empathetic participation in the lives of a study's participants" (p. 8).

The children's narratives that are reconstructed in this paper were produced in the urban primary school *Collaso i Gil* located in Barcelona's old downtown (Raval). The school curriculum at *Collaso i Gil* focuses on managing the arriving population—over 90% of the children are from immigrant families. There is a variety of nationalities, languages, and cultural backgrounds within each classroom (e.g., from Pakistan, Morocco, Ecuador, Rumania, Dominican Republic, Colombia, China, Bangladesh, Brazil, and other countries). Overall, I wished to examine the creation of curriculum spaces and times to empower new places of learning through performing diversity, biography, community, and visuality, using film for ethnographic evidence, reflecting on narratives produced by the ninth- through twelfth-grade students. I will summarize the standards selected during the art educational project based on Catalan national standards for visual arts in

Grades 9-12 Visual Arts Standards	The Catalan Visual Arts Standards	The National Visual Arts Standards, NAEA
Achievement Standard, Proficient	Explore and converse with images, audiovisual texts and objects that can narrate the world and ourselves (1.5a) Use progressively images and objects from our local context with the aim of narrating any aspect of our life (popular culture, media, memories, every day life, local history) (2.3a) Elaborate art proposals as a result of sensorial perception, imagination, experiences, reality, ideas and emotions, using appropriate resources and exploring self-confidently new materials and possibilities (2.4a)	Conceive and create works of visual art that demonstrate an understanding of how the communication of their ideas relates to the media, techniques, and processes they use (1b) Reflect on how artworks differ visually, spatially, temporally, and functionally, and describe how these are related to history and culture (3a) Describe the function and explore the meaning of specific art objects within varied cultures, times, and places (4b)
Achievement Standard, Advanced	Identify life styles and modes of social organization by images and objects: perceive and understand their ideas, values or beliefs; understand the relationship between cultural context and the artists' lives in creating images and objects (1.5b) Understand and communicate ways of life, ideologies and conceptions, through the objects and images. Perceive and understand concepts of times, places, gender and class that these images promote according to the social context (1.7b) Elaborate art productions as a result of sensorial perception… (2.7b)	Initiate, define, and solve challenging visual arts problems independently using intellectual skills such as analysis, synthesis and evaluation (1d) Describe the origins of specific images and explain why they are of value in their art-work and in the work of others (3c) Analyze common characteristics of visual arts evident across time and among cultural/ethnic groups to formulate analyses, evaluations, and interpretations of meaning (4e)

Comparing Catalan and American Visual Arts Standards for students' understandings on contemporary art.

order to compare them with the American Visual Arts Standards (NAEA), and to evaluate students' achievements at the end of the chapter.

Working with Students' Understandings of Cultural Self-Representation

To start by analyzing students' previous knowledge on exploring and understanding visual representations, the teacher invited them to represent themselves with a picture from their family album and talk about it. During this process, the educators and researchers carried out personal inquiry-based teaching methods; therefore, collective conversations were promoted to avoid predetermined/stereotypical cultural knowledge from students' autobiographical narratives. In other words, we avoided classifying and unifying immigrant students' identity and culture, because we wanted to construct authentic diversity and learning through the promotion of an intercultural dialogue. The official stereotypes about immigrant population in urban schools were dismantled by the students' production of non-fixed identity texts across the mixture of diverse geographical, cultural, racial, gender, visual, and historical subjective positions (Rifà-Valls, 2008). In

addition, the dialogic curriculum generated new modes of teaching and learning, in which identity and difference were negotiated, and students' hybrid, multiple, and contradictory experiences were mediated by both local and global representations.

After the students' presentations, different contemporary artworks that addressed identity and difference were pinned up on the wall in front of the classroom. Art pieces by Gilliam Wearing, Meysam Mohammadi, Shadi Ghadirian, Alexander Apóstol, Miquel Angel Gaüeca, Dieter Appelt, Youssouf Sogodogo, Rineke Dijkstra, Pooyan Alimohamadi, and Jo Spence were selected in order to visualize different geographical, cultural, gender, and social contexts (Freedman, 2003). Students interacted with this collection with the aim of promoting a conversation based on artists' subjective positions. Some of the pieces did not raise any specific comment or interest— the students just answered the teacher's questions—but other pieces, like the couple composed by *Qajar* (1999) by Shadi Ghadirian, and *Then as Fountain* (2004) by Alexander Apóstol, elicited in-depth discussion. Most of the students were impressed by these two artworks, and the sentence by the art critic Tania Pardo, "Someone else's personal experience can become ours" (2003, p. 30) started up an interpretative process characterized by identification and displacement. For instance, Oumayma and Gabriela interactively produced reflective statements that relocated their identities as

immigrant students moving from real life stories to virtual scenarios, from past to present and future, and negotiating gender and cultural subjective positions.

Gabriela: It seems like he is on a balcony, in a city.

Oumayma: And she is in a garden.

Teacher: Which objects does she have that you can also have?

Gabriela: Pepsi.

Oumayma: It could also been made by computer.

Gabriela: No, it is like a temple, it is like a temple. It looks to me like, I don't know, as if it is a temple.

Teacher: Do you think she is in a real place or is it drawn?

Gabriela: It is drawn, because there is no distance between here and there. They have modified it.

Teacher: Why do you think that? You said before that there is a difference between modern and old pictures, and I can see a portrait in sepia in an old place and a Pepsi.

Gabriela: I think that it is now but they've changed the color.

Teacher: And would you like to represent yourself like she does?

Oumayma: When my sister wears the chador she has a similar face.

Gabriela: I would like to know, for example, how my picture that I took now would be seen in the future.

Oumayma: In my case, I don't know if pictures in the future will be like now, but I would like to watch myself in the past.

Teacher: Well, if I have understood, you want to see yourself in the future but like you are now, and in your case, you want to know how you will be in the future, is that right?

Gabriela: Yes. It is because our teachers say that we often talk like we are advanced.

The art teacher and the researchers became mediators between the contemporary art representations and the students' stories. We often promoted a conversational process by posing a range of open-ended questions and interpretative assertions, through which we addressed the students' identities and life experiences. In the case of social landscape that Alexander Apostol's artwork represents, we asked: "Do you think he is in a poor area of the city? Do you know a barrio like this?" Students responded that "he is in a public space" and "in a poor area of the city" possibly in Colombia, Barcelona, or Bangladesh. Simultaneously, students compared the Raval as a barrio with other districts and other countries, because they had recognized the precarious materials for building houses in poor areas. They discussed as immigrant children the idea proposed by Apóstol: "people make a city." By contrast, students considered that the woman portrayed by the Iranian artist "is inside, at home," lives in Pakistan or Morocco, and the chador made her seem like a close relative or a friend to these students. In fact, the students reconstructed their own subjectivities when they compared the two artworks, because different identity positions were available in terms of historical, geographical, social class, gender, and cultural diversities.

Teacher: Someone else's personal experience can become ours. What does their dress look like?

Beira: He is nude!

Teacher: And how is she?

Beira: Is she dressed like this because she lives in another age?

Carolina: Because she lives in Morocco.

Oumaïma: Or in Pakistan.

Teacher: Do you think he is in the same place?

Carolina: He is in a city, at the top of some place. I like this picture very much. It reminds me of my country and their houses. I used to climb up the stairs to go to a similar place when I was seven or eight. The boy is also handsome and I like his body position and trousers.

School curriculum practices produce identity and difference similar to that of how visual culture addresses the students as readers and consumers according to gender-constituted pleasure, and satisfaction. Our children's interpretations of global images of identity revealed that the majority of the students wanted to represent themselves like the muchacho portrayed by the Venezuelan artist. Masculine and feminine, public and private, and urban and rural themes came out in the children's interpretation of clothes and body representations, such as when Carolina indicated: "He looks like a strong boy. He does a lot of exercise, like in the TV series. They practice weight training." Oumaïma added: "Yes, he does one, two, three, and repeats."

According to Freedman (1994), we must distinguish different levels of how others interpret the relationship between gender and visual culture. Principally, we can analyze at one level the representations of women in various forms of visual culture and we can consider women as respondents to visual culture at another level, but we can also deconstruct the characteristics of gender in the students' cultural production as well. Therefore, after the interpretation of Ghadirian and Apóstol's images, the students analyzed other artworks that provided different racial and gender themes: *Untitled* (1984) by Youssouf Sogodogo, and *Odessa* (1993) by Rineke Dijkstra. The caption for Dijkstra's image focused the discussion: "I do not take pictures of people who think they are beautiful … They cannot surprise me." This sentence dismantled the visual pleasure device that is reinforced by representing women as fetishes, both in reading and writing visual narratives.

Kevin: Who is she/he?

Aracely: She showed her hairstyle.

Kevin: He looks like a woman.

Teacher: Why do you say that?

Kevin: Because she looks like a woman and like a man. Look at his face.

Mahbuh: He looks like a woman, like a transsexual.

Aracely: He has a delicate face, and his hair is…

Teacher: It could be because he is from the Ukraine. Where is she from?

Aracely: From the Dominican Republic.

Kevin: From Africa.

Teacher: Do you know anybody who looks like her?

Naima: Beira.

Teacher: It is a practice from Beira's culture, and also from Oumayma's friend's …

Aracely: In my family the habit is to comb long hair.

The teacher next invited the students to create a dialogue between an autobiographical image and one of the contemporary art pieces. During this process, students decided how they wanted to represent themselves using a range and variety of visual modes of production they had learned from contemporary artists. This also included a conversation with a Brazilian artist who created a new space at school with the aim of sharing, exploring, and interpreting his autobiographical images and objects. This dialogue also raised questions on visual modes of production; the artist represented himself as an immigrant photographer who reflects on contemporary world topics from a personal approach.

Students' Visual Narratives Engaged in Dialogue with Contemporary Artworks

During the second part of the project, students experimented with different modes of creating contemporary art while they negotiated school knowledge, artists' geographies, and identities. In researching contemporary art understandings, I will focus on analyzing the tactics that the students transferred from the artworks they had interpreted to their own studio practices.

Most of the students utilized and reinterpreted some of the visual tactics of the contemporary artists after identifying with the art stories they had seen, a process that also incorporated the identification with the artists' subjective cultural and gender positions. The children's nostalgia often emerged when they linked their family album pictures with the artworks. For example, Gabriela and Carolina represented themselves with an object

in their hands¬ as an offering—similar to what Ghadirian and Apóstol had done with the Pepsi and the fountain—in a natural, cultural, or autobiographical landscape, in either a new or old place. However, in some cases the students learned from the process what they did not want to select. For instance, a group of students developed visual narrative strategies based on the implementation of a visual effect to narrate the introspective self—such as the man reflected in the mirror in Appelt's *Der Fleck auf dem Spiegel, den der Atemhauch Schafft* (1977). On the other hand, despite that the immutable mask in Wearing's *Self-portrait 2000* displeased some of them, other students used a mask as an object to reflect multiple emotions (sadness, violence, joke, suffering), after they had completed the contemporary art selection with Balanza's (2003) *El lobo Solitario*.

In fact, diverse tactics for producing visual autobiographical narratives challenged the role of visual arts in the neocolonial and disciplinary educational system (Spivak, 1993), replacing it with aspects of deconstructive postcolonial pedagogy and visual culture. Gabriela's autobiographical narrative also reveals a complex process of identity dislocation by immigrant girls. She comes from South America, and as a result of living in many houses during the migration trip, she decided to represent herself as the main character of a glamorous scene for Catalan bourgeois society in

images, the strategies they used to create a visual autobiographical narrative were different in the position of their body, the scene, and the gaze.

Beira: I like very much how she is dressed and how she wears her hair. I like this image because I didn't know it was possible to wear your hair like this. I like it.

Teacher: How do you want to represent yourself?

Beira: I would represent myself with a red curtain at the back.

Teacher: What thing can you bring to represent yourself?

Beira: A saint. And I will wear my skirt, and I will bring the saint, I have it in my room at home.

Teacher: And, would you like to have a hairstyle like this?

Beira: With plaits, my mom knows how to plait hair.

Analyzing the production of autobiographical narratives further, Beira, as a Catholic Latin girl, identified with Sogodogo's portrait and decided to represent herself religiously holding a candle and a saint. In Beira's portrait, the icon of an archangel also coexists with Barbie, the fashion doll she showed in her jacket, as an example of hybridization between religion and postmodern popular culture. The autobiographical visual narrative by Beira also altered the framing and the perspective that Sogodogo used to create the African portraits, Beira's final image dialogues with the adolescents' bodies and scenarios represented by Dijkstra. Eventually, Oumayma and Oumaïma—who are both from Morocco and are "almost white" Muslim girls—identified with Latin idols through the visual and musical culture to become European girls.

Conclusions

Developing contemporary art-based curriculum practices generates new opportunities for immigrant students to construct their own knowledge about social class, culture, and gender positions. In this chapter, I have suggested that a dialogic curriculum for social justice and diversity through art and visual culture implies the reorganization of multiple spaces, times, and knowledge. In addition, future work in performing the curriculum as process can empower students' learning based on the understanding of visual arts and culture, and it can facilitate the acquisition of a sophisticated

the 19th century. After looking at Ghadirian's artwork and her own visual narrative, she challenged all the hegemonic representations about immigrant citizens in Western Europe when she concluded that she is interested in "the wish to learn from the cultures of past." By contrast, her colleague Oumayma decided to represent herself like a princess in an invented galaxy in the future. In this situation, performance and photomontage worked as creative strategies but also as spaces and tools for reconstructing students' identities.

In addition, contemporary art empowered the students' visual narratives as in the case of Beira's identifying with the body in Sogodogo's image, which usually portrayed his daughter's friends' hair plaits and other women from his Malian community, in a quotidian Africanist photographic gesture that resists a eugenic gaze. In their stories, as immigrant girls who come from the Dominican Republican and Morocco respectively, both Beira and Oumaïma presented themselves with an image from their family album that represents a birthday celebration. In both their pictures, they are dressed with similar tiaras and long white dresses made by their grandmothers. The two girls selected these photos because they have parents who were usually absent. However, although they chose similar images from their family album to represent themselves, after interpreting Apóstol and Sogodogo's and advanced level of cultural awareness. By experimenting with the interpretation and production of multiple and complex visual narratives, this project has contributed to visualizing the autobiographical and communitarian needs in Barcelona's old downtown, when different cultural stories and spaces for social justice coincide. Finally, this project invites us to reflect on how arts-based educational research provides new modes of narrating and representing educational data and participants in a collaborative educational process.

AUTHOR NOTE

Photos of students' artworks used with permission.

REFERENCES

Apple, M. W., & Buras, K. L. (2006). The *subaltern speaks: Curriculum, power, and educational struggles.* New York and London: Routledge.

Barone, T., & Eisner, E. (2006). Arts-based educational research. In J.L. Green, G. Camilli, & P.B. Elmore, *Handbook of complementary methods in education research.* Washington, DC and New Jersey: AERA, Lawrence Erlbaum.

Cahnmann-Taylor, M. (2008). *Arts-based research: Histories and new directions. In* M. Cahnmann-Taylor & R. Siegesmund (Eds.), *Arts-based research in education: Foundations for practice.* New York and London: Routledge.

Greene, M. (2000). *Releasing the imagination: Essays on education, the arts and social change.* San Francisco: Jossey-Bass.

Freedman, K. (1994). Interpreting gender and visual culture. *Studies in Art Education, 35*(3), 157–170.

Freedman, K. (2003). *Teaching visual culture: Curriculum, aesthetics and the social life of art.* New York and London: Teachers College, Columbia University.

Pardo, T. (2003). Lo doméstico: territorio (des)conocido. *Lápiz,* 192, 30–37.

Rifa-Valls, M. (2008). Narrating subaltern identities and diversity in a dialogic curriculum for an urban primary school. Paper presented at the *2008 AERA annual meeting, Research on Schools, Neighborhoods and Communities, Towards a Civic Responsibility,* New York.

Sleeter, Ch. E. (2005). *Un-Standardizing curriculum: Multicultural teaching in the standards-based classroom.* New York and London: Teachers College, Columbia University.

Spivak, G. (1993). Marginality in the teaching machine. *Outside in the teacher machine.* New York and London: Routledge, 53-76.

Stuhr, P.L. (1994). Multicultural art education and social reconstruction. *Studies in Art Education, 35*(3), 171–178.

ENDNOTE

[1] I wish to thank Xavier Giménez, Laura Trafí, Irene Tourinho, and Marcelo Schellini for the opportunity to learn from research based on dialogic pedagogy.

Artistic Mentorship with Two Maya Artists: Social Justice and Pedagogy

Kryssi Staikidis

Part One: Working Out of Maya Studios

In this chapter I will present a mentoring project between two Guatemalan Maya painters and me. Together we are three artist-teachers from different cultures who reveal insights into the transmission of cross-cultural painting pedagogy. The study was a collaborative ethnography (Lassiter, 1998, 2004, 2005) with a Maya Tz'utuhil painter, Pedro Rafael González Chavajay, a Maya Kaqchikel painter, Paula Nicho Cúmez, and me. I examine my own perspectives as a North American painter, while also examining the perspectives of my Maya teachers, their philosophies, and the methods they used to teach me in what may be considered non-formal learning contexts—their painting studios. Under their tutelage, we made artwork both in the home and surrounding community.

Up to the time of this study, I had been educated in formal settings, so studying in a situated context such as a painter's studio was new and exciting for me. After I returned home as a professor in art education, I attempted to adapt Maya teaching strategies to foster more inclusive curricula and pedagogy in middle level and high school methods courses for preservice art educators. Such attempts are described here.

Include Me In: Social Justice Perspectives

The need for studies that take place outside of a European model for teaching seems apparent when viewed from a postcolonial perspective. Such a perspective questions the centrality of Western dominant culture in the domain of art pedagogy (Becker, 1996; Ballengee-Morris, 2008; Durham,

> **KEY CONCEPTS**
> - Indigenous Studies
> - Art Education
> - Critical Pedagogy
> - Studio Practice
> - Situated Learning

1995; McMaster, 1998, 2004; Rushing, 1999). University studio art and art education courses are still taught primarily from a Euro-centric skills-based or formalist perspective that tends to exclude multiple perspectives and indigenous epistemologies (Becker, 1996; Deloria & Wildcat, 2001; Dunning, 1998; Efland, 1990; Freedman, 2003; Garber, 2003; Hubbard, 1963; McMaster, 1998; Pio, 1997; Rushing, 1999; Singerman, 1999; Sullivan, 2005). Quinn (2006) observed that working for social justice within art education, "requires attention to the complex contexts of peoples' lives, and then, engaged responses aimed at change" (p. 291). Therefore, providing an inclusive art education curriculum becomes necessary for "analysis and action" (p. 290), where teachers and students are encouraged to "link the arts to social justice or plan arts curricula around conceptions of citizenship in a democracy" (p. 291). Introducing the inseparability of curriculum and pedagogy and a decentralized teaching model to preservice art educators through the teachings of two Maya painters, they learn to incorporate a decentralized model in their own teaching, which empowers their future students. This, in turn, changes student teachers' concepts of citizen as subject to citizen as agent.

Indigenous cultures, whose epistemologies are rooted in the interdependence of the human being and her/his environment, form the basis for understanding a holistic teaching philosophy (Benham & Cooper, 2000; Cahete, 2000; Denzin, Lincoln & Tuhiwai-Smith, 2008; Grande, 2004; Kincheloe & Semali, 1999). My work in the areas of Maya painting and teaching methods through mentoring pairs in Maya art studios (Staikidis, 2006), illuminates processes involved in Maya artmaking and teaching.

Because Tz'utuhil and Kaqchikel Maya mentors guide the research, a study like this can contribute to a broader and deeper understanding of Tz'utuhil and Kaqchikel Maya artistic and pedagogical practices within the fields of art and art education. Historically, art educators have noted that there is sometimes a tendency in the field of art education to inappropriately study cultures under the guise of multicultural teaching (Efland, Freedman & Stuhr, 1996; Ballengee-Morris & Stuhr, 2001; Delacruz, 1996, 2003). Although in theory there has been a shift toward teaching social justice in classrooms, Gall (2006) noted:

> Such strategies recognize diversity, honor differences, and try to redress the inequitable Eurocentric models of the past. Nevertheless, even in their most critical forms they reproduce a scheme of culture that subtly confirms the established order of Modernist hierarchies, and fail to capture the fluid, hybrid, and uneven character of culture. (p. 105)

The literature is replete with interpretations of multicultural education that raise questions about how to teach and represent diverse cultures of students within the art classroom. Desai (2003) categorized multicultural art education as either mainstream or social reconstruction. She argued that mainstream multicultural ideologies have at their core a cultural pluralism rooted in an "essentialist understanding of culture" (p. 148). With regard to multicultural art education curricula, Sleeter (1996) observed, "To my dismay, I found that the great majority of the materials conceptualized multicultural art as the study of folk art, around the world (and usually long ago)" (p. xvi). Cahan and Kocur (1996) asserted that, in contrast, the most effective approaches place the study of art into a broader, cultural, social, political, and historical framework. This study in Maya art studios could be placed in the latter framework, where Maya teaching methods become ways to transform the core of lessons offered in formal classroom settings.

How Do You See Me? Indigenous Voices and Social Reconstruction in Art Education

The Social Reconstructionist movement in art education spanning the 1990s addressed the need for raising democratic citizenry. Quinn (2006) noted that even if social reconstructionism has been connected to social justice goals, this framework has been inadequate because it provides a means, not an end, whereas taking up social justice in art education necessitates a focus on action: "A social justice art education is utopian *and*

practical; it looks ahead to the more democratic society we can practice to build in our classrooms …" (p. 295). If truth be told, examining classroom practices connected to Native American cultures since the social reconstructionist movement in art education began 15 years ago, it seems clear that lessons almost always request students to replicate objects removed from indigenous cultural contexts that do not account for their cultural beliefs, values, aesthetics, function, spirituality, politics, equity, agency, economic/material issues, and power dynamics. There seems to be a need to introduce lessons that respect indigenous cultures and present authorship of practices in first voices rather than constructing lessons that attempt to replicate decontextualized objects, which disrespect the intentions of their makers.

A multicultural curriculum can be used as a platform for educational reform on a global level in which bounded notions of culture, including the notion of "white," are challenged and constantly contested. As Kincheloe and Semali (1999) pointed out, indigenous education, as a microcosm of indigenous experience, would treat the student as part of a greater cosmology, without dissecting it into smaller units of knowledge. Kincheloe and Semali suggested that an appreciation of indigenous knowledge "can inform and transform disciplinary curriculums from elementary schools to graduate studies …" (p. 48). In this context, conversations about two distinct Maya indigenous communities may help students and teachers reflect on their own culturally biased pedagogical and philosophical tendencies, thereby inspiring critical self-evaluation and change. Below I describe two mentoring experiences with Maya painters that aim to provoke thought about teaching in formal classroom settings.

How I Learned

This painting study with two Maya mentors took place in several artists' studios, where knowledge was transformed through artmaking processes (Sullivan, 2005; 2008). Over the course of 5 years the artistic knowledge transmitted by each Maya artist to me, a non-Maya artist, was chronicled. Artists' studios are intimate places where artistic research is made possible. In these spaces, Pedro Rafael and Paula taught me from *inside* their cultures; they did not separate their lives from their art. One day while talking about his grandfather, who was the first painter in San Pedro La Laguna, Pedro Rafael said,

> When I began painting, I engraved my grandfather's themes in my mind. He always worked in customs, traditions and rituals.

I carried all of his ideas inside of me in addition to my own. So when I began, I felt the theme of customs through him. (Personal Communication, July 15, 2007)

Pedro Rafael also viewed teaching as an act related to experiences transmitted through the teacher-student relationship. Teaching methods were one-on-one with Pedro Rafael, but also included his students, who taught me and worked on my canvases. Transmission of knowledge involved being asked to conceptualize creating paintings in an unfamiliar way that involved recording images in my mind to then communicate them to canvas. This required a different experience than the one I was used to. It involved concentrated looking and feeling natural surroundings that encouraged seeing in new ways. Additionally, although personal narrative had always been the basis of my own painting, I was now asked to see and think of cultural customs as ideas for paintings. This was a challenge. Unlike novice Maya painters, I was unfamiliar with cultural customs on a visceral level that made it hard to capture them "realistically." This raised the issue of recognition, or *knowing* something well enough to paint it, very much a part of the Maya cosmovision and not much a part of my experience. One day Luciano, a fellow student, commented:

> Fishermen still exist, but the way fish were sold in the market differed, so I would have to imagine that, and remember how it was done with the ancestors. I would have to use my mind because you cannot see it now. Not see, but imagine how it was before and then capture that reality. (Sitan Sicay, Personal Communication, July 30, 2005)

When I returned to my studio after working with the Maya mentors, I realized that my own artistic ways of knowing were comparable yet different. I had been educated to draw from life, without relying on cultural memory. The idea of rendering from nature is not part of the Maya artistic process yet it was part of my conceptual framework. The Maya concept of ancestors passing down iconography viscerally was nothing previously conceived of by me. Yet, I realized that in many ways I did feel that the Greek side of my family had passed its history of grief down through me, which did appear in my paintings. Studying with Maya mentors enabled me to realize this and view my own work with fresh perspectives. I began to perceive things in new ways. Often times I observed myself making comparisons between how I had been taught while presented with new ways of teaching. Pedro Rafael and Paula did not think of their cultures, life experiences, painting, or teaching as separate categories. Not only were their lived experiences at the center of their teachings, but mine were at the center of mine as well. It was time to take notice (Staikidis, 2009b).

Part Two: Walk the Talk

Because I have been transformed as an educator and an artist by my apprenticeship with Maya painters, Maya teaching practices have begun to inform my own teaching. Two projects are described here that have been used in preservice art education methods courses that incorporate Maya teaching methods, and which combine curriculum and pedagogy into a unified and fluid form (Staikidis, 2008, 2009a). The idea that content is not separate from form comes from mentoring lessons with Pedro Rafael and Paula. The first project involves decentralized teaching, and challenges the teacher-as-expert model (Dunning, 1998; Sullivan & Hawke, 1996; Welker, 1992), enabling students to become novice experts, and teach in groups, creating a forum for democratic teaching. The project also addresses concepts of postmodernity and definitions of the contemporary in art and examines Maya art, its marginalization as "folk art," and its objectification in the wake of cultural tourism. Underlying Maya teaching strategies are used to transform lessons from the text, *Contemporary Art and Multicultural Education* (Cahan & Kocur, 1996). The second project addresses appropriate content for lessons at the middle school level for teaching about Maya Kaqchikel and Tz'utuhil communities using larger social issues as concepts (Jacobs, 1989, 1997; Walker, 2001; Wiggins & McTighe, 2005).

How to Create Innovative Approaches to Teaching: Two Lessons

Teaching teachers means giving them opportunities to reveal their insights into self, as well as helping them design critical lessons for K–12 students that encourage social justice concepts such as agency and action as democratic citizens. Therefore, the designed projects had to be transformative for young adults, and useful in and out of classes in diverse communities with elementary, middle level, and high school students. Maya strategies incorporate mentoring in a non-formal context, and the teaching takes specific forms: personal and cultural narrative, importance of the mentoring relationship, a conceptual framework that I termed *Imagined Realism,* negotiated curriculum, a decentralized teaching model with expert novices, and group collaboration on artworks. These democratic teaching processes were used as models for transformation with preservice art educators, so that they could teach non-essentializing lessons related to two Maya cultures as well as defuse the teacher-as-expert model while disrupting traditions of teacher banking model strategies (Freire, 1970) in formal classroom settings.

One methods class for secondary level preservice art educators was using the text *Contemporary Art and Multicultural Education* by Cahan and Kocur (1996). Because students were using a text that revolved around contemporary art practice and its definitions, the lesson began with questioning assumptions about what it means to be a contemporary artist in a postmodern context. The Tz'utuhil and Kaqchikel painters are contemporary artists whose work might be considered "folk" or "primitive," according to Euro-American mainstream ideologies. As many North American students' versions of the postmodern or contemporary emerged from the course textbook, which tended to present artists as urban, multi-media, and text-based, the issues concerning stereotypes of folk art and their exclusion from certain realms of postmodernity were discussed. In this context, the painting *Pascual Abaj* made in 2004 by Tz'utuhil artist, Antonio Ixtamer from San Juan la Laguna, Guatemala was further examined.

In the absence of any information, and based solely on examining the image, students were asked six questions:

1. Who is the artist?
2. Where is this painting made?
3. When is this painting made?
4. Why is it made?
5. How is it made?
6. What genre?

After viewing the artwork, students were grouped into pairs and asked to develop responses to these questions, presented as assumptions since Maya cultures and their contemporary painting movements had not been discussed in class. Notions of the postmodern and its philosophical European birth and shaping were debated, as well as ideas about what defines the contemporary in art: Urban or rural? Text-based? Male or female? European or indigenous? Is there political commentary? If so, how is the political view expressed and what are the expectations for its expression? Stereotypes about terms such as contemporary art and artists in a postmodern art world were dismantled.

Figure 1. *Pascual Abaj*, Antonio Ixtamer, Oil on Canvas, 2004.

My research in Maya studios was presented and reviewed, focusing on the form and content of teaching practices and the studio as site for research and pedagogy. I explained that I had studied with two Maya painters, one male and one female, in order to bring to the higher education table philosophical thoughts and teaching outside of a Euro-American model for art education. Students were also asked to think about "artistic language as a means of communicating across and through cultures" (Staikidis, 2006), adding that this study indicated that characteristics often associated with situated learning were in part transferable to a formal art teaching setting.

Emerging out of Maya studios were the following teaching practices:

- *Decentralized Teaching: Novices*
- *Collaboration*
- *Negotiated Curriculum*
- *Personal and Cultural Narrative*

I led a discussion about these concepts and how they are defined within the context of the Maya painting schools and how we might define them in our own classrooms. I described the decentralization of teaching in Tz'utuhil and Kaqchikel Maya teaching practices: As the mentor guides according to learner input and level, novice students gradually become novice experts who go on to teach student colleagues. Collaboration, another teaching strategy, took place when Paula Nicho Cúmez and I worked on the images and surfaces of paintings together. Negotiated curriculum took the form of consensus between artists as we developed themes through initial dialogue before beginning paintings. Finally, there is a unity between the author and the piece of work, his/her culture, and daily life. Paintings, and the teaching of painting, become vehicles for the transmission of culture.

After we examined the Maya teaching structures, assignment folders were distributed to groups composed of four to five students. In each folder were copies of a lesson plan from their text, *Contemporary Art and Multicultural Education* (Cahan & Kocur, 1996). I asked students to consider the Maya teaching structures and to brainstorm ideas for the transformation of this particular lesson plan. Lesson 32, *Creating an Enemy*, became a vehicle for practicing curricular transformation. The teaching objectives of this lesson stated that students will learn how racism, directed toward people of Asian descent, is used to mobilize support for war. The students would use works of art and personal testimonies to analyze the impact of racism on individuals and society as a whole. Also, students were asked to create mixed-media projects that challenged racist imagery in mass media. The assignment folders contained artist statements and examples of work by artists Ken Chu, Kristine Yuki Aono, and *Epoxy Art Group*.

Students were asked to review the lesson plans and to change the objectives incorporating at least one, and as many as four, of the Maya teaching structures discussed. In groups of four, the students were asked to deconstruct the lesson plans and apply them to middle or secondary level students.

Solutions varied. One group incorporated the idea of personal and cultural narrative by asking students of similar cultural backgrounds to gather and discuss stereotypes associated with their own histories, creating mixed-media pieces that disrupted such stereotypes. Another group incorporated the idea of collaboration by having students work on collages in pairs. One group integrated decentralized teaching by having students conduct class critiques in groups with facilitators rather than having a single teacher who led the discussion. Another group created a scenario in which students held discussions about racism and decided on an art project via consensus using negotiated curriculum for the art lesson. Each group of preservice educators reported their transformations of the original lesson plan back to the larger group. As students listened, they became excited by each other's ideas.

When asked what they believed were the teaching objectives at the end of class, students' first comments were that teachers are often given a standardized curriculum and told to follow it. Yet, in order to accommodate individual learning needs, it is important to consider how to transform lesson plans and curriculum units, rather than accepting standardized lessons as non-negotiable. They realized that thinking creatively was an important first step for beginning teachers. Second, they appreciated the holistic Maya model in which teachers do not separate form from content or curriculum from pedagogy. Teaching democratically involved changing form (decentralizing the teacher as expert model), as well as content. They also liked the idea that teaching multiculturally could involve learning about artistic and teaching processes of cultures without emulating content. The students stated that, based on prior experiences of so-called multicultural art lessons, they assumed at first that this lesson would involve painting or weaving. Instead, the lesson incorporated Maya approaches to teaching and painting, which were more integrally related to the lessons they themselves would be teaching. This was the first time that students had experienced a more holistic approach to teaching that involved indigenous communities.

Larger Issues as Metaphors

The following lesson has been presented several times to undergraduate preservice art education students in both elementary and middle level methods classes, as well as elementary art teachers. After the lesson, the general response from the teachers was that they had never thought to work with indigenous artworks looking at the concepts underlying the works, rather than focusing on form. Many Native American contemporary artists

Figure 2. *Certeza*, Paula Nicho Cúmez, Oil on Canvas, 2005.

like James Luna, Edgar Heap of Birds, Jimmy Durham, and Jaune Quick-to-See-Smith work with postmodern concepts such as "*cultural critique, recycling and transformation, cultural conflict, double coding*" (Freedman, 2003, p. 95). Ironically, art teachers on the elementary level are still using formal approaches, decontextualizing objects, and studying them as if indigenous communities are long ago and far away (Ballengee-Morris, 2000, 2002), which reflects a disconnect between school art and contemporary art and also supports institutionalized racism. The purpose of this lesson therefore was to break such habits.

At the beginning of the lesson, I gave a presentation to the students on my studies with Paula Nicho Cúmez and discussed teaching and mentoring strategies that emerged from our work together. Afterward, the students were shown a video of Paula talking about each one of her paintings. The group was shown a PowerPoint presentation that included Paula's descriptions in text form next to her painted images (see Figure 2). As seen here, Paula's images and oratory were displayed side-by-side. For example, in describing her painting *Certeza* (2003), Paula stated,

> Rigoberta Menchu speaks about the indigenous peoples and our human rights, and so the idea came to me to make this painting. We see that this part of the painting is dead, but it has flowered once again over here. Like Rigoberta said, pull out all of our roots, pull out everything that we have been and are, go ahead, yet a day will arrive when everything that we are will flower again. These images are fused to the canvas and fused into peoples' hearts. That is the meaning of this work. (Paula Nicho Cúmez, personal communication, June 25, 2003)

As students discussed visual clues in the piece related to concepts or possible ideas that artists' works reflect, they were reminded that this is an alternative approach to the generic discussion about the works of indigenous artists and communities where works are customarily studied by applying formal principles or attempting to replicate the styles of indigenous artists. The literature in the field of art education is full of replicating dream catchers, kachina dolls, and Aboriginal dot paintings. In contrast, here, ideas and concepts behind the works were discussed. The mainstream notions of contemporary and the resulting marginalization of indigenous works made by artists in rural areas who had not received training in the academy were also examined.

Figure 3. *Mural*, 2006.

Conclusion

The methodology underlying the study with Maya painters is one example of a teaching model that derives from an indigenous aesthetic and pedagogical philosophy that employs a holistic learning experience at its center. Maya artists do not separate curriculum as content and pedagogy as form and so the projects that I have designed integrate what is taught with how it is taught. In studying indigenous cultures and their works, educators often study the art objects by removing them from their contexts and their functions. The results become uninformed studies about cultural artifacts with little or no connection to the cultures that created them.

In the two projects described, I attempted to incorporate Maya holistic teaching models in the classes of preservice art educators. In this way, I address social justice issues as they relate to multicultural education, as they relate to marginalization of indigenous communities, and as they help to transform the majority white dominant perspectives of preservice art education students involved. Many university students come from cultures that possess their own traditional art systems that are still very much alive, but are excluded from art education curricula in the schools. These students will also face the same issues of invisibility. Immigrants, as well as ethnic and Native American groups, are expected to study the Western art system and the ideology that goes along with it. In this chapter, I have questioned, and thus hope to disrupt such traditions by describing two projects involving preservice art educators in learning experiences that will, in turn, inform their own desires to foster social justice approaches to the teaching of art.

Following the presentations of the artists' work in first voices, the students received a worksheet that listed issues or concepts related to the themes in each painting. Some difficult issues such as the one cited by Paula Nicho Cúmez—the discriminatory treatment of indigenous communities—were also tackled. Students were asked to use larger concepts with individual paintings and to look for broad issues underlying images, rather than examining only formal aspects or visual symbols.

Students then looked at a variety of individual paintings and their corresponding texts in small groups and created lesson sketches based on larger concepts and issues connected to these works. The lesson sketches were presented to the entire class as each group reported which concepts they had chosen to connect with each painting. At the middle school level, social justice issues raised might be marginality, power dynamics, and privileging voices of first nation's artists and thinkers. Topics related to Native cultures such as dynamic, living, and contemporary might also be integrated.

Ballengee-Morris, C. (2000). Decolonialization, art education, and one Guarani nation of Brazil. *Studies in Art Education, 41*(2), 100–113.

Ballengee-Morris, C., & Stuhr, P. (2001). Multicultural art and visual cultural education in a changing world. *Art Education, 54*(4), 6–13.

Ballengee-Morris, C. (2002). Cultures for sale: Perspectives on colonialism and self-determination and the relationship to authenticity and tourism. *Studies in Art Education, 43*(3), 232–245.

Ballengee-Morris, C. (2008). Indigenous aesthetics: Universal circles related and connected to everything called life. *Art Education, 61*(2), 30–33.

Becker, C. (1996). *Zones of contention: Essays on art, institutions, gender and anxiety.* Albany: State University of New York Press.

Benham, M. K., & Cooper, J. E. (Eds.). (2000). *Indigenous educational models for contemporary practice: In our mother's voice.* New Jersey: Lawrence Erlbaum Associates.

Cahan, S., & Kocur, Z. (Eds.). (1996). *Contemporary art and multicultural education.* New York: The New Museum of Contemporary Art.

Cahete, G. (2000). Indigenous knowledge: The Pueblo metaphor of indigenous education. In M. Battiste (Ed.), *Reclaiming indigenous voice and vision,* (pp. 181-191). Vancouver: UBC Press.

Deloria, V., & Wildcat, D.R. (2001). *Power and place: Indian education in America.* Golden, Colorado: Fulcrum Resources.

Delacruz, E. M. (1996). Approaches to multiculturalism in art education curriculum products: Business as usual. *Journal of Aesthetic Education, 30*(1), 85–97.

Delacruz, E. M. (2003). Racism American style and resistance to change: Art education's role in the Indian mascot issue. *Art Education, 56*(3),13–20.

Desai, D. (2003). Multicultural art education and the heterosexual imagination: A question of culture. *Studies in Art Education, 44*(2), 147–161.

Denzin, N. K., Lincoln, Y. S., & Smith, L. T. (Eds.). (2008). *Handbook of critical and indigenous methodologies.* Los Angeles, CA: Sage Publications.

Dunning, W. V. (1998). *Advice to young artists in a postmodern era.* Syracuse: Syracuse University Press.

Durham, J. (1995). *Jimmie Durham.* London: Phaidon Press.

Efland, A. D. (1990). *A history of art education: Intellectual and social currents in teaching the visual arts.* New York: Teachers College Press.

Efland, A. D., Freedman, K., & Stuhr, P. (1996). *Postmodern education: An approach to curriculum.* Reston, VA: National Art Education Association.

Freedman, K. (2003). *Teaching visual culture.* New York: Teachers College Press.

Freire, P. (1970). *Pedagogy of the oppressed.* New York: Continuum International.

Gall, D. (2006). Multicultural reservations, hybrid avenues: Reflecting on culture in art education. *The Journal of Social Theory in Art Education, 26,* 105–131.

Garber, E. (2003). Teaching about gender issues in the art education classroom: Myra Sadker day. *Studies in Art Education, 45*(1), 56–72.

Grande, S. (2004). *Red pedagogy.* New York: Rowman & Littlefield Publishers, Inc.

Hubbard, G. A. (1963). *The development of the visual arts in the curriculums of American colleges and universities.* Dissertation Abstracts International. (Stanford University)

Jacobs, H.H. (1989). *Interdisciplinary curriculum: Design and implementation.* Alexandria, VA: Association for Supervision and Curriculum Development.

Jacobs, H.H. (1997). *Mapping the big picture: Integrating curriculum & assessment K–12.* Alexandria, VA: Association for Supervision and Curriculum Development.

Kincheloe, J., & Semali, M. (Eds.). (1999). *What is indigenous knowledge?: Voices from the academy.* New York: Falmer Press.

Lassiter, L. E. (1998). *The power of Kiowa song: A collaborative ethnography.* Tucson, AZ: University of Arizona Press.

Lassiter, L. E., & Campbell, E. (2004). *The other side of Middletown: Exploring Muncie's African American community.* Lanham, MD: Altamira Press.

Lassiter, L. E. (2005). *The Chicago guide to collaborative ethnography.* Chicago: University of Chicago Press.

McMaster, G. (Ed.). (1998). *Reservation X: The power of place in Aboriginal contemporary art.* Washington: University of Washington Press.

McMaster, G. (Ed.). (2004). *Native universe: Voices of Indian America.*Washington DC: National Museum of the American Indian, Smithsonian Institution.

Pio, F. (1997). *The creation and development of a program of study derived from Ojibwe philosophy for a proposed center of learning and research in the arts.* Dissertation Abstracts International. (New York University)

Quinn, T. (2006). Out of cite, out of mind: Social justice and art education. *The Journal of Social Theory in Art Education, 26,* 282–301.

Rushing, J. (1999). *Native American art in the twentieth century.* New York: Routledge.

Singerman, H. (1999). *Art subjects: Making artists in the American university.* Berkeley: University of California Press.

Sleeter, C. (1996). Introduction. In S. Cahan & Z. Kocur (Eds.), *Contemporary art and multicultural education.* New York: The New Museum of Contemporary Art.

Staikidis, K. (2006). Personal and cultural narrative as inspiration: A painting and pedagogical collaboration with Maya artists, *Studies in Art Education, 47*(2), 118–138.

Staikidis, K. (2008). Artistic mentorship with two Maya artists as a source for curricular and pedagogical transformation in higher education. In J. Caruso (Ed.), *Creating multicultural communities through art and music.* Berlin: Deutsche Nationalbibliothek.

Staikidis, K. (2009a). Learning outside the box: How Maya pedagogy informs a community/university partnership. *Art Education, 62*(1), 20–24, 33.

Staikidis, K. (2009b). Paths in as lived experience: Transformations of a painter as a result of collaborative ethnography and mentoring with Maya artists. In D. Caracciolo & A. Mungai (Eds.), *In the spirit of Ubuntu: Stories of teaching and research.* Rotterdam, Netherlands: Sense Publishers.

Sullivan, G. & Hawke, D. (1996). *Inquiry into artistic practice: The artist as expert and novice.* Unpublished Manuscript. School of Art Education, University of New South Wales.

Sullivan, G. (2005). *Art practice as research: Inquiry in the visual arts.* New York: Sage.

Sullivan, G. (2008). Painting as research: Create and critique. In A. L. Cole & J. G. Knowles (Eds.), *Handbook of the arts in qualitative research: Perspectives, methodologies, examples, and issues,* (pp. 239–250). Thousand Oaks, CA: Sage.

Walker, S. (2001). *Teaching meaning in artmaking.* Worcester, MA: Davis Publications.

Welker, R. (1992). *The teacher as expert: A theoretical and historical examination.* Albany, NY: State University of New York Press.

Wiggins, G.P., & McTighe, J. (2005). *Understanding by design.* Alexandria, VA: Association for Supervision and Curriculum Development.

Breaking Out of the "Isolation Malaise": The Story of an Asian Minority Art Educator in Rural, Midwestern America

Ryan Shin

Introduction

Many Asian friends of mine, immigrants such as myself who have not been raised in North America, have expressed the opinion that blatant racial oppression and discrimination does not seem a significant part of their lives. I generally agree. However, a more serious problem I have faced as a minority and an Asian immigrant is isolation or alienation within the school and professional environment. Many times, we are left alone in social gatherings, schools, work places, or community activities. My Asian friends have had similar experiences. For them, a sense of belonging to a group is very critical. It keeps us from participating in our local communities and professional organizations.

For example, Lily Yeh is a Chinese immigrant and practicing artist who had felt a deep sense of alienation since she moved to the United Sates. She could not find any value and meaning to her life in America until, in 1986, she began a project that transformed an abandoned inner-city lot into an outdoor art park in a hard-hit neighborhood of North Philadelphia. Even though she was an outsider who could leave the city after the project was completed, she returned every summer to help the inner-city neighborhood make art. She developed an ongoing relationship with the neighborhood, such as when she taught mosaic art to an alcohol-addicted American, who later became an excellent mosaic artist in the area. She founded the Village of Arts and Humanities, a community-based organization for arts, education, and neighborhood development. Annual participation in the village programs and activities now number over 10,000 children, teenagers, and

KEY CONCEPTS

- Social and Professional Isolation
- Dialogue and Collaboration
- Community Outreach and Service
- Community Art Project
- Self-Identity

adults (Knight & Schwarzman, 2006). When I found out about this, I realized I too had engaged community through constructing it as described in the following story.

The Beginning

While working at a small teaching college in Wisconsin, I often felt professionally isolated because I felt that I could not rely on or seek advice from others who might not understand what we as art educators do, feel, or often struggle with in our professional lives. I have come to discover that I am not alone. Many art education professors have communicated similar experiences to me, as they were the only art educator in their department. This kind of professional isolation can become an unexpected yet significant issue for recently graduated art educators embarking on their new careers. Contrarily, with this isolation comes a tremendous sense of freedom; such circumstances allow us to do what we want and determine how to design and teach our courses. This includes defining a teaching philosophy, choosing a theoretical approach, and adapting texts. However, without meaningful professional interactions with other art educators, we may feel disempowered or marginalized (Young, 2000).

In this chapter I describe my effort to break out of what I call isolation malaise: that lonely sense of professional and personal marginalization. This transformation process I recently experienced has taught me that even my minority status could not keep me from changing the social dynamic of the small, local art education world I inhabited, and that I can assume a leadership role and take an initiative to make a positive impact on the field.

Chapter 30. Breaking Out of the "Isolation Malaise": The Story of an Asian Minority Art Educator in Rural, Midwestern America

221

When I began teaching art education courses at the University of Wisconsin at La Crosse in January 2002, there was no established relationship between the university and local area schools, museums, or community art centers. Since the university had not employed a full-time art educator for more than 5 years, and the previous art educator was not available to offer support or advice, I had no resources available to facilitate meeting art professionals in the area. As a result, my first year at UW-La Crosse was stressful, and because of the teaching responsibilities, I did not have enough time or energy to visit local schools. My responsibilities included maintaining a four-course load, with three different course preparations. Since I had to spend more time on campus to address these responsibilities, I was unable to make any significant connections with community art teachers, museums professionals, or artists.

My infrequent and informal meetings with local art educators, such as my colleagues' spouses or retired art teachers, gave me the impression that local area art teachers were also busy with their teaching and thus did not have time for social networking. During the summer break, they were generally busy creating their own artwork. They seemed not to have any interest in developing a formal network or local art teachers' group.

Local art educators' shows and university art faculty exhibitions provided an infrequent opportunity to meet some art teachers. When I asked if there were official meetings or unofficial gatherings among art teachers, I was surprised and frustrated to discover that no such relationship existed. Even though some of the artist/teachers seemed to know each other through attending exhibitions, such art openings seemed to be one of their few social gathering opportunities.

My confusion and anxiety as to what my role would be in the community and how I would fit into this world only increased when the art department put pressure on me to make the university visible to the community in an effort to recruit graduating high school seniors. Also to benefit my preservice students, I had to think of a way to develop a consistent relationship between the university and art specialists in the community.

For the first several years, I struggled to build up a strong professional relationship with the art professionals in the community. Because I was not supervising student teachers, I had difficulty meeting local art teachers; I had hoped there would be social gatherings or official meetings for art educators in the area. However, once I had time to ponder the situation and to gain a clear perspective on the local art education landscape, I developed an idea of connecting the La Crosse art education community through technology.

Making Connections

The project was initiated in the spring of 2006, by which time my anxiety developed into uneasy feelings of powerlessness and disconnectedness from others; I had reached the deepest point of my isolation malaise. The idea for this project was simple: I was going to connect art teachers electronically. However, when I presented my idea of developing an electronic dialogue with my university colleagues, their responses were less than positive. Despite this response, I still believed it would be the most effective way to develop community outreach. Although I was not sure how many art teachers in the area were interested in a La Crosse art educators' electronic forum, I knew I had to try something.

The first thing I did was to list the art teachers whom I had met or had come to know through various events. I then added the names of several of my former students who were now teaching in K–12 schools in the area, and included my daughters' school art teachers. I then collected local art teachers' e-mail addresses after searching local districts' and schools' websites to gather art teachers' e-mail addresses. Even though the population of the La Crosse metropolitan area is only a little over 10,000 with few public and private schools, it took me several days to compile a list of 40 art teachers.

While I was working on contact information, I also developed an introductory letter, proposing an electronic dialogue among art educators. The letter explained why I thought such a thing would be a positive and worthwhile experience. I stressed that this forum would allow us to talk about issues in art education, to create stronger connections in our learning community, and to use this forum to share what art teachers might plan and achieve in the local community.

After sending the first e-mail letter to the 40 teachers, I received approximately a dozen responses within a couple of days. Most agreed that connecting the professional art education community electronically was a good thing. Their feedback confirmed that I was onto something. I now knew there were others who wanted to be connected and wanted to be part of a larger professional community. One art teacher said, "I have never known college faculty to want to network with public school teachers. You should be commended for your efforts." Several of them expressed that they also felt isolated, and they wanted to hear about what projects other people taught in their classes.

Some of the art teachers were enthusiastic about this forum and were even willing to provide more contact information. One teacher sent me several more art teachers' e-mail addresses to be included in the list. An art teacher working as a school liaison to the regional art center sent me several more names of art teachers who were on her personal contacts list. A fine arts superintendent of one of the local school districts in the area sent me his list of art teachers. In no time, the list snowballed to include some 80 La Crosse-area art educators. Whenever I received new contact information, I sent them the introductory letter. I even received an e-mail from two art teachers several months later, one who was serving as a Wisconsin regional representative, expressing an interest in becoming involved in our local discussion, even though her school was 150 miles from La Crosse.

Electronic Discussion

In the beginning of the electronic discussion, I invited art teachers to use the forum to raise any issues, share their experiences, and seek information. I reiterated several times that I did not intend to lead discussions, but that the forum should be used as a communal chatting room similar to a Web blog. Even though blogging was becoming popular around that time, I decided not to use it simply because most people will read e-mail, but do not bother to open a blog website. I also suggested using this dialogue to write about their exhibitions, local art events, school student art shows, and artist lectures and workshops, including what they may have learned at state or national conferences. After some time, I began receiving e-mails from teachers asking me to forward flyers or announcements for them as their computers were limited in their ability to send e-mails to multiple recipients.

The discussion became active within a week. Many participants were asking questions or seeking advice. One person sought out guest artists or speakers to invite for her school diversity week. One needed information about becoming a cooperating teacher to work with student teachers. One even invited me to visit her school to share what she had done.

There was no way to predict what issues would be important to this community. For example, one focused on developing an after-school art club, and issues on funding and establishing a budget to cover an honorarium payment for the art teacher's preparation, teaching time, and other expenses were discussed. Although I did not think this topic would generate much interest because it seemed to of minor importance, I was wrong. After reading the discussion proceed over a long period of time, I realized that this was an important issue that mattered to members of the community.

The issue started simply enough. The teacher who raised the question seemed to seek advice on how to develop an after-school club. However, her question raised many related concerns; the discussion soon included the issue of the value of art education in schools and dealing with administrators and the public. The first response, put forth by a teacher with 30 years of experience in the local schools, was keen and strong. The following is part of her e-mail:

> The athletic Dept. doesn't run sports using unpaid coaches… nor does the Music Dept. I think we do need to make a case for the value of our area, and in our culture, that value seems to equate pay. When you continually give your services away, it seems that you end up feeling resentful because other folks don't value what you are doing (and maybe it is really that we don't value what we are doing enough to put our services on a par with athletics and music???). In our District, the Visual Arts Classic coach is paid as an extracurricular coach or club advisor. Talk to your union folks about how to get included in the extracurricular pay group, like Yearbook, Jazz Band, etc.

Many agreed with her, and argued for equal treatment and the value of art in school and society. Others stressed that school administrators should not take advantage of art teachers who are willing to voluntarily contribute their time and energy to her club and students. Another teacher pointed out that the promotion of art in the community and for school boards, including collecting documentation that focuses on the value of art for students' development and creativity, was important. She promoted the need to be active in media relations as it would allow "you to reach a wide audience," and emphasized that "school boards loved PR." One retired art teacher even suggested going to the school board to promote art programs.

It soon became apparent that the forum bonded the local teachers together as art educators, strengthening a sense of professional community. It also developed a consensus that art teachers need to do something to make people take notice of and learn to value art education in schools and the community.

Another topic caught the attention of many of the art teachers; it was the story of an art teacher who took her students on a museum field trip in Dallas, Texas, and was subsequently fired. In the *New York Times* article "Museum Field Trip Deemed Too Revealing" (Blumenthal, 2006) sent to me by a member of the electronic community, it became clear that the teacher was fired because she exposed her students to artwork of nude images. The art teacher who sent the article to me commented that the article was disturbing to her, and she hoped there were no school districts in Wisconsin that would fire someone in similar circumstances.

Although the art teacher had sent it only to me, I thought it was an important enough issue to forward the article to the other members of our group. The first response came from an art teacher who taught art at a middle school in Eau Claire. Although her school district was two hours away from La Crosse, she was an active member of our community. She voiced concern because she had a field trip scheduled to the Minneapolis Institute of Art the following spring. She wondered if it was necessary to get a disclaimer from all parents, stating that there would possibly be nude images to which the students could be exposed, a seemingly natural and logical reaction to the article.

Within the next couple of days, there were about 10 e-mail responses to this issue. Several of them told of their own experiences taking their students to big city museums, which usually resulted with no protests or complaints. Yet one teacher advised that having the parents sign a disclaimer was probably a good idea. Another community member raised the issue of censorship:

> We have to also realize that TV advertising underwear and such already has made it impossible for parents to screen everything their child sees. Do they expect the art teacher to screen every museum? How much censorship can we stand?

A response soon followed; a teacher shared her own experience after having received a parent's call following a class where she had presented examples of Renaissance art with her seventh grade students. She said that she had explained to the parent the reality in the art world and her desire to prepare her students for real life. She suggested on the forum that the issue of nudity should be introduced in the classroom as a safe place. A teacher agreed with her, and then stressed that "nothing is more powerful than good teaching with honest intention." Another teacher put forth that we should support each other in the view on this. Such dialogue underscores the strength of networking among art teachers.

While I was reading these comments, an art educator who teaches at the University of North Texas came to mind. I have known her personally for some time, and I thought that I might be able to gain some more information and advice from her. I sent her our discussion thread. She responded that it was quite a hot issue in Texas, and further indicated that the art teacher in question had, in fact, worked with UNT student teachers and had been a good mentor. She also said that the school district that suspended the teacher had always been very supportive of art education and had recently issued a statement saying that the firing was related to the teacher's daily performance. Thus, it was not related to the museum field trip. I then shared this information with the Wisconsin forum. Within 2 months, I learned that the Texas art teacher had reached a settlement with the school district, agreeing to resign with her salary paid until the end of school year. Unfortunately, no one in our Wisconsin forum could provide an adequate set of guidelines or legal information for dealing with the presentation of the nude figure within elementary and high school art classrooms. The issue was too vast for our small group to address sufficiently within a limited time frame. Hopefully, the National Art Education Association can work on this issue and provide guidelines that will protect art teachers in similar circumstances and also educate parents and children about such an uncomfortable issue.

Art teachers have used the electronic forum actively for a wide variety of purposes: to distribute invitations to gallery openings and non-art related events; to seek advice on computer software for school purchases; to encourage each other to become members of the Wisconsin Art Education Association; to announce local and university art classes; to motivate others to submit works to local art educators' shows; and to inquire about information regarding gallery field trips. I was active in sharing information whenever I felt the need to. For example, after I acquired a CD-ROM that included the Wisconsin Art Education Association (WAEA) 2006 Fall Conference presentation handouts and after getting permission from the WAEA, I distributed the CD to members of the online community.

Many of the art teachers provided very positive comments on using these electronic dialogues whenever I met them at local gallery openings and other art events. Many of them expressed that such dialogue helps them stay connected and prevents them from feeling isolated from other art teachers. The online forum resulted in the opportunity for me to meet other local art teachers as they regularly invited me to their school art events and gallery openings.

Collaborative Projects

The connection I enjoyed through the electronic dialogue also helped me develop several collaborative projects with local art teachers. In this section, I will present one project initiated by a middle school art teacher, and another collaboration project between my university art education students and some local high school students.

The first project in which I collaborated with a local art educator occurred after the launching of the electronic dialogue. It was called the *Pinwheels for Peace* project and was suggested in May 2006 by art teacher Pam Shaw of Trempealeau Middle School in Wisconsin. Mrs. Shaw had gotten the idea for this project when she attended a Chicago NAEA Convention presentation by two Florida art teachers, who had initiated the nationwide project in 2005. The basic idea of *Pinwheels for Peace* was fairly simple: to make pinwheels as public symbols promoting peace, tolerance, harmony, and unity against the everyday violence witnessed on television, or in video games, magazines, or wars going on in other countries. After returning from the NAEA conference, Mrs. Shaw had initiated the project at her own school. Various participants were instructed to make pinwheels. One side was to be decorated with any kind of written expression, such as a haiku or an essay; the other side of the pinwheel would feature a drawing, painting or collage for visual expression. Once all of the pinwheels were completed, they were arranged in an outside installation on the International Day of Peace.

Mrs. Shaw's grander vision, as presented to our electronic forum, was to expand *Pinwheels for Peace* beyond Trempealeau Middle School to include all of the schools in the La Crosse area in an effort to generate publicity for the children and the schools. Furthermore, she believed that *Pinwheels for Peace* was a good way to help the community reflect on what peace meant to them. She presented the previous year's experience, when students and staff members at her school had participated in a ceremony in which they read their peace poems alongside the pinwheel installations. She added that it was a solemn and beautiful experience to see all of the brightly colored pinwheels spinning. Four other teachers soon indicated they would like to join the project. However, there were some concerns expressed by others.

Another forum member, who had directed the project at her school in the past, communicated to the group an unexpected resistance from people who considered the project an anti-war protest.

Her concern became real to us when we tried to launch the project. Her precaution of possible conflicts seemed to scare off others who might have joined the project. Rather than picking up more art teacher participants, a few teachers who had previously agreed to participate in the project declined to take part. Mrs. Shaw and I encouraged more art teachers to participate. However, there were no other volunteers. Even Mrs. Shaw's school principal did not want to draw national attention or news coverage. The principal made it clear that only the town newspaper was to cover the event, with no additional or expanded media release. Nonetheless, three art teachers in the area continued to work on the project and wrote about their progress with other members on the list. At UW-La Crosse, I invited students taking my Elementary Art Methods class to participate; and I made a sign with a description about the pacifist intent of the project for passers-by. There were about 40 pinwheels made by the students. We celebrated International

Students made and installed pinwheels on the University of Wisconsin—La Crosse campus, and celebrated International Peace Day. Photo by Ryan Shin.

Peace Day on September 21, 2006 with the pinwheels, and shared some pictures with other members.

The second project was a collaborative mural project with a local high school art teacher and her students. After I talked with university NAEA student chapter members about possible community projects, everyone agreed that it would be a good idea to paint a mural in a public school. However, they were concerned with how to select a school for the project. Since I was connected with local art teachers through the electronic forum, it became my happy responsibility. Within a few days, five art teachers, from the elementary through high school levels, contacted me. We exchanged emails and discussed potential mural subjects and sites. After careful consideration of all sites, we decided to work with Tomah High School, a 30-minute drive from La Crosse. The teacher, Mrs. Genrich, was eager to work with us, and at that time, she was developing an art project to design stage banners for the performance of *Thumbelina* by a community theatre and a local symphony orchestra. We thought this would be a worthy project, as the play's organizer did not have funding for the stage decora-

Student volunteers and high school students painting the stage decoration murals. Photo by Ryan Shin.

tion; our job was to provide 12 panels (each measuring 4 x 12 ft.) for the backdrops.

We had painting sessions on two Saturdays: one was held at the university campus, and the other at Tomah High School. There were about 25 university and high school students involved in the project. Painting on the large canvases was fun, and all of the participants were enthusiastic about using the paints.

The project also provided an opportunity for the college and high school students to interact. The high school students asked the college students about college life and taking classes, and appreciated whatever answers they received. Later, I learned that the art teacher valued how the college students treated her students with respect and care.

Actively working with art teachers provided me many opportunities to break out of my "isolation malaise." Along with the above mentioned projects and interactions, I worked with the Mississippi Valley Gifted and Talented Network, a nonprofit organization that focuses on special art events for students in the western Wisconsin area. I invited my art education students to serve as judges for their art show, and to teach art classes for them. I also was invited to judge student art pieces for Youth Art Month for the West Central Region Competition. The opportunities for interactions are numerous. One potential collaborative project discussed was an international artist trading card project, which is to help students design a two-dimensional 2.5 by 3.5 in. miniature artwork in any medium and then trade it by mail between schools in two countries.

Conclusion

Lily Yeh, whom I described in the introduction, has done a tremendous job in transforming many lives through art. Yet her commitment and contribution to society was made, in part, for herself. She said that she was not doing it only for the community; she was also doing it for herself. She found her sense of place in the community, and provided an excellent example of how a minority member in American society can contribute and be a positive force for social change. Like her, I believe that a social change does not have to start from someone who occupies a position of power and privilege in the society. Everyone has it within them to construct community.

As an Asian immigrant, I have experienced Lily Yeh's anxieties of moving to a new place and working with new people with different cultural and belief systems, as well as expressive modes. I believe that I undertook the tasks described in this essay not only for the benefit of the art education community but also for me: to find a sense of my place in the world.

I enjoyed working with art teachers in Wisconsin and I am happy that I overcame my feelings of marginalization and alienation through constructing an electronic and as a result a real-world community. Even though I did not have art education colleagues at UW-La Crosse, through reaching out, I felt that I worked with people who shared my interests and goals. I was happy to be connected with them, and the dialogues and projects provided positive incentives and support to keep me going in teaching art education. I also enjoyed being part of the La Crosse community of art educators, which also benefited my students for their site placement. Once I had taken the step of contacting local art educators, my students had little difficulty finding good teachers with a convenient locations for their student teaching. I still appreciate how much the electronic forum participants interacted even though we taught on different levels.

I learned that an active professional community is critical to the development of art educators who are beginning their careers. Most schools have one or two art teachers who have the task of designing and teaching the school art curriculum. Beyond school walls, it is necessary to support others and share common interests. We need to open the channels of communication and encourage an open dialogue on all levels of the educational hierarchy.

My outreach project demanded much time to develop to sustain professional relationships. Given the current emphasis on junior faculty's workload and the demands of developing a scholarly publication record, some may argue that I should have spent more time on teaching and research. However, I believe that working with art educators has had a positive impact on my approach to the classroom and facilitates my research. While talking and chatting with art teachers, I was able to develop several projects that could be written up as research. It also helped my teaching by allowing me to share with my students the real-life issues in our field. In so doing, I could involve them in community outreach projects. They learned how an art educator can tie together teaching, research, and service. What I learned from my personal experience working with art teachers in La Crosse, Wisconsin, is that a belief in social change can begin with me. More than that, it helped me construct a life in my community here in what had been a foreign land that I now call home.

REFERENCES

Blumenthal, R. (2006, September 30). Museum field trip deemed too revealing. *New York Times*. Retrieved October 8, 2006, from www.nytimes.com/2006/09/30/education/30teacher.html?ei=5090&en=72efd1846b3947bd&ex=1317268800

Knight K., & Schwarzman, M. (2006). *Beginner's guide to community-based arts.* New Village Press: Oakland, CA.

Young, I. M. (2000). Five faces of oppression. In M. Adams et al. (Eds.), *Readings for diversity and social justice: An anthology on racism, sexism, anti-semitism, heterosexism, classism, and ableism* (pp. 35–49). New York: Routledge.

Chapter 30. Breaking Out of the "Isolation Malaise": The Story of an Asian Minority Art Educator in Rural, Midwestern America

227

Author Biographies

Future Akins-Tillett (Future.Akins@ttu.edu), BA General Art (1972) and MFA Printmaking (1977), is an assistant professor in the School of Art, College of Visual and Performing Arts at Texas Tech University where she coordinates the Master of Art Education Program and oversees student teaching. Her credentials include time as a university museum curator and as a public secondary school teacher. She is a practicing artist constantly involved in visual studies community outreach projects.

Tom Anderson (tanderson@fsu.edu) holds the Jessie Lovano-Kerr Chair of Art Education at Florida State University. He received the National Higher Education Art Educator of the Year award from NAEA in 2006 and the Edwin Zeigfeld National Art Educator of the Year award from The United States Society for Art Education in 2004. He also won the Barkan Award, with Sally McRorie, in 1998 for outstanding scholarship in art education. He is former editor of *The Journal of Social Theory in Art Education* and *The Journal of Cultural Research in Art Education*. Author of *Art for Life* (with Melody Milbrandt), Anderson has had about 100 scholarly papers published. He is a founding member of the *Kids' Guernica Peace Mural Project* and has been an advocate of art education for social justice for his entire career.

Katy Barrington (katy.barrington@gmail.com) is an art therapist who teaches in the Art Therapy Department at Adler School of Professional Psychology in Chicago, Illinois. She has earned a Certificate of Aging Studies from the Claude Pepper Institute on Aging and Public Policy, which is affiliated with Florida State University. She also has an interest in death education and is a certified thanatologist (CT). She is concerned with the well-being of older adults and volunteers for hospice and at assisted living facilities.

Christine Ballengee-Morris (Morris.390@osu.edu) was the founding director of The Multicultural Center, and is Associate Professor in the Art Education Department and the American Indian Studies Coordinator for The Ohio State University. She was president of the United States Society for Teaching through Art. In 2007, she co-authored *Interdisciplinary Approaches to Teaching Art in High School*. She has received the 2008 National Art Education Higher Education Western Division Award, the 2007 Zeigfeld Award for Diversity, and the 2006 National Art Education Grigsby Award.

B. Stephen Carpenter, II (bscarpenter@tamu.edu) is Associate Professor of Art Education and Visual Culture at Texas A&M University, and teaches courses in creative inquiry through the arts, curriculum development, curriculum theory, cultural foundations of education, art education, and visual culture. His articles and book chapters have appeared in numerous publications including *Art Education, Ceramics:* *Art and Perception, Educational Leadership, The Journal of Aesthetic Education, The Journal of Cultural Research in Art Education, The Journal of Curriculum and Pedagogy, The Journal of Educational Multimedia and Hypermedia, Studies in Art Education,* and *Visual Arts Research*. He is co-author of *Interdisciplinary Approaches to Teaching Art in High School* (with Pamela G. Taylor, Christine Ballengee-Morris, and Billie Sessions) and co-editor of *Curriculum for a Progressive, Provocative, Poetic, and Public Pedagogy* (with Jennifer Milam, Stephanie Springgay, and Kris Sloan). Carpenter is past editor of *Art Education*, the Journal of the National Art Education Association, and co-associate editor of the *Journal of Curriculum and Pedagogy*.

Min Cho (mcho@admin.fsu.edu) is an Assistant Professor in the Department of Art Education, School of the Arts, Virginia Commonwealth University in Richmond. She sits on the Board of the International Association of Research of Service-Learning and Community Engagement and her current research includes program evaluation, curriculum integration, and teacher professional development. She recently co-authored the premiere arts-based service-learning handbook for K–12 teachers.

Miwon Choe (miwon.choe@wku.edu) is Associate Professor and Chair of the Art Education Program at Western Kentucky University. In 2004, Choe conducted a field study in Cuba: "Cross-cultural studies of Cuban art: Implications for art education." Her examinations of Cuban artists and art have resulted in a number of presentations at NAEA.

Kristin G. Congdon (kcongdon@mail.ucf.edu) has taught art in a variety of settings, including public schools, correctional settings, treatment facilities, museums, and universities. She is Professor of Film and Philosophy at the University of Central Florida and Director of the Cultural Heritage Alliance. She is currently Senior Editor of *Studies in Art Education*.

Kimberly Cosier (kcosier@uwm.edu) is associate professor of art education at the University of Wisconsin-Milwaukee. Her research interests are focused on the interconnected issues of alternative education for at-risk youth, anti-biased teacher education, urban education, and art and education for social justice.

Michelle S. Creel (creelms@yahoo.com) has worked with at-risk children for many years incorporating art, creative writing, environmental science, and multiculturalism experiences. She received her Bachelor's in Creative Writing and Painting from the University of South Florida in 1982, a Master's in Creative Writing from the University of Houston in 1991, and a PhD in Art Education at Florida State University in 2005. In Houston and South Florida, she worked with at-risk children and young adults as artist-in-residence in public schools, museums, and at a juvenile detention center.

Since moving to northern Florida, she has taught art in public schools. In addition to currently teaching art and creative writing to at-risk children at a school for the visual and performing arts, she has written numerous grants, presented workshops to teachers, published fiction in several small presses and an article in the *Art Education* journal, and was a recipient of the Fulbright Memorial Fund Teacher Program to Japan.

Vesta A.H. Daniel (Daniel.4@osu.edu) is Professor of Art Education at The Ohio State University focusing on community-based art education. Daniel has been an international visiting scholar, researcher, and speaker. She is currently writing a book about community-based art education and the significance of race.

Melanie Davenport (meldavenport@gsu.edu) is currently on faculty in the Welch School of Art and Design at Georgia State University in Atlanta, Georgia. She is a member of the World Council of the International Society for Education through Art and serves on Delegates Assembly of the National Art Education Association.

Miriam Davidson (miriamdavidson@trentu.ca) is an Assistant Professor and Coordinator of Integrated Arts at Trent University in Ontario, Canada. She earned her PhD in Art Education from Concordia University in Montréal. Her research focuses on the role of the arts in enhancing student engagement in learning, the connection between the production of visual imagery (photography in particular) and students' literacy practices, and artistic practices found in non-formal community-based settings. Her qualitative studies bring together underserved communities of learners with preservice teachers and artists through the implementation of arts enrichment outreach and service learning projects. She is an active documentary photographer.

Elizabeth M. Delacruz (edelacru@illinois.edu) is Associate Professor of Art Education at the University of Illinois at Urbana Champaign and Editor of *Visual Arts Research* journal. She has authored numerous scholarly texts, presented before national and international audiences, served as consultant to schools, museums, foundations, and governmental agencies, and received numerous awards, including the UIUC Vice Chancellor's Teaching Scholar's Award, a Center on Democracy in a Multiracial Society Fellowship, and a National Endowment for the Arts grant. Delacruz is co-editor of the NAEA anthology, *Globalization, Art, and Education.*

Dipti Desai (dd25@nyu.edu) is an Associate Professor and Director of the Graduate Program in Art Education at New York University. As a scholar and artist-educator, she is committed to addressing the formative role of visual representation and its politics in order to affect social change. She has published widely in the field of art education and her forthcoming book is titled *History as Image, Image as History: Visual Knowledge and History in the Classroom.* She is currently the Associate Editor for the *Journal of Cultural Research in Art Education.*

Carolyn Erler (c.erler@ttu.edu) is an Assistant Professor of Visual Studies in the School of Art at Texas Tech University. She has written extensively on the visual culture of grassroots movements for economic and environmental justice worldwide. She works at the intersections of visual culture, social studies education, and critical pedagogy.

Hatto Fischer (www.poieinkaiprattein.org) is a poet and philosopher, and coordinates the NGO Poiein Kai Prattein ("to create and to do") in Athens, Greece, and has organized Kids' Guernica events in Crete (2006), Chios (2007), and in conjunction with the ECCM Symposium, *Productivity of Culture*, a Kids' *Guernica* exhibition in Athens (2007).

Terry Galloway's (TLGalloway@aol.com) memoir, *Mean Little Deaf Queer*, was published by Beacon Press in 2009. An NEA [grant] recipient, she is a performer as well as a writer and tours her shows all over the globe. Her performance texts, monologues, poems, and personal essays have appeared in numerous anthologies about queerness, deafness, disability, theater, and Elvis, most recently in *Sleepaway: Writings on Summer Camp* (Riverhead, 2005).

Karin Gunn (karingunn@gmail.com), born and raised in São Paulo, Brazil, has been working for the past 4 years as an animation and photography teacher at West Port High School in Ocala, Florida. She earned both a Bachelor of Fine Arts in Electronic Intermedia and a Master of Arts in Art Education from the University of Florida. In addition to teaching, Gunn has worked as a professional photographer, videographer, and animator on several projects in Florida and Mexico. She has presented her work in local, regional, and national professional conferences. Examples of her work can be seen in her award winning website, www.teachanimation.org

David Gussak, PhD, ATR-BC (dgussak@fsu.edu) is Associate Professor and Chairperson for The Florida State University Department of Art Education and Clinical Coordinator for its Art Therapy Program. He has been an art therapist for almost 20 years. Gussak has been conducting extensive research on the effectiveness of art therapy with prison inmates, and has published and presented extensively nationally and internationally on art therapy in correctional settings. His most recent work involved working with the Florida Department of Corrections to develop the statewide Arts in Corrections program, and creating the Inmate Mural Arts Program.

Mary Hafeli (mhafeli@mica.edu) is the Dean for the School of Fine and Performing Arts State University of New York, New Paltz. Her research examines how artists, both adults and children, describe their studio practices and thinking and how they respond to works of art and culture. Her research also investigates the pedagogical conditions that promote students' development of independent artistic judgment. Recent awards for scholarship include the NAEA Manuel Barkan Award (2009), Women's Caucus

Mary Rouse Award (2006), and the Marilyn Zurmuehlen Award for Research in Art Education (2005).

Kara Kelley Hallmark (kkhallmark@gmail.com) received a PhD in Art Education, with a minor in Women's Studies from Florida State University. She earned a MA in Art Education with a certificate in Gender Studies from the University of Central Florida and a BFA in Art History from Southern Methodist University. Publications include a series of artist encyclopedias for Greenwood Press. She is currently under contract to co-author a two-volume project on U.S. folk artists with Kristin G. Congdon. Hallmark lives in Austin, Texas, and teaches art at Union Hill Elementary in Round Rock.

Lisa Hochtritt, EdD (lhochtritt@rmcad.edu) is Chair of the Department of Art Education at Rocky Mountain College of Art and Design (RMCAD) in Denver and former MAT Program Director at the School of the Art Institute of Chicago.

Robin Houdek (robinhoudek@gmail.com) is currently living in Portland, Oregon and teaching middle and high school art and technology classes at the International School of Beaverton in the Beaverton School District.

Karen Hutzel (hutzel.4@osu.edu) is an Assistant Professor of Art Education at The Ohio State University where she teaches courses on computer art, multicultural art education, and research. She utilizes asset-based service-learning strategies to build community learning environments and approaches research through a collaborative artmaking process founded on participatory action research.

Takuya Kaneda (kaneda@otsuma.ac.jp), a professor of art education at Otsuma Women's University in Tokyo, is very active as a representative of the International Children's Peace Mural Project and has organized many workshops for children in different parts of the world. He co-authored *Peaceful Children: Beyond War, Violence and Bullying* (Osaka, 2004).

Esther Eunsil Kho (ekho@korea.ac.kr) was born in South Korea and studied Western painting and art education (BFA) and French literature (BA) at Korea University. She moved to the United States where she earned an MA from NYU and a PhD from FSU in Art Education. She teaches Korean art, contemporary art, and Western art history at Korea University, Kyunghee University, and Korea National University of Education.

Linda McConaughy (lmcconaughy@bcps.org) has taught K–12 art for over 20 years and her accomplishments include National Board Certification. She has taught preservice and in-service teacher education courses at Maryland Institute College of Art and Towson State University, and is currently a doctoral student at Florida State University.

Jeanne Nemeth (nemeth@uwm.edu) is an assistant professor in the Visual Arts Department at the University of Wisconsin Milwaukee. She received a PhD in Curriculum and Instruction from Indiana University and a MFA in Photography and Digital Media from the University of Cincinnati. Her research interests include material culture studies, contemporary art practices, and environmental psychology.

Allison Paul (allisonspaul@gmail.com) recently graduated from the Department of Art Education at Florida State University and earned her master's degree and K–12 Art Certification in the Spring of 2009. She earned a BA from Earlham College, which helped inspire a belief in nonviolence and the power of community. Her vocation includes a commitment to art education as a tool for social justice and a passion for community-based art education and environmental education.

Isabelle Potts, J.D. (ipcbavs@yahoo.com) is an attorney, community organizer, and educator. Her forte is recognizing talent and using it, particularly when it can help children and bring about social justice.

Therese Quinn (tquinn@saic.edu) is Associate Professor of Art Education at the School of the Art Institute of Chicago (SAIC), where she also serves as Undergraduate Division Chair and Director of the BFA with Emphasis in Art Education Program, which prepares undergraduates for teaching.

Loring Resler (Resler.4@osu.edu) is a doctoral student in art education at The Ohio State University. Her research interests include community-based art as a catalyst for transformation of the individual and of social structures.

Montserrat Rifà-Valls (Montserrat.Rifa@uab.cat) is an assistant professor at the Universitat Autònoma de Barcelona (UAB). She is developing visual research projects on art curriculum, identity, and diversity. She prepares future K-12 educators and she also teaches in the Intercultural Education (UAB) and Research in Visual Arts education (UAB) at the graduate level.

Marcia L. Rosal (mrosal@fsu.edu) is Professor and Director of the graduate art therapy program at Florida State University. She is a Fulbright Fellow and past-president of the American Art Therapy Program. Her current research interests include art therapy with survivors of natural disasters, using the museum as a tool in art therapy, and group art therapy.

Lynn Sanders-Bustle (lsb@louisiana.edu) is Associate Professor of Art Education at the University of Louisiana at Lafayette. She holds a PhD in Curriculum and Instruction from Virginia Tech University. She has taught art in public schools working with students across the K–12 spectrum and is editor of the book, *Image, Inquiry, and Transformative Practice* (2003).

Talicia V. Scriven (Tvs2636@fsu.edu) is currently an art teacher at a Title I elementary school in the metro Atlanta area working with many children at risk of educational failure. Her areas of interest include curriculum research and development, teaching art using interdisciplinary teaching methods, and helping students at-risk of educational failure through art. She is also a member of the National Art

Education Association. Her doctorate is in art education from Florida State University. Her Master's in Art Education was completed at the University of Southern Mississippi and her BS in Art Education from South Carolina State University. She currently resides in Riverdale, Georgia.

Ryan Shin (shin@email.arizona.edu) is an assistant professor in the School of Art at the University of Arizona. He received his PhD in Art Education from the Florida State University in 2002, and taught at the University of Wisconsin at La Crosse from 2002 to 2007. His research has focused on Asian folk art and performance art, Asian visual culture, and digital media technology in art education.

Debrah Sickler-Voigt (dsickler@mtsu.edu) became a professor so that she could mold preservice teachers into effective instructors and assist current teachers in bettering their teaching practices. In 2008, she earned the *Outstanding Achievement in Instructional Technology Award* at Middle Tennessee State University. In 2007, she received the *Outstanding Art Educator in Higher Education Award* from the Tennessee Art Education Association. Currently, Sickler-Voigt is co-authoring a textbook, *Teaching Art: Methods for Real World Elementary and Middle School Art Education.* Additionally, her research has appeared in diverse scholarly journals and she regularly presents her research at professional conferences.

Kryssi Staikidis (kstaikidis@niu.edu) is an assistant professor in art education at Northern Illinois University. She holds a Doctor of Education Degree in Art and Art Education from Teachers College Columbia University and a Master of Fine Arts from Hunter College in New York City. Her research interests include indigenous pedagogy, studio practice as a site for research, and critical pedagogy.

Mary Stokrocki (Mary.Stokrocki@asu.edu), Professor of Art, Arizona State University, received the 2007 College of Arts & Architecture Alumni Award, Pennsylvania State University; the 2007 Women's Caucus June King McFee Award presented by the National Art Education Association; the 2005 Lowenfeld Award; and the 1995 Manuel Barkan Award. Her qualitative research focuses on multicultural teaching/learning in inner-city Cleveland; Rotterdam, Holland; Ankara, Turkey; Sao Paulo, Brazil; Warsaw, Poland; Barcelona, Spain; Evora, Portugal; and the Yaqui, Pima/Maricopa, Ak-Chin, Apache, and Navajo Reservations in Arizona. Her recent research involves explorations in empowering students and disenfranchised people in cyber worlds.

Patricia L. Stuhr (Stuhr.1@osu.edu) is Professor and Chair of the Art Education Department at The Ohio State University. She received her PhD from the University of Wisconsin-Madison in 1987. Before coming to OSU, she taught art in Wisconsin K–12 public schools for 14 years and evening art classes in maximum and medium security prisons for 11 years. Stuhr had done extensive research and publication in the area of contemporary Wisconsin Native American visual culture and artists, multicultural art education, and the arts in integrated curriculum. In 1998, she received a Fulbright Award to teach and research on the topics of multicultural art education and integrated curriculum at the University of Art and Design in Helsinki, Finland. In 2000, she was named an NAEA Distinguished Fellow. She also received the Zeigfeld Award from the United States Society for Education through Art (1999) and the NAEA Women's Caucus June King McFee Award (2008) for her contributions to multicultural art education and issues of social diversity.

Pamela G. Taylor (pgtaylor@vcu.edu) is Chair and Associate Professor in the Department of Art Education, School of the Arts, Virginia Commonwealth University in Richmond. She earned her PhD from Penn State in 1999, served as Editor of *Art Education* from 2007–.08, and researches service-learning, interactive digital technology, emerging media, visual culture, curriculum, and criticism.

Anne Thulson (annethulson@odysseydenver.org) earned an MFA from Cranbrook, and teaches at the Odyssey School, a K–8 Expeditionary Learning School in Denver. Through the role of curious artist-teacher, she works to re-enchant the world with her students. Apart from them, she intervenes into the continuous narrative of Denver history through site-based performances and painting.

Alexandria W. Zettler (awz08@fsu.edu) is currently working on her PhD in Art Therapy at Florida State University. Zettler's passion is working with adolescents from maladaptive family systems. She hopes to develop an expressive art therapies intervention to assist in issues of self-esteem and locus-of-control to break the cycle of abuse. Alexandria earned a master's in teaching degree from City University, WA, in 1996, and a BA from Oberlin College, OH, in 1983. She has taught in a range of positions from Pre–K to 12th grade, including exceptional, elementary, technology, and visual arts education. Additionally, Zettler has traveled, lived, and/or worked from Brazil to the coastal waters of Alaska. She lives with her family in Tallahassee, Florida.

Editors' Note

We understand that this anthology provides only a sampling of the many phenomenal art education and social justice oriented initiatives that exist. Join our online forum at **www. arteducationforsocialjustice.org** and provide feedback regarding the content and ideas in *Art Education for Social Justice* as well as exchange current information concerning community projects, schools, art organizations, and research that strives to address social justice through the arts.